THE TWENTIETH CENTURY

1890–1945

The Twentieth Century
1890-1945

RAYMOND FURNESS

CROOM HELM LONDON

BARNES & NOBLE NEW YORK
(a division of Harper & Row Publishers, Inc.)

© 1978 Raymond Furness
Croom Helm Ltd, 2-10 St John's Road, London SW11

British Library Cataloguing in Publication Data

Furness, Raymond
    The twentieth century. – (Literary history
    of Germany; vol. 8)
    1. German literature – 20th century – History
    and criticism.
    I. Title.   II. Series.
    830'.9'00912   PT401

ISBN 0–85664–361–0

Published in the USA 1978 by
Harper & Row Publishers, Inc.
Barnes & Noble Import Division

ISBN 0–06–492310–X
LC 77–10037

Printed and bound in Great Britain

CONTENTS

ACKNOWLEDGEMENTS

For permission to quote copyright and other material acknowledgement is made to the following: Edith Hasenclever (Walter Hasenclever), Artemis and Winkler Verlag (Stanislaw Przybyszewski), Langen-Müller Verlag (Frank Wedekind and Gustav Sack), Insel Verlag (Rainer Maria Rilke), Niedieck Linder A.G. (Alfred Döblin), Aufbau Verlag (Heinrich Mann), S. Fischer Verlag (Thomas Mann, Hugo von Hofmannsthal, Franz Werfel and Arthur Schnitzler), Schocken Books Inc. (Franz Kafka), Suhrkamp Verlag (Hermann Hesse, Ödön von Horváth, Bertolt Brecht, Walter Benjamin and Hermann Broch), Verlag Die Arche, Peter Schifferli (Jakob van Hoddis), Internationaal Literatuur Bureau (Ernst Toller), Ellermann Verlag (Georg Heym), Hoffmann und Campe Verlag (Hans Henny Jahnn), Limes Verlag Max Niedermayer (Gottfried Benn, Johannes R. Becher and August Stramm), Herr Otto Rosenthal and the heirs of the estate (Robert Musil), R. Piper and Co. Verlag (Ernst Barlach and Christian Morgenstern), Ernst Klett Publishers (Ernst Jünger and Rudolf Pannwitz), Bouvier Verlag (Stefan George), Ullstein Verlag (Gerhart Hauptmann), Carl Hanser Verlag (Elias Canetti), Hermann Luchterhand Verlag (Carl Sternheim and Arno Holz), Melanchthon Verlagsbuchhandlung (Fritz von Unruh), Kösel Verlag (Karl Kraus, Alfred Mombert and Theodor Däubler), Glock und Lutz Verlag (Reinhard Sorge), Otto Müller Verlag (Georg Trakl), Verlag Lambert Schneider (Oskar Loerke), Verlag Annedore Leber (Oskar Maria Graf), Dr Charles Wassermann (Jakob Wassermann), and Professor Oskar Kokoschka. The final form of the manuscript owes much to the tactful suggestions of Dr R.T. Llewellyn, Christ's College, Cambridge, but above all the patience of my wife must be acknowledged, without whose serenity and forebearance the writing of this book would have proved a much more arduous task.

Manchester, April 1977

1 AN INTRODUCTION: NATURALISM AND ITS DECLINE

In a famous passage in Book One of *Der Mann ohne Eigenschaften* Robert Musil portrays with accuracy and irony the intellectual atmosphere in which the 'man without qualities' and his friends passed their formative years. The plethora of artistic styles and movements, the rich confusion, with no clear-cut tendency or direction is described as follows:

> Aus dem ölglatten Geist der zwei letzten Jahrzehnte des neunzehnten Jahrhunderts hatte sich plötzlich in ganz Europa ein beflügelndes Fieber erhoben. Niemand wußte genau, was im Werden war; niemand vermochte zu sagen, ob es eine neue Kunst, ein neuer Mensch, eine neue Moral oder vielleicht eine Umschichtung der Gesellschaft sein solle ... Es wurde der Übermensch geliebt, und es wurde der Untermensch geliebt; es wurden die Gesundheit und die Sonne angebetet, und es wurde die Zärtlichkeit brustkranker Mädchen angebetet; man begeisterte sich für das Heldenglaubensbekenntnis und für das soziale Allemannsglaubensbekenntnis; man war gläubig und skeptisch, naturalistisch und preziös, robust und morbid; man träumte von alten Schloßalleen, herbstlichen Gärten, gläsernen Weihern, Edelsteinen, Haschisch, Krankheit, Dämonen, aber auch von Prärien, gewaltigen Horizonten, von Schmiede- under Walzwerken, nackten Kämpfern, Aufständen der Arbeitssklaven, menschlichen Urpaaren und Zertrümmerung der Gesellschaft.[1]

There seemed to be at this time, Musil implies, a profound uncertainty in man's emotional response to the world around him: it appeared that a new man was needed, or a new morality, or else a radical dislocation of society. The superman was hailed, the subhuman was extolled, the sun was worshipped, as were consumptive girls; one praised the hero, and also the humble working man; one had faith, one was sceptical, one was naturalistic, also precious; one was robust, yet also morbid, dreaming one moment of autumnal gardens, old castles, remote pools, opium, and decay, and at the next of prairies, immense horizons, foundries, factories, naked warriors, revolution, primitive communities and social upheaval. A better description of the fertile, even febrile, artistic and intellectual concoction with which the nineteenth century ended and the twentieth century began would be difficult to find. Nietzsche, naturalism, symbolism, decadence and the beginnings of expressionism – the 1890s appear more and more to be a fascinating and crucial decade in German literature where creative imitation and original contribution, rejection of past models and anticipation of future developments are extraordinarily juxtaposed. This book will therefore begin by considering the salient features of that decade. The fact that one year, 1892, saw not only the appearance of Stefan George's *Algabal* poems, but also Hofmannsthal's lyrical drama *Der Tod des Tizian* and the completion of Hauptmann's *Die Weber*, bears out Musil's description of the coexistence of disparate artistic tendencies. Although the chief feature of the calendar of the 1890s would be the rise of aestheticism and neo-romanticism, the impact of Hauptmann's *Vor Sonnenaufgang* (1889) was not short-lived. Musil specifically mentions the word 'naturalistisch', contrasting this with 'preziös', and although naturalism, with its belief in biological determinism and mechanical laws, seems to smack more of the nineteenth century than the twentieth, it must stand at the beginning of this introduction, for its great value may be seen in its claim to being the 'Entbindung der Moderne'.

As the nineteenth century drew to its close the avant-garde in Germany realised more and more that German literature, particularly lyric poetry, was dull and unimaginative when compared with that of France: the circle of writers in Munich, of whom Emanuel Geibel and Paul Heyse were the most eminent, seemed of slight stature when juxtaposed with such names as Baudelaire, Verlaine, Mallarmé and Rimbaud; the novelists Spielhagen and Freytag cut sorry figures indeed when measured against the great French, English and Russian masters. The monumentalising grandeur of the *Gründerjahre* and the historicising sentimentality of much of the art of those years confirmed the parlous nature of the German cultural situation when compared with that of other countries: as early as 1871 Nietzsche had warned of the 'Niederlage, ja Exstirpation des deutschen Geistes zugunsten des deutschen "Reiches" '.[2] It was France particularly which served as a cultural model: Zola, vilified and rejected by the bourgeoisie, was hailed by the younger writers as the great liberator, as was Tolstoi (and, later, Dostoevski), and in the theatre it was Henrik Ibsen who represented the breakthrough to a new daring.

As so often in Germany, the theoretical justification for an

uncompromising modernity in the arts preceded the actual works
themselves. The 1880s were characterised by a wealth of periodicals,
pamphlets, journals and manifestoes, each attempting to define the
basic position. Modernity and naturalism became the watchwords,
and Zola's much quoted dictum 'une oeuvre d'art est un coin de la
nature vu à travers un tempérament'[3] provided the apparent
justification for mimesis, for a portrayal of man and nature without
recourse to metaphysical doctrines, and a determination to describe
without sentiment or embellishment. But Zola's prodigious and
exuberant imagination, indeed, his reference to a 'tempérament', by
no means precluded subjectivity; although the scientific writings of
Darwin and Haeckel, and the positivist-materialism of Comte and
Taine were widely extolled, the German literary imagination did not
feel entirely at ease in the observation of the minutiae of day-to-day
living. Empirical analysis of environment and heredity was very much
the order of the day, but the excessive emphasis upon determinism
would soon prove irksome to the more imaginative writers. The social
concerns of the day were deemed worthy of artistic portrayal: the
plight of the proletariat, and man as an economic or political cipher,
were to be described with possible amelioration in mind, and yet
(and here Ibsen is the over-riding influence) naturalist drama would
deal predominantly with middle-class problems and preoccupations.
From the outset it must be made clear that naturalism in Germany
was an elusive phenomenon: a recent study has rightly seen that as
soon as the movement became creative rather than theoretical, then it
fell apart, unable to resolve the tensions between the specifically
German and the more radical European manifestations.[4]

The two centres associated with what may be called naturalism were
Berlin and Munich. The former city, with its slums and concomitant
social problems, apparently offered enough material for the writer
bent on a discussion of modern industrial problems; Munich, although
relatively unspoilt by industrialisation, had been associated with the
pallid school of poets gathered by Maximilian for his symposia, and
here was all that the avant-garde rejected. In Berlin the brothers
Heinrich and Julius Hart founded the *Kritische Waffengänge* (1882–
1884), a periodical concerned predominantly with the drama and the
lyric, and looking above all to Tolstoi, Ibsen and Strindberg; in Munich
Michael Georg Conrad founded, in 1885, *Die Gesellschaft*, a vital
organ for the new mentality in the arts, and one more allied to Zola's
work and aims than the Berlin venture. The Hart brothers stressed
the need for an 'Ideal-Realismus', and propounded their admiration

for the 'natural', meaning basically the spontaneous and the anti-formal, in a manner which derived more from Nietzsche; the Polish-German writer Stanislaw Przybyszewski, in his *Erinnerungen an das literarische Berlin*, described his meeting with the Hart brothers in the Berlin suburb of Friedrichshagen, and spoke slightingly of their attempts to emulate the great figures of Russia and Scandinavia.[5] In 1885 appeared the anthology of new poetry *Moderne Dichter-charaktere*, to which the brothers Hart contributed, as did such writers as Hermann Conradi, Karl Henckell, O.E. Hartleben and Arno Holz. Karl Henckell called the new poetry 'durchtränkt vom Lebensstrom der Zeit und der Nation',[6] but it had little in common with Zola and the French naturalists; it betrays the influence of Nietzsche (as does Hermann Conradi's desire for 'eine Zeit der großen Seelen und tiefen Gefühle')[7] and moves in the direction of *Heimat-dichtung*. The Hart brothers also attempted to publish the *Berliner Monatshefte für Literatur, Kritik und Theater* which, however, only survived six months and came to an end in October 1885. The younger writers, the 'Jüngstdeutschen', were dissatisfied and defected to the far more radical Conrad and his Munich journal.

In 1886 there appeared in *Die Gesellschaft* an article by Julius Hillebrand entitled 'Naturalismus schlechtweg!'. The author proclaimed: 'Ist doch Realismus nichts anderes als die künstlerische *Zurückspiege-lung* des Seienden, was ja die echten, großen Dichter von jeher bewußt oder unbewußt als ihre Aufgabe anerkannten . . . Ist denn die künstlerische Arbeit des Realisten ihrer *inneren* Natur nach eine andere als die des Idealisten?'[8] Hillebrand attempted to refute the view that the writer is a mere camera, registering with absolute objectivity the real as a purely perceptual entity: he stressed 'Individualität' as, indeed, Zola had stressed the 'tempérament' and had betrayed at all points an abundant imaginative power. The German theorists moved away from the concept of passive registration of phenomena, which approximated to a form of impressionism, towards the emphasis upon subjectivity and individuality. An important document is Karl Bleibtreu's *Revolution der Literatur*, which appeared in Leipzig in 1886. Bleibtreu discusses the new tendency in literature (which he calls realism) and takes pains to stress that this is invalid if it merely con-centrates upon the ugly and the depraved: 'Dem Realismus allein gehört die Zukunft der Literatur. Allerdings nicht dem Pseudo-Realismus . . . Der Mensch ist weder Maschine noch Tier, er ist halt ein — Mensch, d.h. ein rätselhaftes, unseliges Wesen, in dem sich psychische Aspiration und physische Instinkte bis in den Tod und bis an den Tod befehden.'[9] Bleibtreu puts forward a balanced view: he cannot condone the tendency which he and others see in Zola, the tendency to concentrate upon the bestial rather than the spiritual. Of interest also is the essay by Konrad Alberti which appeared in *Die Gesellschaft* in 1889, entitled 'Zwölf Artikel des Realismus', where 'das Natürliche' is again emphasised, but the writer O.J. Bierbaum, in the same number, points back to Böcklin as a realist (with the editor adding, in a footnote, that Richard Wagner was one likewise).[10] There is little clarity as to what 'naturalism' actually means, and the 1880s end with conflicting doctrines, with the overall tendency, however, to move away from Zola and Ibsen should their probing prove too harrowing.

But 1889 saw at last the emergence of a work of art in Germany which could stand comparison with the best of the new works from abroad. Gerhart Hauptmann (1862–1946) had moved to Erkner, a suburb of Berlin, in 1885; he had met many of the contributors to the *Moderne Dichtercharaktere*, an anthology which had a profound effect upon him. In 1889 the *Freie Bühne für modernes Leben* was formed in Berlin, a society whose members included Wilhelm Bölsche, Eugen Wolff, Otto Brahm, Paul Schlenther and the brothers Hart. The society produced private performances of the newest plays, beginning in fact with a production, on 29 September, of Ibsen's *Ghosts*; less than a month later Hauptmann's *Vor Sonnenaufgang* was staged. The editors of *Die Gesellschaft* had rejected the work; Theodor Fontane, then in his seventieth year, recommended the play to Otto Brahm. It has been claimed that the work owes much to Arno Holz and Johannes Schlaf, whose *Papa Hamlet*, a group of three prose sketches verging on the dramatic (for it was believed that the narrative should be as close as possible to dialogue in order to be as objective as possible), had appeared in the same year. The first edition of Hauptmann's play is dedicated to 'Bjarne P. Holmsen' (the pseudonym used by Holz and Schlaf – such was the impact of Scandinavian literature on the German literary scene at that time), 'dem konsequentesten Realisten, Verfasser vom *Papa Hamlet* . . . in freudiger Anerkennung der durch sein Buch empfangenen, entscheidenden Anregung'. It should, however, be remembered that Hauptmann's stories *Bahnwärter Thiel* and *Fasching* had appeared in 1888, before Hauptmann had met Holz; the idea of literary influence is often an unsubtle one. Holz had indeed suggested the title (in place of Hauptmann's *Der Sämann*), but the play itself springs from an original talent of undoubted stature.

Vor Sonnenaufgang was produced immediately after *Ghosts* in the
Freie Bühne's first season, and the famous first night, with a doctor
(a certain Dr Kastan) in the audience offering the forceps to the
doctor on the stage, before walking out in disgust, during the scene
where the alcoholic mother gives birth to a stillborn child, has gone
down in German theatrical history. A critic has written: 'Indeed the
crassness and horror of Hauptmann's realism and the profound
humanity of his portrayal of suffering, coupled with his uncanny
skill for reproducing the feel of a situation, the intonation of a voice,
the latent instincts of a human being, at last revealed what splendours
Naturalism was capable of'.[11] The violent hostility caused by
Anzengruber's *Das vierte Gebot* in 1877 was as nothing when
compared with Hauptmann's *succès de scandale*; in 1886 Hillebrand
had proclaimed Ibsen to be the Marlowe, destined to prepare the way
for Shakespeare, and Theodor Fontane, in his review of *Vor Sonnenaufgang*, wrote as follows:

> Er [Gerhart Hauptmann] erschien mir einfach als die Erfüllung
> *Ibsens*. Alles, was ich an *Ibsen* seit Jahr und Tag bewundert hatte
> . . . alles das fand ich bei Hauptmann wieder; und alles das, was ich
> seit Jahr und Tag bei *Ibsen* bekämpft hatte . . . alle diese Fehler
> fand ich bei Gerhart Hauptmann nicht. Kein von philosophisch
> romantischen Marotten gelegentlich angekränkelter Realist, sondern
> ein stilvoller Realist, d.h. von Anfang bis Ende derselbe.[12]

Hauptmann as 'ein stillvoller Realist', Hauptmann as the playwright
who portrayed with uncompromising honesty the social habits of the
Silesian *nouveaux riches* (who may dine off lobster, oysters and
champagne and yet whose table manners and conversation betray
coarser origins), and the fatal consequences of an intrusive idealist
without compassion — here was the young dramatist who was seen
as the heir and successor to Ibsen. It is surely invidious to criticise
Hauptmann for remaining within the conventions of the 'well-made
play' here;[13] Wedekind's *Frühlings-Erwachen*, written shortly after
Vor Sonnenaufgang, certainly seems more 'modern', but Hauptmann
could scarcely have chosen a better model than Ibsen for his first
masterpiece: to call the ending predictable and contrived is to under-
estimate the tragedy of Helene's position. Loth is by no means a flat
character: the fusion of altruism and egoism which characterises him is
acutely observed by Hauptmann, who sees the Nietzschean desire for
self-fulfilment active beneath his ostensibly progressive views on social

conditions. With great skill Hauptmann sees that the radical and the reactionary often coexist in an uneasy truce within a single character; it is also of interest that Loth could advise Helene to read Felix Dahn rather than Zola, whereas it is Hoffmann, apparently the aggressive parvenu of the Second Reich, who has a degree of sympathy unknown to Loth. Pascal calls Loth 'a compendium of nationalist ideals':[14] he was modelled to some extent on Alfred Ploetz, so-called expert on eugenics and founder of the 'Archiv für Rassen- und Gesellschaftsbiologie', and his reasons for abandoning Helene (he fears the possibility of tainted blood due to alcoholism) have a disquieting flavour. Hauptmann's neutrality, however, is admirable: his interest in Loth is above all a *dramatic* one, and ten years later he was to explain: 'Die dramatische Kunst ist gleichsam auf einer produktiven Skepsis errichtet: sie bewegt Gestalten gegeneinander, von denen jede mit ihrer besonderen Art und Meinung voll berechtigt ist'.[15] This is not to deny Hauptmann sympathy and compassion, but the *idées fixes* of his characters provide dramatic impetus rather than a stimulus for social or political thought.

Hauptmann explored in his next two plays, *Das Friedensfest* (1890) and *Einsame Menschen* (1891) problems concerned with middle-class situations — here Ibsen, as has earlier been stated, had prepared the way. In the former play he analysed with subtlety and tautness the lack of communication within a family, a family based rather too closely on the Wedekind household in Zurich. If *The Wild Duck*, with the theme of the idealist whose intrusion into the family brought disaster, provided the impetus for *Vor Sonnenaufgang*, then the influence of *Ghosts* may be discerned in *Das Friedensfest*, particularly in Robert Scholz's statement: 'Wir sind alle von Grund auf verpfuscht'.[16] (The conflict between rather and son, found also in such plays as Ernst Rosmer's *Dämmerung* (1893) and Wilhelm Weigand's *Der Vater* (1894), anticipates the far more violent expressionist preoccupation.) *Einsame Menschen* is more reminiscent of *Rosmersholm*, and also contains biographical elements, namely the relationship between Carl Hauptmann, his wife (the sister of Gerhart Hauptmann's first wife Marie Thienemann) and a young Polish student Josepha Kodis-Krzyzanowska. (It also prefigures certain problems to arise in Hauptmann's own marriage, which would be discussed in *Das Buch der Leidenschaft* in 1929.) Johannes Vockerat, 'der moderne Übergangsmensch', is caught between traditional beliefs on the one hand and more progressive views on the other (the photographs of Darwin and Haeckel in his room are juxtaposed with those of eminent theologians).

The young student Anna Mahr is not a seductive temptress *à la* Strindberg, nor an anticipation of Hanna Elias in *Gabriel Schillings Flucht*: she is as sensitive and lonely as Johannes, and has assumed a shell of hardness to protect herself against a hostile world. Her fascination lies in her combination of intellectual acumen and sexual power, with which Käthe, the tired young mother, cannot compete: it is not only the bee which is attracted to Anna's well-developed figure.[17] Hauptmann is here concerned with personal and psychological problems, which demonstrates once again the reluctance of the German writers — particularly those living in Friedrichshagen at this time — to contemplate the social predicament as the truly 'naturalistic' writer is often expected to do. It is not until Hauptmann's fourth play that the proletariat appears — indeed, it is that play which linked his name with the European movement more than any other.

It may not be too fanciful to see a likeness between the emancipated woman Anna Mahr and Lou Andreas-Salomé (1861–1937), who had been living in Berlin since 1889 and had met many of the avant-garde there, including Richard Dehmel, Arno Holz, Max Halbe and, in October 1889, Gerhart Hauptmann himself. Lou Andreas-Salomé provided many reviews for *Die Freie Bühne*, including those of Sudermann's *Heimat* and Max Halbe's *Die Jugend*. Her admiration for Hauptmann contrasts sharply with Przybyszewski's coolness: he had attended the opening night of *Vor Sonnenaufgang*, and spoke scathingly of the play in his *Erinnerungen*, where Hauptmann generally received short shrift: 'Arm das Deutschland, das sich nur Hauptmanns rühmt'.[18] But Przybyszewski's voice is the solitary one, and Hauptmann's fame was assured by the success of *Die Weber*, produced on 26 February 1893 in the *Freie Bühne*. This is indeed Germany's classic drama of hunger, exploitation, strike and abortive revolution — the hero has been replaced by the people themselves who speak with a natural force and directness which came over even more forcibly in the Silesian dialect version *De Waber*. Here is no simple *pièce à thèse*, but an intensely human document of great power and compassion; the critic Herbert Ihering, seeing the play in 1921, stressed the theme of humanity above all, rather than any political element: 'Die Revolution als Aufruf, als Protest, als brennender Haß ist in dem fortreißenden Gedicht von Heine *Die schlesischen Weber*. Die Revolution der Menschenliebe, die Empörung des Erbarmens ist in Hauptmanns Drama'.[19]

The first public performance of the work took place on 25 September 1894 in the Deutsches Theater in Berlin, the Kaiser having cancelled his box in disapproval. But although this is a genuine working-class drama the play is, in Hauptmann's own words, 'wohl sozial, aber nicht sozialistisch'.[20] Old Hilse sees that no political agitation can remove the ultimate suffering of the world (as Büchner himself had seen, a dramatist the young Hauptmann greatly admired). The revolt is not carefully planned by the workers, who do not act according to any particular ideological commitment; Moritz Jäger acts as a catalyst upon them to release their pent-up energy, much as Anna Mahr acted upon Johannes Vockerat. The irony of the death of Old Hilse is that the quietist is killed, not the revolutionary: blind chance and a malevolent destiny seem to thwart all human actions. What is remark-able above all in Hauptmann at this time is his ability to portray the vulnerable nature of human existence, his 'achievement in giving dramatic shape to the painful oppression of the trapped and the pursued'.[21] This is seen most strikingly in *Rose Bernd* (1903), whose heroine knows that her struggle against an inexorable destiny is fruitless, and that 'kee himmlischer Vater hat sich geriehrt'.[22] In *Michael Kramer* (1900) the preoccupations of naturalism seem to have been completely ignored; the cult of suffering and death (greatly admired by Rilke) and the elevation of words above mere 'Alltagsleben' demonstrate an almost metaphysical awareness of human existence.

A good example of the complex and ill-defined nature of German naturalism is provided by Arno Holz, who, at one time, provided the most extreme formulation of the 'scientific' approach to literature, exemplifying a desire to go beyond Zola in the quest for an absolute, consistent, 'konsequenter Naturalismus'. In 1891 appeared his *Die Kunst. Ihr Wesen und ihre Gesetze* which contained the notorious declaration: 'Die Kunst hat die Tendenz, wieder die Natur zu sein. Sie wird sie nach Maßgabe ihrer jeweiligen Reproduktionsbedingungen und deren Handhabung'.[23] This sentence was reiterated and the formula was added: 'Kunst = Natur $- x$', where 'x' is, presumably, to be identified with Zola's 'tempérament'. It has been cogently argued that Holz is by no means clear as to the relationship between the objective forms of experience and the subjective response: what is meant by 'nature' also seems to include emotional reactions and sensations. Respect for an external world gives way to a form of solipsism, and 'an apparent demand for realistic literature becomes a sanction for complete subjectivity'.[24] The 'Sekundenstil' devised by Holz and Schlaf is likewise an ambiguous phenomenon: a desire for mimetic verism is not far removed from a *pointillisme* and hence a fragmentation of reality, a situation which Hofmannsthal's Lord Chandos, as chapter 5 will describe, will well comprehend. The attempt to capture the very essence of an object or a situation by minutely detailed, photographic reproduction led inevitably to disintegration, sterility and absurdity.

It is perhaps in the drama that 'konsequenter Naturalismus' achieved success: both Arno Holz (1863–1929) and Johannes Schlaf (1862–1941) claimed that 'novellistische Skizzen' were to be the paradigm, and used the technique in *Die Familie Selicke* (1890) and *Meister Ölze* (1892), a grim portrayal of murder and fraud written by Schlaf alone and hailed as a veritable breakthrough. *Die Familie Selicke* is a bleak account of the death at Christmas of a young girl in a wretched, petit-bourgeois family, where mediocrity and helpless resignation triumph. As a portrayal of sordid drabness the play is effective; an added poignancy is found in the fact that Toni Selicke feels obliged to remain in such surroundings. It was probably the exact reproduction of ordinary speech, fragmented and formless, that made Theodor Fontane claim that *Die Familie Selicke* was a more progressive work even than *Vor Sonnenaufgang*.[25] Ihering, seeing the play in 1913, was impressed by its effectiveness and wrote that, above the sordid greyness of the monotony, 'erhebt sich der Sinn eines Kunstgesetzes. Der äesthetische Wille wird zum ethischen Ereignis. Vater Selicke entwickelt sich aus der Trinkerstudie zum vereinsamten, zerrütteten Menschen. Und Larmoyantes, Kleinbürgerliches wird nun durch diesen Willen seiner Banalität entfremdet.'[26] Przybyszewski went as far as to praise both Holz and Schlaf at the expense of the 'Zögling, ihr anglegentlich protegierter und verhätschelter Schüler Gerhart Hauptmann',[27] and Paul Ernst, discussing *Meister Ölze*, believed that 'Hinter den Trivialitäten der Erbschleicherei, des gemeinen Verbrechens aus elendsten Motiven, steht eine Natur von gewaltiger Größe, unbeugsamer Energie, höhnischer Menschenverachtung'.[28] As examples of naturalistic technique these two plays may well have a certain merit, but Hauptmann reaches far greater prominence than either Holz or Schlaf because of the vital energy of his talent and his potentiality for organic development.

The peak of German naturalism may also be called its collapse: M.G. Conrad, who had done much to promote the new tendency, used *Die Gesellschaft* to attack the concentration on themes of squalor and drabness ('diese traurige Asphaltpflanze der Großstadtgasse'[29]). He rejected both Holz's and Hauptmann's work as being the 'nüchternste, gemütloseste und geistig armseligste Form' of literature;[30] he likewise deplored the imitation of foreign models (for all that his own cycle of novels *Was die Isar rauscht* was unthinkable without Zola), and adopted themes of patriotism and bucolic *Heimatdichtung*. A reaction is underway, a rejection of mechanical, scientific observation in favour of something less jejune; an article in *Die Gesellschaft* of 1891 recommended the movement away from naturalism towards a 'symbolische Romantik'[31] (but one which, the writer stresses, must be within the limits prescribed by the natural sciences). Mere scientific reproduction of reality no longer satisfied, and the imagination, released from its straitjacket, was about to assume bizarre and fascinating forms.

Certainly the theatre had been revitalised, thanks above all to Hauptmann, and the immense success of Sudermann's *Heimat* (1893) was not entirely due to Eleanore Duse's portrayal of the famous singer: the well-made plot and the defence of women's rights to self-determination helped it to an international reputation. The modern writers had shown what 'realism' meant after the pallid attempts at veracity made by the Poetic Realists of the mid-nineteenth century. They had the courage to face the themes of squalor, violence, revolt, heredity and prostitution, and may therefore be called the first 'modern' German writers, at least as regards their choice of theme. But if modernism is taken to mean the direction towards abstraction in the arts, towards the use of the autotelic image and the independent metaphor, towards a rejection of mimesis and the creation of subjective, inner states, then naturalism seems more firmly rooted in the nineteenth century, closer, indeed, to impressionism rather than expressionism. And yet the 'Sekundenstil' of the naturalists and the *pointillisme* of impressionism, where the surface textures of reality are captured in minute detail, are both, as has been stated, associated with a loss of familiarity and a movement towards dissolution which must surely anticipate the bolder, more modern experiments. Clemens Heselhaus has indeed argued that the poetry of what is called impressionism in German literature (particularly in that of Liliencron and Dauthendey), although apparently concerned with the sensual surface textures of reality (as were the 'Skizzen' of Holz and Schlaf), contributed much to the movement towards the disintegration of hitherto fixed forms and he claims that 'die Impressionisten waren eigentlich die großen Auflöser und Zerlöser in der modernen Dichtung'.[32] What is of great interest in this context is to discover in the work of Arno Holz those tendencies to be discussed in later chapters: this writer who demanded the most 'consequential' naturalism, who had, as he described in a letter to Max Trippenbach (26 December 1887) reached such an exactitude in his artistic demands 'daß mir z.B. selbst Zola als Idealist passiert',[33] created in his *Phantasus* of 1898 and 1899 a world

composed of impressionistic, *Jugendstil*, vitalistic elements which
would, together with their mixture of Whitman, Japanese poetry and
Pre-Raphaelitism, prove a remarkable crucible for much that was to
come.

Holz's early collection of poems *Gedenkbuch* (1884) was much
influenced by Emanuel Geibel; in the *Buch der Zeit* (1885) he
demanded the aggressively modern, yet also portrayed the dreaming
poet, homeless in the modern world, who exulted in the tension
between art and society in a very traditional fashion. (This ambivalence
can also be seen in the *Moderne Dichtercharaktere* collection, where
the traditional existed side by side with the more experimental.)
In 1893 Holz contributed nine poems to O.J. Bierbaum's *Modernes
Musen-Almanach* which ignored the themes of 'Großstadtlyrik' and
created an impressionistic world flavoured with Böcklin and chinoiserie;
although in his drama Holz may be seen as adhering to the main tenets
of naturalism, he explored in his poetry a less rigorous, far more
exotic world. Johannes Schlaf likewise moved towards a sentient,
cosmic mysticism; his *Frühling* (1896) opened up new vistas which
Holz and others would later explore:

> Ich habe mit Christus, dem Herrn, die Leidenschaft in Gethsemane
> durchlitten, und mit Buddha das Innerste der Welt erkannt . . .
> Ich wurzele in einer süßen, feuchten Kühle, und dehne mich sacht
> in ein laues, fächelndes Schweigen hinein, spreize mich, ringend und
> nachgebend, mit hundert Formen in sanften, neckischen Widerstand
> hinein, etwas Heißem, Lichtem sehnend entgegen.[34]

In 1898 and 1899 appeared the first version of Holz's *Phantasus*
(a cycle of poems in the *Buch der Zeit* had borne that name) in two
parts, consisting of fifty poems each with a highly ornamental title
page and in a decorative script not entirely unlike that of Stefan George.
(The whole concept of the 'Mittelachse', that exact symmetry of lines
upon which Holz insisted here, also betrays a decorative quality.) The
theoretical writing of Holz, *Revolution der Lyrik*, which appeared
also in 1899, demanded a form of poetry which, 'rein formal, lediglich
durch einen Rhythmus getragen wird, der nur noch durch das lebt,
was durch ihn zum Ausdruck ringt';[35] the *Phantasus* collection was to
exemplify the new freedom of rhythm and the new freshness of tone,
a perfect concordance, Holz believed, between sound, rhythm and
image.

The first part is a 'Jahr der Seele' *à la* George; naturalistic elements have been left far behind, and the stylised impressions of a dreamer, a nature-worshipper, are revealed:

Durch die Friedrichstraße
– die Laternen brennen nur noch halb,
der trübe Wintermorgen dämmert schon –
bummle ich nach Hause.

In mir, langsam, steigt ein Bild auf.

Ein grüner Wiesenplan,
ein lachender Frühlingshimmel,
ein weißes Schloß mit weißen Nymphen.

Davor ein riesiger Kastanienbaum,
der seine roten Blütenkerzen
in einem stillen Wasser spiegelt![36]

The imagery of 'Aus weißen Wolken' points forward to neoromanticism, while 'Auf einem vergoldeten Blumenschiff combines exoticism with chinoiserie. The impressionistic sketches of a Peter Altenberg are fused with the sensuous vitalism of a Richard Dehmel in the following:

Lachend in die Siegesallee
schwenkt ein Mädchenpensionat.

Donnerwetter, sind die chic!

Wippende, grünblau schillernde Changeantschirme,
lange, buttergelbe schwedische Handschuhe,
sich bauschende, silbergraue, von roten Tulpen durchflammte
    Velvetblousen.

. . .

Und ich kriege die schönste, die sich nicht sträubt, um die Taille,
die ganze Gesellschaft stiebt kreischend auseinander,
Huuch! die alte Anstandsglucke fällt in Ohnmacht –
und rufe:

Mädchen, entgürtet euch und tanzt nackt zwischen Schwertern![37]

The 'zweites Heft' of *Phantasus* exemplifies the movement away from the scientific interests of naturalism towards a more poetic, lyrical Darwinism, a cosmic phantasy:

Sieben Billionen Jahre vor meiner Geburt
war ich eine Schwertlilie.

Meine Wurzeln
saugten sich
in einen Stern.

Auf seinem dunklen Wasser
schwamm
meine blaue Riesenblüte.[38]

Holz's letter to Karl Strobl (25 June 1900) elucidates this fusion of the self with the vastness of cosmic processes in a manner greatly reminiscent of Schlaf, yet alongside this cosmic synthesis of soul-migration and material transfiguration there exists the jauntiest modernism, which again recalls Peter Altenberg:

So eine kleine Fin-de-siècle-Krabbe, die Lawn tennis schlägt!

Rote, gewellte Madonnenscheitel,
eine lichtblaue Blouse aus Merveilleux
und im flohfarbnen Gürtel ein Veilchensträuschen,
das nach amerikanischen Zigaretten duftet.

Um ihren linken Seidenknöchel,
wenn sie die weißen Bälle pariert,
klirrt ein Goldkettchen.

Abends ist Feuerwerk.

Man drängelt sich mit ihr in eine möglichst dustre Ecke,
läßt sie sich schmachtend an seinen Busen lehnen
und sieht zu, wie die Sterne zerplatzen.

Ah!

Ein Fünfminutenkuß und gar kein Fischbein.[39]

But the collection ends, as it began, in the gulf of inter-stellar space, in the manner of Mombert and Morgenstern:

In rote Fixsternwälder, die verbluten,
peitsch ich mein Flügelroß.

Durch!

Hinter zerfetzten Planetensystemen, hinter vergletscherten
    Ursonnen
hinter Wüsten aus Nacht und Nichts
wachsen schimmernde neue Welten — Trillionen Crocusblüten![40]

Holz returned obsessively to the *Phantasus* material and would later, in 1925, publish a grotesquely inflated version (over fifteen hundred pages in three volumes in the 1961 Luchterhand edition) in an attempt to represent every possible range of emotion and to allow infinite imaginative exploration of every conceivable situation. The juxtaposition of very long lines and monosyllables, the neologisms, the almost Dada-like dislocation of language and the puns (which can only be compared with those of *Finnegans Wake*) create a gargantuan *oeuvre* which narrowly escapes absurdity.

Holz has been quoted extensively in this introduction not simply because his lyrical work is relatively unknown but to demonstrate a remarkable *volte-face*: scarcely had naturalism arisen in Germany than its exact antitheses asserted themselves in bewitching and fascinating forms. In the first version of *Phantasus* are found not only elements of impressionism, which are related to naturalism, but forms of neoromanticism, *Jugendstil* and cosmic poetry which are utterly remote from it. Following chapters will examine these reactions against naturalism more fully; it is in Vienna that the 'Überwindung des Naturalismus' achieved its most memorable formulations, and it is the situation in that city during the 1890s which must now be investigated.

24   An Introduction

Notes

1. Robert Musil, *Der Mann ohne Eigenschaften* (ed. Frisé), Hamburg, 1952, 55.
2. Friedrich Nietzsche, *Werke* (ed. Schlechta), Munich, 1954, I, 137.
3. Emile Zola, *Mes Haines*, 1866, also *Salon de 1866* and *Le naturalisme au théâtre (Le roman expérimental)*, Paris, 1923, 111.
4. John Osborne, *The Naturalist Drama in Germany*, Manchester, 1971, 170.
5. Stanislaw Przybyszewski, *Erinnerungen an das literarische Berlin*, Munich, 1965, 113.
6. Erich Ruprecht (ed.), *Literarische Manifeste des Naturalismus*, Stuttgart, 1962, 5.
7. Ibid.
8. Op. cit., 63.
9. Op. cit., 84.
10. Op. cit., 7.
11. Furst/Skrine, *Naturalism* (The Critical Idiom Nr. 18), London, 1971, 65.
12. Theodor Fontane, *Gesammelte Werke*, Berlin, 1905–1911, 2, Serie, VIII, 300-310.
13. Osborne, 80.
14. Roy Pascal, *From Naturalism to Expressionism*, London, 1973, 96.
15. Hauptmann, *Sämtliche Werke* (Centenar-Ausgabe), Frankfurt/Main and Berlin, 1962, VI, 698.
16. Hauptmann, I, 121.
17. Ibid., 200.
18. Przybyszewski, 84.
19. Herbert Ihering, *Von Reinhardt bis Brecht. Eine Auswahl der Theaterkritiken 1909–1923*, Hamburg, 1967, 97-98.
20. Osborne, quoted 119.
21. Osborne, 142.
22. Hauptmann, II, 256.
23. Arno Holz, *Werke*, Neuwied/Rhein, 1962, V, 15-16.
24. Osborne, 41.
25. Theodor Fontane, *Sämtliche Werke*, Munich, 1959–1967, XXII, 731-735.
26. Ihering, 18.
27. Przybyszewski, 84.
28. Paul Ernst, quoted Frenzel, *Daten deutscher Dichtung*, Munich, 1963, 115.
29. Ruprecht, *Literarische Manifeste des Naturalismus*, 10.
30. Ibid.
31. Op cit., 226.
32. Mann and Rothe (eds.), *Deutsche Literatur im 20 Jahrhundert*, Berne and Munich, 1967, 16.
33. Quoted Jost Hermand, *Phantasus*, Johnson Reprint, New York and London, 1968, xiv.
34. Ibid.
35. Holz, *Revolution der Lyrik*, Wiesbaden, 1951, 35.
36. *Phantasus* (no pagination).
37. Ibid.
38. Ibid.
39. Ibid.
40. Ibid.

2 JUNG-WIEN

In 1888 Hermann Bahr, the Austrian critic, essayist, poetaster and *littérateur* visited Munich, where he met Henrik Ibsen and the circle around Michael Georg Conrad, and moved on to Paris. With acute sensitivity, and a remarkable openness to the literary scene in that city, Bahr sensed that the old watchwords and slogans had had their day, and that something new was in the air. The great names, Zola, Maupassant and the Goncourts, no longer had the resonance of even a few years before: it was Bourget, Barrès and above all Huysmans and Maeterlinck who were now read and admired. Bahr travelled back to Berlin, and also made a journey to St Petersburg; returning to Vienna, he soon grouped around himself a circle of young poets and novelists who met in the Café Griensteidl and who were known as 'Jung-Wien'. This circle included such names as Arthur Schnitzler, Hugo von Hofmannsthal, Richard Beer-Hofmann and the lesser known writers Leopold v. Andrian, Felix Salten (later to achieve fame not only as the creator of the deer Bambi but also as the writer of the hilariously pornographic *Josefine Mutzenbacher*), and the decadent Felix Dörmann. The satirist Karl Kraus and the *enfant terrible* Peter Altenberg had little respect for Bahr (Kraus delighted in referring to Bahr as 'der Herr aus Linz', and mocked the 'Linzer Gewohnheit, Genialität durch eine in die Stirne baumelnde Haarlocke anzudeuten',[1] a hair-style avidly copied), but although Bahr's novel (*Die gute Schule*) and his plays are now forgotten, his three collections of essays, *Zur Kritik der Moderne* (1890), *Die Überwindung des Naturalismus* (1891) and *Studien zur Kritik der Moderne* (1894) are indispensable in any account which attempts to analyse the movement away from naturalism towards symbolism, or neo-romanticism (Neuro-Mantik!) or decadence, which occurred in the 1890s.

Writing one year *before* Hauptmann's *Die Weber* was completed, Hermann Bahr proclaimed: 'Die Herrschaft des Naturalismus ist vorüber, seine Rolle ist ausgespielt, sein Zauber ist gebrochen . . . Ich glaube also, daß der Naturalismus überwunden werden wird durch eine nervöse Romantik; noch lieber möchte ich sagen: durch eine Mystik der Nerven.'[2] Bahr stressed the movement away from a faithful reproduction of reality to the cultivation of an inner vision: 'Wir haben nichts als das Außen zum Innen zu machee',[3] and wrote that 'Sensationen,

nichts als Sensationen, unverbundene Augenblicksbilder der eiligen
Ereignisse auf den Nerven — das charakterisiert die letzte Phase'.[4]
In 1894, in his chapter on 'Die Décadence' in the *Studien zur Kritik
der Moderne*, Bahr formulated succinctly and with considerable
insight the preoccupations of the new generation of poets:

> Eines haben sie alle gemein: den starken Trieb aus dem flachen
> und rohen Naturalismus weg nach der Tiefe verfeinerter Ideale
> ... Sie wollen *modeler notre univers intérieur*. Darin sind sie wie
> neue Romantiker und auch in dem höhnischen Hochmuth gegen
> den gemeinen Geschmack der lauten Menge, in der ehrlichen
> Verachtung des 'Geschäftes', in dem zähen Trotze gegen alles
> *ce qui est demandé* ... Ein anderes Merkmal ist der Hang nach
> dem Künstlichen ... Dazu kommt drittens eine fieberische Sucht
> nach dem Mystischen. *Exprimer l'inexprimable, saisir l'insaisissable*
> — das ist immer und überall ihre Losung. Sie suchen Allegorieen
> und schwüle, dunkle Bilder. Jedes soll einen geheimen, zweiten
> Sinn haben, der sich nur dem Eingeweihten ergibt ... Endlich ist
> an ihnen immer ein unersättlicher Zug ins Ungeheure und
> Schrankenlose ... Sie sind nicht unsonst Wagnerianer. Alles
> Gewöhnliche, Häufige, Alltägliche ist ihnen verhaßt. Sie suchen die
> seltsamste Ausnahme mit Fleiß.[5]

This passage gives an excellent description of the new preoccupations
and aversions: of paramount importance is the debt to French
symbolism and French decadence, the neo-romantic cult of the soul,
the Wagnerian element (again derived, paradoxically, from France)
and the Nietzschean vision of the spiritual aristocrat remote in azure
loneliness. The jewels, opium, autumnal gardens and strange sicknesses
of which Musil spoke are now to the fore: it is not for nothing that
Thomas Mann tells us that Hanno Buddenbrook's young friend, Kai
Graf Mölln, is secretly reading Edgar Allan Poe.[6]

Symbolism, neo-romanticism, decadence — can these labels be
attached indiscriminately to the literature of the 1890s? Symbolism,
as a literary movement, was not defined, even in France, till 1886:
when Hermann Bahr described the new anti-naturalistic tendencies in
France he tended to use the term 'decadence', and even when
'symbolist' became a generally viable term the two areas overlapped
almost completely as far as the German literary imagination was
concerned. And neo-romanticism? The relationship between
symbolism and romanticism is a close one: the idea that the external

event is somehow an emblem of an event taking place elsewhere, in a realm hidden from man, is a famous romantic conceit, to be found in almost all of the great romantic poets. The symbolist, through the manipulation of evocative symbols, strives to make available to himself and his readers an invisible, arcane reality — the word becomes a magic entity in itself, and its manipulation a priest-like function. German romanticism knew full well of the correspondence between inner and outer, of the mysterious power of words, which do not merely possess an evocative power but which recreate reality itself, and which tap a vast and fecund unconscious. The term 'neo-romanticism' may be applied to the predilection, by Maeterlinck and others, for those misty regions of the soul, for mystical yearnings and exquisite refinements, frequently with an imaginatively medieval setting. Ricarda Huch's *Blütezeit der Romantik* struck a resonant chord in the imagination of many of the writers at the turn of the century, and a revival of myth, legend and the fascination of the supernatural was perhaps not surprising at this time. After the lean years of naturalism, where the imagination had been harnessed to social issues, the time had come for a return to crumbling castles, to silent swans on sombre waters, for Musil's 'brustkranke Mädchen' and 'heimliche Gärten'. An aesthetic religiosity also became apparent at this time, influenced greatly by Wagner's *Parsifal*; the prevalent atmosphere of yearning, of sultry eroticism and a fascination with death owe much to 'old Klingsor'. Somewhat later in the century the publisher Eugen Dieterichs will claim to have been the guiding light in the neo-romantic movement, hailed by him as the 'neue Geistesrichtung', in which the banausic and the social were rejected. Samuel Lublinski, the Berlin critic, used the term 'Neuromantiker' to describe Hugo von Hofmannsthal and, more surprisingly, also proclaimed, in his *Bilanz der Moderne* (1904), that 'Nietzsches *Zarathustra* ist ein durch und durch romantisches Werk, ein Gipfel der modernen Romantik . . . Einem Nietzsche ist gelungen, was ein Novalis vergeblich erstrebte: als ein Einzelner eine Mythologie, eine Symbolik, eine Religion zu erzeugen'.[7] Nietzsche's tone seems too imperious and defiant for the neo-romantic velleities and lassitudes, but his insistence on vision, on imaginative daring and the rejection of the banal certainly appealed to the writers of the 1890s. As far as decadence is concerned (a concept which fascinated Nietzsche, who saw in Wagner its supreme example), it may be claimed that the hermetic and precious aspects of symbolism become decadent when cultivated for their own sakes, and when the *goût de l'artificiel* became more pronounced, extolling the extravagant and the sterile at the expense of the natural and the vital. Both neo-romanticism and decadence may be subsumed under the category of *fin-de-siècle*, or aestheticism; the terms, however, remain blurred and frequently overlap.

Other writers and critics, apart from Hermann Bahr, sought to describe the literary atmosphere of the time. The Viennese writer and critic Franz Servaes preferred to use the term 'Impressionismus'; he explained in 1899: 'Die Erneuerung in der Kunst des neuenzehnten Jahrhunderts hat überall beim Impressionismus gelegen. Den momentanen Eindruck zu fixieren: keine Zeit hat in dem Grade diese Leidenschaft gehabt, als die unsrige.'[8] This so-called impressionism may be looked upon as a development of photographic naturalism, as chapter 1 has already mentioned: the subtle reproduction of sensuous impressions, the delicacy of the nuance, the attempt to characterise in a few deft touches leads on from certain tendencies in Johannes Schlaf and also Arno Holz who, however, rejected the term 'Impressionismus' as being one of the many 'Seifenblasenworte'[9] of the day. In Austria the philosophy of Ernst Mach exerted a powerful influence; his most famous work, entitled *Analyse der Empfindungen*, appeared in 1886 and put forward the thesis that 'reality' is, in fact, simply a conglomeration of sense-impressions. Robert Musil was a student of Mach, and his description, in *Die Vollendung der Liebe*, of the tea which 'aus einer matten silbernen Kanne jetzt in die Tasse fiel, mit einem leisen Klingen aufschlug und dann im Strahle stillzustehen schien, wie ein gedrehte, durchsichtige Säule aus strohbraunem, leichtem Topas'[10] shows the subtlety and precision of Musil's registration of these impressions, both aural and visual. On a more popular level the prose sketches of Peter Altenberg, the Viennese *bohémien* who was mentioned in connexion with Karl Kraus, sought to capture the particular quality of a person or a situation in a most succinct and telling way: his *Was der Tag mir zuträgt* (1901), with its 'fünfundsechzig neue Studien' catches the different facets of life in Vienna, Munich and elsewhere, ranging from the effects of listening to Wagner's *Walküre* to the ingredients of *Sauce Cumberland*.[11] Literary impressionism may be seen as deriving from naturalism, but its sensitive registration of the nuances of finely wrought sensibilities merges into the world of aestheticism. Servaes even claims that Nietzsche, the brilliant forger of aphorisms, was an impressionistic philosopher, 'der die zeitlose Abstraction und Construction verwarf und die Weisheit in der prismatischen Strahlenbrechung ihres ersten unmittelbaren

Aufleuchtens zu zeigen verstand'.[12] As well as Servaes, the critic and
linguist-philosopher Fritz Mauthner attempted to describe the literary
manifestations around him, and particularly poured scorn on the term
fin-de-siècle, which he found on every street-corner, and which he
rejected as being 'das leerste und sinnloseste Wort von den Pariser
Boulevards'.[13] Amusing in this context is the attack by the young
Theodor Lessing on the effete young decadents of the day; in the
Munich journal *Jugend* he described with malicious humour the
exhausted young *poète maudit* who, in the cafés, proclaimed:

> 'Und die Kunst ist die große Müdigkeit
> In sensitiven Symbolen'.
> Er lispelt's und ließ von der dienenden Maid
> Sich das vierte Stück Punschtorte holen.[14]

But of all the attempts to describe the particular aspects of aestheticism,
whether they be called impressionism, symbolism, neo-romanticism or
decadence, it is Hermann Bahr, chameleon-like and over-flexible though
he may have been, who came closest to the temper of the age, and it
was in Vienna, the city in which naturalism had never gained a foothold,
that Bahr experienced personally a talent of the highest order that
perfectly exemplified the new mentality.

The youthful precocity of Hugo von Hofmannsthal (1874–1929),
who used the pseudonym Loris, amongst others, for boys still at
school were forbidden to publish, is one of the miracles of literary
history. Stefan Zweig, writing much later in his *Erinnerungen,*
describes the astonishment of Arthur Schnitzler that a long-legged
young schoolboy, who had been introduced to his Sunday gatherings,
should be able to write verses of such perfection. Amongst the lamps
with red shades, the brandy, the latest yellow-bound French novels
on the tables, Hofmannsthal read aloud a small play in verse, and
Schnitzler and his companions exchanged astonished, almost
frightened glances. Verses of such loveliness, such flawless plasticity
and deep musicality were something that had never been heard in
Schnitzler's rooms before: equally extraordinary was the magical
intuition that this boy felt with all things. After he had finished reading,
the company sat speechless.

Hugo von Hofmannsthal was saturated with the rich Viennese
cultural tradition and, even as a schoolboy, was keenly aware of the
modern trends in the literary movements of most European countries.
The *Moderne Rundschau* mirrored all the recent developments in

literature: for the Viennese naturalism had had little impact, and the
new names were Maeterlinck, Huysmans, D'Annunzio, Wilde and Poe.
The lyrical drama *Gestern*, which made the seventeen-year-old
Hofmannsthal famous in 1891, shows French and Italian influences
and also the undeniable presence of Nietzsche; the hero, a hedonist
untroubled by moral or religious scruples, proclaims:

> Wie süß, die Lüge wissend zu genießen,
> Bis Lüg und Wahrheit sanft zusammenfließen;
>
> . . .
>
> Eintönig ist das Gute, schal und bleich,
> Allein die Sünde ist unendlich reich![15]

The aesthete, beyond good and evil, announces that he loves criminals
and those men who spring like panthers; he hates those who tame their
instincts and bow beneath the yoke of honourable behaviour. It is so
charming, he muses, to betray and injure people for no motive or
reason, but purely for the beauty of it. He welcomes the flagellants
into his house for the sake of their blood-stained whips and the
atmosphere of death and crucifixion which would thrill the jaded
appetite for extreme sensations.

The Nietzschean gestures, the beauty and blood cult of some
fictional Renaissance are part of the stock in trade of *fin-de-siècle*
aestheticism, and the young poet has absorbed much of the fascinating
poison. (Later, in a letter to Richard Strauss of 27 April 1904,
Hofmannsthal will lament the prevalence of this type of Renaissance
drama on the German stage; Thomas Mann's *Fiorenza* is another
example.[16]) To be still at school, to go to mass dutifully on Sunday
with his parents, and yet to revel in the heady atmosphere of Viennese
neo-romanticism was a unique experience. Towards the end of 1891
occurred an event which was to have a profound influence on his life
and work: sitting reading in the Café Griensteidl he was approached by
a stranger with a very striking head, wearing a square monocle of a
type fashionable in Paris, who:

> fragte mich, ob ich der und der wäre — sagte mir, er habe einen
> Aufsatz von mir gelesen, und was man ihm sonst über mich
> berichtet habe, deute darauf hin, daß ich unter den wenigen in
> Europa sei (und hier in Österreich der einzige), mit denen er

Verbindung zu suchen habe; es handle sich um die Vereinigung
derer, welche ahnten, was das Dichterische sei.[17]

The stranger was Stefan George (1868–1933) who was only twenty-
three at that time, but who seemed far older, and who radiated an
uncanny, even sinister, yet fascinating influence. George gave
Hofmannsthal a copy of Mallarmé's *L 'Après-midi d'un faune*, and also
a book of his own poems *Hymnen* (1890); Hofmannsthal donated
Gestern and also dedicated a poem to 'Herrn Stefan George, einem,
der vorübergeht' which contains the lines:

Du hast mich an Dinge gemahnet
Die heimlich in mir sind
Du warst für die Saiten der Seele
Der nächtige, flüsternde Wind.[18]

But Hofmannsthal sensed that there was something disquieting about
George, about his very strong views on the poet's duty, about the
need for a spiritual élite. The young man felt flattered by George's
visits and discussions, but also felt an instinctive fear, an intuitive
knowledge that George's way was not necessarily his. He admired
George's purity of vision and extensive knowledge of modern poetry,
but knew that his own background and premises were totally different;
he, Hofmannsthal, had been born in an imperial city, the centre of a
traditional culture and not in an out-of-the-way town on the Rhine
(Bingen), and he sensed as early as this that at least a part of him
wished to belong to a particular living society, to a particular generation, and not to be in total isolation, or in a hot-house atmosphere of
cultivated aestheticism. The sonnet *Der Prophet*, written in
Hofmannsthal's diary in 1891, expresses the fascination and the
reservations:

In einer Halle hat er mich empfangen,
Die rätselhaft mich ängstet mit Gewalt,
Von süßen Düften widerlich durchwallt:
Da hängen fremde Vögel, bunte Schlangen,
Das Tor fällt zu, des Lebens Laut verhallt,
Der Seele Atmen hemmt ein dumpfes Bangen,
Ein Zaubertrunk hält jeden Sinn befangen
Und alles flüchtet, hilflos, ohne Halt.

Er aber ist nicht wie er immer war,
Sein Auge bannt und fremd ist Stirn und Haar.
Von seinen Worten, den unscheinbar leisen,
Geht eine Herrschaft aus und ein Verführen,
Er macht die leere Luft beengend kreisen
Und er kann töten, ohne zu berühren.[19]

An atmosphere of mysterious danger is conveyed, of violence pervaded
with sweet, sickening perfumes; the young man feels suffocated and
drugged, spellbound by the Prophet-Magus who dominates and seduces.
The futile din of life is excluded from the Master's hall, where exotic
birds and snakes hang and coil; at his soft words the air seems to spin
in magic circles, drawing in closer and closer, until an intolerable
tension is reached.

Hofmannsthal saw the possible danger of George's influence, and
also he noticed the somewhat ludicrous nature of his exclusiveness.
The deliberately cultivated sartorial style and the arrogant bearing
seemed more appropriate to Munich than to Vienna: in Germany such
eccentricity might help in literary circles to enhance the poet's prestige
and strengthen the artistic aura, but in Vienna it would seem false, even
ridiculous. Hofmannsthal later contributed to George's *Blätter für die
Kunst*, but tensions and differences of opinion increased to the point
of being insurmountable. Hofmannsthal felt an intuitive reluctance to
sever his ties with tradition, with society, with vital human emotions
and this theme, the writer *vis-à-vis* society, became of paramount
importance to him, indeed, it is a theme which will beset so many
writers at this time. A favourite literary topos of Hofsmannthal (and
others) is that of the metallic, crystal garden, and this artificial
construction is juxtaposed with the natural, living one. The poem *Mein
Garten* describes the garden which the poet now inhabits, a park full
of golden trees, silver leaves and diamond dew-drops, with streams
made of topaz and full of heraldic, metallic beasts, yet also introduces
the memory of some more natural place:

Schön ist mein Garten mit den gold'nen Bäumen,
Den Blättern, die mit Silbersäuseln zittern,
Dem Diamantentau, den Wappengittern,
Dem Klang des Gong, bei dem die Löwen träumen,
Die ehernen, und den Topasmäandern
Und der Volière, wo die Reiher blinken,
Die niemals aus dem Silberbrunnen trinken . . .

So schön, ich sehn mich kaum nach jenem andern,
Dem andern Garten, wo ich früher war.
Ich weiß nicht wo . . . Ich rieche nur den Tau
Den Tau, der früh an meinen Haaren hing,
Den Duft der Erde weiß ich, feucht und lau,
Wenn ich die weichen Beeren suchen ging.
In jenem Garten, wo ich früher war.[20]

The other garden, which the poet cannot quite remember, nor quite
forget, is full of natural fragrance, dew, tender berries and soft, warm
earth: it is to this natural garden that his thoughts turn time and time
again. A similar theme is that of the contrast between the sinister,
exotic hothouse and the innocence of natural beauty; the poem 'Die
Töchter der Gärtnerin' portrays two daughters, each filling their vases
with very different flowers:

Die eine füllt die großen Delfter Krüge,
Auf denen blaue Drachen sind und Vögel,
Mit einer lockern Garbe lichter Blüten:
Da ist Jasmin, da quellen reife Rosen
Und Dahlien und Nelken und Narzissen . . .
Darüber tanzen hohe Margeriten
Und Fliederdolden wiegen sich und Schneeball
Und Halme nicken, Silberflaum und Rispen . . .
Ein duftend Bacchanal . . .

Die andre bricht mit blassen feinen Fingern
Langstielige und starre Orchideen,
Zwei oder drei, für eine enge Vase . . .
Aufragend, mit den Farben, die verklingen,
Mit langen Griffeln, seltsam und gewunden,
Mit Purpurfäden und mit grellen Tupfen
Mit violetten, braunen Pantherflecken
Und lauernden verführerischen Kelchen,
Die töten wollen.[21]

The loose sheaf of bright blossoms in the one vase is contrasted with
the tall, strangely complicated orchids, purple and seductive, in the
other, blooms which are fascinating and perverse. (Theodor Wratislaw's
poem 'Orchids', also his 'Hot-house Flowers', dating from 1896, come
to mind here; the theme of the hothouse with rank, bizarre growth

becomes a popular literary topos of aestheticism, from Wagner's song 'Im reibhaus' to Ernst Stadler's early poem of the same name.)

In December 1892 the *Blätter für die Kunst* published poems by Hofmannsthal, including 'Erlebnis', 'Wolken' and 'Vorfrühling'. The first of these three is a perfect example of the neo-romantic lyric, with its mellifluous imagery, and its equation of death with beauty. The silvery-grey fragrance of the valley, the pellucid sea, the glowing flowers and radiant light of the radiant topaz — all this and the deep surging of sad music is, in fact, a vision of death: death, for the young poet, has become music itself. The beauty of this is beyond question, but the poet feels nostalgia for his home, for life, for normality, as in that metal garden he thought of the warm earth. Life beckons, yet he is irresistibly drawn away by the magnetic fascination of his magical vision, luxurious, slightly sinister, yet full of haunting euphony. The vision in 'Erlebnis' is indeed like something conjured up by music: the theme of the proximity of music and death is, of course, a quintessentially romantic one, found as early as Wackenroder. Hofmannsthal himself was intensely musical, as opposed to George, who had comparatively little feeling for music and who rejected it as being inferior to the creation of plastic images. From the beginning it is clear than Hofmannsthal was very sensitive to the kind of natural beauty that moves past like music: this is apparent in 'Wolken', a poem in which momentary, transient impressions are captured. Similar to 'Wolken' is the better known 'Vorfrühling', more highly developed and richer in themes, suggesting a close communion between nature and human beings, between natural beauty and human emotions. The wind, invisible and ever-moving, is charged with memories, evocative perfume and a whole variety of human experience, tears, desire and laughter: it is as if the wind had connected all those different human beings who suffered and desired, so that they all belong to each other, just as all belong to nature. The wind seems to stand for the poetic insight itself, elusive and yet cogent, aerial and yet charged with human life. Hofmannsthal was very fond of the wind as a poetic image, using it again in 'Regen in der Dämmerung' where the natural processes are again enfolded in human emotions; alliteration is used to good effect in this and in 'Vorfrühling' to create a form in incantation.

The same year, 1892, saw the publication of Hofmannthal's lyrical drama *Der Tod des Tizian*, a dramatised lament for the death of the Renaissance Venetian painter, who is used to exemplify the artist generally. The verse has a languorous beauty, and the theme shows George's influence: art is a secluded domain, remote from vulgarity, and is superior to nature, which has no significance until form has been bestowed. But it is the short play *Der Tor und der Tod*, which appeared in the following year in *Der moderne Musenalmanach* that continues to demonstrate in a more sincere manner the problems facing Hofmannsthal: the problem of the aesthete and his attitude to life. Böcklin's painting may well have provided the initial impetus: Death the musician calls, and the artist pauses to review the meaning of his own life. The work may be called the literary elaboration of a certain confession and awareness, and the poet is reported to have said at the time of writing this work: 'Ich bin alles Feinen, Sübtilen, Zerfaserten, Impressionistischen, Psychologischen recht müde und warte, daß mir die naiven Freuden des Lebens wie Tannenzapfen derb und duftend von den Bäumen herunterfallen'.[22]

The play opens with an almost Faustian monologue in which the young man, Claudio, looks out of his richly furnished room into the evening darkness. He sees that his life has been empty of meaning; he has never experienced powerful emotion, preferring instead to observe life from afar and to cultivate an exquisite aloofness. Now he feels that his beautifully appointed room is 'Die Rumpelkammer voller totem Tand'.[23] The crucifix means nothing; his old Italian painting has never revealed life to him but has been something simply around which he can weave his imagination. (The year before, in *Der Tod des Tizian*, the young men had claimed that their eyes had been opened by the Master's paintings, but now Claudio has passed beyond this to a tragic disillusionment.) He turns to the ornately carved chest, full of rare beauty, but now he realises that the precious objects have only given an emotion at second hand: Claudio has never known the primary creative joy of the true artist, but only the sensitivity of the aesthete — a situation well described by Thomas Mann a few years later. In his musings Claudio is interrupted by his servant who, alarmed, tells of shadowy figures in the park: the mysterious sound of the violin is also heard, and Death enters the room. Death brings the awareness that Claudio's life has been a sham, devoid of meaning. The shades of mother, beloved and friend appear before him, those who had lived and suffered; at the point of death (death not as medieval skeleton, but 'Aus des Dionysos, der Venus Sippe'[24]) Claudio becomes intensely alive, and learns that before this ultimate mystery, akin to love and a form of ecstasy, the self is obliterated and a communion with all things is anticipated: 'Erst, da ich sterbe, spür ich, daß ich bin'.[25]

The aesthete is forced to a vital awareness of existence by death itself in this short play, but a far more sombre, more tragic exploration of this theme is found in the story *Das Märchen der 672. Nacht*, begun in 1894 and completed the following year. Hofmannsthal had been reading the *Thousand and One Nights* at this time, and the story does have an almost Oriental fatalism about it: 'Wo du sterben sollst, dahin tragen dich deine Füße . . . Wenn das Haus fertig ist, kommt der Tod'[26] (words which, incidentally, Thomas Buddenbrook will quote in a moment of tragic awareness). The young man, son of a wealthy merchant, devotes his life to aesthetic contemplation, and thinks much of death, death associated always with beauty and a strange joy: 'und sah sich schön, wie ein auf der Jagd beirrter König, in einem unbekannten Wald unter seltsamen Bläumen einem fremden, wunderbaren Geschick entgegengehen'.[27] But the gulf between dream and reality is vast: he will not be lost in a forest, but in dismal streets (and a sombre green-house); there is no elegant bridge to death, but a plank over a ditch; death does not reside in a palace, but in the barracks, and the moment of extinction is not beautiful, but terrible. In this remarkable story Hofmannsthal combines a naturalistic description of ugliness, stench and oppression with a symbolic extension: the drab streets become the Underworld, and the barracks Hell itself. As the young man had lived alone, so he must die alone; kicked in the groin by an ugly, sullen horse, he is carried by soldiers on to a mean, iron bed. 'Zuletzt erbrach er Galle, dann Blut — und starb mit verzerrten Zügen, die Lippen so verrissen, daß Zähne und Zahnfleisch entblößt waren, und ihm einen fremden, bösen Ausdruck gaben.'[28]

From this time dates Hofmannsthal's period of military service, spent in Moravia and Galizia. Periods of depression, caused by the squalor and ugliness of the Eastern provinces and the dull hopelessness of so many lives (the 'totes dumpfes Hinlungern der Dinge im Halblicht'[29]), alternated with moments of happiness, the realisation of his own privileged position and also the awareness that culture, if it means anything at all, must mean communication, awareness of other lives and a sense of commitment. His military experiences prompted the *Reitergeschichte* of 1899, a short and masterful account of one day in the life of Anton Lerch, a non-commissioned officer who meets a violent death after being corrupted by thoughts of sordid sexual adventures and the role of domestic bully. Here is no aesthete whom life destroys, but a man conquered by his baser self, by lust and greed. Also contained here is the eternal struggle between the privileged and the lower orders, between aristocratic discipline and elegance on the one hand and more brutal, less polished desires on the other. The story is again a brilliant fusion of naturalistic detail and symbolic meaning; the filthy village and the greasy streets, the terrible dogs and the dull, brutish life perfectly reflect Anton Lerch's own depravity; the fat fly on Vuic's comb, and the perplexing glimpse of a figure in the mirror set up a host of associations. The use of omens and anticipations is most effective, and the romantic *Doppelgänger* motif blends effortlessly with the clipped, military tone of the beginning and the end.

The juxtaposition of love and death in the *Märchen* has given way to a portrayal of the proximity of sex and violence. Beneath the poised and beautifully wrought surface of Hofmannsthal's writing there lurks frequently an awareness of the possible eruption of atavistic forces — his *Elektra* (1903) may be regarded as an anticipation of expressionistic excess in the portrayal of hysteria and revenge. *Das Bergwerk zu Falun* (1899), a dramatisation of Hoffmann's story is, however, a quintessentially neo-romantic work in its symbolism: the descent into the mine becomes a journey into the soul, a mystical process of self-exploration and revelation; *Der Kaiser und die Hexe* (1897) is also very much of its time in its craving for redemption and also its awareness of dark, disruptive forces. But the work which stands at the beginning of the twentieth century and which is regarded as a vital document in any account of Hofmannsthal and his exploration of one of the central problems facing the modern writer — that of language — is the famous *Ein Brief* of 1901; it is this work above all which links Hofmannsthal with such Viennese writers and thinkers as Karl Kraus and Ludwig Wittgenstein and the dilemma of the *Sprachkrise*, which will be discussed in chapter 5.

Before examining the literary situation in other cities, mention must be made of the other habitués of the Café Griensteidl who were regarded as the avant-garde writers of the city, and many of whom had met Lou Andreas-Salomé when she visited Vienna in 1895. Richard Beer-Hofmann (1866–1945) attempted a Novelle *Der Tod Georgs* which was very much in the style of Hofmannsthal, but which also used the technique of inner monologue which Schnitzler would perfect in his *Leutnant Gustl*. Beer-Hofmann's fastidious care when writing led Karl Kraus to comment that he 'seit Jahren an der dritten Zeile einer Novelle arbeitet, weil er jedes Wort in mehreren Toiletten überlegt'.[30] His poetic drama *Der Graf von Charolais* (based on Philip Massinger's *The Fatal Dowry*) failed to achieve a satisfactory unity and was met with Alfred Kerr's devastating remark that the work was, in fact, two dramas: 'Das eine dieser Dramen war von Beer, das andere von Hofmann — zu dem ersten war der Schluß nicht gedichtet, zu dem zweiten war der Anfang nicht gedichtet'.[31] Leopold

von Andrian (1875–1951) contributed to the *Blätter für die Kunst*
and published his Novelle, *Der Garten der Erkenntnis*, in 1895; Felix
Dörmann (i.e. Felix Biedermann) (1870–1928) assumed the role of
decadent in his anthologies *Neurotica* (1891) and *Sensationen* (1896).
His poem 'Was ich liebe' may stand as a piece of typical Viennese
fin-de-siècle:

> Ich liebe die hektischen, schlanken
> Narcissen mit blutrotem Mund;
> Ich liebe die Qualengedanken,
> die Herzen zerstochen und wund;
> Ich liebe die Fahlen und Bleichen,
> Die Frauen mit müdem Gesicht,
> Aus welchen in flammenden Zeichen
> Verzehrende Sinnenglut spricht;
>
> Ich liebe die schillernden Schlangen
> So schmiegsam und biegsam und kühl;
> Ich liebe die klagenden, bangen,
> Die Lieder von Todesgefuhl; . . .
>
> . . .
>
> Ich liebe, was Niemand erlesen,
> Was keinem zu lieben gelang:
> Mein eig'nes, urinnerstes Wesen
> Und alles, was seltsam und krank.[32]

This poem called forth a tirade from *Die Gesellschaft* in 1894; a certain
Ottokar Stauf von der March (that is, the Viennese poetaster Fritz
Chapulka) in his article 'Décadence' inquired:

> Was soll uns solch eine Dichtung? was soll uns, den Lebenwollenden,
> das Evangelium des Siechtums? Ist das irritierende Zucken in den
> Nervengeflechten vielleicht doch ein Vorzeichen des Lebens, wie
> die Dekadenten meinen? Und wenn — wie kann eine Poesie, die
> absolut kein Interesse für die sozialien und künstlerischen Kämpfe
> der Gegenwart besitzt, die sich ganz ins Sexuelle einspinnt — wie
> kann eine solche Poesie auf Geltung im XX. Jahrhundert Anspruch
> erheben?[33]

Chapulka seemed unaware of Dörmann's conventionally naturalistic plays *Ledige Leute* (1897) and *Zimmerherren* (1900).

But the most famous name of this Viennese group after that of Hofmannsthal was Arthur Schnitzler (1862–1931), the success of whose plays allowed him, an eminent doctor, to devote his life to his writing. Mach's *Analyse der Empfindungen* might have been an appropriate name for Schnitzler's artistic method which was qualified, however, with a typical brand of Viennese self-deprecating irony and gentle scepticism. The seven dialogues or 'playlets' *Anatol* (which Schnitzler began in London in 1888 and finished three years later) were given a prologue by the young Hofmannsthal, in which the atmosphere of Schnitzler's world is brilliantly conveyed:

> Also spielen wir Theater,
> Spielen unsre eignen Stücke,
> Frühgereift und zart und traurig,
> Die Komödie unsrer Seele,
> Unsres Fühlens Heut und Gestern,
> Böser Dinge hübsche Formel,
> Glatte Worte, bunte Bilder,
> Halbes, heimliches Empfinden,
> Agonien, Episoden.[34]

The seven dramatic episodes have much of the impressionistic sketch about them and Anatol, the self-indulgent bachelor, weak, and with an almost morbid capacity for self-analysis, is a typical product of the Viennese *fin-de-siècle*. In conversations with Max and Grabriele his thoughts revolve around the possibility of a fleeting *affaire* without the necessity of lasting commitment; too sophisticated to enjoy the present, too burdened with the memories of the past, he demands of the 'süßes Mädl' what he himself can never give – a fresh, generous, emotional response. 'Das Episodenhafte der Geschichte kam mir so deutlich zum Bewußtsein. Während ich den warmen Hauch ihres Mundes auf meiner Hand fühlte, erlebte ich das Ganze schon in der Erinnerung. Es war eigentlich schon vorüber. Sie war wieder eine von denen gewesen, über die ich hinweg mußte. Das Worte fiel selbst mir ein, das dürre Wort: Episode.'[35] Schnitzler, acknowledged by Freud to be his *Doppelgänger*, is expert at analysing Anatol's erotic egotism, his insufficiency in any emotional response. Yet the charm of this cycle resides in Schnitzler's refusal to adopt a moral position: Anatol's inability to feel deeply is viewed with an ironic detachment. In *Reigen*, started in 1896, sex is the force before which all levels of society are equal: the ten scenes show how sexual desire is concealed behind subtle — and not too subtle — prevarication. Man's desires may be squalid, and his excuses totally inadequate, but at least in sex some form of communion is made. Schnitzler's tone is delicate here: he greatly admired, as did Karl Kraus, Offenbach's librettist Halévy, and was able to combine this lightness and subtlety of tone with Viennese charm and irony in his portrayal of erotic entanglements. This did not, however, prevent the work being banned by the censor of the time, and as late as 1920 the performance in the Kleines Schauspielhaus in Berlin resulted in a notorious scandal. Herbert Ihering was at the performance (on 23 December) and defended the work, claiming that this play would survive, whereas much of Schnitzler's other work would not: 'Reigen ist Wien, ist der betäubende, lockende, verführerische Schimmer dieser herrlichen, fauligen, sinkenden, versunkenen Stadt . . . Viele Dramen von Schnitzler sind veraltet, weil sie Probleme stellten, und die Probleme entweder zu leicht waren oder von der Zeit zerfressen wurden. Reigen ist unproblematisch, und wird in der deutschen erotischen Literatur, die arm ist, bleiben.'[36]

Another scandal surrounded Schnitzler's *Leutnant Gustl* (1900), a story which so enraged the Austrian Imperial Army that Schnitzler was deprived of his military commission. The narrative is in the form of an inner monologue (a technique Schnitzler also used in *Fräulein Else)* and shows the utterly fatuous, shallow, and conformist attitudes of this young lieutenant who, at a concert, treats a civilian discourteously and, after being called 'ein dummer Bub' by him, wanders through the Prater in an overwrought condition, trying to make up his mind whether or not to commit suicide. Lieutenant Gustl's prejudices and ignorance, his mawkish sentimentality and pompous attitudinising are all brilliantly betrayed by Schnitzler's subtle analysis of his mental processes, but again it would be wrong to assume that there is any overt condemnation here on the author's part. Schnitzler observes, and does not pontificate: however trivial and unpleasant this young lieutenant may be, and however superficial the society he represents, the reader is not incensed, but rather saddened, at such a life and at such a way of thinking utterly moulded by society, family and tradition.

Schnitzler observed Viennese society at the turn of the century with the sharp eye of the psychologist but also the humane tolerance of the talented and ironic writer. A wider canvas is given in his autobiographical novel *Der Weg ins Freie* (1908), where the relationship between talented Jews and society as a whole is analysed; the play *Professor Bernhardi* (1912) deals with the clash between the Jewish physician's convictions and the insistence of the Catholic Church upon the administration of extreme unction. But Schnitzler never resorts to cumbersome polemic: Bernhardi realises the unassailable medical rightness of his position yet is loth to become a *terrible simplificateur.* Schnitzler is not a successful writer of *pièces à thèse* for he is prevented by his intelligence and his irony from an all-too-earnest commitment. His reputation quite rightly rests on his ability to give a shrewd assessment of the quality of mind of typically Viennese characters at the turn of the century, where no moral stance is adopted.

Before leaving this account of Austrian *fin-de-siècle* the names of two other poets, Rilke and Trakl, must be mentioned, both firmly lodged in this period as far as their juvenilia and early works are concerned, but both of whom outgrew aestheticism and moved towards a more 'modern' attitude. Neither Rilke nor Trakl owe much to Vienna: Rilke travelled extensively, yet always avoided that city; Trakl was profoundly unhappy there during his brief visits. The two men never met, although Rilke greatly admired Trakl's poety, and both men were indebted to Wittgenstein's financial generosity.

Rainer Maria Rilke (1875–1926) is a poet who, after enormous popularity, has suffered a surprising eclipse. The more aggressive critics condemn him for being precious, pretentious, remote and exquisite – and yet, in 1949, Gottfried Benn praised him for the one line which his own generation, he declared, would not forget: 'Wer spricht von Siegen? Überstehn ist alles'.[37] This is the writer who also, in *Die Aufzeichnungen des Malte Laurids Brigge* (to be discussed in chapter 5) dealt with the problems of modern man in the great city, who faced sickness, ugliness, *Angst* and death in an attempt to distil one drop of beauty from the dross of modern life. This is also the writer who, in the *Duineser Elegien* (see chapter 5), explored the flux and turmoil of human existence in a manner similar to the existential writers of the time, who feared senseless technology and who sought to praise the artefact and the artisan. And Rilke is the poet above all in whose hands the German language achieved miracles of expressiveness, a suppleness and an associative force undreamed of. Those hostile to his art talk of the vapid, self-indulgent musicality of his early work, his insufferable poses, his sycophancy *vis-à-vis* wealthy aristocratic ladies, his indifference to political problems above all, as though the hallmark of a great poet were his strident proclamation of unassailable public attitudes. They ignore the limpid strength of many of his *Neue Gedichte,* his ultimate integrity as *poet,* as creator of powerful, redolent images, and his awareness of the great task of affirmation, of love of the world and the praise of human creativity.

The beginnings are not auspicious. Provincial Prague cannot compare with cultured Vienna: Hofmannsthal, born one year before Rilke, could write such works as *Der Tod des Tizian* and *Der Tor und der Tod* in 1892 and 1893 respectively, whereas Rilke's neo-romantic effusions are derivative and often embarrassing in their mawkishness.Holthsen's description of the twenty-one-year-old Rilke as a literary 'Hans Dampf-in-allen-Gassen' is a telling one, and stands in remarkable contrast to the poet's later insistence on loneliness and silence. In 1896 he tried his hand at writing the obligatory naturalistic drama *(Jetzt und in der Stunde unseres Absterbens* and *Im Frühfrost);* in the following year it is Maeterlinck who is imitated (in *Höhenluft* and *Ohne Gegenwart).* In 1894 and 1895 the collections of poems *Leben und Lieder* and *Larenopfer* appeared; in the following year *Traumgekrönt* and in 1897 *Advent.* The very titles betray the character of the poems included within: a cliché-ridden world of sentimental images, merely adjectival in function, facile *Stimmungsbilder,* maidens, princesses, evening, roses, dreams and distant castles was spun with effortless facility from the young poet and lulled the reading public with its musical, dream-like quality. The sentient waves of feeling, the stock-in-trade neo-romantic settings rarely rise above the level of Patience Strong. It would not be an easy task for Rilke to transmute the themes and pictures of his poetic beginnings into the precise, highly polished images of the *Neue Gedichte* and his latest utterances. The themes of love, death and transience will never leave his work, but will later assume an unprecedented intensity and precision.

His soul-dramas *à la* Maeterlinck, his impressionistic descriptions of Prague and other cities, and the panache surrounding the daring young officer (very much inspired by Liliencron, a poet whom Rilke admired and whom he invited to Prague to give a poetry reading in May 1897), the *Arme-Leute Poesie,* the dash of Bohemian melancholy and the introspection and subtleties of Jens Peter Jacobsen and Sigbjørn Obstfjelder — these are the features which characterise Rilke's work in the 1890s, the work of a perfect epigone. To this must be added the inevitable influence of Nietzsche, felt particularly in *Ewald Tragy* and *Der Apostel.* In Erich Heller's words: '. . . the effects of Nietzsche's hammering and dynamiting are unmistakable; yet there is not the slightest trace of the depth and complexity of Nietzsche's thought and feeling'.[38] Rilke had moved to Munich in 1896: in the following year he met Lou Andreas-Salomé, whose book *Friedrich Nietzsche in seinen Werken* had been published in Vienna in 1894. Frau Andreas-Salomé possessed the highest credentials: she had known Nietzsche

personally, had actually been courted by him, and the notorious
photograph of her with the whip, riding the cart pulled by Nietzsche
and Paul Rée, may well have inspired that line of Nietzsche known (and
misunderstood) by so many: 'Du gehst zu Frauen? Vergiß die Peitsche
nicht!'[39] Heller explains that *Das Florenzer Tagebuch* (1898), written
for Lou's eyes, is entirely Nietzschean in its rapturous vision of the
artist superman. Yet it will not be until the *Duineser Elegien* and the
Sonette an Orpheus, a quarter of a century later, that the Nietzschean
element is found in its true profundity and fervour.

The effect of the meeting with Lou Andreas-Salomé, which took
place on 12 May 1897 in Jakob Wassermann's rooms in Munich, was for
Rilke overwhelming; she is adored and worshipped in a mystical and
ecstatic rapture. The well-known poem from the Stundenbuch cycle
(1899–1903), 'Lösch mir die Augen aus', was, according to Lou,
written as early as the summer of 1897, that is, a few months after their
first meeting, and is meant not for some ill-defined 'God', but for Lou
herself;

> Lösch mir die Augen aus: ich kann dich sehn,
> wirf mir die Ohren zu: ich kann dich hören,
> und ohne Füße kann ich zu dir gehn,
> und ohne Mund noch kann ich dich beschwören.
> Brich mir die Arme ab, ich fasse dich
> mit meinem Herzen wie mit einer Hand,
> halt mir das Herz zu und mein Hirn wird schlagen,
> und wirfst du in mein Hirn das Brand,
> so werd ich dich auf meinem Blute tragen.[40]

In the autumn of the same year, 1897, Rilke moved to Berlin to be near
Lou: on 14 November he went with her to hear Stefan George read his
poems at the house of Reinhold and Sabine Lepsius. This was the year
of George's *Das Jahr der Seele;* seven years older than Rilke, George had
established himself in Munich as the High Priest of poetic purity. The
meeting with Hofmannsthal has already been described; George, after
having been admitted to Mallarmé's Tuesday afternoon gatherings, was
determined to graft the refinements of French symbolism on to the
German literary tradition. Rilke wished to be admitted to George's
circle of acolytes, but, in spite of this meeting, and a brief encounter in
the Boboli Gardens in Florence in the following year, the two men
remained estranged from each other. George's poetry will be discussed
in the next chapter; suffice it to say here that his imperious vision of

the supremacy of art, his Nietzschean pose of spiritual aristocrat, may well have impressed Rilke at that time, but he later sensed that there may well be something forced, angular and harsh about much of George's poetry, something *voulu* and lacking in spontaneity and vividness. George, for his part, later rejected Rilke's Franciscanism concerning 'die Dinge' as being plebeian.

The autumn of 1898 was filled with bare-footed walks with Lou Salomé through the forests outside Schmargendorf; 1899 saw the next collection of poems, *Mir zur Feier,* with its various sections entitled 'Engellieder', 'Mädchen-Gestalten', 'Lieder der Mädchen', 'Gebete der Mädchen zu Maria' and so forth. Rilke is intoxicated with the facility with which rhymes present themselves to him, and indulges in what Holthusen calls 'ein unersättliches Schmachten und Buhlen mit femininen und oft genug infantilen Gefühlslagen'.[41] This collection became well known, as did the prose-poem *Die Weise von Liebe und Tod des Cornets Christoph Rilke,* which appeared in the same year. This latter work became enormously popular, doubtless because of its musicality and its sentimental tale of the aristocratic young cadet who moves through love to death in battle. By today's standards the book is unreadable, but a whole generation was captivated by such passages as these:

Als Mahl beganns. Und ist ein Fest geworden. Man weiß nicht wie. Die hohen Flammen flackten, die Stimmen schwirrten, viele Lieder klirrten aus Glas und Glanz und endlich aus den reifgewordnen Takten entsprang der Tanz. Und alle riß er hin. Und war ein Wellenschlagen in den Sälen, ein Sich-vermischen und ein Sich-vermählen, ein Abschiednehmen und ein Wiederfinden, ein Glanzgenießen und ein Lichterblinden, ein Willigwerden jenen stillern Winden, die wie die Flügel fremder Blüten sind. Aus dunklem Wein und tausend Rosen rinnt die Stunde rauschend in den Traum der Nacht.[42]

The later Rilke was extremely embarrassed by the success of this early piece of writing, which he chose to forget, even if the reading public did not; his reaction to the suggestion that he might make the young hero into a fighter-pilot for patriotic reasons might well be imagined.

In the spring of 1899 Rilke left for Russia with Lou Salomé and her husband: they experienced the Russian Orthodox Easter service and met Count Tolstoi. In the following year Rilke and Lou travelled alone to the south of Russia, visiting Tolstoi at his estates. The vastness and greatness of Russia, its backwardness, apparent anti-Westernism and anti-materialism profoundly affected Rilke: his *Stundenbuch* cycle, which appeared in 1905, dates from this time. The poet, speaking through the mouth of an imaginary Russian monk, uses religious terminology in a very personal way: he arrogates Christian (particularly medieval) symbols into his own aesthetic vision of existence. The word 'God' is used indiscriminately; it soon becomes clear that the 'monk' blesses and affirms in a purely aesthetic immanent manner. The supreme religion would seem to be Art, and a typically neo-romantic confusion between aesthetic and religious concepts is clearly noticeable. The rather vapid spirituality of the cycle is occasionally interrupted by startlingly explicit descriptions of the sexual act:

> Mach Einen herrlich, Herr, mach Einen groß,
> bau seinem Leben einen schönen Schoß,
> und seine Scham errichte wie ein Tor
> in einem blonden Wald von jungen Haaren,
> und ziehe durch das Glied des Unsagbaren
> den Reisigen, den weißen Heeresscharen,
> den tausend Samen, die sich sammeln, vor.[43]

A favourite poetic idea of Rilke, found also in the collection *Buch der Bilder,* is that death is a mystical, almost erotic experience, and that man carries his death within himself, like a fruit which grows towards an ultimate release. He discussed love and death with Lou Salomé with great earnestness and openness (she would later discuss with Freud Rilke's sexual difficulties); these archetypal romantic themes will run throughout the whole of his work, and achieve great importance in the *Duineser Elegien.* The problem of death, particularly, will never leave Rilke; at this time he visited Kleist's grave on the Wannsee in Berlin, and was also profoundly moved by Gerhart Hauptmann's *Michael Kramer.* In December 1900 he met Hauptmann at Lou Salomé's house and on 19 December the two were invited by Hauptmann to a private rehearsal of the play. (Lou Salomé's Novelle *Ein Todesfall* had appeared two years before, and both she and Rilke sensed that Hauptmann may have based his play upon the story.) A related problem is that of affirmation: a quieter variation of Nietzsche's *Ja-sagen* is Rilke's Franciscan acceptance of things, a desire to bless and affirm all in an almost amoral act of worship. The poet-monk stands beyond good and evil, and anticipates the insistence upon *Rühmen* which will play such an important part in Rilke's later poety. Although much of the

Stundenbuch collection is undistinguished the great themes are there, waiting for a more precise, more vital exploration: the neo-romantic self-indulgence of this early writing is fully overcome by Rilke's move to Paris in 1902 and his encounter with Rodin. A clearer, harder line becomes evident in his poetry, which emerges from the misty effulgence of the 1890s towards a new clarity and toughness.

The poetry of Georg Trakl (1887–1914) must be finally considered before the neo-romanticism and *fin-de-siècle* attitudes in Munich and Berlin are considered. Trakl's poetry moves towards a mysterious, almost surrealist exploration of the world; his name has also been linked with that of Stadler and Heym as being a precursor of certain features of expressionism. The early work, however, shows once more a debt to French symbolism: Trakl was certainly able to read Huysmans, Maeterlinck, Louÿs, Rodenbach and Lerberghe in the original, and Baudelaire and Mallarmé came as a revelation to him, particularly the former, whose vision of the *poète maudit*, revelling in the delights of the flesh and the artificial paradise of drugs appealed to the young man's sense of revolt. Imitations of *Les fleurs du mal*, albeit gauche, are to be found in the juvenilia; the short prose work *Verlassenheit* is a typical neo-romantic description of a desolate park, stagnant waters and a silent castle, where a lonely aristocrat, obsessed by transience, silently awaits dissolution.

The description of the Count, surrounded by putrefaction, is indeed reminiscent of Edgar Allan Poe's *The Fall of the House of Usher*: Baudelaire, Mallarmé and Debussy all looked to Poe and Richard Wagner — an extraordinary juxtaposition, but one which Thomas Mann well understood — as forerunners and explorers of a new, disturbing sensitivity. Trakl's *Traumland* is again reminiscent of Poe's *Berenice* in its description of the young woman who fades into death for no known cause. Themes of decay, falling and madness link the two writers, similarly the awareness of some fearful sin — in Trakl's case it is incest, a typically decadent transgression. The poem 'Blutschuld' could not be bettered as an example of that sultry, erotic yearning for redemption which may be found in so much decadent poetry in France and England:

Es dräut die Nacht am Lager unsrer Küsse.
Es flüstert wo: Wer nimmt von euch die Schuld?
Noch bebend von verruchter Wollust Süße
Wir beten: Verzeih uns, Maria, in deiner Huld!

Aus Blumenschalen steigen gierge Düfte,
Umschmeicheln unsere Stirnen bleich von Schuld.
Ermattend unterm Hauch der schwülen Lüfte
Wir träumen: Verzeih uns, Maria, in deiner Huld!

Doch lauter rauscht der Brunnen der Sirenen
Und dunkler ragt die Sphinx vor unsrer Schuld,
Daß unsre Herzen sündiger wieder tönen,
Wir schluchzen: Verzeih uns, Maria, in deiner Huld![44]

Trakl's early poetry, that is, many of the poems published under the title
Gedichte by Kurt Wolff, has an impressionistic quality: the poet is
entranced by the sound and colour of life around him, particularly in
Salzburg and the surrounding villages, and registers his impressions
with a sensitive precision. 'Im roten Laubwerk voll Guitarren', 'Kleines
Konzert' and 'Die schöne Stadt' are good examples; 'Kleines Konzert'
consists of an enumeration of pictures conveyed in conventional
syntax: an atmosphere of summer and midday is evoked, where all
seems tangible and near. The 'you' who is addressed merges into a
profusion of impressions, into the movement, sound and colour of
nature. A haunting harmony is conveyed, and an atmosphere is created
which hints at something beyond the sum of the different components.
Trakl approaches a symbolist position in certain poems, including
'Landschaft', from his second anthology, where soul and landscape
become a mysterious unity:

Septemberabend; traurig tönen die dunklen Rufe der Hirten
Durch das dämmernde Dorf; Feuer sprüht in der Schmiede.
Gewaltig bäumt sich ein schwarzes Pferd; die hyazinthenen Locken
   der Magd
Haschen nach der Inbrunst seiner purpurnen Nüstern.
Leise erstarrt am Saum des Waldes der Schrei der Kirschkuh
Und die gelben Blumen des Herbstes
Neigen sich sprachlos über das blaue Antlitz des Teiches.
In roter Flamme verbrannte ein Baum; aufflattern mit dunklen
   Gesichtern die Fledermäuse.[45]

There seems to be a perfect correspondence between inner and outer
here: the natural descriptions well reflect the poet's inner condition
in the way in which Baudelaire's poet meets 'des regards familiers' in
his dark forest.

The enigmatic figure of Elis fits in well with the mysterious soul-landscapes created by Trakl's poetry; vulnerable and luminous, he moves through a crepuscular world of mysterious euphony, a cipher of poetry itself, threatened by sinister forces. The moonlit landscapes of the dead, invoked by Trakl (and also Rilke) seem very much a product of neo-romantic mysticism, but his work also touches upon an awareness of crisis which is almost expressionistic. Rilke compared the figure of Trakl with that of the mythological Linos: 'Trakls Gestalt gehört zu den linoshaft-mythischen',[46] and hence also with the figure of Orpheus for, as the last lines of the first Duino Elegy describe, it was the death of Linos that caused the Orphic lament to vibrate throughout creation. There is, however, no Orphic *religio intransitiva* in Trakl; a Christian awareness of sin informs many of the poems, and the sense of universal malaise ceases to be merely a decadent flirtation with depravity. Stylistically, his poetry, like Rilke's, outgrows the tired neo-romantic gestures and becomes far more 'modern'; these aspects will be discussed in chapter 5. But before modernism and expressionism are examined, the *fin-de-siècle* literature of Munich and Berlin must be assessed; although the Austrian poets and writers, particularly Hofmannsthal, achieved great eminence at the turn of the century, the situation in Germany is equally fascinating.

Notes

1.   Ruprecht and Bänsch (eds.), *Literarische Manifeste der Jahrhundertwende*, Stuttgart, 1970, 191.
2.   Hermann Bahr, *Die Überwindung des Naturalismus. Theoretische Schriften 1887–1904* (ed. Wunberg), Stuttgart, 1968, 85-87.
3.   Ibid., 37.
4.   Ibid., 84.
5.   *Literarische Manifeste der Jahrhundertwende*, 305.
6.   Thomas Mann, *Gesammelte Werke in 12 Bänden*, 1960, III, 720.
7.   *Literarische Manifeste der Jahrhundertwende*, 274-275.
8.   Ibid., 32.
9.   Ibid., 53.
10.   Robert Musil, *Sämtliche Erzählungen*, Hamburg, 1968, 156.
11.   Peter Altenberg, *Was der Tag mir zuträgt*, Berlin, 1911, 111 and 125.
12.   *Literarische Manifeste der Jahrhundertwende*, 33.
13.   Ibid., 298.
14.   See Manfred Gstaiger, *Französische Symbolisten in der deutschen Literatur*, Berne and Munich, 1971, 77.
15.   Hofmannsthal, *Gesammelte Werke. Gedichte, Lyrische Dramen*, 1970, 158.
16.   Strauss-Hofmannsthal, *Briefwechsel*, Zurich, 1952, 17.

17. The meeting is described in a letter to Walter Brecht, written by Hofmannsthal shortly before his death. See Boehringer (ed.), *Briefwechsel zwischen George und Hofmannsthal* (second edition), Munich and Düsseldorf, 1953, 235.
18. Hofmannsthal, *Gesammelte Werke. Gedichte, Lyrische Dramen*, 1970, 500.
19. Ibid., 502.
20. Ibid., 500.
21. Ibid., 501.
22. Hofmannsthal, *Briefe an Marie Herzfeld* (ed. Weber), Heidelberg, 1967, 37.
23. Hofmannsthal, *Gedichte, Lyrische Dramen*, 202.
24. Ibid., 209.
25. Ibid., 220.
26. Hofmannsthal, *Gesammelte Werke. Die Erzählungen*, 1945, 11.
27. Ibid., 11.
28. Ibid., 35.
29. Hofmannsthal, *Aufzeichnungen*, 1959, 124.
30. Karl Kraus, *Die demolirte Literatur*, Steinbach/Gießen, 1972, 19.
31. Alfred Kerr, *Die Welt im Drama* (ed. Hering), 1954, 86.
32. Quoted Hermann Bahr, *Überwindung*, 152-153.
33. *Literarische Manifeste der Jahrhundertwende*, 304.
34. Hofmannsthal, *Gesammelte Werke. Gedichte, Lyrische Dramen*, 44-45.
35. Schnitzler, *Gesammelte Werke*, Frankfurt/Main, 1962, *Die dramatischen Werke*, I, 62.
36. Herbert Ihering, *Von Reinhardt bis Brecht*, 78.
37. Rilke, *Sämtliche Werke in 6 Bänden*, Wiesbaden, I, 664.
38. Erich Heller, *The Disinherited Mind*, Cambridge, 1952, 102.
39. Nietzsche, *Werke*, II, 330.
40. Rilke, I, 313.
41. Holthusen, *Rainer Maria Rilke*, Rowohlt Bildmonographien, 37.
42. Rilke, III, 298-299.
43. Rilke, I, 349.
44. Georg Trakl, *Dichtungen und Briefe*, Salzburg, 1969, I, 249.
45. Ibid., I, 83.
46. *Erinnerung an Georg Trakl*, Salzburg, 1959, 10-11.

3 AESTHETICISM, DECADENCE AND NEO-ROMANTICISM IN GERMANY

In March 1889, when he was twenty-one years old, Stefan George arrived in Paris, having left Turin almost at the same time that Nietzsche had left it, clinically insane. In the Hôtel des Américains he made the acquaintance of Mallarmé, 'le prince des Poètes', and was invited to his Tuesday afternoon gatherings. After the hopeless provincialism of so much German poetry, George now entered an atmosphere redolent with the names of the great French symbolists and with the presence of Poe, Richard Wagner and Baudelaire, that poet decried by Zola in the Berlin periodical *Die Gegenwart* as a 'Räpresentant des diabolischen Romanticismus'.[1] George returned to Germany with a sense of mission: his goal was nothing less than the vivification and purification of German art — and life. As well as the obvious *l'art pour l'art* elements in George's work there will also later emerge a vast and imperious vision; conscious of the achievement of French symbolism, he will also owe a debt to his German mentors, particularly Hölderlin and Nietzsche. The cult of the spiritual aristocrat, the visionary remote in azure loneliness has already been referred to, and obviously betrays a Nietzschean presence, but on a profounder level it was Nietzsche's views on art which were of vital importance for George. For Nietzsche returned again and again to the problem of art, and passionately believed that art is the highest manifestation of life, that the artist transfigures and thereby redeems by his vision (as Baudelaire had claimed: 'Tu m'as donné ta boue, et j'en ai fait de l'or'[2]), and that life has meaning only as an aesthetic phenomenon. 'Die Kunst und nichts als die Kunst. Wir haben die Kunst, daß wir nicht an der Wahrheit zugrunde gehen',[3] and again: 'Die Kunst ist das große Stimulans zum Leben. Wie könnte man sie als zwecklos, als ziellos, als *l'art pour l'art* verstehen?'[4] — these two aphorisms illustrate his beliefs concerning art at the end of his mental life. Art as an illusion? As *l'art pour l'art*? But it is an illusion that keeps man in life, that enhances life, and it therefore is a manifestation of the Will to Power. The supreme artist is he who blesses, praises and affirms, and Nietzsche's *dicta* will reverberate as none other throughout the German literary scene of the first half of the twentieth century.

In 1890 Stefan George (or Étienne, and with a French pronunciation of the surname) cultivated the prose of the dandy (doubtless with Baudelaire in mind): the monocle, the grain of incense on the burning cigarette, the frock coat all helped to startle and impress. In 1890 the *Hymnen* appeared in one hundred copies, privately printed and circulated to friends; these were poems of a deliberate aestheticism, exquisite and exotic, betraying a deliberately esoteric sensibility. The natural is studiously avoided, the extravagant and the hermetic are stressed — and yet the little poem 'Die Spange' of the following collection, *Pilgerfahrten* (1891) praises not the heavy gold and gorgeous gems that the poet has at his disposal but the coolness of polished steel; the poet regrets that he has not this metal to make the clasp, and that he must indulge in the esoteric and the *recherché*:

> Ich wollte sie aus kühlem eisen
> Und wie ein glatter fester streif.
> Doch war im schacht in allen gleisen
> So kein metall zum gusse reif.
>
> Nun aber soll sie also sein:
> Wie eine grosse fremde dolde
> Geformt aus feuerrotem golde
> Und reichem blitzendem gestein.[5]

As early as this the condensed syntax of George's later work is observable, the reduction of punctuation to a minimum, the centred fullstop and the lack of capitalisation. It seems as though George sensed within himself a tendency towards the bizarre and the exotic which had to be controlled by discipline and order.

The meeting with Hofmannsthal in 1891 was described in the last chapter: the younger man's desire to preserve his own individuality when confronted with George's powerful personality was tempered by his admiration for George's breadth of knowledge, his intense earnestness and dedication to the highest poetic ideals. George's passionate wooing of the younger man, the spiritual, and certainly also erotic, longing for a companion who could share his highest vision ('ein hoffen — ein ahnen — ein zucken — ein schwanken — o mein zwillingsbruder'[6]) was received with remarkable maturity by Hofmannsthal, who kept a respectful distance; George's ultimata and his demands were discreetly ignored, and Hofmannsthal's father sought to clarify the relationship. Meetings between the two men ceased, and their correspondence finally terminated in 1906.

From 1892 date George's *Algabal* poems, highly stylised and of a
ruthless aestheticism. The cruelty and barbaric magnificence of the
boy-emperor Heliogabalus, priest of the sun-god, became a paradigm
for the wanton splendour of art, with the artist-emperor as an *Übermensch* beyond vulgar morality. The decadence of Rome and the cruel
beauty of the Orient fascinated many of the poets of the time:
Mallarmé's *Hérodiade*, the *Shéhérazade* poems of Tristan Klingsor
(a Wagnerian disguise for Léon Leclère) and Oscar Wilde's *Salome*
may be cited as examples. Artifice and a sterile, cruel beauty have been
raised to a *ne plus ultra*; the beautiful, degenerate young emperor
takes care lest his train be spattered with his brother's blood:

> Sieh ich bin zart wie eine apfelblüte
> und friedenfroher denn ein neues lamm.
> Doch liegen eisen stein und feuerschwamm
> Gefährlich in erschüttertem gemüte.
>
> Hernieder steig ich eine marmortreppe.
> Ein leichnam ohne haupt inmitten ruht.
> Dort sickert meines teuren bruders blut.
> Ich raffe leise nur die purpurschleppe.[7]

His will is such that his servants perish rather than feel the remorse
at having disturbed his doves:

> Wenn um der zinnen kupferglühe hauben
> Um alle giebel erst die sonne wallt
> Und kühlung noch in höfen von basalt
> Dann warten auf den kaiser seine tauben.
>
> Er trägt ein kleid aus blauer Serer-seide
> Mit sardern und safiren übersät
> In silberhülsen säumend aufgenäht.
> Doch an den armen hat er kein geschmeide.
>
> Er lächelte: sein weisser finger schenkte
> Die hirsekörner aus dem goldnen trog.
> Als leis ein Lyder aus den säulen bog
> Und an des herren fuss die stirne senkte.
>
> Die tauben flattern ängstig nach dem dache

'Ich sterbe gern weil mein gebieter schrak'
Ein breiter dolch ihm schon im busen stak.
Mit grünem flure spielt die rote lache.

Der kaiser wich mit höhender gebärde . . .
Worauf er doch am selben tag befahl
Dass in den abendlichen weinpokal
Des knechtes name eingegraben werde.[8]

The poems are written 'Dem Gedächtnis Ludwigs des Zweiten' who
became for George at this time a second Algabal, the young king who
devoted his whole life to art, who had adored Richard Wagner and who
had sought release from a banal and stultifying existence in the waters
of the Starnberger See. The *Algabal* poems are probably the finest
examples of German decadence, but in the middle of the Byzantine
posturings may be found the quiet, unpretentious poem 'Weisse
schwalben sah ich fliegen', which betrays the poet rather than the
aesthete.

In 1892 George's plan to found an exclusive journal, modelled on
the French symbolist *Écrits pour l'art* and entirely dedicated to the
cult of beauty came to fruition: the first number of the *Blätter für die
Kunst* appeared. The programme of the *Blätter* was announced as
follows:

Der name dieser veröffentlichung sagt schon zum teil was sie soll:
der kunst besonders der dichtung und dem schrifttum dienen,
alles staatliche und gesellschaftliche ausscheidend. Sie will die
GEISTIGE KUNST auf grund der neuen fühlweise und mache –
eine kunst für die kunst – und steht deshalb im gegensatz zu jener
verbrauchten und minderwertigen schule die einer falschen
auffassung der wirklichkeit entsprang. Sie kann sich auch nicht
beschäftigen mit weltverbesserungen und allbeglückungsträumen in
denen man gegenwärtig bei uns den keim zu allem neuen sieht, die
ja sehr schön sein mögen aber in ein anderes gebiet gehören als das
der dichtung (October 1892).[9]

Appearing intermittently until 1919, the *Blätter*, together with the
associated Jahrbücher, insisted on beauty and purity, and on a total
rejection of any political or philosophical commitment. The novel as
an art form is rejected because of its social preoccupations:

Das *Gedicht* ist der höchste der endgültigste ausdruck eines
geschehens: nicht wiedergabe eines gedankens sondern einer
stimmung. Was in der malerei wirkt ist verteilung linie und
farbe, in der dichtung: auswahl mass und klang . . . Man
verwechselt heute kunst (literatur) mit berichterstatterei
(reportage) zu welch lezter gattung die meisten unserer
erzählungen (sogen. romane) gehören.[10]

A spiritual élite was called for, a sodality dedicated to the cultivation
of beauty in all its manifestations, and to the expression of that beauty
in the noblest verse, regardless of vulgar utilitarianism:

Dass ein strahl von Hellas auf uns fiel: dass unsere jugend jezt
das leben nicht mehr niedrig sondern glühend anzusehen
beginnt: dass sie im leiblichen und geistigen nach schönen
massen sucht: dass sie von der schwärmerei für seichte allgemein-
bildung und beglückung sich ebenso gelöst hat als von verjährter
lanzknechtischer barbarei (November 1897).[11]

There is nothing narrowly patriotic in this programme, certainly
nothing chauvinist. George ignored with disdain the grandiloquence of
the second Reich: his disciples and colleagues came from all over
Europe; the Pole Waclaw Rolicz-Lieder, the Dutchman Verwey, the
Belgian Paul Gérardy and the Englishman Ernest Dowson — all felt
attracted and even magnetised by the hierarchic nimbus which
surrounded George.

Yet, when the sacerdotal ritual is forgotten, poems of a grave and
quiet beauty emerge. A dignified expression of restrained grief is
'Jahrestag' from *Die Bücher der Hirten- und Preisgedichte, der Sagen
und Sänge, der hängenden Gärten* (1895). The language is elevated
and the mourning is ritualised; the scene is probably Grecian, yet the
meaning is universal, and also mysteriously elusive:

O schwester nimm den krug aus grauem ton.
Begleite mich! denn du vergassest nicht
Was wir in frommer wiederholung pflegten.
Heut sind es sieben sommer dass wirs hörten
Als wir am brunnen schöpfend uns besprachen:
Uns starb am selben tag der brautigam.
Wir wollen an der quelle wo zwei pappeln
Mit einer fichte in den wiesen stehn

Im krug aus grauem tone wasser holen.[12]

George's ability to create a clear, and yet elusive situation, with a
possibly symbolic extension, is seen in 'Die Fremde' from the collection
*Der Teppich des Lebens und die Lieder von Traum und Tod, mit
einem Vorspiel* (1899). He uses the quatrains from the German folk-
song, but the heavy tread, the preference for the solid vowel of the
frequently archaic monosyllabic noun and for the strong verb are very
much George's own:

> Sie kam allein aus fernen gauen
> Ihr haus umging das volk mit grauen
> Sie sott und buk und sagte wahr
> Sie sang im mond mit offenem haar.
>
> Am kirchtag trug sie bunten staat
> Damit sie oft zur luke trat . . .
> Dann ward ihr lächeln süss und herb
> Gatten und brüdern zum verderb.
>
> Und übers jahr als sie im dunkel
> Einst lattich suchte und ranunkel
> Da sah man wie sie sank im torf —
> Und andere schwuren dass vorm dorf
>
> Sie auf dem mitten weg verschwand . . .
> Sie liess das knäblein nur als pfand
> So schwarz wie nacht so bleich wie lein
> Das sie gebar im hornungsschein.[13]

The mysterious stranger who arrives at the village, who sings in the
moonlight, incenses the villagers and vanishes, leaving a strange child,
would seem to represent the poetic spirit itself, which leaves a
mysterious gift — the poem — to startle and confuse the world of men.
Who knows from where the poem emerges, what subconscious forces
acted as an impetus? It is not for nothing that the child is associated
with bastardy.

The famous 'Komm in den totgesagten park und schau', from *Das
Jahr der Seele* (1897), also exists on two levels. The portrayal of the
park, by a skilful weaving of associative images, becomes somehow
something more:

Komm in den totgesagten park und schau:
Der schimmer ferner lächelnder gestade.
Der reinen wolken unverhofftes blau
Erhellt die weiher und die bunten pfade.

Dort nimm das tiefe gelb das weiche grau
Von birken und von buchs: der wind ist lau.
Die späten rosen welkten noch nicht ganz.
Erlese küsse sie und flicht den kranz.

Vergiss auch diese lezten astern nicht
Den purpur um die ranken wilder reben
Und auch was übrig blieb von grünem leben
Verwinde leicht im herbstlichen gesicht.[14]

The park is said to be dead, and yet the sensitive eye observes the
pastel shades of autumn: some flowers remain and bloom. Similarly,
the German literary scene, of which George frequently despaired
('Die gestalt des dichters scheint den deutschen ganz verloren zu sein.
Es gibt jetzt den gelehrten beamten bürger – der gedichte macht'[15])
is not to be rejected entirely. His own idealism and quest for poetic
merit would, he hoped, inspire a whole generation of poets: poetry
must become a vehicle for the rejuvenation of the whole national
community. Germany could also look to such figures as Nietzsche
(extolled in the famous poem 'Der siebente Ring' of 1907 and placed
alongside the 'andre führer mit der blutigen krone'[16]), Goethe and
especially Hölderlin, the poet whom George's circle, particularly
Norbert von Hellingrath, rediscovered and made available to the
intelligent reader. Similarly Jean-Paul Richter, a virtually unknown
writer in George's day, was hailed and praised in the collection *Deutsche
Dichtung* compiled by George and Wolfskehl: 'Wenn Du höchster
Goethe mit Deiner marmornen hand und Deinem sicheren schritt
unsrer sprache die edelste bauart hinterlassen hast so hat Jean Paul der
suchende der sehnende ihr gewiss die glühendsten farben gegeben und
die tiefsten klänge'.[17] It is also of interest that George, in the Jean-
Paul volume, reproached those poets who lose themselves in 'euren
mennigroten wiesen euren fosfornen gesichten und euren lilaträumen'.[18]
The 'phosphorescent' visions of the decadents, their lilac and crimson
hues, are rejected in preference to Jean Paul's depth and fervour – and
this in 1900.

The circle of men who gathered around George has given rise to much controversy. His name has been associated with Munich and the group of *littérateurs* and philosophers who gathered there in the early years of this century; George is often portrayed as holding court, surrounded by incense and Byzantine accoutrements, but it should be remembered that he had no fixed place of residence: he travelled widely and stayed in the homes of friends when in Munich and other cities. Munich had been associated with the arts since the 1850s, when King Ludwig had striven to give a classical air to his capital city; Maximilian, as was mentioned in chapter 1, gathered a host of poets around him. Munich later became associated with Richard Wagner and, at the turn of the century, it was Thomas Mann who most brilliantly captured the *fin-de-siècle* atmosphere to be found there. In the early years of the twentieth century the city attracted a whole host of literati, decadents and over-wrought pseudo-philosophers; its quirky atmosphere, compounded of *bonhomie*, aestheticism and irrational *Weltanschauungen* was very different from that of Vienna, with its genuine sense of tradition stretching back for centuries. Munich's *bohème* had an air of self-consciousness not found in the Austrian city.

Thomas Mann (1875–1955) moved from Lübeck to the Bavarian capital in 1893. After a sojourn in Italy with his brother Heinrich he returned to Munich where, from 1898 to 1899 he worked as a reader on the editorial board of the satirical journal *Simplicissimus*, founded by Albert Langen and made famous by the satirical drawings of Thomas Theodor Heine and the Norwegian caricaturist Olaf Gulbransson. Mann's earliest work shows an undeniable debt to the naturalistic vogue: *Gefallen* (1894) was published in M.G. Conrad's *Die Gesellschaft* and *Der kleine Herr Friedemann* (1897) contains the almost obligatory themes of alcoholism and determinism. But the young author's detached, analytic vision was already tinged by an ironic sophistication; the 'Pathos der Distanz', and the pose of the fastidious observer betray the influence of Nietzsche, whose analysis of decadence fascinated Thomas Mann. In Munich he had ample opportunity to study the more extravagant vagaries of the literary mentality, and personally knew many of the aesthetes and *enfants terribles*, including Kurt Martens (1870–1945) and Arthur Holitscher (1869–1941). Martens's *Roman aus der Décadence* (1898) Thomas Mann certainly knew, with its 'hero', Just, who is described in his progress away from bourgeois normality towards anarchist circles, Catholic rites and bizarre séances. Martens portrays Just's friend, Erich von Lüttwitz, as depraved and degenerate: perversion, cruelty and the Salome-figure add a particularly decadent flavour to the novel.

Arthur Holitscher's *Der vergiftete Brunnen* (1900) was read by
Mann and recommended by him for publication. (Holitscher, incidentally, became a model for Detlev Spinell in Thomas Mann's *Tristan*, and
claimed, in his memoirs, that Thomas Mann had watched him through
opera-glasses from his window.) The novel is very much of its time,
with the description of the jewel-encrusted sphinx, with eyes of
turquoise, lips of ark-violet amethysts and nipples of enormous rubies.
The life of the heroine, Desirée Wilmoth, is similar to that of des
Esseintes in its luxury and languor (there is also an echo of 'Melmoth'
in the choice of name).

Holitscher's Novelle *Von der Wollust und dem Tode* (1902) portrays the hero's final achievement of sexual climax after he has cut
his wrists and slides dead upon his partner, thus enacting a grotesque
love-death. A novel by Gerhard Ouckama-Knoop (father of Wera,
whose death inspired Rilke's *Sonette an Orpheus*) entitled *Die
Dekadenten – Psychologischer Roman* (1898) anticipates certain
figures in the early work of Thomas Mann, particularly the officer,
who is analysed thus by his doctor: 'Du bist zwar nicht krank, aber
auch kein normaler Mensch . . . Zwar gehörst du den Entarteten, aber
Entartung ist nicht stets, noch für immer ein Unglück. Du teilst dein
Übel mit einem Drittel der zivilisierten Menschheit . . . Du bist ein
Degenerierter höherer Gattung'.[19] The term 'Entartung' may well
have been taken from Max Nordau's famous attack on modern
literature of five years before; whereas Nordau had rejected indiscriminately the whole of modern writing as being effete and perverse,
novelists such as Martens, Holitscher and Ouckama-Knoop took pride
in their decadence as being the highest, most sophisticated evolution
of the human imagination. Writing later in the *Betrachtungen eines
Unpolitischen*, Thomas Mann admits that this period of decadence
and amoral aestheticism was the period from which he stemmed and
from which he derived many of his ideas concerning the artist, his
triumphs and his insufficiencies: the generation of writers to which he
belonged was destined to become the chroniclers and analysts of the
fin-de-siècle mentality. In *Meine Zeit* he explains: 'was das über
Europa hingehende Schlagwort "Fin de Siècle" nur immer meinen
mochte, Neu-Katholizismus, Satanismus, das geistige Verbrechen, die
mürbe Überlieferung des Nervenrausches – auf jeden Fall war es eine
Formel des Ausklangs, die allzu modische und etwas geckenhafte
Formel für das Gefühl des Endes, des Endes eines Zeitalters, des
bürgerlichen'.[20]

For Thomas Mann this was above all the time of writing *Budden-*

brooks, which appeared in 1901 and is the perfect fusion of realistic observation and subtle, symbolic extension, a novel deeply indebted to European realism, to Fontaine and the Goncourts, to Jonas Lie (*Ein Mahlstrom*) and Alexander Kjelland, but also to Nietzsche, Schopenhauer and Wagner. (Ricarda Huch's first novel, the study of a cultivated Hanseatic family in decline, which appeared in 1892 and was entitled *Erinnerungen von Ludolf Ursleu dem Jüngeren*, may also have played a part, with its portrayal of the fatalistic capitulation before the intoxication of the erotic, and also the outbreak of cholera.) The theme of heredity, certainly, seems reminiscent of naturalism, but, as Thomas Mann later explained: 'Der junge Verfasser von *Buddenbrooks* hatte die Psychologie des Verfalls von Nietzsche gelernt';[21] he also referred to the powerful trio 'Schopenhauer, Nietzsche und Wagner: ein Dreigestirn ewig verbundener Geister'[22] who exerted such a powerful influence over him. 'Robust und morbid' − these two adjectives of Musil are inevitably used when the house of Buddenbrooks is described, where growth in sensitivity and artistic awareness is only achieved at the cost of uncomplicated living and healthy optimism. From Nietzsche's scintillating aperçus Thomas Mann had learned of the relationship between sickness and art, and between vitalism and decadence; this most ruthless of psychologists had called into doubt Schopenhauer's insistence upon the sublimity of art and questioned the motives behind artistic creation. His writings, and Wagner's dubious example, had sharpened Thomas Mann's awareness of the tensions existing between the claims of the spirit and the demands of life, between thought and sensitivity on the one hand and ruthless 'normality' on the other. It is Thomas Buddenbrook (whose character had been adumbrated in the short story *Der Bajazzo*) and his wife Gerda who are 'nervös' and complex; she has the strength of her musical talents, her playing, to sustain her, and also her supreme indifference to the Buddenbrook tradition. But Thomas has to face each day with a supreme effort of will: having seen through the meaningless farce of existence he seeks solace in Schopenhauer, yet a Schopenhauer, as Erich Heller has pointed out,[23] curiously mixed with Nietzschean *Lebensbejahung*. Their son, Hanno, weak and sensitive, can do nothing but swoon to Wagner's heady poisons and finally succumb to the temptations of death, lacking in his final illness the will to live. The family declines, and the *nouveaux-riches* triumph, but is their victory not a hollow one? The strength of the Buddenbrooks is utterly sapped, yet have they not gained in sensitivity and insight? With consummate irony Thomas Mann delineates those who live and those who think about life,

those who are content to live their lives as Hanseatic burghers and
those who move restlessly in the realms of spiritual adventures.
'Verfall einer Familie' – the novel would perhaps have used the term
decadence in its title had not Martens used the word for his novel in
1898. Thomas Mann's indifference to the social and political problems
of his day, certainly up to and including the *Betrachtungen* is well
known, but behind the fate of this one family a larger process may
perhaps be discerned, the decline of the whole bourgeois tradition.
Speaking later, Thomas Mann made the following observations about
his youthful masterpiece: 'daß an seinen Bildern, Charakteren,
Stimmungen und Schicksalen das europäische Bürgertum überhaupt
sich wiedererkannte, sich und seine seelische Situation um die Jahrhundertwende, von wo es knapp anderthalb Jahrzehnte nur noch
bis zum Ausbruch der Weltrevolution und zum Ende des bürgerlichen
Zeitalters waren.'[24] The novel might be called 'ein Werk, dessen
tiefstes Anliegen Psychologie, und zwar die Psychologie ermüdenden
Lebens, die seelischen Verfeinerungen und ästhetischen Verklärungen
war, welche den biologischen Niedergang begleiten'.[25]

Art and its temptations, beauty and its disregard of morality and
convention, the fascination of decadence, of lassitude and perversion:
Thomas Mann experienced the blandishments of the Bavarian capital
with an ironic detachment remarkable for a man in his mid-twenties.
The story *Gladius Dei*, which appeared in 1902, begins with an
incomparable description of a sparkling summer morning in the city:

> München leuchtete. Über den festlichen Plätzen und weißen
> Säulentempelchen, den antikisierenden Monumenten und Barock-
> kirchen, den springenden Brunnen, Palästen und Gartenanlagen der
> Residenz spannte sich strahlend ein Himmel von blauer Seide,
> und ihre breiten und lichten, umgrünten und wohlberechneten
> Perspektiven lagen in dem Sonnendunst eines ersten, schönen
> Junitages. Vogelgeschwätz und heimlicher Jubel über allen Gassen
> . . . Und auf Plätzen und Zeilen rollt, wallt und summt das
> unüberstürzte und amüsante Treiben der schönen und gemäch-
> lichen Stadt . . . Viele Fenster stehen geöffnet, und aus vielen
> klingt Musik auf die Straßen hinaus . . . Junge Leute, die das
> Nothung-Motiv pfeifen und abends die Hintergründe des modernen
> Schauspielhauses füllen, wandern, literarische Zeitschriften in den
> Seitentaschen ihrer Jacketts, in der Universität und der Staats-
> bibliothek aus und ein.[26]

This is the city, Thomas Mann infers, where art flourishes, and yet it is also the city where Tonio Kröger, in 1903, questioned the whole meaning of art, the city in which the artist battens upon healthy, innocent desire as a vampire, drawing the very life blood away in his restless greed for sensations. With a feeling amounting almost to bitterness Tonio Kröger announces: 'Das Gefühl, das warme, herzliche Gefühl ist immer banal und unbrauchbar, und künstlerisch sind bloß die Gereiztheiten und kalten Ekstasen unseres verdorbenen, unseres artistischen Nervensystems.'[27] Does being artistic mean being precious, *raffiné* and morbidly sensitive? Does the artist truly *live*, or is he not rather like an emasculated singer? 'Die Literatur ist überhaupt kein Beruf, sondern ein Fluch – damit Sie's wissen'.[28] Tonio Kröger, at home neither with the burghers of Lübeck nor the aesthetes of Munich, nevertheless proclaims his love for life, for innocence and honesty, but not the cult of Life and Power, not the cult of Cesare Borgia and the demented vitalism of the pseudo-philosophers.

Munich was to remain Thomas Mann's home until his exile in 1933; he married into the wealthy Pringsheim family, and the novel *Königliche Hoheit* and the later story *Unordnung und frühes Leid* provide amusing and penetrating autobiographical details of his marriage and his family life. (*Königliche Hoheit* is an allegorical novel: the poet-prince whose life is inauthentic and unreal until his marriage certainly refers to Thomas Mann's own situation; the chapter 'Der hohe Beruf' is an ironic portrayal of the play-acting indulged in by the prince and anticipates the *Hochstapler*-motif which will be very dear to Thomas Mann, found, of course, in *Felix Krull* and the figure of Joseph in the great tetralogy.) Before his marriage Thomas Mann paid a visit, with his future mother-in-law, to the attic of Ludwig Derleth (1870–1948), whose *Proklamationen* were read out. In 1904 he published the short story *Beim Propheten*, which is an account of this visit; the 'prophet', Daniel, is described, who 'verlor sich in irre Bilder, ging in einem Wirbel von Unlogik unter und tauchte plötzlich an gänzlich unerwarteter Stelle gräßlich wieder empor. Lästerungen und Hosianna – Weihrauch und Qualm von Blut vermischten sich. In donnernden Schlachten ward die Welt erobert und erlöst'.[29] Daniel, to be introduced forty years later as Daniel zur Höhe in *Doktor Faustus*, was certainly based on the figure of Derleth, a young poet who had met George in Paris and who had come to Munich ostensibly to study philosophy. He had published certain poems in 1896 ('Anadyomene' and 'Verwesung und Flamme') and, in the following year, inspired by Sâr Joséphin Péladan, the decadent Wagnerian and 'Grand Maître de la

Rose-Croix du Temple et du Graal', journeyed to Rome to found a
new order, a spiritual-military brotherhood with the Nietzschean vision
of 'Caesar with the soul of Christ' as its watchword. In 1902 Derleth
settled in Munich's Schwabing, in an attic in Destouches-Straße No. 1,
to await revelation; in 1903 he journeyed once more to Rome to await
the announcement of the next Pope, Pius the Tenth (a situation not
unlike that of the English 'Baron Corvo', that is, Frederick Rolfe).
Derleth believed that the Apocalypse was at hand, and that Christus-
Imperator Maximus would come with fire and sword to bring a reign
of terror; in Easter Week 1904 invitations were sent out to an exclusive
circle announcing the reading of his *Proklamationen*. The readings
were to be given by his devoted sister Anna and two other disciples;
Derleth was not present. Thomas Mann and Frau Pringsheim attended
the second reading; a private reading to Stefan George of certain
'Herausschreiungen' had been given previously.[30]

In his *Proklamationen* Derleth called for discipline, obedience,
violence, ecstasy, cruelty, destruction and terror — Thomas Mann saw
here the close proximity of aestheticism and brutality. Derleth's cosmic
visions were similar to the work of Alfred Schuler, also of Ludwig
Klages, both of whom were associated with Stefan George until the
break in 1903: this will be discussed later. The hectic perorations, the
rodomontade of Schuler, and his confused desires (he had hoped to
dance before the insane Nietzsche in copper in the hope of effecting a
cure) seemed typical of the intellectual climate of the Bavarian capital
before 1914, a heady and ominous anticipation of irrational excess to
come.

George's insistence on 'mass und klang', his hatred of turgid hyperbole and his demand for clarity and order must needs have led him to
reject the work of Derleth, Schuler and Klages, erstwhile companions
who broke away to form cults and enact rites of their own. George
shared with Schuler and Klages an aversion to Christianity, but it was
his aesthetic need for perfected mortality, for *kalokagathia*, which
made him turn to the Greek world and to Hölderlin, and not to any
feverish myth or ominous *Deutschtümelei*. George's outlook, it must
be stressed, remained essentially cosmopolitan, his admiration for
certain aspects of German culture being manifestations of that
'vaterländische Umkehr' of which Hölderlin spoke. George felt it
increasingly necessary to assume the role of *Meister*, a magnetic centre
holding the spiritual exercises of his companions together; those who
fled into purely personal gratification, like Schuler and Klages, moved
necessarily towards disintegration:

Wer je die flamme umschritt
Bleibe der flamme trabant!
Wie er auch wandert und kreist:
Wo noch ihr schein ihn erreicht
Irrt er zu weit nie vom ziel.

Nur wenn sein blick sie verlor
Eigener schimmer ihn trügt
Fehlt ihm der mitte gesetz
Treibt er zerstiebend ins all.[31]

The disciples who remained closest to George included Karl
Wolfskehl, Friedrich Gundolf, Ernst Bertram, Max Kommerell, Ernst
Kantorowicz and a host of lesser figures. How far George encouraged
their adulation is uncertain: the young men whom he met seemed all
too ready to use excessive and fulsome praise of his person. The
description by Edgar Salin of the appearance of George on the streets
of Heidelberg may be quoted as representative: 'War es ein Mensch
gewesen, der durch die Menge schritt? Aber er unterschied sich von
allen Menschen, die er durchwanderte, durch eine ungewußte Hoheit
und durch eine spielende Kraft, so daß neben ihm alle Gänger wie
blasse Larven, wie seellose Schemen wirkten. War es ein Gott, der das
Gewühl zerteilt hatte und leichtfüßig zu anderen Gestaden enteilt
war?'[32]

The intellectual fruits of the communion with the *Meister* include
Gundolf's *Goethe*, Bartram's *Nietzsche*, Kommerell's *Der Dichter als
Führer in der deutschen Klassik* and Ernst Kantorowicz's *Friedrich
der Zweite*. The 'monumentalising' attitude of these writers, their
elevation of history to the realm of myth, has been criticised by many,
but whether George himself should be blamed for this tendency which,
after all, stems from Nietzsche, is doubtful. His disgust for Wilhelm's
Reich has already been mentioned: in spirit he moved to France (the
poem 'Franken' of *Der siebente Ring* tells of the great figures Mallarmé,
Verlaine and Villiers de l'Isle-Adam), to classical Greece ('Hellas ewig
unsere Liebe') and the beauty of perfect physical form, to
Shakespeare's sonnets, to Dante, Petrarch, Rossetti, Rimbaud,
D'Annunzio, Dowson and all who strove to transcend the base and the
ignoble. His 'monochrome' poetry, replacing the decadence of the
earliest period, with its aloof punctuation and type-face, spoke, it is
true, solely to initiates, but those who persevered found that the rigid
lines of verse, the welded severities and trochaic tread contained a

sober beauty.

Yet this fascinating man, who insisted upon order and form, was vulnerable, as the Hofmannsthal experience showed, to passionate abandonment. The Maximin incident proved a stumbling block to many readers and disciples: the Dutch poet Verwey felt estranged by George's cult of the dead youth and the elevation of this rather unremarkable young man after his death to the status of a god. The Greek concept of *kalokagathia* had undeniable erotic overtones, and George had sublimated only with difficulty the passionate urges within him. In 1902 he introduced himself on the street to Maximilian Kronberger, then fourteen years old; he had desired to sketch Kronberger's head, and had taken him to a photographer for a portrait. Kronberger later read Klage's book on George, which had appeared that year, and many months later, in January 1903, he met George again on the street, and was invited to the circle. Throughout the year the meetings remained sporadic; Kronberger, at times, infuriated George by his inability to concede to every whim. But Kronberger was present at the famous *Dichterzug*; on 14 February he appeared as a Florentine page-boy, dressed in red stockings and a red smock, bearing a red candle in his hand (made by George, but unfortunately without a wick) and wearing a wreath of red carnations in his hair. George was dressed as Dante (his striking profile resembled the Italian poet greatly), and Wolfskehl as Homer. On 24 March, on the occasion of the appearance of the seventh number of the *Blätter für die Kunst* the *Dichterzug* was repeated, this time Kronberger wearing a simple blue tunic with a wreath of violets in his hair.[33] But this Alcibiades was already touched by death; after the performance he went straight to Vienna, but returned at the beginning of April, suffering from cerebro-spinal meningitis. He died on 15 April, one day after his sixteenth birthday.

The deification of the young man may appear blasphemous, even perverse; what ultimately matters is the quality of the poetry which emerged from this experience. The *Gedenkbuch für Maximin* appeared in 1906: here *Maximin* was seen as the embodiment of the ideal of classical Greece, the perfect blend of the physical and the spiritual, the perfectly formed body containing the Germanic qualities of earnestness, idealism and spiritual fervour. *Maximin* became an ideal which was to provide an inspiration for those who sought beauty in an age of ever-increasing banausic vulgarity. The collection *Der siebente Ring* has the book *Maximin* as its central axis, but it is George's last collection, *Das neue Reich*, which contains the most moving tribute to the young man, the poem 'Du schlank und rein wie eine flamme', an effusion of love that has no equal in George's work; in vigorous iambics he binds the 'du' and the 'ich' together in an insoluble relationship:

> Du schlank und rein wie eine flamme
> Du wie der morgen zart und licht
> Du blühend reis vom edlen stamme
> Du wie ein quell geheim und schlicht
>
> Begleitest mich auf sonnigen matten
> Umschauerst mich im abendrauch
> Erleuchtest meinen weg im schatten
> Du kühler wind du heisser hauch
>
> Du bist mein wunsch und mein gedanke
> Ich atme dich mit jeder luft
> Ich schlürfe dich mit jedem tranke
> Ich küsse dich mit jedem duft
>
> Du blühend reis vom edlen stamme
> Du wie ein quell geheim und schlicht
> Du schlank und rein wie eine flamme
> Du wie der morgen zart und licht.[34]

Here natural and elemental images, appropriate to spontaneous feeling, open and close the poem, holding it in an intense embrace: the youth's presence is hailed everywhere in nature, in sunlight and darkness, in coolness and heat (one thinks involuntarily of Goethe's 'Allgegenwart' here); the third stanza, in its powerful eroticism, moves from 'atmen' to 'schlürfen' to 'küssen', making this one of the most powerful love poems in the German language.

Disruption and passion, homosexual love and the Munich setting – Thomas Mann's *Der Tod in Venedig* springs inevitably to mind. But this remarkable story, this complex crystal,[35] dating from 1911, is not simply an indirect elaboration of George's Maximin experience: other names and situations spring to mind – Richard Wagner, who had died in Venice and had composed much of the *Tristan* music there, the homosexual poet Platen, author of the *Sonette aus Venedig* who had died of cholera in Syracuse, also Gustav Mahler, whom Thomas Mann had met after the performance of the première of the Eighth Symphony in September 1910, and the news of whose death reached Mann on the Lido of Venice, and possibly also Winckelmann, who had devoted his life to 'edle Einfalt und stille Größe' and who was murdered by a young man in Trieste. The biographical details may be of interest: Thomas Mann visited the Lido in 1911, and his passionate feeling for the painter Paul Ehrenberg may have contributed to the story, as it would to the relationship between Schwerdtfeger and Leverkühn in *Doktor Faustus*.

Thomas Mann takes pains to show that definite similarities exist between himself and his Aschenbach, certainly as far as their literary output is concerned: the story, however, becomes a more general statement concerning the dangers of aestheticism, even when that aestheticism presents a classical exterior. Aschenbach, the reader is told, hated the decadent, the ostentatious and the whole *vie bohémienne* and sought to eliminate from his work all that was dubious and suspect. But concentration on pure form also leads to the 'abyss', for form is amoral, indifferent to good and evil. This *Leistungsethiker*, this man who daily took a cold shower before settling down to work, whose timetable was rigorously ordered, realises too late that the Dionysian forces would assert themselves if denied too long and that classical form is no defence against the monstrous and the perverse. Aschenbach had not grasped the saving grace of irony, that ability to see both sides, to refuse to pass unthinking moral judgement – this is the great difference between author and fictional hero. And Mann achieves the *tour de force* of expressing this tale of degradation and disintegration in a flawlessly classical style, in prose which at times verges on the hexameter. A profoundly psychological study of the dangers inherent in the artistic character merges with a mythical extension: the move from north to south, from rock to water, from Wotan's ravens to the sun-god's chariot is grafted effortlessly on to a realistic milieu, and Aschenbach's walk through the Englischer Garten, along the Ungererstrasse to the Nordfriedhof may be traced in the appropriate Baedeker. It is of interest that Thomas Mann read Goethe's *Die Wahlverwandtschaften* several times when at work on *Der Tod in Venedig*: the conflict between civilisation and passionate disruption, between the park and the elements of nature seemed an appropriate dichotomy to him. The essay by Georg Lukács *Die Seele und die Formen* also played a part, particularly in its discussion of the ambiguous nature of Platonic inspiration.[36]

Thomas Mann once described himself as a 'Chronist und Erläuterer der Dekadenz, Liebhaber des Pathologischen und des Todes, einen Ästheten mit der Tendenz zum Abgrund'.[37] His *Wälsungenblut*, published in 1906 but withdrawn by himself for fear of certain misunderstandings is probably the most acute portrayal in German literature of the symptoms of decadence — sterile narcissism, perversion and incest, with Wagner's *Die Walküre* acting as the erotic impetus. Élémir Bourges, in 1884, had described a similar experience in his *Le crépuscule des dieux*; in Mann's story the utterly empty lives of the wealthy twins Siegmund and Sieglinde Aarenhold are portrayed with ruthless precision, and the seductive power of Wagner's music is that force which drives them to sexual intercourse. The description of Siegmund's toilet is masterly, as is that of the meaningless emptiness of his days:

> Siegmund machte Toilette für die Oper, und zwar seit einer Stunde. Ein außerordentliches und fortwährendes Bedürfnis nach Reinigung war ihm eigen, dergestalt, daß er einen beträchtlichen Teil des Tages vorm Lavoir verbrachte. Er stand jetzt vor seinem großen, weißgerahmten Empire-Spiegel, tauchte den Puderquast in die getriebene Büchse und puderte sich Kinn und Wangen . . .[38]

Pampered and cosseted, Siegmund Aarenhold can find only in his twin sister, his mirror-image, a partner who can in any way understand him; the flippant, superior tone with which they address each other conceals darker desires which are liberated after a performance of Wagner's opera whose hero and heroine, bearing the same names as themselves, commit the incestuous act in rapturous abandonment. It is Siegmund Aarenhold's tragedy that what is probably his first spontaneous act should be one of sterility and perversion. Decadence and aestheticism are closely interwoven here; it is also possible to see in this disturbing story an expression of that undeniable narcissism which undoubtedly affected Thomas Mann's writing at this time (the description of certain aspects of the Aarenhold household seemed uncomfortably close to those of the Pringsheim family) and his interest in the more pathological aspects of sexuality, seen also in the later works *Der Erwählte* and *Die Betrogene*.

Three years after the brief appearance of *Wälsungenblut* in the *Neue Rundschau* (1906) there was published in Munich Alfred Kubin's *Die andere Seite. Ein phantastischer Roman*, a fascinating portrayal of a dream-land utterly dedicated to ultra-aesthetic refinements, subtle, exquisite sensations and all kinds of perverse luxury. In this land beyond Samarkand, with its capital Perle, a much magnified *À rebours*

is found, ruled by the millionnaire Patera. The land is described as
being enveloped in mist, through which the sun never penetrates;
a bizarre palace stands above a mass of labyrinthine alleys, each
containing corners where strange and secret lusts are enacted. Patera,
'hegt einen außerordenlich tiefen Widerwillen gegen alles Fortschritt-
liche im allgemeinen';[39] he refuses to allow any machinery into his
domain. The inhabitants of Perle, Kubin explains, consist mainly of
those who had once been the inmates of mental homes: 'Die besseren
darunter waren Menschen von übertrieben feiner Empfindlichkeit.
Noch nicht überhandnehmende fixe Ideen, wie Sammelwut, Lesefieber,
Spielteufel, Hyperreligiosität und all die tausend Formen, welche die
feine Neurasthenie ausmachen, waren für den Traumstaat wie
geschaffen'.[40] This land of eclectic aestheticism, of over-refined souls,
degenerate and blasé, knows that its days are numbered, and the end
comes with the arrival of Hercules Bell, an American who preaches
utilitarianism, equality and progress. Mass copulation, sadism and
frenzy break loose, a *Blutdunst* envelops all, and the town is destroyed.
This work may indeed be prophetic: an over-ripe civilisation, seeking
ever more thrilling *frissons* to spice the jaded appetite, which clings
to the old rather than face the new (every fifth shop in Perle is owned
by an antique dealer) and which indulges in lascivious titillation must
surely by a familiar idea to the modern reader. To return to Thomas
Mann, it is also possible that he found in this work the theme of the
healthy American *vis-à-vis* the moribund which he will later use in *Die
Betrogene.*

Before leaving the artistic and intellectual situation in Munich at
the turn of the century the phenomenon of *Jugendstil* must be briefly
considered, which was associated above all with that city but which
spread out over Germany and Austria. Like so many labels for
literary movements (impressionism and expressionism are the ones
that come most readily to mind) the term was first used in the history
of art, and came to describe a decorative formalism used by the artists
associated with the Munich journal *Jugend*, which first appeared in
1896. The designs were frequently ornamental, using arabesques and
swirling lines, and showed a predilection for tendrils, foliage, birds,
swans and fountains. The tendency is yet another aspect of the anti-
naturalistic movement of the times, and the artists dwelt upon the
exotic, the decorative and all that was remote from the day-to-day:
lakes and islands, the Japanese element (as seen in the Orientalism of
Lafcadio Hearn), dancing maidens with swirling hair, streaming incense
and flying clouds — these became the favourite designs.[41]

In poetry (and the movement, as with so many neo-romantic or anti-naturalistic tendencies, is one in which the smaller artistic forms were preferred) the themes mirrored the designs: it is a poetry of parks and fountains, also of dance, of 'Flöten und Geigen', which seems to stem from the carnival and cabaret, as does the poetry of Otto Julius Bierbaum (1865–1910), who founded and worked for several of the important periodicals (*Pan*, a bibliophile quarterly, and *Insel* were two of these) and who also appeared in *Die elf Scharfrichter* in Munich. The titles of his works, *Lobtanz* (1895), *Der bunte Vogel* (1896), *Pan im Busch* (1900) and the *Irrgarten der Liebe* (1901) show the preoccupation with the arabesque, the dance, the labyrinth and the plumage of exotic bords. Rilke's 'Lieder der Mädchen' and such poems as 'Das war der Tag der leichten Chrysanthemen' fit well into the *Jugendstil* atmosphere, as does much of the poetry of Stefan George's beginnings; the lettering on Detlev Spinell's one and only novel (in *Tristan*) is also very much in the *Jugendstil* manner.

It is commonly believed that Vienna and Munich were the centres of neo-romantic aestheticism, and that Berlin was untouched by this reaction against naturalism. The novel of Heinrich Mann (1871–1950), *Im Schlaraffenland. Ein Roman unter feinen Leuten* (1900), gives a satirical account of the literary and fashionable life in Berlin at this time; most diverting is the lively description of the performance of a naturalist play before an expensively exclusive audience, where the proletariat's cry for vengeance on the stage is greeted by tumultuous applause from the audience: 'Es war eine Szene, der niemand widerstand. Der Racheschrei des ausgesogenen, geschändeten Volkes ging durch das ganze Haus. Er durchschüttelte die Damen, daß ihre Brillanten klirrten . . . Die Millionäre auf den Stehplätzen schrien da capo. Ihre weißen Handschuhe klafften bereits, und infolge ihres minutenlang aushaltenden Beifallssturmes war man genötigt, den Vorhang herabzulassen'.[42] But it is unsubtle to assume that Berlin had been the centre of naturalism: Munich had also had *Die Gesellschaft*, and M.G. Conrad's advocation of Zola was far more radical than the naturalism of the Hart brothers in Berlin, as chapter 1 has already pointed out. Berlin certainly had the *Freie Bühne*, but the Prussian city, capital of Wilhelm's Reich, likewise showed that naturalism could not satisfy on a profound level: scarcely had *Vor Sonnenaufgang* and *Die Weber* made their impact on the German stage than Gerhart Hauptmann turned his attention to symbolic, poetical dramas, and the Pole Stanislaw Przybyszewski became the centre of a group of bohemian aesthetes no less bizarre or inclined to decadence

than their Munich counterparts. The brashness and ugliness of much
of the Prussian city, the arrogance of a militaristic caste and the
Philistinism of the established society made the need for a flight from
reality and a deliberate flouting of Wilhelmine taboos more marked
than elsewhere.

The memoirs of Stanislaw Przybyszewski (1868–1927) are an
indispensable account of the Berlin situation at the beginning of the
century. In Friedrichshagen Przybyszewski met Ola Hansson, the
Swedish poet who had married the German authoress Laura Marholm
in 1889 and had settled in Berlin after the hostile reception of his work
in Sweden. Both he and Hansson shared an admiration for Strindberg
and Nietzsche; Lou Salomé lived close by and, in her meetings with
Hansson and Strindberg, provided first-hand information on the tragic
philosopher. Strindberg had corresponded briefly with Nietzsche at
the time of his mental collapse, and Przybyszewski had, in fact,
caught a glimpse of the insane Nietzsche during a visit to Weimar:
'Es war ein schrecklicher Augenblick: Als wenn eine machtvolle,
heilige, gotische Kathedrale zusammengestürzt wäre – eine riesenhafte
Ruine und Trümmer, die den Betrachter mit dem Schauder des Ungeheuren durchdringt!'[43] Przybyszewski, as has been pointed out, took
pains to denigrate Hauptmann and, in fact, most of the attempts at
drama instigated by the naturalists; he poured scorn on Max Halbe's
Jugend ('gibt es ein elenderes, dümmeres, flacheres dramatisches
Machwerk?'[44]), but made an exception of *Die Familie Selicke*. He
turned increasingly to a morbid, decadent aestheticism or satanism:
his *Totenmesse* (1893) and *Satanskinder* (1897) brought him the
reputation he so avidly sought.

In 1894 Przybyszewski met Strindberg in Berlin, and the tavern
'Zum schwarzen Ferkel' became the Berlin equivalent of the Café
Griensteidl, although the Scandinavian element (the painter Edvard
Munch was also an habitué) lent an intensity and a crudeness not found
in the Viennese circles. Symptoms of paranoia associated with
Hansson and Strindberg are also to be found in Przybyszewski, together
with a flaunting of 'demonic' powers, immorality and genius: 'Immer
habe ich die Wahnsinnigen geliebt, die Psychopathen, Degenerierten,
Entgleisten, die unvollständigen und verkümmerten Menschen.'[45]
It is not without a certain pride that Przybyszewski claimed that
Peter Altenberg held him responsible for the suicide of Otto Weininger,
author of the immensely popular *Geschlecht und Charakter*, after
Weininger had read *Totenmesse*; it would seem, however, that the young
man's suicide (at the age of twenty-three he had shot himself in the

room in which Beethoven had died in Vienna) was a flamboyant
gesture of *Weltschmerz* and repugnance.

Przybyszewski later made the acquaintance of Sigbjørn Obstfjelder,
the Norwegian *fin-de-siècle* poet greatly admired by Rilke, and also
Knut Hamsun, but the most vital of his friendships was with Richard
Dehmel (1863–1920). Dehmel achieved great popularity during his
lifetime: he was hailed by Liliencron, Emil Ludwig, Frank Wedekind
and others as being Germany's greatest poet at that time ('Nietzsche
philosophus, Dehmel poeta'), and many composers, including Strauss,
Reger, Pfitzner and Schönberg, set his poems to music. Gustav
Landauer wrote of him: 'Er empfindet urweltlich, ursprünglich . . .
alles Geistige, bloß Geistige, Kulturliche, will immer wieder im Triebe
baden, ins Ursprüngliche hinabsteigen, zur Natur werden'.[46] Dehmel's
work encompassed not only naturalism, but also a form of *Jugendstil*
and even expressionism (see *A Literary History of Germany*, vol. 7,
pp. 149-152); from what might be called a popular Darwinism he
moved to an aesthetic transfiguration of reality and a fervent pantheism,
a Dionysian affirmation *à la* Nietzsche. His *Erlösungen: eine
Seelenwanderung in Gedichten und Sprüchen* had appeared in 1891:
certain of these poems, 'Der Rächer' and 'Landung', with their swan
imagery, seem to presage *Jugendstil*; the Kaspar Hauser poem (a translation, like that of Wolf Graf von Kalckreuth, of Verlaine)
demonstrates the fascination that this figure had for the neo-romantic
generation. But the 'Nachruf an Nietzsche' and the fervour of many
poems, with their imagery of light, flame and morning, proclaim an
affirmation, ecstatic and frequently erotic, which transcends delicacy
and refinement. The poems of *Aber die Liebe* (1893) explore the
relationship between the sexes with passion and occasional pathos;
social awareness is also present (for example, in the popular 'Der
Arbeitsmann'), yet there is no crude socialism, rather an awareness of
the true nature of the human personality, of the joy felt in sexual love
and the hope for true emancipation in the future. *Die Verwandlungen
der Venus* seems more reminiscent of Przybyszewski (the poem 'Venus
bestia', with the description of the slimy slugs sucking the damp fungus
is, fortunately, not typical[47]), but Dehmel is far removed in his basic
attitudes from the cult of the morbid and the perverse; there is in his
poetry a healthy sexuality and a pantheistic eroticism akin to
Whitman's. The collection *Zwei Menschen* also achieved great popularity
(Schönberg's *Verklärte Nacht* derives from it), as did *Weib und Welt*;
the rhapsodic rhetorical style of many of the poems may indeed be
regarded as prefiguring certain aspects of expressionism.

'Wirklich der erste, der den Naturalismus völlig zerbrach, vielleicht weil er nie tief in ihm gesteckt hatte, war Richard Dehmel': thus Przybyszewski claimed.[48] He dedicated to Dehmel his *Totenmesse* ('Meinem Freunde, dem Dichter der *Verwandlungen der Venus*'), and spoke frequently of Dehmel's charitable nature, his support of Liliencron, Mombert, the hapless Peter Hille and many others. Przybyszewski's rejection of Hauptmann may have been symptomatic of the envy felt by the less successful for the man who, apparently, can succeed in many genres and different styles. One year after the success of *Die Weber* Hauptmann's *Hanneles Himmelfahrt* was performed in Berlin: the theme, however, may be found as early as 1885 in *Das bunte Buch*. (It is also possible to draw parallels between this work and Kleist's *Käthchen von Heilbronn*; Hauptmann's comedy *Der Biberpelz* is also cast in the same mould as *Der zerbrochene Krug*.) The opening scenes with the wretched house, the bare walls and dirty bed prepare the audience for another naturalist work, but the mystical, religious visions of the child at the end (curiously reminiscent of Mahler's Fourth Symphony) lift the drama on to a very different plane. The work is indeed a 'Traumdichtung' where the teacher Gottwald becomes an angelic messenger who proclaims:

> Die Seligkeit ist eine wunderschöne Stadt,
> Wo Friede und Freude kein Ende mehr hat.
> Ihre Häuser sind Marmel, ihre Dächer sind Gold,
> roter Wein in den silbernen Brünnlein rollt . . .
> auf den weißen, weißen Straßen sind Blumen gestreut,
> von den Türmen klingt ewiges Hochzeitsgeläut.[49]

The faith of Old Hilse in *Die Weber* has here become translated into actual vision, a reality transfigured by fairy-tale elements (the glass coffin) taken from Silesian folk-lore. Those present on 14 November in the Königliches Schauspielhaus in Berlin may well have wondered if this were indeed by the same playwright who had written *Vor Sonnenaufgang*, yet Lou Andreas-Salomé reviewed the play with great enthusiasm and, indeed, her novel *Ruth*, which appeared in 1895, may well, in part, have been suggested by it. She was present at a performance of *Hanneles Himmelfahrt* in St Petersburg on 23 May 1895, and spoke of the charm of the Byzantine settings.[50] (Much later in his life Gerhart Hauptmann wrote in his diary (14 February 1937) that of all the early reviews of this play, Lou Salomé's were without doubt the most perceptive.) In 1896 the 'deutsches Märchendrama' *Die versunkene*

Glocke appeared at Christmas in the Deutsches Theater; in *Hanneles Himmelfahrt* the spirit world was present only in Hannele's feverish visions but now, in *Die versunkene Glocke*, the elemental spirits, dwarfs and elves are as real as Heinrich the bell-founder, his wife and their neighbours.

'Gerhart Hauptmann cashed in on the vogue for debased fairy-tale with his "Deutsches Märchendrama" ', writes one critic;[51] another praises Hauptmann for being able to graft the world of phantasy and mystery onto the everyday.[52] The contrast between valley and mountain, the dichotomy between Heinrich's everyday world and the realm of the mountain-nymph Rautendelein owes much to Ibsen (who likewise had left the drama of social criticism and moved into the world of poetic symbolism) and also to German romanticism, particularly Tieck and his *Runenberg*. (It is also tempting to see certain biographical details in the drama: the 'sunken bell' becomes a symbol for that other work, *Florian Geyer*, which had been rejected by the public and cast into oblivion.) Certain elements may have been taken from *Zarathustra*, for the mountain represents freedom, fulfilment and sun-lit joy as opposed to the mundane existence in the valley: the creative artist can only find himself, his true meaning, in elemental loneliness. Heinrich's death in Rautendelein's arms, his transfiguration, the dawn and the *Sonnenglockenklang* seem to indicate that ultimate fulfilment is only possible at the point of death, but a death bathed in radiance and joy. It is of interest that, amongst the neo-romantic aspects of this play certain expressionistic elements are apparent, particularly in Act 4, where the six elves represent different facets of Heinrich's psyche; similarly Hauptmann's *Und Pippa tanzt!* (1906), 'Ein Glashüttenmärchen', which appeared to be a typical portrayal of the clash between spirit and nature, seemed to prefigure, particularly in the Max Reinhardt production and with Ida Orloff's dancing, definite expressionist developments. (Alfred Kerr, in the *Deutsches Tageblatt*, claimed that 'Dieses Werk war expressionistisch vor dem Expressionismus'.[53]) Lou Salomé had travelled from Göttingen to Berlin for a private reading of the play by Hauptmann, and in January 1906 encountered Frank Wedekind (whom she had met in Paris in the previous year) at the dress rehearsal. She sent an enthusiastic review of the play to Max Harden, editor of *Zukunft*, notwithstanding the fact that Harden was one of Hauptmann's arch detractors. The romantic topoi of mountain and mine give way, in *Gabriel Schillings Flucht* (1907), to the sea, which assumes an almost mythical quality as the background to the destruction of the artist-figure, torn between two women on a remote island: the realistic portrayal of the coastguard station with the figure-head upon it merges imperceptibly into an awareness of vastness, myth and dissolution.

The development away from naturalism in Arno Holz was discussed in chapter 1; his play *Sonnenfinsternis* (1908), a portrayal of aestheticism and incest, may also be mentioned in this context, also *Ignorabimus* (1913), where a powerful, Oedipus-like situation ends in suicide and occult practices. The development of the drama towards expressionism will be examined in chapter 6; it should, however, be noticed at the end of this chapter that Carl Hauptmann's play *Der Krieg* (1913) is in an entirely different category from his *Die armseligen Besenbinder*. As the new century advances it becomes increasingly apparent that the neo-romantic's dream world, the aesthete's flight into the rarefied and the bizarre, and the decadent's cultivation of artificial paradises are being supplanted by a more intense, extreme and hectic portrayal of reality or, rather, recreation of reality. The search for the true self, implied in certain of the works mentioned in this chapter, will become a search for a new Man of a new Life: the eponymous hero of Hermann Hesse's *Peter Camenzind* (1904), a sensitive, introspective young man, may eventually find his place in society, but others will demand a new society itself. This first major work by Hesse, with its theme of the flight from society into the realms of nature, and the hero's muddled decision to become a country inn-keeper, is blurred, sentimental and over-lyrical; an atmosphere prevails which more astringent writers would reject as intolerable. Musil's 'Zertrümmerung der Gesellschaft' is not far away, and fascinating experiments will radically alter the stylistic features of all genres of literature; Hesse, however, reserved his self-indulgent neo-romantic attitudes until well into the First World War, when his dabbling into psychology would give his works a specious modernity. Perhaps the last great outburst of the fantastic is *Der Golem* by Gustav Meyrink (1868–1932), with its descent into horror through subterranean passages, its portrayal of the sombre corners of the city where the Golem lurks and its constant confusion between drama and reality in the battle between the cabbalist Schemaja Hillel and the evil demon Aaron Wassertrum. But here again the threshold of expressionism is reached: the obsession with waxworks, trances and demonic possession is a fascination that certain expressionists will exploit, particularly in the new art form of the cinema.

The last two chapters have attempted to trace the various forms that the literary reaction against naturalism took in the German-speaking world; the different labels used demonstrate the difficulty in describing accurately the precise forms of the reaction. It may be claimed that the tendency between 1890 and 1910 to create works of dream and nightmare, of pseudo-medievalism and prurient eroticism betokens the condition of the writer during the last stages of bourgeois culture; the 'machtgeschützte Innerlichkeit'[54] described by Thomas Mann provided a fertile breeding ground for the cultivation of the precious and the recondite, the ornamental and the perverse. The next chapter will attempt to examine the literary prophets and seekers after myth and vision who went beyond neo-romanticism not towards expressionism, but towards the contemplation of cosmic patterns in a manner which has no equal in European literature.

Notes

1. Quoted Gstaiger, *Französische Symbolisten*, 23.
2. *Oeuvres complétes de Charles Baudelaire. Oeuvres posthumes*, Paris, 1939, XI, 27.
3. Nietzsche, *Werke*, III, 832.
4. Ibid., II, 1,004.
5. Stefan George, *Gesamtausgabe der Werke. Endgültige Fassung*, Berlin. *Hymnen. Pilgerfahrten. Algabal*, 83.
6. *Briefwechsel zwischen George und Hofmannsthal* (second edition), 13.
7. *Hymnen. Pilgerfahrten. Algabal*, 103.
8. Ibid., 98-99.
9. *Blätter für die Kunst. Zum Jubiläumsjahr*, Düsseldorf and Munich, 1969, Folge I, 1.
10. Ibid., Folge II, 34.
11. Ibid., Folge IV, 4.
12. George, *Die Bücher der Hirten und Preisgedichte der Sagen und Sänge und der hängenden Gärten*, 11.
13. George, *Der Teppich des Lebens und die Lieder von Traum und Tod*, 44.
14. George, *Das Jahr der Seele*, 12.
15. *Blätter für die Kunst*, Folge V, 2.
16. George, *Der siebente Ring*, 12.
17. *Blätter für die Kunst*, Folge III, 2.
18. Ibid., III, 59.
19. Gerhard Ouckama-Knoop, *Die Dekadenten-Psychologischer Roman*, Munich, 1898, 81.
20. Thomas Mann, *Gesammelte Werke*, 1960, XI, 311.
21. Ibid., XI, 556.
22. Ibid., XII, 79.
23. Erich Heller, *The Ironic German*, London, 1958, 60.
24. Mann, XI, 553.
25. Ibid., 554.
26. Ibid., VIII, 197.
27. Ibid., VIII, 295.
28. Ibid., VIII, 297.

29.   Ibid., VIII, 369.
30.   For information on Ludwig Derleth see Winkler, *George Kreis* (Sammlung Metzler), also Dominik Jost, *Ludwig Derleth*, Stuttgart, 1965.
31.   George, *Der Stern des Bundes*, 84.
32.   Edgar Salin, *Um Stefan George*, Godesberg, 1948, 14.
33.   See R. Boehringer, *Mein Bild von Stefan George*, Munich, 1951, Tafeln, 88 and 89.
34.   George, *Das neue Reich*, 138.
35.   Mann, IX, 123.
36.   T. J. Reed, *Thomas Mann. The Uses of Tradition*, Oxford, 1974, 143.
37.   Mann, XII, 153.
38.   Ibid., VIII, 390-391.
39.   Alfred Kubin, *Die andere Seite. Ein phantastischer Roman*, Munich, 1909, 4.
40.   Ibid., 51.
41.   See Jost Hermand's introduction to *Lyrik des Jugendstils*, Stuttgart, 1964.
42.   Heinrich Mann, *Im Schlaraffenland*, Hamburg, 1966, 115-116.
43.   Przybyszewski, *Erinnerungen*, 196.
44.   Ibid., 86.
45.   Ibid., 97.
46.   Gustav Landauer, in *Der Demokrat* (1909–1911), Jg. 2, 22.
47.   Richard Dehmel, *Gesammelte Werke*, Berlin, 1918, I, 297.
48.   Przybyszewski, *Erinnerungen*, 153.
49.   Gerhart Hauptmann, *Sämtliche Werke*, I, 582.
50.   Rudolph Binion, *Frau Lou*, Princeton, 1969, 189.
51.   Malcolm Pasley (ed.), *Germany. A Companion to German Studies*, London, 1972, 568.
52.   Herbert Ihering, *Von Reinhardt bis Brecht*, 36.
53.   H. Daiber, *Gerhart Hauptmann*, Vienna, 1971, 142.
54.   Mann, IX, 419.

4 THE COSMIC DIMENSION

In *Der Fall Wagner,* written a few months before his mental collapse, Nietzsche described the enormous influence that Wagner's music had had upon him, and the struggles with which he strove to free himself from its powerful seductiveness. Wagner seemed to Nietzsche to be the perfect exemplification of what he called decadence: the hysteria, brutality, ambiguous eroticism and dubious morality left an indelible impression on the literature of *fin-de-siècle:* 'Wie verwandt muß Wagner der gesamten europäischen décadence sein, daß er von ihr nicht als décadent empfunden wird? Er gehört zu ihr, er ist ihr Protagonist . . . Man ehrt sich, wenn man *ihn* in die Wolken hebt . . . Denn daß man nicht gegen ihn sich wehrt, das ist selbst schon ein Zeichen der *décadence'.*[1] Nietzsche admitted his own debt to the musician, but also acknowledged his own strength in overcoming Wagner. It may not be too much to claim that the break with Wagner represents a rejection of *fin-de-siècle* and the opening of new vistas; if Wagner was an inspiration for so much music and literature at the turn of the century, then it is Nietzsche who dominated the period leading up to the First World War. The naturalists had applauded Nietzsche's attack on bourgeois complacency; the symbolists had thrilled to his vision of the poet-prophet remote from the vulgar wranglings of the market place. But many writers before 1914 would extol in Nietzsche the creator of life-enhancing myths, and the thinker who insisted upon self-awareness, self-mastery and self-fulfilment. His emphasis on idealism, strength, affirmation and joy, together with the dark halo of his madness, made him the spokesman, at once glorious and forbidding, of the new century. (For a discussion of Nietzsche's work see *A Literary History of Germany 1830–1890.*)

Nietsche is, of course, all things to all men; for some he is the brilliant aphorist *à la* Rochefoucauld, for others the psychologist *par excellence,* for others the myth-creating visionary of *Also sprach Zarathustra.* It was this latter role that found the greatest resonance in Germany after Nietzsche's death, regardless of the fact that *Also sprach Zarathustra* is by no means Nietzsche's greatest work, with its lapses into bathos, its repetitiveness and the undeniable longueurs of the second half. Yet the flashes of brilliance undoubtedly made up for its shortcomings, and the images of mountain, eagle, hammer, lightning, fire and dance, and its dithyrambic ecstasies thrilled a whole generation grown tired of naturalistic drabness and the refinements of symbolism. The mythologising, monumentalising tendencies of the Second Reich, described in a recent study, also found in the creator of *Zarathustra* a subject suitable for elaboration: the short-sighted, sickly Professor of Classical Philology became the prophet of the mountain tops, dwelling amidst ice and fire, from which he hurled thunderbolts into the valley beneath. Even his madness and increasing paralysis, probably caused by syphilis, became 'ein Hinaufgehen ins Mythische';[2] Rudolf Steiner (1861–1925), who had moved to Weimar to edit Goethe's works on natural history for the Goethe-Schiller Archive, worked also on the arrangement of Nietzsche's manuscripts, and wrote of the awful feeling that the sight of Nietzsche inspired within him. Steiner described in fulsome terms Nietzsche's immortal gaze, his transcendent sublimity, his unfathomable exultation;[3] the authoress Gabriele Reuter (1859–1941) wrote in similar fashion of the solitude in which Nietzsche's spirit dwelt, and the terrible power of his gaze.[4] Even Przybyszewski compared Nietzsche's collapse with that of a Gothic cathedral and described Nietzsche's gaze thus: 'Die Augen, blind geworden für das törichte Außen, höhlten sich scheinbar hinein in eine andere Welt – in jene Ewigkeit, die er so liebte'.[5] In 1896 Richard Strauss composed his *Also sprach Zarathustra,* doubtless as a token to the power of Nietzsche's work; in the same year Gustav Mahler composed his Third Symphony, the fourth movement of which was a setting of the 'Mitternachtslied' from the same work. Another artist, the painter Paula Modersohn-Becker (1867–1907), confided to her diary her feelings after reading *Also sprach Zarathustra,* and yet again used hyperbole and excessive expressions ('Riesenmensch'[6]) to portray its effect.

Depths of suffering, loneliness, eternity, gigantic power, heroism and affirmation – these are the expressions used to describe the man and his work. There is felt to be something Christ-like about his agony, in spite of his tirades against orthodox Christianity, and his emphasis upon the affirmation of the here and now. Mahler's Third Symphony moves from pantheism, through the setting of Nietzsche, to a rapturous proclamation of love, and somehow Nietzsche was felt, by many people, to represent some elemental force of joy which asserted itself in spite of pain, even because of it. This Dionysian acceptance of all life, including its futility and bestiality, provided a fascinating answer to those who wished to exclude nothing and who refused to apply moral categories in their work and their thinking. To those starved of symbols and lacking the sustaining power of a religious faith, Nietzsche's own fusion of poetry, myth and cosmic vision offered a stimulating and awe-inspiring substitute: Dionysus-Zarathustra inspired, uplifted and challenged the imagination of many who found no fulfilment in the contemplation of jejune social doctrines. The reception of Nietzsche in Germany prior to 1914 demonstrates yet again the German tendency to prefer the idea to the man, and the mythical to the actual; where Wagner's treatment of myth seemed to lack the life-enhancing quality, then Nietzsche's emphasis on vitality, creativity and the will struck away the moribund and brought energy and joy.

As is appropriate in such a work, images of the dawn predominate: the book opens with Zarathustra's praise of the sun, and ends with his imperious proclamation: 'Dies ist *mein* Morgen, *mein* Tag hebt an: *herauf nun, herauf, du großer Mittag!* '[7] Almost half-way through the work, in the section 'Von der unbefleckten Erkenntnis' the glowing orb is again greeted: 'Denn schon kommt sie, die Glühende – *ihre* Liebe zur Erde kommt! Unschuld und Schöpfer-Begier ist alle Sonnen-Liebe! Seht doch hin, wie sie ungeduldig über das Meer kommt! Fühlst du den Durst und den heißen Atem ihrer Liebe nicht? . . . Wahrlich, der Sonne gleich liebe ich das Leben und alle tiefen Meere'.[8] Sun, sea and the South – above all a halcyon world of limpid radiance, the bay at Rapallo, the pine trees, the blue and silver of the glittering Mediterranean – this is the world of Zarathustra, infinitely remote from the Nordic turbulence of Wagner. Nietzsche's letter to Peter Gast (10 October 1886) enthusiastically describes the landscape in which the first part of *Zarathustra* was written: 'Denken Sie sich eine Insel des griechischen Archipelagos, mit Wald und Berg willkürlich überworfen, welche durch einen Zufall eines Tags an das Festland herangeschwommen ist und nicht weiter zurück kann. Es ist etwas *Griechisches* daran, ohne Zweifel: andrerseits etwas Piratenhaftes, Plötzliches, Verstecktes, Gefährliches; endlich, an einer einsamen Wendung, ein Stück *tropischen* Pinienwaldes'.[9] The traditional German longing for the South, particularly Italy, receives in Nietzsche its keenest impetus; it was in that country that his happiest days were spent and from which his friend Overbeck would collect him at the end of his mental life.

A cosmogony or mythopoeic vision composed after Nietzsche's *Also sprach Zarathustra* must needs have felt the centripetal pull of that powerful creation; such was the force and directness of Nietzsche's language (the language, according to Gottfried Benn, of 'der größte Sprachgenie seit Luther') that his imagery is indelibly impressed upon the poetry of the next twenty years. The expressionist generation – Gottfried Benn's own – saw in Nietzsche its greatest precursor, and a

recent study has examined the close links between Nietzschean vitalism
and early expressionism.[10] Gustav Sack's fragmentary *Paralyse* may be
cited as a perfect example of the fascination exerted by the powerful
myth created by Nietzsche's life and madness; the notes explain: 'Ein
Dichter-Philosoph [*à la* Nietzsche] : "Herr der Welt" . . . erkrankt mitten
auf seiner Höhe an *dementia paralytica*. Erste Anzeichen! Er erkennt
sie – körperlich vollkommen elend, ohne Fähigkeit der Erinnerung und
logischen Denkens fällt er in die wildesten, phantastischsten Wahnideen'.
Sack also portrays 'ein alter Jäger . . . der sich schließlich, als er –
körperlich nichts als ein elender Klumpen faulen Fleisches – einen
Sonnenuntergang in leuchtendsten Hyperbeln "besingt" und schließlich
von der Ewigen Wiederkehr jubelt, seiner erbarmt und ihn mit der Axt
niederschlägt'.[11] The prevalence of titles containing the words 'Sonne',
'Licht', 'Leben' during the early years of the century (*Triumph des
Lebens, Es lebe das Leben, Gesang des Lebens* and so forth) shows the
dual presence of Whitman and Nietzsche: there is also an undeniable
tendency to reject the neo-romantic moonlight in favour of the solar
deity, with its virile and fervid energy. Schickele's proclamation in
Sommernächte may serve as an example:

> Nichts ist herrlicher als die Sonne!
> Wenn sie die schlummernde Kraft weckt
> Und das Gehirn entzündet zum Rausche der That,
> Zum blutroten Ringen vom Sieg.
> Nicht falten kann ich die Hände zu ihr –
> Geballt streck' ich die Fäuste in all das Glühen
> Hinauf . . .
> Und bete, Sonne, zu dir . . .[12]

as may Stadler's early, Wagnerian *Baldur,* published in the Alsatian
journal *Stürmer:*

> Baldur – Prometheus – Christus –
> Heiliges Leben
> In Licht, in Schönheit,
> Nie sterbender Götterrausch
> Glühendster Trunkenheit! . . .
> Nur füllen, atmen, schwelgen. Seligstes
> Nirwana und
> Aus tausend Himmeln tausend Morgensonnen.[13]

Expressionism, however, will be discussed in chapter 6; the point of this chapter will be to look briefly at what an eminent critic has termed the 'lost post-Nietzschean generation', also the 'post-Nietzschean archipelago of German literature which no one mind can hope to map, let alone inhabit'.[14] The task is daunting but fascinating: the gap between poetry and prophecy is frequently blurred by obfuscations both forbidding and fertile, and the works which come to mind include those of Däubler and Mombert, Morgenstern and Rudolf Steiner, Ludwig Klages and Alfred Schuler, and certain aspects of the work of Holz, Pannwitz and Gerhart Hauptmann.

Theodor Däubler (1876–1934) spent his formative years in Trieste; the Mediterranean world and proximity of Venice provided unforgettable visual impressions. Yet it was the music of Mahler which overwhelmed the poet: the Second Symphony (1895), with its enormous cosmic sweep, and the Third (1896), with its rapturous sense of panic — also Nietzschean — affirmation, seem to anticipate the music which Däubler later achieved in his giant work *Das Nordlicht*. (The uneven quality of Mahler's music, his juxtaposition of the banal and the glorious, his undeniable lapses of taste are also to be found in Däubler's cosmic mythology: Ernst Barlach's fragmentary novel *Seespeck,* dating from 1913–1916, gives a very perceptive portrayal of Däubler, with Seespeck's reactions and reservations.) Däubler mentions also Beethoven and Wagner, and the profound effect that they made upon him: talking of his stay in Vienna he wrote: 'Dann bin ich zweimal von Wagner's Siegfried bezaubert worden. Von nun an konnte ich nur noch in Versen grübeln, schließlich denken: Wahngebilde hat die Musik in mir zu Gestalten vereinfacht. Die deutsche Sprache ist abermals meine Muttersprache geworden. Dann bin ich von Wien abgereist. In Neapel fand ich Wort für meine Bilder . . . *Das Nordlicht* habe ich am Fuß des Vesuvs in deutscher Sprache angefangen'.[15] Däubler had hesitated whether or not to compose an *Impero del Sole:* the music of Beethoven, Wagner and Mahler, however, released a flood of images in German.

In a 'Selbstdeutung' printed with the so-called 'Genfer Fassung' of *Das Nordlicht* in 1921, and frequently more esoteric than the epic-lyric itself, Däubler explains:

Ich fühlte glücklich, die Erde birgt in sich noch viel Sonne, die mit uns, gegen die Schwere verbunden, selbst wieder zur Sonne zurück will. Überall. Sogar im Eis. Gerade dort, an den Polen, wo die Nacht am tiefsten, am längsten, besonders mächtig! Eine leuchtende

Umschlingung von erlöster Sonne aus der Erde und himmlischer
Sonne bringt den monatelangen Nächten um die Pole das Polarlicht!
Die Erde sehnt sich, wieder ein leuchtender Stern zu werden.[16]

All things yearn for the light, and even in the polar realms of ice and
darkness the intense striving towards the sun kindles the *Nordlicht,*
which becomes a symbol for the earth's longing for redemption, a
guarantor even of the earth's eventual transformation into a radiant star.
The idea is wholly Nietzschean (and also Christian): he who struggles
against a hostile and adverse environment for *Selbstüberwindung* is more
heroic, and has a greater potential for heroism, than he whose path has
been an easy one. Däubler's private, possibly eccentric, cosmogony has
as its base a plausible psychological truth.

The work, loosely constructed, took twelve years to complete: it
was written during Däubler's extensive journeys and finally delivered
into the hands of Moeller van den Bruck in 1910, a vast compendium of
literary styles, some thirty thousand lines long. The first part, entitled
'Das Mittelmeer', contains a prologue which emphasises the yearning of
the earth to return to the sun and, almost like Walt Whitman, greets the
miners who penetrate into the earth for fuel to ignite and thereby to
emulate the solar radiance:

Die Erde treibt im Norden tausend blaue Feuerblüten
Und übermittelt ihren Sehnsuchtstraum der Nacht,
Drum soll der Mensch auch seinen Flammenkelch behüten,
Wenn er, durch ihn belebt und lichterfüllt, erwacht . . .
Der Sonne könnt ihr bloß im Erdenschoße nahen,
Dort unten stoßt ihr auf den Sinn von dieser Welt,
Und auch das Licht der Dinge, die noch nie geschahen,
Wird, urbestimmt, durch euch in uns hervorgeschwellt.[17]

The reader is reminded forcibly of Novalis here: the 'Reich Arcturs' of
Klingsohr's *Märchen* is the 'Reich des Nordens', and the miners in
Novalis's work are those who find in gold the elemental equivalent of
the divine essence. As regards Walt Whitman, it was Johannes Schlaf in
his essay in the *Freie Bühne* of 1892 who praised, in psalm-like adulation,
the effect of Whitman's poetry; Schlaf's book on Whitman, which
appeared in 1904, announced him as being a man 'mit dithyrambischem
Jubel und in der Vollgesundheit herrlichster Barbarei in eine neue,
frische, und werdende Welt tretend: hinein in das große Brausen und
Jubeln neuer und unerhörter Anfänge'.[18] The cosmic embrace of

Däubler has indeed something of Whitman about it, although the extent to which he may have known Whitman's work remains uncertain.

The short section 'Hymne der Höhe' is a portrayal of a sunrise much indebted to *Zarathustra,* or even Wagner, with its 'wildwabernde Fackeln, die qualmend verglühen': as in *Zarathustra,* the language, stretched to an extreme intensity, collapses into bathos:

Noch einmal zersprengen die Sonnenscheinlanzen
Den Mantel, die Mauern von Schattentitanen;
Auf Gipfeln gewittern Davonkrauchungspflanzen:
Granithart der Alpen basaltalte Ahnen![19]

Neologisms, frequently grotesque, are the hall-mark of Däubler's work, as are the bizarre rhymes, particularly in the descriptions of elemental activity. More satisfactory are the sections of *Das Nordlicht* with an autobiographical quality – the invocations of Venice, Rome, Florence and Naples, which take up most of Part One. Poems such as 'Farbenstadt Venedig', 'So flammt denn auf, ihr goldenen Hallen!' and 'Auf des Tages Abendschleppe' have a more lyrical aspect which is frequently more successful than the attempted portrayal of gigantic forces. The poems of the Roman section strive to capture the monumental dignity of the Imperial City; Däubler also shares with his time the fascination with Nero (Oskar Panizza's play dates from 1898; Alfred Schuler, as will be described later, dwelt long upon the notorious Emperor). The Tuscan landscape particularly is portrayed in loving detail, with the sun-symbolism of early Renaissance painting (and St Francis's 'Hymn to the Sun') neatly fitting into Däubler's vision; Ghiberti's bronze doors in Florence, gleaming in the sun, link, for Däubler, the spiritual with the elemental. The figure of Christ becomes the supreme example of the desire to return to the Father, to the Sun: the incarnation and resurrection are interpreted always with the sun-myth in mind. The final section *Pan. Ein Orphisches Intermezzo,* salutes the pagan forces in Dionysian vitalism, for Christian and pagan are embraced in Däubler's poetic myth: the poet, as Orpheus, moves among the dead and awakens them with his song – an almost Rilkean world is adumbrated here (although Rilke rejected the 'schlackenhafte Wort-Monstren' in which Däubler indulges[20]). Orphic and Christian elements fuse: again, images of light predominate in the movement away from the grave towards transfiguration.

In the second part of *Das Nordlicht,* entitled 'Sahara', Däubler's 'Gigantomachie der Bildlichkeit' exceeds all bounds; the earthquake is hailed, a chthonic eruption which bursts from the depths:

> Eingeklemmt von alterstarrter Erdenkruste,
> Sträubt sich sonnenwonnig noch ein Erdenkern.
> Ihr hört ihn oft; des Drachen Wutgepruste
> Sagt und warnt: Ein Erdbeben ist nimmer fern!
>
> Sehnsucht nach der Sonne, Heilung für den Himmel
> Nagt als flackernde Gefahr am Starrsinnsrand;
> Geist der Liebe wirft sich auf den Hilfeschimmel,
> Bringt der Nacht entflammten Tanz von Schwerterkranz.
>
> Langsam wird der Drache wieder zahmer,
> Bis auch bald sein Bad aus Glut und Tunke ruht;
> Seines Umrucks Schatten schweift durch ihn – Umahmer,
> Und der Kotklops wimmelt drum von Aufruhrbrut.[21]

Such dynamism of imagery, such play of assonance and creation of compound nouns verges upon the absurd, as a wanton revelling in language which strives for baroque grandeur but which achieves at best a hyperbolic impressiveness. The section 'Der Weltbruch' masses together gigantic images of apocalyptic destruction, a *dies irae* compounded of the Book of Revelations, Nietzsche's *Zarathustra* and Mahler's Resurrection Symphony. Section three, 'Das Ra-Drama' returns to the Egyptian world, where Ra the sun-god was elevated to the highest divinity. Däubler's imagination moves through history to portray those times when the sun was extolled, or when heroic figures fought to bring mankind closer to spiritual transfiguration; the solar energy, for Däubler, being synonymous with spiritual truth. 'Der Ararat' invokes Buddha, the Indian priests, the Parsees, to whom Zarathustra belonged; Perseus, St George, Roland and Parzifal are seen as symbols of the external struggle for perfection on earth. An 'Astraler Gesang' is reminiscent of Faust's 'Walpurgnisnachtstraum' with its 'Zeichendeuter', 'ein plötzlich auftauchender Komet', 'eine dahinwehende Seele', 'die plötzlich stehenbleibende Sonne' and 'ein Schwarm berauschender Gefühle'; it culminates in the final section, 'Der Geist', which is a vision of ultimate redemption. Written in terza rimas, with obvious echoes of Dante, the final utterance of this amazing work is the belief that: 'Die Welt versöhnt und übertönt der Geist!'[22]

This cataract of verses, spread over one thousand two hundred pages in the 'Genfer Fassung', is a work so extraordinary, at times even

grotesque, that the reader is baffled and confused. But the basic
concept, as has been stated, is not an alien one — man's longing for
redemption, for absorption into the wider whole, into a cosmic scheme
sustained at all points by the sun-symbol, whose radiance is sought
most avidly in darkness. The megalithic work alienates above all by the
excess of its language, particularly the compound nouns ('Wutschlund-
eingeburt', 'Schlummerebbungsschleim', 'Raschelwahrheitseschenäste')
and tasteless rhymes ('vermutet — man tutet', 'Sonnenscheinlanzen —
Protuberanzen', and so on), and the cosmic flight which only a
Klopstock or a Hölderlin could execute. It is essentially a youthful
work, with its ecstasy and chaos, its nimiety and its bathos. The works
which followed *Das Nordlicht* are more accessible; it seems that, once
the colossus was written, then Däubler was able to write in a more
restrained and ordered form. The collection of sketches *Mit silberner
Sichel* (1916) contains much talented prose writing, where the
monstrous hyperboles have given way to an unsuspected delicacy.
From this time also date the sixty-eight poems of *Der sternhelle Weg*,
which include those which are held to be Däubler's most successful:
the tree poems above all ('Die Fichte', 'Die Buche') and the 'Goldene
Sonette', with lines that inevitably bring Trakl to mind, whom Däubler
had met at the end of 1912:

> Vertändelt ist das ernste Gold der Garben.
> Auf alten Mauern schlafen rote Schlangen . . .
> Das Jahr vollendet seinen Kranz der Farben.
> Die Lauben sind mit Schattenblau behangen,
> Der Äcker Todesgold ist aufgegangen:
> Wie wahr, daß wir schon alle lange starben![23]

It would be false to see in Däubler an isolated literary figure: his
extensive travels, his membership of the Prussian *Akademie der Künste*
and his presidency of the German PEN club brought him into close
contact with the literary figures and movements of his day. Trakl and
Barlach have been mentioned (it may not be too far-fetched to see in
certain of Barlach's sculptures the cosmic weight of Däubler's presence,
for example *Die Vision* of 1912; Barlach had also started work on a
model for Däubler's tomb), Moeller van den Bruck and Rudolf Pannwitz. Däubler was in Paris between 1903 and 1910 (this was exactly
the same time as Rilke's sojourn); Cézanne and Van Gogh were an
overwhelming experience for him, particularly the great Cézanne
exhibition of 1905. He is 'voll Anbetung vor Cézanne', and Van Gogh

is praised as the 'Sänger des Ackers und der Sonne'.[24] The most perceptive of Däubler's articles and essays show his admiration for Chagall, Paul Klee and above all Edvard Munch; a most important essay is his *Expressionismus*, with its famous opening sentence:

> Der Volksmund sagt: Wenn einer gehängt wird, so erlebt er im letzten Augenblick sein ganzes Leben nochmals. Das kann nur Expressionismus sein! Schnelligkeit, Simultanität, höchste Anspannung um die Ineinandergehörigkeiten des Geschauten sind Vorbedingungen für den Stil. Er selbst ist Ausdruck der Idee. Eine Vision will sich in letzter Knappheit im Bezirk verstiegener Vereinfachung kundgeben: das ist Expressionismus in jedem Stil. Farbe ohne Bezeichnung, Zeichnung und kein Erklären, im Rhythmus festgesetztes Hauptwort ohne Attribut: wir erobern unsern Expressionismus![25]

It is also characteristic of Däubler that he should also stress the mystical tendencies of the movement, the 'mystische Perspektive, Auftakt zu einer Hierarchie, Rückfluß in den Ichkristall'.[26] A recent book on expressionism has stressed too much Däubler's affinity with the young writers associated with that particular art form,[27] but it is at least salutary that this writer should not be relegated to the 'lost generation': the mythomania may have found little resonance, but the rest of the work is still a fruitful source.

Däubler's name is inevitably linked with that of Alfred Mombert (1874–1942); both writers are commonly held to be creators of vastly inflated, cosmic-symphonic utterances remote from the basic trends of twentieth-century writing. Mombert, as Däubler, owes much to Nietzsche, but there is nothing in his work to compare with the elephantine proportions of *Das Nordlicht*. Däubler's 'Italian' qualities are lacking in Mombert, who is indebted more to the Grecian and Persian worlds; there is, rather, in Mombert a German-Oriental axis, which is reminiscent of Hölderlin's 'vaterländische Umkehr', also a cosmic proportion more intellectually elaborate than Däubler's vision. (Mombert's famous claim: 'Ich bin über die Plejaden und den Orion an den Rhein gelangt'[28] is not a whimsical pleasantry, but a serious comment on the cosmic view-point which he came to see as his particular position.) There is in Mombert a more dedicated, almost obsessive concentration on his mythical realities; he rejected his legal profession to concentrate entirely on his writing, finishing his last work, as chapter 8 will describe, in the concentration camp itself.

His claim 'Ich habe keine Zeit, mich mit der "Zeit" herumzuschlagen. Mein Amt ist, dauernde Harmonien zu schaffen'[29] and his seeing in the flash of light in a turmalin crystal ultimate truth itself, are not the capricious records of a poet unable to 'face reality' but the beliefs of a man who would not be distracted by arbitrary historical manifestations from his task of praise and creation. 'Wenn alle Schöpfungen, alle Kosmen vergehen, vergangen sind, bleibt der in den Kosmen schöpferische Geist: Er, der Traum ist das Maß aller Dinge. Ihn wage darzustellen!'[30]

The early collection *Tag und Nacht* (1894) contains much of what could be termed impressionist-naturalistic, but an individual tone soon emerges. 'Die Stadt' depicts the squalor of the town, yet also its rapturous transfiguration beneath the lambent radiance of the sun:

> O die Stadt!
> Noch eben schwarz gewitterschwül —
> schwindsüchtiges Gesindel, hungrig elend —
> Fabrikenqualm und Elend — Kot Kot Kot —
> Und es brach die Sonne durch! — und blauer Himmel!
> Des Domes Riesenkuppel glänzt im Golde!
> Karossen sprengen an mit weißen Hengsten![31]

The poem 'Abend', the depiction of the dark, fervent conversation between man and woman owes much to Dehmel, a poet whom Mombert greatly admired, and with whom he remained on friendly terms; 'Schwüle' is reminiscent of Conrad Ferdinand Meyer, and also betrays a certain *Jugendstil* quality in the portrayal of the dark lake, the slim youth and the rose petals. Mombert also demonstrates in the early collection a remarkable ability to create dramatic pictures of a concentrated intensity: 'Mondaufgang', with its depiction of the rising moon, and the murder of the man who had scorned the rapt fervour of those watching it, creates an atmosphere of menace and strange beauty; 'Die Nacht' is a succinct but impressive portrayal of the mad king upon his balcony, demanding proof that the sun would rise again, and the grinning crowd beneath.

The next collection, *Der Glühende* (1896), is dedicated to Dehmel; it was an anthology which greatly impressed Przybyszewski who, in the following year, dedicated his *Auf den Wegen der Seele* to 'Dem Magier, dem "Glühenden" Alfred Mombert' and who also printed in his journal *Zyćie* a fervent appreciation of Mombert and his work: 'Seit ein paar Jahren verfolgt ich die Entwicklung dieser erstaunlichen

Seele, versunken in Träumen vom urewigen Sein, lauschend und horchend auf Gesänge nicht von dieser Erde'.[32] Martin Buber likewise demonstrated the high esteem in which he held Mombert by dedicating his *Ekstatische Konfessionen* to him and quoting him verbatim in *Daniel*. Nietzsche's *Dionysos-Dithyramben* (1888) supplied much of the imagery for Mombert's collection, for example pain, ecstasy, torture and frenzied joy, and the desert as a scene of fearful enlightenment. The ability to create, with a few deft touches, a tangible situation which possesses a baleful, symbolic extension is found in the following:

> Ich saß auf rotem Pfühl im Prunkgemach.
> Es mochte Mittag sein, war ganz hell.
> Ich schaute träumend starr nach einer Frau,
> die sich am Fenster hin und her bewegte.
> Die warme Lustgestalt im Morgenkleid,
> der Hügelbusen und das Sonnehaupt;
> das weiche Wellenspiel der starken Arme . . .
> Plötzlich hört' ich meine Stimme sprechen:
> 'Was machen Sie denn dort?'
> Sie hielt ein wenig an und sprach verwundert:
> 'Ich putze die Scheibe.
> Sie ist trüb.
> Ich putze immer.
> Aber sie wird nie hell.
> Sie ist ganz trüb . . .'
> Und träumend sah ich, wie sie immer rieb.[33]

Mombert's letter (22 November 1896) to Otto Haas explained that the poem expresses 'die Stimmung eines Menschen, der unsonst nach Erkenntnis der tiefsten Rätsel seiner selbst und der Welt geforscht hat und dem nun eine böse Trübung unterschleicht. Das ist der Moment unheimlichsten Klarsehens und furchtbarster Melancholie. Die Ahnung des Untergangs, mitten im sonnigen Gemach. Ich habe dies Gedicht in einer bösen − und doch herrlichen − Stunde geschrieben'.[34]

Mombert speaks of melancholy and the presentiment of decline − 'der Glühende' knows of such moments, of the 'Marmortraurigkeit des Daseins' − and portrays these in a manner not dissimilar to Kafka's:

> Wann der Zug einrollt in den schwarzen Tunnel
> mit sprühenden Nüstern

auf dröhnender Schiene,
der Fahrgast angstbleich,
bei flackerndem Lämpchen,
es bebt der Finger,
im Reisebuch sucht, sucht:
wie lang — wir lang der Tunnel!? —
Er keuchend sich klammert
an ein schwarzumrändert Blatt,
drauf stehn
schwarze große Lettern:
'In die Ewigkeit'.[35]

and in the sombre dread of the following:

Im Hintergrund des Zimmers zurückgewichen,
kauernd in der Dunkelheit,
hör' ich eine Leiter leise anlegen.
An der Außenwand.
Dunkle Gestalten huschen herauf . . .
Man vergittert mir das Fenster.[36]

Yet in the darkness the poet feels also within himself the potential for transformation and radiant illumination, and he insists that his task is as follows:

Mein Haupt zu heben aus den Kissen.
Mein Haupt zu heben in die Herrlichkeit.
Mein Haupt zu heben in den Gesang.[37]

The collection *Die Schöpfung* of 1897 contains the poem which is frequently quoted in expressionist anthologies: 'Stürz' ein, o Seele, und erwache im Chaos!'. The imagery is again Nietzschean; Zarathustra's cry that 'Man muß noch Chaos in sich haben, um einen tanzenden Stern gebären zu können'[38] emphasises the need for amoral energy, for daring vitality which is at the heart of all creation, and certain of the expressionist writers, as will be shown, demanded a similar passion. The rhapsodic, cosmic sweep of Mombert's poetry, together with Whitman's pantheistic fervour and Nietzsche's vitalism, fed many of the sources of early expressionism; it is also worth noticing that Herwarth Walden, later to be editor of the vitally important journal *Der Sturm*, organised a reading of Mombert's poetry on 19

January 1906 in Berlin, and that Alban Berg set to music three of
Mombert's poems from *Der Glühende*. In *Die Schöpfung* the Oriental
atmosphere predominates in an ethos compounded of Goethe's Hafis
poetry and Nietzsche's Zarathustra, also of the work of the thirteenth-
century Persian mystic Dschelâl-eddîn-Rumi, who stressed the need
for creativity and love and for a rebirth into total being. The ecstatic
tone is much apparent: 'Du Glut und Pracht! Du meine Schöpfermacht!
Du Meer! Du Sonne! Adlerschrei!'; Mombert describes how the vital
tension between complementary opposites pulses throughout eternity,
and through the eternal recurrence of all things:

> Sonne, Feuer, Weib, und Meer:
> Das sind die heiligen vier Schöpferwunden,
> die bluten in den glänzenden Traumstunden
> und singen ein Lied von ewiger Wiederkehr.[39]

The words 'Schaffen', 'Glut' and 'Kraft' are found in practically every
poem: the vision may be sublime, but a certain monotony is also
evident. (Mombert's humour, however, should not be forgotten; the
picture of the Lord urinating upon the objectionable Professor Adolf
Bartels, which he longed to include in the collection, is an amusing
one.[40])

The cycle *Der Denker* (1901) is dedicated to the constellation of
Orion, and consists of the meditations of twelve Thinkers; although
this work is called a 'Gedicht-Werk' the personification of different
elemental entities reflects Mombert's dramatic talents (the reference
to the 'Feuerschlund des Ätna' reminds the reader of Hölderlin's
Empedokles, a dramatic venture of another essentially lyrical poet).
Der Sonne-Geist (1905) is entitled 'Mythos': its 'Chor schwirrender
Kometen', 'Chor kreisender Sterne' and 'Die Himmlischen' is
reminiscent of Däubler, who was writing his *Das Nordlicht* at the
same time. (The two men only met in 1931, in Venice, after Däubler's
return from Greece.) Mombert turned more and more to the
dramatic: his *Aeon. Dramatische Trilogie* occupied him between 1907
and 1911, after *Die Blüte des Chaos* of 1905. The Aeon trilogy consists
of *Aeon, der Weltgesuchte, Aeon zwischen den Frauen* and *Aeon vor
Syrakus*, and portrays the emergence of the highest potentiality of
man, Sfaira, from the human psyche. It may be called a soul-drama,
and, as such, would anticipate many of the expressionist *Stationendramen*, yet it also has much in common with the colossal mystery-
dramas of Rudolf Steiner (his *Der Seelen Erwachen*) and Albert Steffen

(*Das Todesereignis des Manes* and *Der Sturz des Antichrist*), works
performed in the Goetheanum at Dornach in the septennium 1909–
1916.[41] Steiner's theory of the ultimate unity of science, art and
religion, his indebtedness to Goethe the scientist, and his work in the
Nietzsche Archive bring Mombert very much to mind, as does Steiner's
work on the spiritual-scientific cosmogony *Occult Science – An
Outline*. But Mombert's references to Steiner (see the letter to Hans
Reinhart of 13 December 1927) are disparaging: 'Der Auslauf aller
Bächlein und Wässerlein in den Ozean STEINER wirkt auf einen
Nicht-Dornachianer ganz unerträglich. Ob Dornach allein Kosten und
Mühe lohnt, entzieht sich meiner Beurteilung'.[42] (Mombert is here
referring to the rebuilt Goetheanum, after the first, built entirely of
wood according to a clay model designed and moulded by Steiner and
based upon his principles of gravitation and levitation, was burnt to
the ground on New Year's Eve 1922.) The concept of Sfaira, emerging
in this trilogy, is best understood as a creative, spiritual act, one which
Mombert identified with a divine act of play; in December 1920 he
confided: 'Dichtung ist erst vorhanden, wenn alles Geheimnis, alle
Wissenschaft und Religion *Spiel der Welt* geworden sind – *Alles ein
Spiel* – Das ist dann: SFAIRA'.[43]

Mombert felt the pressing need to view all human experience *sub
specie aeternitatis*, to link crystal, rock and stone with star and meteor,
to see the vital forces within the psyche acting and pulsing against the
vaster forces without. But it would be erroneous to claim that the
historical situation of man was incomprehensible to him: the two
collections *Der Held der Erde* (1914–1919) and *Atair* (1925) reverberate with the historical upheavals of the times, and show that Mombert
was a patriot in Hölderlin's sense, a man for whom the highest
achievements of German culture were embraced after a spiritual
journey into the remoteness of esoteric realms: the section 'Asia
erscheint' from *Der Held der Erde* has unmistakable echoes of 'Patmos'
('Abende. Asia erschien: vergoldet von Blumen . . . An dem Rande der
steinernen Hochebene erfaßte mich ein jäher Sturmwirbel'[44]), and the
praise of the 'junger deutscher Held' in *Atair*, whose poems were
dedicated to the memory of Heinz Dehmel, who fell in 1917, remind
the reader forcibly of *Germanien*. What is of interest here is the section
from *Der Held der Erde* written in 1916, entitled 'Umlagert von
Dämonen!', in which demons are described who surround the tower
and proclaim apocalyptic destruction:

Völker kämpfen tosend unter mythischen Schleiern,

die wolkengleich hinwallen,
von Nacht-Gewitter-Blitzen überzuckt:
manchmal stößt eine gepanzerte Faust durch die Decke,
und brennende Städte schleudern Funken durch sie.[45]

The entry of the Thinker into the tower, and the portrayal of the
First Demon ('wirft traumhaft sein Haupt zurück – hält einen langen
Augenblick lauschend inne – auf seinem Antlitz erglänzen Himmel –,
dann beugt er sich, vom Herzen überwältigt, heftig über die Zinne des
Turms hinab – ruft: Schlacht!'[46]) could have been taken directly from
Georg Kaiser. Mombert served on the Eastern front after the end of
the hostilities there; even in Czenstochau a musical setting of one of
his poems by an unknown lieutenant reached him from Macedonia.

It has been common in critical circles to dismiss Mombert's work as
being a gigantic monologue; indeed, Mombert himself was aware of
the difficulties confronting the potential reader, but he realised also
that he was not the only 'outsider' in German literature. In a letter to
Rudolf Pannwitz he wrote: 'Das wissen Sie selber genau so gut wie ich:
Sie sind als Dichter wie als Denker für die Menschen eine schwer zu
erklimmende Hochspitze . . . sehr oft von Wolken und Nebel umzogen,
vereist, mit grausigen Steilabstürzen und ständiger Steinschlag-Gefahr,
nur den schwindelfreien unbeirrten Kletterern und professionellen
Waghälsen zugängig'.[47] The letter goes on to describe the absolute
loneliness in which Mombert was living in Heidelberg, a loneliness
possibly even greater than Nietzsche's: 'Mit der Universität habe ich
nicht die geringste Verbindung. Studenten wagen sich höchst selten
zu mir; Dozenten überhaupt nicht',[48] and yet, with characteristic
generosity and interest he wished Pannwitz well with his new work
Kosmos Atheos. The correspondence between Mombert and Pannwitz
is a lively one, and lasted until Mombert's internment in the
concentration camp at Gurs in the South of France.

Rudolf Pannwitz (1881–1969), together with Otto zur Linde
(1873–1938), had edited the journal *Charon* from 1904 until its
demise during the First World War. The love of mythical terminology
is seen in the very title of the journal – Charon, who ferried the dead
across the river Styx without questioning their origins or their
destination, becomes the mythological symbol for the poetic act
itself, an act of pure devotion. The programme of the first number
explained: 'Wir wollen nichts; aber es liegt uns daran, unserem Sein
wie es in Leben und Werk sich von selbst Form giebt, durch dieses
Unternehmen auch ein äußeres Zentrum zu verschaffen. Wir sind keine

Mystiker; sondern wir geben einfache Wirklichkeit'.[49] The laconic opening, and the insistence 'Wir sind keine Mystiker' may well have been an attempt to avoid hyperbole and excess, but the *Charontiker* soon used Nietzschean terminology in their demand for a new Society, a new Man; Rudolf Paulsen, one of the most avid contributors, wrote in 1907: 'Denn im Uebrigen will der Charon alles: ein Geisterstaat ganz neuer Art sein, eine Stätte für alle Echten, eine Schule für die Werdenden, ein neues Kulturzentrum, der Träger der Blüten und Ruheplatz der Früchte. Er will sogar eine neue Welt schaffen, indem er neue Menschen schafft'.[50] The diffuse sentiments and high-flown rhetoric betray the post-Nietzschean situation, and Otto zur Linde's own *Charontiker Mythos* (1913), a collection of gnomic visions ('Urvater', 'Urgeburt', 'Ballade vom Tod und der nackten Seele' and 'An den Wurzeln des Raums'), by no means exemplifies his 1904 programme. Similarly the declaration in that programme that the emphasis would be upon facts and 'reality' changes five years later to the praise of *idealism*: 'Und sich einsetzen für die Idee, mit seinem ganzen inneren Menschen einsetzen, das heißt Charontiker sein'.[51] Otto zur Linde stressed the task as being 'den deutschen, freiheitsstolzen und weltfrommen Idealismus wieder zu erwecken';[52] although zur Linde rejected what he called the 'menschenhasserische Optimismus eines Nietzsche' he nevertheless utters the full *credo* in an unmistakably Zarathustrian fashion: 'So meine ich: eine Zeit ohne Idealismus ist krank oder stumpf, und so meine ich: ein Leben ohne Taten, und ein Leib ohne Lebenslust, und eine Seele ohne Schwunghaftigkeit sind krank oder stumpf'.[53]

If Otto zur Linde denied the Nietzschean presence, then Rudolf Pannwitz proclaimed himself to be Nietzsche's most fervent disciple. 'Meinen einzigen freund sah und sprach ich nie. als der äon ihn schlug ward ich geboren. *ein* jahr erzeugte zweimal einen zarathustra. neun jahre war ich alt da verwaiste das erbe . . . Nie verwand ich meines freundes sonnenlosen untergang'.[54] Nietzsche is 'his only friend'; when Nietzsche was struck by the 'aeon', the world-shattering idea of the Eternal Recurrence (1881), Pannwitz was born, and he was nine years old when Nietzsche collapsed into insanity. The second mentor was Stefan George, as the lack of capitalisation in Pannwitz's writing demonstrates; Pannwitz was a close associate of Karl Wolfskehl and had been a member of George's circle before joining Otto zur Linde, and never forgot the impact that George had made. The poem 'Das Totengedicht' was greatly admired by George, who called it 'Musik für Unglückliche':

Nicht berührt von allem körperhaften
Fristet ich ein abgetrenntes leben
Ruhelos in alten leidenschaften
Einer hirtenflöte hingegeben/
Deren goldnes singen ich erfuhr
Zu den schrecklich abgelegenen zeiten/
Als ich ging auf einer grünen flur
Ausgeschmückt mit allen menschlichkeiten.[55]

At the very end of his life Pannwitz described how it was George who had created order and form: 'ich habe in jungen jahren den zusammenstoss des epigonischen stils mit dem naturalistischen/das durchdringen der westlichen dichter von Poe an/die bewegung des ersten expressionismus und die welten des symbolismus und der mystiker erlebt . . . George bändigte das chaos und schuf normen'.[56] Pannwitz kept George's orthography and punctuation, and continued to praise and extol him, and Nietzsche, in his poetry. 'An Stefan George' keeps an appropriate Alcaic form, whereas 'Auf Zarathustra' swells with a cosmic surge. The cosmic dimension is seen further in 'Die Rückehr des Saturn'; elemental forces are invoked in 'Unter dem Wetterstein', where Aion seems, *à la* Mombert, to represent the highest potential in man, the creative urge and *daimon*. As both Mombert and Däubler, Pannwitz experienced Venice as a myth, rather than a reality (he lived on the Dalmatian island of Kolocep); Mombert, 'der alte Sfaira' is greeted in 'An Mombert zwischen Ragusa and Venezia' and 'Auf Däublers Tod' hails the creator of *Das Nordlicht* as a spiritual companion and source of inspiration. A late poem, cast very much in the mould of Stefan George, portrays the mystery of beauty, an experience beyond analysis, even beyond understanding:

Ich bin die blaue blume und ich bitte
Lasst mich und tastet nicht und fragt und wollt nicht.
Bin ich euch wunder bleib ich selbst mir rätsel
Nur dass ich da bin frommt — das andere quält
Ich blühe meine stund am innern rand
Walds oder volkes sehnend dass ich doch
Das wachsende geheimnis ganz entfalte.
Solang wir leben sind wir ja unendlich
Vermögen immer mehr. nur diese himmel
erretten mich / mich töten jene stimmen.
Ich sagte bloss: ich bin die blaue blume.[57]

Pannwitz, as has been stated, was a member of George's circle in Munich; he was a frequent visitor at the house of Karl Wolfskehl (1869–1948) and came into contact with the *Kosmiker*, that group of writers who broke with George and developed their own often highly eccentric *Weltanschauungen*. Wolfskehl's insistence upon an ecstatic, visionary quality of life, his Orphic, Dionysian attitudes, compounded with a Jewish apocalyptic Messianism, are found in his *Saul. Ein Spiel in vier Teilen* (1905) and *Sanctus. Orpheus. Zwei Mysterien* (1909). The rhapsodic prose of *Der Künstler der Heiland* (1897) equates the creative force with a religious act of redemption, and sees the artist as creator, liberator and lover of all things. The inflated claims, the arrogation of superhuman powers and of abilities beyond the attainments of normal man characterise the so-called *Kosmiker*, who were briefly mentioned in chapter 3, but who must now be examined, particularly Ludwig Klages, Alfred Schuler and, once more, Ludwig Derleth, for here the most extreme, and even dangerous, pseudo-intellectual excesses may be found. The 'proliferation of prophets' finds here its most perverse nucleus.

Alfred Schuler (1865–1923) published nothing in his lifetime: his *Cosmogoniae Fragmenta* and *Neronis Domini Fragmenta Selecta* were inscribed in gold Byzantine lettering on purple tablets, from which readings were permitted. (The tablets were, apparently, intended for the Empress Elizabeth of Austria, who was murdered before their completion.) Schuler had studied J.J. Bachofen's *Versuch über die Gräbersymbolik der Alten* (1859) and *Das Mutterrecht* (1861, reprinted 1897) and was obsessed by the world of later antiquity, firmly believing that he was a reincarnation of a Roman patrician of Nero's time. He announced that he could, by magic and ritual, invoke the dead, and he insisted upon reintroducing the cults of Eros and Thanatos, praising beauty and blood. The Jewish-Christian world was utterly rejected by Schuler, who saw in Nero the highest embodiment of human culture. Progress, enlightenment and rationalism were equally despised as resulting from Christian ethics: Ludwig Klages joined with Schuler here in an attack upon mind at the expense of 'life', and the presence of Nietzsche is here most potently felt. (Schuler's plan to perform corybantic dance before Nietzsche was mentioned earlier.) For Schuler the swastika, the ancient sun-symbol, represented the vital powers of creation, the destruction of the moribund Jewish-Christian tradition and the hope for the future: a vast 'Blutleuchte' would destroy the rottenness of Europe and introduce an era of violence, ecstasy and Dionysian frenzy. Ludwig Derleth's *Proklamationen* had likewise

revelled in pictures of smoking carnage, but Derleth had extolled
Christ-Napoleon; he rejected Schuler ('der Kupferhund') because of
Schuler's paganism, although the two men had much in common. They
are linked by what may be called the aestheticising of violence; at the
same time as the production of Schuler's *Cosmogoniae Fragmenta*
Derleth was translating the New Testament with Machiavelli's *Principe*
at hand, and emphasising not charity, but harshness and terror: his
titanic Christ-figure bore the features of Alexander, Hannibal,
Mahomed, Luther, Wallenstein and Nietzsche. Derleth's famous invitation to the *Proklamationen*, described in chapter 3, may well have
been copied from Schuler's notorious readings. On 29 April 1896
Klages, George, Wolfskehl and his wife were invited to a peroration by
Schuler in candlelight and incense; very much later, in his introduction
to Schuler's fragments, published in 1940, Klages described the scene:

> Die seelenatmosphärische Spannung wird unerträglich. Keiner
> vernimmt noch genau, was Schuler kündet; doch aus dem Dröhnen
> seiner Stimme wächst ein Vulkan, der glühende Lava schleudert,
> und aus der Lavaglut steigen purpurne Bilder, besinnungraubend,
> entrückend — wann es vorbei ist, wie es vorbei ist, bleibt unfaßlich
> . . . Auf der nächtlichen Straße stehe ich plötzlich mit George
> allein. Da fühlte ich mich am Arm ergriffen: 'Das ist ja Wahnsinn!
> Ich ertrage es nicht! Was haben Sie getan, mich dorthin zu locken!
> Das ist ja Wahnsinn! Führen Sie mich fort.'[58]

Schuler's world of blood, myth and orgiastic rodomontade was utterly
remote from Stefan George: George certainly esteemed Schuler's vast
knowledge of Roman antiquity, but sensed the hysteria and megalomania of Schuler's vision, and rejected his 'Lingualorgien'. It is interesting that Rilke, during the First World War, heard Schuler lecture in
Munich and was greatly impressed; a letter dated 18 March 1915 to
Marie von Thurn und Taxis describes the experience: 'stellen Sie sich
vor, daß ein Mensch, von einer intuitiven Einsicht ins alte kaiserliche
Rom her, eine Welterklärung zu geben unternahm, welche die Toten
als die eigentlich Seienden, das Toten-Reich als ein einziges, unerhörtes
Dasein, unsere kleine Lebensfrist aber als eine Art Ausnahme davon
darstellte'.[59] Rilke learned much from Schuler's view of death; after
Schuler's funeral he laid narcissi on the altar of a disused chapel near
Muzot, and acknowledged Schuler's contribution to the *Sonette an
Orpheus*. But George had had first-hand experience of Schuler's
eccentricity: a note left on Wolfskehl's writing desk declared: 'Sezet

nicht für den Priester den fakir/für den vates den magus/für die geister
die gespenster'.[60] Wolfskehl likewise saw the danger of Schuler's
brooding, and forbade him and Klages to enter his house. (Wolfskehl's
Jewishness was, of course, anathema to Schuler.) George wisely
ignored the rumours associated with his name and his dealings with
the *Kosmiker*; stories of satanism, orgies and sacrifice were rife in
Schwabing, particularly after the *Dichterzug* and the various carnival
celebrations, and George disdained to comment, or else ironically
elaborated on them. Another member of the circle, a companion of
Ludwig Klages, the young Theodor Lessing, wrote in his memoirs:

> Es wurde viel Nebel um ihn gebreitet, und die harmlose
> Symposien seines Ordens wurden von den Mißgünstigen als
> fantastische Orgien gedeutet. Das gab ihm einige Genugtuung,
> und wenn erzählt wurde, die letzte Vorlesung im bescheidenen
> Atelier Ludwig Derleths oder der dünne Maitrunk bei Karl
> Wolfskehl sei eine satanische Messe bei violetten Lichtern unter
> Ambraampeln gewesen, so mahnte er: 'Vergeßt nicht, daß eine
> Schüssel rauchenden Blutes vor mir stand'.[61]

Ludwig Klages (1872–1956), more intellectual than Schuler, was a
more tenacious enemy. He had been one of George's closest associates,
had shared George's reservations after the Schuler reading in 1896,
and his book on Stefan George (Berlin, 1902) had praised George's
poetry as representing the finest flowering of the German lyric. Klages,
encouraged initially by Wolfskehl, contributed firstly to the *Blätter
für die Kunst* a fragmentary drama *Desiderata* and then *Der Eroberer*,
a short piece of prose extolling the great military genius, the hero who,
utterly alone, can subdue half the globe: 'In steinerner unbeweglichkeit
harrt der eroberer auf seinem regungslosen roß. Seine züge sind von
der pracht verwitternder dolomiten. In seinem blick ist der kalte
schein des nordlichts. Auf dem haupte trägt er einen reif aus
bläulichem stahl'.[62] The conqueror is Tamburlane, but more the
myth of the superman than the historical figure, an archetypal man
of destiny who imposes his will upon the inchoate mass: 'Die schatten
zukünftiger feuersbrunst scheinen ihm vorauszufliehen, und hinter
ihm wälzt sich die dumpfe wucht der kräfte-schwangeren masse der
sein zerstörer-wille eine seele lieh'.[63] Like Schuler, Klages came more
and more to reject the modern world: Nietzsche's *Kulturpessimismus*
found in Klages a most fervent disciple, who rejected democracy,
utilitarianism and virtually all twentieth-century institutions. (Again it

is Thomas Mann, in his descriptions of Sixtus Kridwiss and Helmut Institoris in *Doktor Faustus*, with their derisive rejection of progress and their cult of the Italian Renaissance as being a time which 'von Blut und Schönheit geraucht hat', who has given a good portrayal of Schuler and Klages.[64]) George knew that Klages's way was not his; in 1903 his poem *Porta nigra*, which portrays a Roman youth whose desires were not always exemplary, led to altercations; George showed magnanimity by still publishing certain poems by Klages in the *Blätter für die Kunst*, firmly believing that art need not suffer because of differences of opinion, but the breach widened, and finally proved unbridgeable.

Klages's early essays *Aus einer seelenlehre des künstlers* and *Vom schaffenden* which appeared in the *Blätter* describe the artist as an instrument of vital, often monstrous forces; an artist-superman is proposed, in terms similar to those used by Rilke in his *Florenzer Tagebuch*, written at the same time. The Nietzschean images are unmistakable: the artist resembles 'dem mann der that, dem feldherrn, dem helden', yet also dwells in a 'bezirk erträumter sensationen'.[65] Klages's exaggerated claims for the superiority of the artist, his praise of vitalism, rejection of objectivity and insistence upon intuitive consciousness prepared the way for his later psychological studies *Ausdrucksbewegung und Gestaltungskraft* (1913), *Das Wesen des Bewußtseins* (1921), *Vom kosmogonischen Eros* (1922) and the notorious three volume study *Der Geist als Widersacher der Seele*, a discussion of which lies outside the compass of this book. Suffice it to say that Klages's praise of chaotic ecstasy, the 'soul' as opposed to the 'Geist', was anathema to George, whose insistence upon ordered structures in poetry and upon the 'male' principle of discipline and form was consciously a polemical counterblast to the chaotic and primitive fantasies of Klages. (The figure of Meingast, the 'prophet' in *Der Mann ohne Eigenschaften* is plainly modelled on him: his belief 'daß der Erlösungs-Gedanke immer anti-intellektuell gewesen sei', and 'Also ist nichts der Welt heute mehr zu wünschen als ein guter kräftiger Wahn'[66] could be direct quotations from Klages.) His seminar for 'Ausdruckskunde' in his academy near Zurich, his insistence upon expressiveness and drama in movement and gestures brought some of his thinking into the practices of expressionist dance; indeed, certain features of expressionism were undeniably anticipated by Klages.

Before terminating this discussion of the Munich circle of *Kosmiker* a few final remarks must be made on Ludwig Derleth, Carl J. Burckhardt's 'homo magus sive divinans'.[67] After the reading of the

Proklamationen Derleth moved, with his sister Anna ('die böse Nonne')
to a room high above the Marienplatz, decorated with pictures of
Napoleon, the Virgin Mary and a head of the Medusa; the table with
the carved eagle, from which the *Proklamationen* had been delivered,
took pride of place. Derleth contributed to the *Blätter*, but devoted
himself more and more to the writing of *Der Fränkische Koran*. After
the war he moved to Rome, and led an itinerant life, much as Däubler
and Mombert. *Der Fränkische Koran* was a work which occupied
Derleth for at least twenty years, and which grew so unwieldy that he
was forced to publish part one separately in 1932; the complete work
was to consist of over two thousand poems. It is a work which can be
compared with, if anything, Däubler's *Das Nordlicht*, in its vast cosmic
sweep, its movement through world history culminating in an
apocalyptic vision. The work begins with the section 'Anrufungen und
Gebete', where Christian ritual and superior powers are extolled; the
sections 'Weinlieder' and 'Liebeslieder' invoke the pagan deities. The
obligatory criticisms of modernity follow in 'Kritik der Wissenschaft'
and 'Kritik der Geschichte' where sybilline utterances, in gnomic
grandeur, condemn the hubris of all intellectual endeavour which lacks
a life enhancing Christology. The lightning imagery derives from
Revelations, and also *Also sprach Zarathustra*; Spitteler's *Der
Olympische Frühling* (1900) has also left its mark with its pretentiously
mystical grandeur. The publication of part one met with little interest;
George remained silent, yet Wolfskehl responded warmly, and much
later in life, in his New Zealand exile, he recalled the effect that the
work had had upon him: 'Sie wissen doch, wie Rausches voll ich über
den *Fränkischen Koran* war . . . Ein nachttrunknes Sonnenbad in
Purpur, mit einigem Ätzkalk versetzt, aber Duft und Donner!'[68] Of the
second part of Derleth's vast work only 'Der Tod des Thanatos' and 'Die
seraphische Hochzeit' were published in his lifetime: other sections, such
as 'Die Posaune des Kriegs', 'Der chymische Herkules', 'Die apokalyptische
Schlacht' and 'Von Wingert zur Kelter' are virtually unknown despite the
six volume publication of *Das Werk* in 1971. In 1933 a concert of contemporary music in Vienna included Egon Wellesz's opus 46, *Fünf kleine
Männerchöre*, based on texts from the first part of the work.[69]

It is a welcome relief to move out of the lutulent waters of the
literary scene in Munich, from that overwrought atmosphere of
Nietzscheanism, Messianism, inflated aesthetic claims and grotesque
posturing. (Roderich Huch, a nephew of Ricarda Huch, who was
once admired by both Klages and Schuler as the 'Sonnenknabe' and was
painted by Sabine Lepsius, gives a good portrayal of his dismissal from

the circle for betraying 'cosmic secrets': he had been rejected by
George for refusing to stand naked before him and physically
attacked by Klages's henchman.[70]) It has been emphasised that George
did not share in the excesses of irrationalism, but the cultic ritualisa-
tion of his Maximin experience also betrays a semi-religious yearning
for initiation and redemption. The theme of the quest, the longing
for mystical illumination, is characteristic of so much German literature
of this time; it is paradoxically the vision of the superman, that most
'godless' of creatures, that stimulated so much of this writing. No sooner
had God been declared dead, and man to have assumed His attributes,
than a quickening of the religious faith was felt, a religiosity derived
partly from *fin-de-siècle* decadence (Wagner's *Parsifal*) and the
Dionysian paganism unleashed by Nietzsche; George's cultic play *Die
aufnahme in den orden* has a theme which is reminiscent of Wagner's
Bühnenweihfestspiel.[71] Themes of mystical yearning, an *imitatio Christi,*
or a sun-worship, or a quest for the Grail, proliferate in German
literature more than in the literature of any other country; the
millennial fantasies would partly feed the Messianic elements of
expressionism and, in a more sinister way, stimulate the more
irrational elements of National Socialism.

Gerhart Hauptmann's novel *Der Narr in Christo Emanuel Quint*,
started in 1901 and published in 1910, shares the theme of the quest,
the religious yearning and the imagery of mountain heights. The
Christ-figure had been anticipated by Hauptmann's short story *Der
Apostel* (1890), but the novel is a far vaster, far more sympathetic
portrayal of a man who, confused and limited in his mental powers,
achieves a Christ-like humility and love for all things. Dostoevski may
well have given the impetus to this novel (his reception in Germany will
prove of interest during the discussion of expressionism); Quint, the
Fool in Christ, is hounded by authority and orthodoxy and perishes
upon the St Gotthard pass. Hauptmann assumes the position of the
objective narrator, ironically uncommitted; is Quint a pathetic figure,
ignorant and abject, or is there greatness in his simplicity? Are his
followers likewise deluded, fanatical *Schwärmer*? The narrator cannot
tell us, yet must admit to being touched by Quint's obvious sincerity:

Auf einem Briefbogen, den man in seiner Tasche fand, waren die
Worte noch deutlich zu lesen gewesen: 'Das Geheimnis des
Reichs?' die keiner beachtete noch verstand, die aber den
Chronisten, als er das traurige Dokument in Händen hielt, eine
gewisse Rührung abnötigten. War er überzeugt oder zweifelnd

gestorben? Wer weiß es? Der Zettel enthält eine Frage, sicherlich!
Aber was bedeutet es: Das Geheimnis des Reichs?[72]

The meaning is not understood, and whether Quint died in exultation
or despair is likewise unknown. Deluded and deranged Quint may well
have been in his quest for Christ-like illumination, but his most intense
moments of ecstasy are derived from contact with elemental forces —
the mountains and the sun. The sun as a symbol for Christ is superseded
by its role as a guarantor of older, more elemental forces: as a remote
and splendid deity it fills Quint with an overwhelming sense of power,
almost as Zarathustra was transfigured by its appearance.

The year after the completion of *Der Narr in Christo Emanuel Quint*
Hauptmann started his *Sonnen-Meditationen* at Portofino, near
Rapallo, that very place described so glowingly by Nietzsche in his
letter to Peter Gast. In rapturous terms the 'alternde Dichter' greets the
radiant orb rising above the sea:

> Hinter einer riesigen Wolkenbank ging sie auf. Sie glich einem
> rosafarbenen Pilz — einer Feuertulpe — einer Seerose — einer
> ungeheuren Rubinschale.
> Die Rubinschale bricht. Unter ihrem ungeheuren Lichtausbruch
> entsteht die Welt.[73]

(The same description is found, almost word for word, in *Die Insel der
großen Mutter*, in the scene where the naked Laurence greets the
sunrise; her awareness that 'Wir leben ebensosehr und mehr auf der
Sonne als auf der Erde'[74] could have been derived from Däubler's
gigantic epos.) The poet walks through the luminous landscape,
entranced by the joy of the morning:

> Mit allen Diademen reich beladen,
> schwingt sich der Morgen her in meine Seele.
> Lautlos entsteigt er, klaren Adels voll,
> Mit Frische angetan, mit Licht gesegnet.[75]

The worship of the sun, the life force, fuses with a pantheistic
awareness of indwelling powers, a pan-erotic urge to seize and embrace
all: Hauptmann's poetic world is here not far removed from that of
D.H. Lawrence. (The 'Sonnenaufgang' section of Richard Strauss's
Alpensymphonie, written at the same time, would be an equivalent
experience in music to Hauptmann's descriptions in *Sonnen*.) The

sun-god, and Eros, kindle, sustain and inspire to creativity — this 'der alternde Dichter' knows as he admires the beauty of the girl who appears before him. Thoughts of inadequacy, the awareness of mutability and transience are swept away as 'Helios [fegte] selber mit seinem goldenen Wagen und seinem Gespann aus dem Meer wie ein Sturmwind des Lichts und verjagte mit eins Chimaira, Dämonen und Götter'.[76] The dithyrambic sentiments expressed here prepare the way for *Der Ketzer von Soana*, begun roughly at the same time, bearing the original title *Die syrische Göttin*. Hauptmann's visit to Greece in 1907, a stay of three months in all, encouraged the new, Dionysian *Weltanschauung*; Harry Graf Kessler, writing in 1909 on Hauptmann's *Griechischer Frühling*, links Hauptmann's name with that of Kleist and stresses the musical, rhapsodic element of his work at this time: 'daß seine Kunst . . . aus demselben Born fließt wie die Musik, nämlich aus dem Urquell der Gefühlsphantasie, den Nietzsche den dionysischen genannt hat; Hauptmanns Kunst ist, wenn man sie schon Naturalismus nennen will, ein dionysischer Naturalismus'.[77] Lou Salomé, who visited Hauptmann in 1915 and again in 1917, also esteemed *Griechischer Frühling* highly and wrote perceptively on it in her diary; Thomas Mann, however, spoke disparagingly of Hauptmann's cult of life and 'health' in this work.[78]

The dark violence of the Greek myths profoundly impressed Hauptmann, who at the end of his life, as chapter 8 will describe, composed his *Atriden Tetralogie* in the most sombre and ruthless period of German history. The heliocentric Mexican civilisations also exerted a powerful influence. Montezuma, son of the Sun-God, is portrayed in *Der weiße Heiland*, but it is *Indipohdi*, begun in Portofino in 1913, and first performed under the title *Das Opfer* in 1922, which is Hauptmann's most powerful description of pagan sun-worship; although the setting is a volcanic island, and not Mexico, the references to the 'possibly toltec palace', the obsidian altar and the blood sacrifice are sufficiently reminiscent of the world of the Aztecs and Mayas. Yet it is also in this work that Hauptmann seeks for a synthesis between the creative . activity of the heretic of Soana and the passivity and self-denial of Emanuel Quint; the pagan-dionysian element is felt to be insufficient, and an almost Christian humility is reinstated. It seems as though Hauptmann had seen the dangers in Nietzschean vitalism, in pagan substitutes for Christianity and in myth-making and sun-worship. But life-denial and self-deprecation likewise are unsatisfactory — Prospero's resignation and tiredness are contrasted with the youthful vitality of his son Ormann, who demands the right to rule. The fierce rumbling of the volcano, the threat of human sacrifice, the barbaric splendour of the temple provide a powerful background to the father-son conflict. Yet it would be true to say that both learn from the other: Prospero is able to lay down his life to appease the chthonic powers and to enact a Christ-like sacrifice, and Ormann respects and loves his father's sublime act of self-abnegation. Prospero reconciles himself to nature's vitalism and passes, much like Hölderlin's Empedocles, into the divine fire; Ormann's vitality is tempered by knowledge and love. The last words of the play are Prospero's magnificent address to the sun:

> Titan! Titan! Du schleppst zum letztenmal
> die Welt von Licht, die Welt voll Glut herauf
> in deines Schöpfers Seele. Brausen fegt
> die Feuersturmflut über alle Gipfel
> und stürzt, ein Tönenmeer, in alle Tiefen.[79]

But a Nietzschean vitalism gives way to a Schopenhauerian quietism, oblivion and reabsorption into the Whole at the end.

The mythomania and yearning for cosmic illumination, the sun-worship, pantheism and atavistic irrationalism of the writers and thinkers mentioned in this chapter give to German literature and thought a fascinating and often disquieting flavour. The rejection of the historical in favour of myth, the emphasis on vitalism and pantheism in place of orthodoxy and the institutional provided the sanction for untrammelled subjectivity and a perverse idealism. It would, however, be false to claim that the quest for metaphysical illumination was wholly amoral in any Nietzschean sense: writers such as Christian Morgenstern and Ernst Barlach exemplify a quest for religious experience which merges into Christian mysticism. As Christian Morgenstern (1871–1914) is frequently considered to be simply the writer of amusing and often grotesque verse it is well to be reminded that he dedicated his early work *In Phantas Schloß* (1895) to 'dem Geiste Friedrich Nietzsches', that he translated Ibsen for the S. Fischer edition, having travelled to Norway to meet the great dramatist, and that for several years he was the editor of *Das Theater* in Berlin. In the winter of 1905–1906, after reading Dostoevski and Meister Eckhart in the loneliness of Birkenwerder, he underwent certain mystical experiences and began his *Tagebuch eines Mystikers*; three years later he became a fervent disciple of Rudolf Steiner, and became a member of the Anthroposophical Society, travelling to Oslo

and Budapest to be present at Steiner's lectures. His tuberculosis
became critical in 1914, and after his death in the spring of that
year he was cremated, his ashes being deposited in the Goetheanum
at Dornach.

Morgenstern's development from Nietzschean life-affirmation to
Christian mysticism was similar to Steiner's; in 1897 Steiner had
edited, with Hartleben, *Das Magazin für Literatur*, and had defended
the ideas of Nietzsche, Stirner and John Henry Mackay. He had
propagated an anarchic-individualism and rejected what Freud had
termed the 'black ooze' of spiritualism and theosophy.[80] But after his
work in the Goethe and Nietzsche archives in Weimar Steiner became
increasingly fascinated by theosophy and, in 1901, he became the
German Secretary of the Theosophical Society. It was after the
increasing difficulties of working with Annie Besant that he left and
founded his own Anthroposophical Society and, in 1913, started to
build the Johannistempel — later to be named the Goetheanum —
at Dornach. Like Steiner, Morgenstern also succumbed to the powerful
intoxication of *Zarathustra*, and many of the early poems reflect the
Nietzschean imagery of sunrise, mountain, chalice, fire and ice.
His Norwegian experiences are reflected in such poems as 'Farbenglück'
and 'Dagny': his meditations on the natural world in *Stufen* are similar
to Däubler's heliotelluric fantasies: 'Warum sollte die Erde nicht
innerlich durchleuchtet sein? Warum die Gold- und Silberadern nicht
im Geheimen von den Strahlen eines Lichtes leuchten, für das wir
keine Augen haben? So wuchtet mächtigen Gesanges die Erde ihre
Ätherbahn'.[81] The future poet, for Morgenstern, must be the creator
of myth: 'Ich betrachte als eine Aufgabe kommender Dichter-
geschlechter, neue Mythen zu schaffen . . .';[82] this poet likewise would
conceive of a drama describing the clash between Newtonian physics
(analysis) and Goethean science (synthesis), in which the latter is
triumphant. This reference to Goethe's *Farbenlehre* brings Steiner to
mind, for he had edited and published Goethe's scientific writings in
Kürschners deutsche Nationalliteratur (1895–1897); it is therefore not
surprising that Steiner is compared to the sun which eternally gleams in
spite of the sombre darkness of the dismal day. In his *Bild meines
Lebens* Morgenstern describes the development of his spiritual life in
the image of a chalice containing the sacred blood, where the stem is
the 'weltliche Periode [Nietzsche]' which continued until his tuberculosis, the cup itself is his awakening ('Öffnung durch Johannëisches')
and the blood is his redemption.[83] His last collection of poems *Wir
fanden einen Pfad* is dedicated to Rudolf Steiner, and a Christian

mysticism, tinged with anthroposophy, prevails.

At the time that Morgenstern was reading Dostoevski and the German mystics in Birkenwerder, the sculptor Ernst Barlach (1870–1938) travelled to Russia and, much as Rilke had six years before, experienced a fervent quickening of his religious-aesthetic sensibilities. After his return he began, in 1907, to write his play *Der tote Tag*, which was published in 1912 and which received its first performance in Leipzig in 1919. Barlach is frequently considered to be a precursor of expressionism: he certainly represents the transition between the religious-prophetic mysticism which this chapter has attempted to describe and the yearning for transcendence which is found in certain of the works of early expressionism. Barlach's sculpture, earth-bound yet striving for mystical illumination, has already been mentioned in connection with Däubler; his 'Der Ekstatiker' (as well as Edvard Munch's 'The Shriek') meant much to the expressionist generation. In March 1913 he wrote the following about his play: 'Heute entdeckte ich mir selbst, daß mein Drama *Der tote Tag* so etwas ist wie eine Phantasie über unbefleckte Empfängnis, d.h. geistige Abstammung des Menschen im Gegensatz zur leiblichen, die so befleckt sein mag, wie man nur wünscht'.[84] The emphasis on the 'immaculate spiritual conception' demonstrates the play's religious intention; it is also of interest that the last sentence of the play, which emphasises this point, was quoted by Jung in his *Seelenprobleme der Gegenwart* to refute the doctrines of Sigmund Freud.[85]

The play examines the conflict between the principle of transcendence (the Father) and immanence (the Mother), with the son as the battlefield. (Barlach's own struggle to gain his son from the boy's mother provided the impetus; Barlach wrote: 'Die Mutter wollte den Knaben nicht hergeben. Auf diese Weise mußte ich früher oder später notwendig Gott für ihn werden. Das war der Anstoß. Unter den Händen wuchs die Idee von selbst ins Mythische'.[86]) The Son is portrayed as yearning for release from the clinging maternal influence; he dreams of the divine horse which is to take him home to his Father. The horse is brought by a blind figure who incites the Son to flee; the Mother destroys the horse, which 'wittert schon die Sonne',[87] and a dead greyness, a 'dead day' surrounds the lonely house. The Son, confused and troubled, lights candles to dispel the sombre anguish; in spite of the Mother's apparent triumph he hears mysterious voices – 'Ich hörte die Sonne sausen überm Nebel'.[88] The Mother exults at having destroyed the magic horse, but kills herself in a frenzy of hatred because the Son cannot forget the Father; in madness the Son follows her example. The blind figure sets forth to proclaim that God is the Father of mankind: man's spiritual yearning for transcendence cannot be stifled by physical realities. A similar problem is examined in Barlach's next play, *Der arme Vetter*, which, unlike *Der tote Tag* with its ghosts and mists, starts with a realistic setting – the arrival of a party of Easter trippers in a country inn on the Elbe – but then moves towards a mystic transfiguration and Ascension. The man-made lantern may appear to give a brighter light than the splendour of Sirius, but spiritual illumination, 'der Abglanz vom Jenseits',[89] triumphs to bring about a mystical excarnation.

A recent study has well described the 'yawning abyss between poetry and prophecy that after *Zarathustra* engulfed so many'.[90] The undoubted sincerity of Mombert, and the frequently lumbering solar-Christology of Däubler, the Charontic mysticism of Pannwitz, the ecstatic raptures of Wolfskehl, the anthroposophical yearning of Morgenstern and the fervent longing for transcendence of Barlach betray an idealism, however private, where Zarathustra, St Francis, Meister Eckhart and Rudolf Steiner fuse in an uncomfortable synthesis; Schuler, Klages and Derleth on the other hand exemplify an atavistic vitalism derived from Nero, Tamburlane, Loyola and Napoleon. That redemption should be sought in such disparate (and dubious) figures betrays a profound spiritual malaise, the origins of which lie with the theologian rather than the literary critic, who points finally to yet another example of monumentally aesthetic religiosity, *Das Mirakel*, by Karl Vollmoeller (1878–1948), which enjoyed enormous success after being staged in the Schumann-Zirkus in Berlin by Max Reinhardt in 1912. Vollmoeller's collection of poems *Parcival* (1897–1900) belongs more in a discussion of neo-romanticism rather than religious yearning, where 'Montsalwatsch' is portrayed as a city of sun and beauty rather than spirituality. Vollmoeller chose to live in the Palazzo Vendramin in Venice where Wagner had died, and in obvious imitation of D'Annunzio flew aeroplanes with reckless abandon; he later wrote film scripts. *An den Toren des Lebens*, by Ernst Hardt (1875–1947), extolled 'unser heiliges, großes glühendes Leben' in that Nietzschean-religious manner which has been described so often; his *Tantris der Narr* and his Grail dramas (*Gawân, Lanwâl* and *Lanzelot*) are again examples of what could be called neo-romantic religiosity at its most precious. The imagery – grailsblood, grail-flowers, ruby and opals – derives from Wagner's *Parsifal*; Hofmannsthal's *Jedermann* (1911) represents a further triumph of showmanship over sincerity, a debased form of theatrical spirituality.

The cosmic element which this chapter has attempted to describe derives basically from Nietzsche; it overlaps to a certain extent with certain elements associated with neo-romanticism and shares many of the premises of early expressionism. But sun-worship, *Lebensrausch* and vitalism also assumed more sinister properties: the formation of such societies as the *Gralsbund*, the *Sankt Georgs Bund*, *Thulegesellschaft* and *Mittgart-Kreis* presuppose the cult of *völkisch* tendencies which prepared the way for National Socialism; Zarathustra's sun-worship will find its perverse conclusion in the theosophical paintings of Fidus (Karl Höppner), who portrayed sun-drenched nudes striding towards the sun, about to embrace the cosmos, in the writings of Ellegard Ellerbeck (Erwin Leiser), whose *Sönne Sönnings Söhne auf Sönnensee* is a most remarkable mixture of theosophy, occultism, spiritualism and astrology, and in Lanz von Liebenfels's amazing work *Theozoologie oder die Kunde von den Sodoms-Äfflingen und dem Götter-Elektron. Eine Einführung in die älteste und neueste Weltanschauung und eine Rechtfertigung des Fürstentums und des Adels*. But these turgid waters need not be sounded here; what is of far greater importance is Germany's considerable contribution to twentieth-century Europe's literary excellence, and this will be discussed in the next chapter.

Notes

1. Nietzsche, *Werke*, II, 912.
2. Bertram, *Nietzsche. Versuch einer Mythologie*, Berlin, 1919, 361.
3. See Hollingdale, *Nietzsche*, London, 1965, 304.
4. Ibid., 303.
5. Przybyszewski, *Erinnerungen*, 196.
6. Paula Modersohn-Becker, *Briefe und Tagebuchblätter*, Munich, 1925, 76.
7. Nietzsche, *Werke*, II, 561.
8. Ibid., 380.
9. Haufe (ed.), *Deutsche Briefe aus Italien*, Hamburg, 1965, 464-465.
10. Gunter Martens, *Vitalismus und Expressionismus*, Stuttgart, 1971.
11. Gustav Sack, *Prosa. Briefe. Verse*, Munich and Vienna, no date, 426-427.
12. Quoted in Martens, 128.
13. Ibid., 132.
14. Paul Hamburger, *From Prophecy to Exorcism*, London, 1965, 57.
15. Däubler, *Dichtungen und Schriften*, Munich, 1956, 868.
16. Däubler, *Das Nordlicht* (Genfer Ausgabe), Leipzig, 1921, I, 11.
17. Ibid., 52.
18. See Thomke, *Hymnische Dichtung im Expressionismus*, Berne, 1972, 21.
19. Däubler, *Das Nordlicht*, I, 67.
20. *Rainer Maria Rilke–Katherine Kippenberg Briefwechsel*, Frankfurt/Main, 1954, 178-179.

21. Däubler, *Das Nordlicht*, II, 9.
22. Ibid., 622.
23. Däubler, *Dichtungen und Schriften*, 234.
24. Däubler, *Wir wollen nicht verweilen*, Dresden, 1915, 141.
25. Däubler, *Dichtungen und Schriften*, 853.
26. Ibid., 854.
27. John Willett, *Expressionism*, London, 1970.
28. Alfred Mombert, *Dichtungen*, Munich, 1963, II, 609.
29. Ibid., 617.
30. Ibid.
31. Ibid., I, 24.
32. Mombert, *Briefe 1893–1942* (ed. Morse), Heidelberg, 1962, 210, 211.
33. Mombert, *Dichtungen*, I, 80.
34. Ibid., III, 79.
35. Ibid., I, 93.
36. Ibid., I, 94.
37. Ibid., I, 103.
38. Nietzsche, *Werke*, II, 284.
39. Mombert, I, 200.
40. Ibid., III, 116.
41. See the *Bühnenbilder* of these plays published by the Goetheanum, Dornach, 1938.
42. Mombert, *Briefe*, 81.
43. Mombert, III, 290.
44. Ibid., I, 426.
45. Ibid., I, 495.
46. Ibid., I, 506.
47. Mombert, *Briefe*, 73.
48. Ibid., 74.
49. *Literarische Manifeste der Jahrhundertwende*, 476.
50. Ibid., 477.
51. Ibid., 497.
52. Ibid., 491.
53. Ibid., 492.
54. Pannwitz, *Trilogie des Lebens*, 96. Quoted Konrad Hess, *Von Nietzsche zu Pannwitz*, Langnau, 1963, 12.
55. Pannwitz, *Wasser wird sich ballen*, Stuttgart, 1963, 9.
56. Ibid., 359.
57. Ibid., 236.
58. Quoted F. Schonauer, *Stefan George in Selbstzeugnissen und Bilddokumenten*, Reinbet, 1960, 80.
59. *Rainer Maria Rilke–Marie von Thurn und Taxis Briefwechsel*, Zurich, 1951, I, 409.
60. See Schonauer, 81.
61. Theodor Lessing, *Einmal und nie wieder*, Gütersloh, 1969, 309.
62. *Blätter für die Kunst*, Folge IV, 88.
63. Ibid., 90.
64. Thomas Mann, *Doktor Faustus*, chapters 34 and 35.
65. Winkler, *Der George-Kreis* (Sammlung Metzler), 35.
66. Musil, *Der Mann ohne Eigenschaften*, 834.
67. Quoted in Dominik Jost, *Ludwig Derleth*, 9.
68. Karl Wolfskehl, *Zehn Jahre Exil. Briefe aus Neuseeland*, Heidelberg, 1959, 275.
69. Quoted Jost, 178.
70. See Roderich Huch, *Alfred Schuler. Ludwig Klages und Stefan George.*

Erinnerungen an Kreise und Krisen der Jahrhundertwende in München-Schwabing, Amsterdam, 1973, 39 and 46.

71. Pascal, *From Naturalism to Expressionism*, 101 and 189.
72. Hauptmann, *Sämtliche Werke*, V, 414.
73. Ibid., VI, 665.
74. Ibid., V, 787.
75. Ibid., VI, 676-677.
76. Ibid., 686.
77. Quoted in K.L. Tank, *Gerhart Hauptmann in Selbstzeugnissen und Bilddokumenten*, Reinbek, 1959, 168.
78. See note 103 in Thomas Mann's projected *Geist und Kunst*. I am indebted to Mr T.J. Reed for this point.
79. Hauptmann, II, 1435–1436.
80. Pascal, *From Naturalism to Expressionism*, 176.
81. Christian Morgenstern, *Gesammelte Werke*, Munich, 1965, 369.
82. Ibid., 375.
83. Ibid., 440.
84. Ernst Barlach, *Das dichterische Werk*, Munich, 1958, II (*Die Prose I*), 328.
85. Barlach, *Briefe* I (ed. F. Dross), 800.
86. *Barlach im Gespräch*, Munich, 1963, 32.
87. Barlach, *Das dichterische Werk*, I, 44.
88. Ibid., 87.
89. Barlach, *Die Dramen*, I, 162.
90. Pascal, *From Naturalism to Expressionism*, 179.

'Modernism' is a vexed and controversial term; almost every new generation of writers has claimed that its own way of experiencing and describing the world is more up-to-date or 'relevant' than that of its predecessors. The German romantics felt themselves to be more modern than the *Stürmer und Dränger*, and the adherents to the *Jung Deutsch-land* school doubtlessly felt the same *vis-à-vis* such writers as Novalis, Tieck and Brentano; the uneasy compromise between poetry and reality which may be discovered in much of the writing of the Poetic Realists was felt to be hopelessly antiquated by the new generation of writers who were the heirs of French symbolism and naturalism. To be 'modern' at the end of the nineteenth century meant to write poetry like Mallarmé, or prose like Zola, or to write drama like Ibsen; it meant that, formally, the poet could experiment with syntax and create inner worlds of esoteric resonances, and that, with regard to content, the novelist and playwright could deal with the outcast, the depressed proletariat and with the effects of congenital syphilis.

In Munich and Berlin it was the naturalists who prided themselves on their modernity, as chapter 1 has shown; in Vienna it was *Jung Wien* which felt that the *dernier cri* was neo-romanticism, symbolism and a nervous decadence. But naturalism, neo-romanticism and those inordinate self-inflations into cosmic realms described in chapter 4 — the equivalents in prose and poetry of the music of Richard Strauss, Gustav Mahler and early Schönberg — were rejected by a generation grown tired of social reporting, exquisite refinements and self-indulgent bombast. It is usual to see expressionism as being the form which 'modernism' took in Germany, a complete break with all the former canons of artistic experience, but that extraordinarily complex movement, to be discussed in chapter 6, owes much to the social concerns of the naturalists and to the inflated egocentricity of writers described in the last chapter. The German-speaking writers who have entered the European consciousness as being somehow spokesmen of the modern situation are not expressionists: Kafka and Rilke and, to a lesser extent, Robert Musil and Karl Kraus are the names which seem to belong legitimately to the twentieth century and can compete with the great modern writers of England and France.

It was Vienna, as a recent study has shown, that centre of the conservative, ossified Habsburg domains and of the neo-romanticism analysed in chapter 2, which became, at the beginning of the twentieth century, the testing-ground for practically all the modern movements in the arts.[1] By 'modern' is meant here the reaction against neo-romanticism, against self-aggrandisement, self-indulgence, intellectual muddle and complacent mediocrity. In 1897 Gustav Klimt seceded from the Imperial Academy, objecting to the heavy, mythologising tendencies of Makart; the architect Adolf Loos moved further than Klimt in his rejection of that which was unnecessarily ornate and cumbersome. Arnold Schönberg, after passing through the post-Wagnerian harmonies of Strauss and Mahler, sought a new clarity, an inherent logic which would replace the quest for ever-greater theatrical effects in music (although his admiration for the authenticity and integrity of Mahler led Schönberg to dedicate to him his *Harmonie-lehre*). In his fortnightly periodical *Die Fackel*, which he edited from 1899 until 1936, and to which he became the sole contributor, Karl Kraus sought to expose the narcissistic arrogance of the aesthete and the portentous claims of the literary experts; in Ludwig Wittgenstein the seeds were sown for a thorough-going critique of the muddle between logic and metaphysics: a new, more vital, more precise way of writing and thinking was prescribed. The escapism of the aesthetes of the Café Griensteidl, their cultivation of exquisite worlds was not enough: both Kraus and Wittgenstein realised that egocentric self-indulgence which lacked an earnest integrity was the end of art, just as Loos had seen that the pompous mythological encumbrances betrayed an escapism which resulted from an inability to come to terms with the premises of the present. Discussions of architecture and philosophy lie outside the scope of this book; what can be discussed, however, is the vital problem concerning language and its limitations which became the most crucial issue and the truest symptom of modernisation at this time.

It is Nietzsche who, as so often, provides the most enlightening *aperçus*. As early as *Menschliches Allzumenschliches* he explained:

Die Bedeutung der Sprache für die Entwicklung der Kultur liegt darin, daß in ihr der Mensch eine eigene Welt neben die andere stellte, einen Ort, welchen er für so fest hielt, um von ihm aus die übrige Welt aus den Angeln zu heben und sich zum Herren derselben zu machen. Insofern der Mensch an die Begriffe und Namen der Dinge als an *aeterna veritates* durch lange Zeitstrecken hindurch geglaubt hat, hat er sich jenen Stolz angeeignet, mit dem er sich

über das Tier erhob: er meinte wirklich in der Sprache die Erkenntnis der Welt zu haben.[2]

A perfect correspondence seemed to prevail between language and
world – but, Nietzsche explains, this cannot last. 'Sehr nachträglich –
jetzt erst – dämmert es den Menschen auf, daß sie einen ungeheuren
Irrtum in ihrem Glauben an die Sprache propagiert haben'. Is language
a mirror-image of the world, or simply a monstrous delusion, leading
man ever further from the 'truth'? The death of God means the
collapse of *all* meaning and order, linguistic ones included: to believe
in grammar, Nietzsche startlingly claims in *Götzendämmerung*, means
to believe in God.[3] To deny the Logos, the Word, means to deny
absolute validity to any human activity or institution, and man's faith
in language as an adequate means of 'portraying reality' is utterly
discredited. That 'Nachtgeist' which Hölderlin had feared and which
'hat unser Land/Beschwätzet, mit Sprachen viel, unbändigen und/
Den Schutt gewälzet/Bis diese Stunde'[4] would become increasingly
apparent as the twentieth century advanced.

One year after Nietzsche's death appeared two works by the
Bohemian journalist-philosopher Fritz Mauthner (1849–1923), the
Wörterbuch der Philosophie and the *Beiträge zu einer Kritik der Sprache*.
Mauthner saw with ever-increasing clarity that words were not 'things'
but activities, whose meanings are in a constant state of flux: to use
such unreliable guides in an attempt to understand reality was to
court disaster. Language was but a game; it could not grasp or alter
the real world but, by its metaphorical tendencies, it was well suited
to the creation of poetry. It would seem that Mauthner was putting
forward a justification of aestheticism, that is, that only in the creation
of works of art can language be said to have any meaning at all, in a
manner not dissimilar to that of Ernst Mach. (Ernst Mach's
phenomenalism, his belief that the world was simply the sum total of
appearances to the senses, and that 'inner experiences', for example
dreams, were of equal importance to 'outer' ones, for example sense
impressions, had a great influence on the young Viennese writers;
both Hofmannsthal and Hermann Broch attended his lectures, and
Musil wrote a doctoral thesis on him.) But Mauthner does not extol
language as the sole arbiter or aesthetic legislator; in art, also, it
comes up against limits which it cannot transcend. In his *Beiträge* he
quotes Maeterlinck's comment on the inability to speak meaningfully
on the things that appear of greatest importance, and the need for
silence, sentiments which Wittgenstein endorsed in the last sentence of

his *Tractatus*: 'Worüber man nicht sprechen kann, darüber muß man schweigen'. To speak with authority and integrity on any subject seemed impossible in a language inflated to megalomaniac proportions or rarefied to the point of exquisite and unnatural delicacy. And the man who would experience this predicament in its full earnestness was the poet who had used the German language with such effortless grace but a few years before – Hugo von Hofmannsthal.

The situation is described with great clarity in *Ein Brief*, first published in October 1902; letters to Stefan George and R.A. Schröder testify to the seriousness of the issues at stake. A historical mask is chosen, a means of alienation to bring the central problem – that of language – into a sharper focus. Hofmannsthal had read Bacon's essays frequently in the summer of that year and describes his own essay as 'der Brief, den Philipp Lord Chandos, jüngerer Sohn des Earl of Bath, an Francis Bacon, später Lord Verulam and Viscount St Albans, schrieb, um sich bei diesem Freunde wegen des gänzlichen Verzichtes auf literarische Betätigung zu entschuldigen'.[5] Young Lord Chandos, aged twenty-six (Hofmannsthal was born in 1874), author of works which had been praised to the skies, now complains of a 'geistige Starrnis', 'eine Krankheit meines Geistes'; he feels, he explains, separated as by an abyss from those earlier works and from the plans he had made for the future. He had, in his earlier years, felt at one with all things, spiritual and temporal; he had moved as in a magic harmony (what Hofsmannthal had called elsewhere a state of 'Präexistenz'), able to register the sensuous impressions of all phenomena and to express their meaning in verses of flawless perfection. Using a beautiful image he explains that formerly 'Mir haben sich die Geheimnisse des Glaubens zu einer erhabenen Allegorie verdichtet, die über den Feldern meines Lebens steht wie ein leuchtender Regenbogen, in einer stetigen Ferne, immer bereit, zurückzuweichen, wenn ich mir einfallen ließe hinzueilen und mich in den Saum seines Mantels hüllen zu wollen'. But suddenly and with consternation Chandos realises: 'Es ist mir völlig die Fähigkeit abhanden gekommen, über irgend etwas zusammenhängend zu denken oder zu sprechen'.[6]

The ability to think and speak coherently about anything has been lost to Chandos: language has suddenly failed him, and hence the power to conceptualise, and to pass any value judgements. First the abstract general terms became impossible for him: 'Ich empfand ein unerklärliches Unbehagen, die Worte "Geist", "Seele", oder "Körper" nur auszusprechen ...'; those words which are glibly used to pronounce certain evaluations crumbled, he writes, in his

mouth like 'modrige Pilze'.[7] (A very similar situation is described by
Thomas Mann in his *Enttäuschung*, written in 1896, and which describes a nocturnal conversation in St Mark's Square, Venice, where
the narrator learns of the lonely figure's hatred of 'diesen großen
Wörtern für Gut und Böse, Schön und Häßlich, die ich so bitterlich
hasse' and his rejection of 'diese Dichter, die ihre großen Wörter an
allen Wänden schreibe'.[8]) Chandos looked at the activities of men
from a fresh angle, accepting nothing at its face value, and everything
dissolved into meaninglessness. It has been rightly pointed out that
here is a criticism of Ernst Mach's atomic sensationalism: not only
abstractions but *all* sensuous impressions became problematic and
ineffable. The disease spread 'wie ein um sich fressender Rost', and
Chandos continues: 'Es zerfiel mir alles in Teile, die Teile wieder in
Teile, und nichts mehr ließ sich mit einem Begriff umspannen. Die
einzelnen Worte schwammen um mich; sie geronnen zu Augen, die
mich anstarrten, und in die ich wieder hineinstarren muß: Wirbel sind
sie, in die hinabzusehen mich schwindelt, die sich unaufhaltsam drehen
und durch die hindurch man ins Leere kommt'.[9] Words have lost all
coherence and order, and the pattern of reality is totally fragmented:
all is flux, or, rather, a vortex which swirls in vertiginous confusion.

The manipulator of words is now at their mercy or, rather, at the
mercy of a Babel of apparent meanings which communicate nothing.
One is here forcibly reminded of Kafka, who knew the Chandos *Brief*
and respected the earnestness of Hofmannsthal's self-analysis: Kafka
himself knew of vertigo, labyrinth and the rust and fungoid decay
which blights all attempts at communication. The aesthete who
responded with an almost voluptuous self-abandonment to the seductive power of words and who used them as though they were jewels
set in rare velvet now fears them, for their promise turns to nought.
Lyrical subjectivity leads either to solipsism and ultimate sterility or to
a dazzling display of linguistic virtuosity in a vacuum. What hope
remains for Chandos-Hofmannsthal is beyond language; only in rare
moments of intuitive harmony with all things is anything like the
previous state of oneness restored, and joy is given now not by
exquisite artistry but by dumb, simple objects — a beetle, a stunted
apple tree, a mossy stone. As Van Gogh (a painter greatly admired by
Hofmannsthal and whose work he described in the 'Briefe eines
Zurückgekehrten') found the beauty of authenticity and integrity in
the humblest of objects, so now does Chandos-Hofmannsthal: in a
'Sprache, in welcher die stummen Dinge zu mir reden', a language
beyond silence, he finds an ultimate reality, as he does in the 'Denken

in einem Material, das unmittelbarer, flüssiger, glühender ist als Worte'.[10] And Chandos abjures writing, so he explains to Lord Bacon, because of its utter meaninglessness and its inability to reflect the ultimate truth of any situation: silence and reverence are all that a man of integrity can permit. The closing proposition of Wittgenstein's *Tractatus* will reach the same conclusion.

Chandos abjured writing: Hofmannsthal did not. He attempted to 'overcome' the problem by bringing it into sharper focus, and he succeeded admirably; he strove likewise to go beyond the subjectivity of the lyric and acknowledged his debt to the Austrian theatrical tradition. If words were insufficient, then music, allegory and opera would reach out to more fruitful acts of communication: this was Hofmannsthal's fervent hope. His collaboration with Richard Strauss demonstrated the sincerity of his desire to transcend solipsism and reach out to a wider audience; his military service and his awareness of a vast hinterland behind the capital city are quoted by those of sociological bent as also having contributed to his desire to become more aware of man's social concerns. But the years following the Chandos letter were not happy ones for Hofmannsthal, and it is questionable whether he received ultimate fulfilment in his collaboration with Strauss. The Salzburg festivals, as Karl Kraus so rightly saw, became mere spectacle, with Max Reinhardt as the consummate ringmaster. There seemed to be almost a resurrection of the Wagnerian *Gesamtkunstwerk* in the festival plays and in a work like *Die Frau ohne Schatten*, and the imitation of the Barock became an anachronism, almost an absurdity. The flirtation with expressionism in *Elektra* betrays a profound uncertainty of direction in Hofmannsthal, whose increasing weariness and resignation became more and more apparent.

The narcissistic solipsism of the aesthete is rejected by Hofmannsthal, as it had been rejected by Tolstoi four years before in *What is Art?*: a more energetic and yet also more precise and less inflated form of expression was needed. Where words are deemed unsatisfactory as agents of communication, then the German mentality turns to music, the highest art form for a philosopher like Schopenhauer, who saw it as being able to pierce mere phenomena and reveal the ultimate beat and rhythm of existence itself. But Arnold Schönberg, who sent a copy of his *Harmonielehre* to Karl Kraus, acknowledged that 'Ich habe von Ihnen vielleicht mehr gelernt, als man lernen darf, wenn man noch selbständig bleiben will';[11] he found in Kraus an intellectual probity which he desired that music should regain. For musical neo-romanticism

had likewise overreached itself, and the time for a new clarity, a new
sincerity, was long overdue. His relationship to the expressionists,
above all to Kandinsky and his paintings, will be mentioned in a later
chapter; here let it be noticed that Schönberg's modernism grew
out of a need to be free of suspect subjectivity and rodomontade.
The central theme, in fact the only theme, of his opera *Moses und
Aaron* is one of great profundity – a clash between the ineffable
vision of transcendence and the temptation of self-indulgent
expressiveness. In this most remarkable work the central figure, Moses,
does not sing, for God's message is not to be cast in beauty, but is an
ethical absolute. In the Golden Calf episode the operatic audience is
given its orgy of voluptuous neo-romantic sound, and is made aware
that the desire is nothing more than self-indulgent aestheticism,
decadent and ultimately despairing.[12] And Moses sees that it is not
only song that is false, but words themselves, that all expression is
inadequate, and that there is an ineradicable gulf between words and
the Word. The unfinished work *must* remain unfinished, for it could
not boast of completion and fulfilment: Moses's last, despairing cry,
'O Wort, Wort, das mir fehlt' is the last, most poignant utterance.
Perhaps this was also the truth that the stuttering Wendell Kretzschmar,
the music teacher of Adrian Leverkühn, was attempting to explain to
his small audience in Thomas Mann's *Doktor Faustus*: Beethoven's
opus 111 does not, need not have a last movement, for 'der Schein –
der Kunst wird abgeworfen – zuletzt wirft – immer die Kunst – den
Schein der Kunst ab'.[13] Great art, even in its fragmentariness, is
always profounder than the most perfectly modelled artefact.

At the same time that Hofmannsthal published his *Ein Brief* another
work was in preparation which, published in 1906, has been claimed as
being 'vielleicht das hellsichtigste Buch, das vor dem ersten Weltkrieg
geschrieben wird'.[14] *Die Verwirrungen des Zöglings Törless* by Robert
Musil (1880–1942), a short novel of barely one hundred and fifty
pages, brought instant notoriety to its author who, having trained
(like Wittgenstein) as an engineer, turned to the study of philosophy
and finally devoted over twenty years to the writing of his vast,
unfinished novel *Der Mann ohne Eigenschaften*. *Törless* was read
first and foremost as a study of the problems of puberty, particularly
of homosexuality, in a distinguished private academy for young
gentlemen. The book has virtually nothing in common with the rash of
descriptions of pedagogic cruelty and ruthless authoritarianism to be
found in German literature at this time, for example Hesse's *Unterm
Rad*, Emil Strauss's *Freund Hein* and Friedrich Huch's *Mao* (neither

the school authorities nor the parents are in any way repressive);
neither is it a study of homosexuality or sadism (yet Musil's
understanding of psychological tensions is profound, as is his
prophetic description of future demagogues and irrationalists
who would later humiliate and torture men's bodies and minds).
Behind the respectable façade of the Academy was concealed the
'red room', where unspeakable practices are enacted, just as beneath
the surface of society, as Freud had analysed, atavistic wish-
fulfilments lurked and festered. But the central problem of Musil's
book is again one of communication; its motto is taken from
Maeterlinck:

> Sobald wir etwas aussprechen, entwerten wir es seltsam. Wir glauben
> in die Tiefe der Abgründe hinabgetaucht zu sein, und wenn wir
> wieder an die Oberfläche kommen, gleicht der Wassertropfen an
> unseren bleichen Fingerspitzen nicht mehr dem Meer, dem er
> entstammt. Wir wähnten eine Schatzgrube wunderbarer Schätze
> entdeckt zu haben, und wenn wir wieder ans Tageslicht kommen,
> haben wir nur falsche Steine und Glasscherben mitgebracht; und
> trotzdem schimmert der Schatz im Finstern unverändert.[15]

To describe means to debase, for human experience is ultimately
ineffable, a mystery which is made banal and meaningless by man's
crude forms of portrayal. Young Törless feels that silence may be
more valuable than language, that it *is* a form of language: 'Dieses
plötzliche Schweigen, das wie eine Sprache ist, die wir nicht hören'.[16]
Reiting and Beineberg exult in their sexual abuse of the pusillanimous
Basini: Törless, at first, is fascinated that such a world of violence and
terror can exist side by side with normal behaviour and muses: 'War
diese Kammer möglich . . . dann war es auch möglich, daß von der
täglichen Welt, die er bisher allein gekannt hatte, ein Tor zu einer
anderen, dumpfen, brandenden, leidenschaftlichen, nackten,
vernichtenden führte'.[17] But the Basini affair disgusts him and confuses
him, because he cannot put into words his feelings for Basini: his
disdain, his pity and the realisation that he might well have been in a
similar predicament. Clarity of judgement is lost, in the world of
morality as well as in other worlds, such as mathematics and philosophy.
The concept of irrational numbers disturbs Törless, who does not
desire to progress over uncertain foundations; Kant's insistence on the
unknowable nature of the numinous world would likewise have
dismayed him, had he advanced beyond the first bewildering pages of

that philosophy in his Reclam edition. At a crucial stage of his adolescent development Törless has to reassess his intellectual and emotional situation; bestiality lurks behind respectability, rigorous disciplines apparently admit of tenuous connections, the silent may speak with greater eloquence than the articulate, a prostitute reminds him of his mother and the wall in the school grounds seems not be not solid, but moving and rustling. How can one express the ultimate sense of a world where the boundaries are blurred and indeed lost? Is reason to be abjured utterly? The mystagogue Beineberg scorns Törless's need for clarity and articulation, and delights in obfuscations which erupt into brutality; but this is not Törless's way. The voluptuous feel of bed-linen and the almost prurient dallying with fantasies that he was a young girl may well drive the rigours of the categorical imperative from his mind while lying in bed, but not permanently. Does sensuality bring a greater wisdom than rationality? Is the sexual excitement that Törless feels at Basini's maltreatment a justification for this brutality? The fastidious Törless knows that it is not; he likewise feels shame at having been seduced by Basini's soft, white flesh. Is there a 'pathological inhibition or an ideological stance in Törless's unwilling-ness for so long to carry out a simple human action to help a victim', as a recent critic believes?[18] Hardly: Törless's non-intervention results from a paralysis which is by no means abnormal; something of value, rather, is gained from the whole experience. (If blame is to be allotted, then Basini must bear it for his cringing servility.) Törless has learnt of the limits of language and of the intellect in the expression and understanding of certain crucial aspects of life, and also that which appears to be one thing may indeed be something different when viewed from an oblique position. The members of staff at the end are baffled by his contention: 'Es gibt gewisse Sachen, die bestimmt sind, gewissermaßen in doppelter Form in unser Leben einzugreifen. Ich fand als solche Personen, Ereignisse, dunkle, verstaubte Winkel, eine hohe, kalte, schweigende, plötzlich lebendig werdende Mauer'.[19] They had expected an explanation for bullying and truancy, and instead received an adolescent's sophisticated awareness of the dual nature of things, of what Musil will later define as 'der andere Zustand'. The dark and light exist side by side; that neat image of the jet black crow against the dazzling white of the fields shows that a certain clarity *has* been achieved, a sharper focus and a sensitive precision. In later life Törless will become, the reader is told, 'ein junger Mann von sehr feinem und empfindsamem Geiste',[20] a man and, presumably, a writer, characterised by a certain 'ironischen Korrektheit' who will admit that the experience left behind in him 'jene kleine Menge Giftes, die nötig ist, um der Seele die allzu sichere und beruhigte Gesundheit zu nehmen und ihr dafür eine feinere, zugeschärfte, verstehende zu geben'.[21] It is difficult not to be reminded of Thomas Mann.

Much later in his life, during the writing of *Der Mann ohne Eigenschaften*, Musil will again think about language and its limitations, and ironically posit a possible 'language' which might be both more imaginative *and* more precise. Ludwig Wittgenstein likewise, as has been pointed out, attempted to provide a distinction between the spheres of reason and fantasy, the world of facts and the world of values: 'the *Tractatus* becomes an expression of a certain type of language mysticism that assigns a central importance in human life to art, on the grounds that art alone can express the meaning of life'.[22] As a scientist Musil sought exactitude and clarity: as an artist and a thinker he sought not merely to describe, but to recreate in striking images the world of sense impressions. The story *Tonka* illustrates most clearly the problems of communication and the limits of reason: there can surely be no doubt about her infidelity – and yet what, ultimately, are 'facts' in the face of love? The two stories *Die Vereinigungen* (1911) which, Musil claims in his own *Curriculum vitae* 'leiteten, vielleicht durch Irrtum, den literarischen Expressionismus in Deutschland ein, mit dem er aber weiterhin nichts zu schaffen haben wollte',[23] move towards an irrational experience of self-abasement and self-obliteration, where reason is totally superseded by Claudine in her adultery and Veronica in her indulgence in animal sensuality: Otto Weiniger's views on female psychology are not far removed from Musil here. Yet Musil regarded these stories as experiments in narrative form, poised as they are between the subtleties of impressionism described in chapter 2 and the expressionist predilection for extreme psychic states, which will be described later, as will the journey of Ulrich, the ironic, elegant 'man without qualities' into the 'tausendjähriges Reich', the Millennium, with his own sister and beloved. Their love, however perverse in the eyes of the world, transcends the garrulous attitudinising of a totally bankrupt society, a society where the mediocre are elevated to the heights of adulation and where both thinking *and* loving lack clarity and imagination.

It is Musil's contemporary and compatriot Karl Kraus who immediately springs to mind during any discussion concerning the cheapening of concepts and the debasement of language; indeed, Kraus is unique in his constant vigilance and devastating satire against clichés of all kinds. He was born in 1874, the same year as Hugo von

Hofmannsthal, and the centenary of the birth of that most implacable
enemy of Austrian (or, rather, Viennese) attitudinising and 'charm'
was, unthinkably, celebrated by both civic recognition and a host of
articles written for the Kraus symposium by admirers and detractors.
The *enfant terrible* of the Austrian literary world has been welcomed
into the fold and given the blessing of academic recognition: *Die
letzten Tage der Menschheit*, the *monstrum* which Karl Kraus would
allow neither Piscator nor Reinhardt to produce, and which he
declared suitable only for a theatre on Mars, has been adapted for the
radio, and the complete *Fackel* has been reprinted. For many, Karl
Kraus was filled with an almost Messianic vision, a vision of the truth
and an insatiable desire to uphold the greatest values of civilisation
against insidious hypocrisy and mendacity; for others he appeared to
be an almost demented misanthropist, whose antics Walter Benjamin
compared to the frenzied dance of Rumpelstiltskin. ('Denn wie im
Märchen hat der Dämon in Kraus die Eitelkeit zu seinem Wesensaus-
druck gemacht. Auch die Einsamkeit des Dämons ist seine, der da auf
dem versteckten Hügel sich toll gebärdet.'[24]) Kraus is important in this
chapter in that he was in touch with the avant-garde literary figures
of his day and, in many cases, defended them against the complacent
mediocrity of the established literary canons; what is of equal
importance was his passionate concern with the defence of the word,
with the guardianship of literary and moral integrity. And, as for
Wittgenstein, the two were one. For Kraus, in the profoundest sense of
all, *le style c'est l'homme même*: Walter Muschg has written, somewhat fulsomely, of him:

> Das Wort wurde ihm zur heiligen Waffe, die Kritik an den
> Schändern des Wortes zum religiösen Bekenntnis. Der tödliche
> Schliff seiner sprachdialektischen Witze, der Einfallsreichtum seiner
> Wortspiele, der kontrapunktische Bau seiner Sätze müssen vor
> diesem theologischen Hintergrund gewürdigt werden. Es ist ein
> gebundener, gezeichneter Geist, der in höherem Auftrag handelt.
> Das Urteil über ihn fällt nicht in die Kompetenz des Ästheten.[25]

Kraus and Hofmannsthal, it is said, matriculated on the same day, but
their literary futures were to be very different. Kraus, who greatly
respected Liliencron, Arno Holz and Gerhart Hauptmann, detested
what he considered to be the spurious nature of Hermann Bahr's
influence in the Café Griensteidl, particularly Bahr's self-appointed
role as leader and spokesman of the *Moderne*. A letter to Arthur

Schnitzler of March 1893 admits 'Ich hasse und haßte diese falsche, erlogene "Décadence", die ewig mit sich selbst coquettiert, ich bekämpfe und werde immer bekämpfen: die posierte, krankhafte, onanierte Poesie!'[26] An attack on Hermann Bahr in the *Gesellschaft* ('Die Überwindung von Hermann Bahr') was followed by the famous *Die demolirte Literatur*, published in the *Wiener Rundschau* in 1896 (the external impetus for this satire was the destruction of the old Café Griensteidl, but Kraus saw that Bahr and the aesthetes were equally negative in their precocity and deliberate *Nervosität*). What the young Kraus despised most in Bahr was his lack of integrity, his ability to assume any pose, to adopt any role, and the conviction would grow in him that a man's art — or his aesthetic pretensions — are intimately bound up with his moral character. It is in a man's use of language that Kraus found a clue to his ethical core, and the language of most of his Viennese contemporaries he found either cliché-ridden, hollow, pretentious or inflated beyond measure. Not yet twenty-five years old, Kraus was offered the post of chief satirist in Vienna's most prestigious paper, the *Neue Freie Presse*; he refused to accept, and decided instead to found his own satirical journal.

The first number of *Die Fackel* appeared at the beginning of April 1899: modelled on Maximilian Harden's *Die Zukunft* and written mainly by Kraus himself, *Die Fackel* made an enormous impression on the Viennese intellectual public. It was to survive until 1936, the year of Kraus's death, and from 1911 onwards would be written entirely by himself (apart from the one-act play *Eselschaf* by Strindberg, which appeared in 1912, coincidentally on the day of his death). Such writers as Peter Altenberg, Richard Dehmel, Else Lasker-Schüler, Detlev von Liliencron, Heinrich Mann, Frank Wedekind and Franz Werfel were to appear in the early issues; Adolf Loos, Arnold Schönberg and Hugo Wolf were also contributors. But the literary establishment, men such as Hermann Bahr, Felix Salten and Roda Roda, and the composer Franz Léhar, were ruthlessly denounced; the aesthetes of the Café Griensteidl, 'die aus Lebensüberdruß Gift nehmen könnten, weil es grün ist und die einen Pavian um den roten Hintern beneiden'[27] were castigated without mercy, and even men like Max Reinhardt and Hugo von Hofmannsthal ('der vom Rausch bei goldenen Bechern, in denen kein Wein ist, ernüchtert dahin lebt'[28]) were not spared. Writing, like Kafka, at night, and besieged by spectres of human folly, vanity and viciousness, Kraus took it upon himself to be, like Søren Kierkegaard (the comparison was made by Theodor Haecker) the Cassandra of his age and the champion of the new, the vital and that which was honest above all.

The poem 'Nach zwanzig Jahren' succinctly summarises the position; Kraus takes stock of what the great themes and preoccupations of his life had been:

> Geschlecht und Lüge, Dummheit, Übelstände,
> Tonfall und Phrase, Tinte, Technik, Tod,
> Krieg und Gesellschaft, Wucher, Politik,
> der Übermut der Ämter und die Schmach,
> die Unwert schweigendem Verdienst erweist,
> Kunst und Natur, die Liebe und der Traum —
> vielfacher Antrieb, sei's woher es sei,
> der Schöpfung ihre Ehre zu erstatten!
> Und hinter allem der entsühnte Mensch,
> der magisch seine Sprache wiederfindet.[29]

The nobility of these sentiments is irrefutable, and the nine hundred and twenty-two numbers of *Die Fackel* plus the other works of Kraus testify to the unceasing energy with which he pursued his task. He defended Frank Wedekind's work and organised the first performance of *Die Büchse der Pandora* in Vienna on 29 May 1905 (appearing, incredibly, as Kungu Poti!); of Wedekind he wrote 'Er ist der erste deutsche Dramatiker, der wieder dem Gedanken den langentbehrten Zutritt auf die Bühne verschafft hat',[30] and he saw that many of the naturalists, who strove to portray 'life in the round' failed strikingly when compared with Wedekind. Kraus quite rightly saw that Lulu is not a personification of destructive sensuality: it was the selfishness and arrogance of man which debased her. The words of Schigolch at the end were essentially valid: 'Sie kann von der Liebe nicht leben, weil ihr Leben die Liebe ist'.[31] Kraus could not endorse the extreme views of Otto Weininger, whose *Geschlecht und Charakter* (and whose flamboyant suicide) had amazed Vienna; neither could he accept the misogyny of Strindberg, the power of whose writing, however, he always admired. Femininity was to be respected and defended against double standards (as well as against aggressive 'emancipated' women), for the emotional female element of the psyche was the well-spring of creation. The humourless probing of psychoanalysts was also rejected: the hysterical condition of certain middle-class Viennese ladies could not be taken as a human norm. 'Psychoanalyse ist jene Geisteskrankheit, für deren Therapie sie sich hält',[32] and 'Den Weg zurück ins Kinderland möchte ich, nach reiflicher Überlegung, doch lieber mit Jean Paul als mit S. Freud machen'[33] have, quite rightly, become two of his most famous aphorisms.

His defence of Adolf Loos, Georg Trakl, Oskar Kokoschka and the avant-garde writers associated with the *Brenner* journal of Ludwig von Ficker, his support of Peter Altenberg and Przybyszewski and his comments on Alfred Kerr's self-satisfied discovery that Bertolt Brecht had used certain lines translated from Villon in his work ('Im kleinen Finger der Hand, mit der er fünfundzwanzig Verse der Ammerschen Übersetzung von Villon genommen hat, ist dieser Brecht originaler als der Kerr, der ihm dahintergekommen ist'[34]) must be matched by his courage to be conservative, his love of late Goethe (his public readings, particularly of *Pandora*, were exemplary) and deep devotion to Nestroy — like Kraus himself a writer, stage-manager and star performer with an amazingly acute ear for the finer points of language. To quote Toulmin and Janik: 'Here, in the plays of Nestroy, one can understand the Krausian notion that the *language* of a satirist contains the "origin", as it lays bare the moral character of the person who speaks . . . the man and his work were so perfectly integrated that he expressed his character through the very nuances of the grammar that he used to expose the foibles and hypocrisies of society'.[35] The joys of Offenbach as opposed to the cheap vulgarities of Léhar, the profundity of Jean Paul as opposed to the specious glitter of Heine — above all the emphasis is upon authenticity and integrity, upon respect for that which was truly vital and life-enhancing. Time and time again Kraus turned to Shakespeare for the most vital and miraculous re-enactment of life (his last letter to Sidonie Nádherný von Borutin, dated 16 May 1936, avows that 'Die Weltdummheit macht jede Arbeit — außer an Shakespeare — unmöglich'[36]), and for a unique sense of corruption and human frailty: how appropriate must the Duke's lines (Act 5, Scene 1) of *Measure for Measure* have seemed to him: 'My business in this state/ Made me a looker-on here in Vienna,/Where I have seen corruption boil and bubble/Till it o'er-run the stew'. The triumph of the mendacious, the ignorant and the banal Kraus feared above all, particularly through the medium of the press, for he saw with remarkable prescience that the manipulation of words by thoughtless, third-rate minds blurred the reader's critical receptivity, and the unscrupulous have their way prepared for their more sinister purposes. In a welter of confused notions, obfuscation and cant the nations of Europe seemed blind to the obvious — their destruction of all that was natural and beautiful. Kraus's greatest work *Die letzten Tage der Menschheit*, written during the war, is a forerunner of 'documentary theatre' in that it incorporates within its five enormous acts plus epilogue ('dessen Umfang nach irdischem Zeitmaß etwa zehn Abende umfassen würde'[37]) the speeches of politicians, scientists and generals as well as the petty chit-chat of officers' clubs, cafés and the Ringstraße. There is none of Robert Musil's ironic detachment in the description of Kakania but a biting satire born of disgust and bitter disappointment at the corruptibility of all human institutions. Karl Kraus lets men condemn themselves by their own phrases (as Brecht realised in his famous aphorism[38]), which are born of greed, stupidity and gullibility rather than evil. For evil, Kraus senses, was too portentous a word for the twentieth century: hence his pronouncement on Hitler: 'Mir fällt zu Hitler nichts ein'[39] – a statement incomprehensible to those who wish to see Kraus as a champion of the Left, but so profound in its realisation of the utter banality and ignorance of that leader.

Scene 36 of Act 5 of *Die letzten Tage der Menschheit* consists of a letter written by 'Der Freund' in Galizia. The friend's voice is the only constructive one in the whole Babel which accompanied the apocalypse, and it is that of Ludwig von Ficker, whose *Der Brenner* was esteemed by Kraus as being the only honest journal to appear in Austria. Wittgenstein had asked Kraus the best way in which to distribute one hundred thousand Kronen: Kraus suggested Ludwig von Ficker as an intermediary best suited to understand how the money should be used. Ficker encouraged and supported such writers as Rilke, Trakl and Else Lasker-Schüler, and his sympathy and generosity were rare qualities in any editor and publisher; his financial resources, however, were practically exhausted by 1914 and Wittgenstein's intervention was providential. The journal itself, on Wittgenstein's suggestion, was allotted ten thousand Kronen, and Rilke and Trakl were to be given twenty thousand each. But this was in the late summer of 1914; Trakl had already been enlisted in the Medical Corps. Ficker's visit to the psychiatric ward of the military hospital in Cracow to see Trakl is symptomatic of the man's decency and humanity; he was alerted to the mortal danger in which he had found Trakl and immediately sent a message to Wittgenstein, who was serving in the army not far away; the message arrived too late and, although Wittgenstein found the ward, Trakl was already dead, having committed suicide.

Trakl had hailed Kraus in the following words:

Weißer Hohepriester der Wahrheit,
Kristallne Stimme, in der Gottes eisiger Odem wohnt,
Zürnender Magier,

> Dem unter flammendem Mantel der blaue Panzer des Kriegers
>   klirrt.[40]

He had dedicated the poem 'Psalm' to him (this had appeared in *Der Brenner* in October 1912) and Kraus had acknowledged this in *Die Fackel*. The early works of Rilke and Trakl were discussed in chapter 2, and their debt to European *fin-de-siècle* aestheticism was noted. The task in this present chapter is to acknowledge their rejection of neo-romanticism, or decadent versifying and the emergence of a clearer, purer and profounder tone in their works, a sharper focus and a more authentic voice. The problem of language, communication and expression continues to be of importance, not overtly, as in the case of the thinker Wittgenstein, but subconsciously. Rilke's development is more subtle and complex than that of Trakl, who was only twenty-seven when he died, and it is therefore to him that we look first to assess the significance of the emergence of his later tone.

In June 1902 Rilke was commissioned to write a monograph on Rodin, and later in that year left for Paris which, in spite of many journeys to most European countries, was to remain his home until the outbreak of the First World War. What Rilke learned from Rodin, and from the canvases of Cézanne, is that the poet must, like the sculptor and the painter, be a *craftsman*, a patient worker who respects his art, the manipulation of words, rhymes and rhythm. The movement away from effusion and self-indulgence in his poetry towards a greater hardness, sharpness and clarity was paralleled elsewhere in Europe by the Imagist demand for a rejection of flabby Georgian verse: Rilke's admiration for the ruthless objectivity of Cézanne and the fearless truth of Baudelaire's 'Une charogne' reminds the reader of Ezra Pound's plea for the imitation of Gautier's *Émaux et Camées*, of Eliot's appreciation of Laforgue and ultimately of his rejection of all imprecise effusion, particularly in the famous lines describing the difficulty of the poet's task and lamenting his having to use 'shabby equipment always deteriorating/In the general mess of imprecision of feeling./Undisciplined squads of emotion . . .'.[41] Rodin's insistence on craftsmanship, upon persistence and dedication ('Il faut travailler, rien que travailler') led to a corresponding tautness and muscular suppleness in Rilke's poetry and the emergence of images which, fresh and vivid, intensified and clarified the poetic vision. The famous *Requiem für Wolf Graf von Kalckreuth* of 1908 expresses Rilke's new-found conviction:

> . . . O alter Fluch der Dichter,
> die sich beklagen, wo sie sagen sollten,
> die immer urteiln über ihr Gefühl
> statt es zu bilden; die noch immer meinen,
> was traurig ist in ihnen oder froh,
> das wüßten sie und dürftens im Gedicht
> bedauern oder rühmen. Wie die Kranken
> gebrauchen sie die Sprache voller Wehleid,
> um zu beschreiben, wo es ihnen wehtut,
> statt hart sich in die Worte zu verwandeln,
> wie sich der Steinmetz einer Kathedrale
> verbissen umsetzt in des Steines Gleichmut . . .[42]

The intense subjectivity and introspection of the young Kalckreuth,
Rilke believed, led to his suicide at the age of nineteen, and in this
Requiem there is almost a reprimand; he would certainly have
endorsed Eliot's late pronouncement that 'Poetry is not a turning loose
of emotions, but an escape from emotion: it is not an expression of
personality, but an escape from personality'.[43]

The *Neue Gedicht* collection of 1907–1908 contains what are
acknowledged to be masterpieces of lyric poetry, an elegance and a
subtlety combined with profundity and clarity, with only rare lapses
into a manneristic self-consciousness. Above all there is observation
and precise rendering of that observation in entirely appropriate images.
The famous *Dinggedichte* are recreations of objects (often animals,
patiently observed) in a language that is precise and evocative, objective
and allusive. The poet is now not concerned with emotions, but with
experiences and objects which, as well as being precisely portrayed,
paradoxically contain a subtle symbolism. There is no sterile *l'art
pour l'art* here: the famous 'Archäiser Torso Apollos' is the description
of what is almost a collision between the fragmentary torso and the
beholder, a piece of stone sculpted with such mastery that it challenges
one's very existence. 'Du mußt dein Leben ändern'[44] – this is the
'message' of the stone, for great art such as this is life-enhancing in its
authenticity, and ruthless in the absolute clarity of its statement. A
poem like 'Blaue Hortensie' recreates, with absolute fidelity and
sensitivity, the colours to be seen in a fading hydrangea; Rilke's use of
the simile is found to great effect in 'Spanische Tänzerin': it is not
merely decorative, but expressive of those associations which his
subjects have for him, and establishes unseen connections for the reader
(the spurting match and the movements of the dance). Rilke also

demonstrates that he is a master in the use of enjambement; alliteration and assonance are likewise not abused, but carefully controlled to create a necessary statement. 'Spätherbst in Venedig' is a highly successful evocation of that city and that time of year and, by subtle symbolic extension, demonstrates how art, like Venice itself, rises from unknown depths, with a disquieting force of impact:

> Nun treibt die Stadt schon nicht mehr wie ein Köder,
> der alle aufgetauchten Tage fängt.
> Die gläsernen Paläste klingen spröder
> an deinen Blick. Und aus den Gärten hängt
>
> der Sommer wie ein Haufen Marionetten
> kopfüber, müde, umgebracht.
> Aber vom Grund aus alten Waldskeletten
> steigt Willen auf: als sollte über Nacht
>
> der General des Meeres die Galeeren
> verdoppeln in dem wachen Arsenal,
> um schon die nächste Morgenluft zu teeren
>
> mit einer Flotte, welcher ruderschlagend
> sich drängt und jäh, mit allen Flaggen tagend,
> den großen Wind hat, strahlend und fatal.[45]

The tension between intensity and peace, between creativity and rest, which underlies many of the famous poems of this collection, demonstrates the curious synthesis of Nietzscheanism and Franciscanism (or Buddhism: there are three poems to Buddha in the *Neue Gedichte*) which characterises much of Rilke's work at this time.[46]

'Denn Verse sind nicht, wie die Leute meinen Gefühle (die hat man früh genug), – es sind Erfahrungen';[47] this is what Rilke has learnt, and what the *Neue Gedichte* exemplify. The words are spoken by Rilke's *alter ego* Malte Laurids Brigge, whose *Aufzeichnungen* he started as early as 1904 in Rome and on which he worked intermittently for nearly five years. The book (or, rather, 'notes') appeared in 1910 and the work is undoubtedly the expression of a crisis in the poet's life, a coming to terms with the problems of aestheticism and reality. Those who denounce Rilke for being precious and mannerist should not lose sight of the fact that he was one of the first in German literature to register the full terror of loneliness, dread and isolation, of *Grenzsituationen* and the predicament of 'faceless' modern man. A great many of the themes which would come to dominate twentieth-century fiction are adumbrated here, as well as certain existentialist preoccupations. The fragmentary nature of the work betrays its inconclusiveness: it might well be claimed that Malte Laurids Brigge is the scapegoat on whom Rilke wished to unburden his unresolved problems concerning art and human existence in general. The frequency with which he strove, particularly in letters, to elucidate the meaning of the novel demonstrates that he was not entirely sure of the outcome of the struggle himself: did Malte perish, or was he able to come to terms with his problems by objectifying them, externalising them into an art work, or, rather, the notes which could precede one? In a letter of February 1912 he warns that the sensitive reader would be well advised to read the book 'gewissermaßen gegen den Strom';[48] there must be no emulation, but pity and even admiration for Malte's tenacity.

The book deals with the experiences of a young Dane in Paris. Rilke's book is another example of the European interest in — and indebtedness to — Scandinavian literature at the beginning of this century; Rilke had greatly admired the work of Jens Peter Jacobsen, and even started to learn Danish in order to read him (and Kierkegaard) in the original. Malte's references to his own writing, particularly a play entitled *Die Ehe*, bring to mind the work of the Norwegian Jonas Lie, but it is of greater interest that Rilke, in 1904, wrote a review of certain papers by Sigbjørn Obstfjelder that were discovered after his death. Rilke sensed that behind the apparent confusion lay a certain unity: that of Obstfjelder's personality. A letter of 11 May 1910 later described the impression of reading *Malte Laurids Brigge* as being 'als fände man in einem Schubfach ungeordnete Papiere und fände eben vorderhand nicht mehr und müßte sich begnügen';[49] the same could be said of Obstfjelder's jottings, whose unfinished work *A Priest's Diary* (1900) could also have been in Rilke's mind. Ellen Key's invitation to visit her home in Sweden in the summer of 1904 strengthened the Scandinavian atmosphere of the book, but the echoes of Jacobsen and Obstfjelder are not the most successful parts: the descriptions of the minor Danish aristocracy show that Rilke has not entirely succeeded in exorcising those *précieux* and somewhat effete aspects associated with his earlier work. But the descriptions of the Paris streets, of decaying buildings, squalor, sickness, loneliness and death bring a directness totally lacking in the earlier writings: here is no sentimental 'Arme-Leute-Poesie' but dread and darkness. And Malte, alone, five floors up in his dismal room, broods on his experiences in an attempt to derive some meaning from the ugliness and futility of modern life. Not only modern life: he seeks in historical sources descriptions of death and mutilation in order to be able to affirm in a Nietzschean act of praise.

He is twenty-eight years old — this was Rilke's age when starting to write this work. He begins to question man's former beliefs and attitudes: 'Ist es möglich, daß man noch nichts Wirkliches und Wichtiges gesehen, erkannt und gesagt hat? Ist es möglich, daß man trotz Erfindungen und Fortschritten, trotz Kultur, Religion und Weltweisheit an der Oberfläche des Lebens geblieben ist? . . . Ist es möglich, daß die ganze Weltgeschichte mißverstanden worden ist?'.[50] Malte answers in the affirmative; men have accepted unthinkingly interpretations of life which have been utterly meaningless, mere husks of former beliefs. A radical reappraisal is needed, particularly of love and death, of joy and suffering, not so violent as Nietzsche's *Umwertung*, but nevertheless a reshaping and a refeeling. The way is prepared here for the *Duineser Elegien*, whose Angel bears many of the features of Nietzsche's *Übermensch*; yet Malte, stunned by what he has seen in the streets of Paris, can affirm and praise only with great difficulty, if at all; *fin-de-siècle* aestheticism and the most brutal naturalism produce an intolerable tension.

How is Malte to accommodate within his vision the experience of the broken, rotting wall of such repulsive ugliness? It is surprising to remember that the following passage was written so soon after the maiden-and-angels poetry of the earlier collections:

Man sah ihre Innenseite. Man sah in den verschiedenen Stockwerken Zimmerwände, an denen noch die Tapeten klebten, da und dort den Ansatz des Fußbodens oder der Decke. Neben den Zimmerwänden blieb die ganze Mauer entlang noch ein schmutzig weißer Raum, und durch diesen kroch in unsäglich widerlichen, wurmweichen, gleichsam verdauenden Bewegungen die offene, rostfleckige Rinne der Abortröhre . . . Und aus diesen blau, grün und gelb gewesenen Wänden, die eingerahmt waren von den Bruchbahnen der zerstörten Zwischenmauern, stand die Luft dieser Leben heraus, die zähe, träge, stockige Luft, die kein Wind noch zerstreut hatte. Da standen die Mittage und die Krankheiten und das Ausgeatmete und der jahrealte Rauch und der Schweiß, der unter den Schultern ausbricht und die Kleider schwer macht, und das Fade aus den Munden und der Fuselgeruch gärender Füße.

> Da stand das Scharfe vom Urin und das Brennen vom Ruß und
> grauer Kartoffeldunst und der schwere, glatte Gestank von
> alterndem Schmalze. Der süße, lange Geruch von vernachlässigten
> Säuglingen war da und der Angstgeruch der Kinder, die in die
> Schule gehen, und das Schwüle aus den Betten mannbarer
> Knaben.[51]

This expression of the very grease and stench of human life must be
accepted, as Baudelaire accepted and described the putrefying carcass
in the road. 'Was sollte er tun, da ihm das widerfuhr? Es war seine
Aufgabe, in diesem Schrecklichen, scheinbar nur Widerwärtigen das
Seiende zu sehen, das unter allem Seienden gilt. Auswahl und Ableh-
nung gibt es nicht.'[52] The true artist is not one who escapes into rarefied
worlds, but who observes the sick and the dying, the deformed and the
rejected, and yet transforms all this through a manipulation of
appropriate images into an objectified, recreated reality. The sensibility of aestheticism and the precision of naturalism fuse at this stage
of Rilke's life into a unique synthesis: nuance and exactness,
refinement and precision must co-exist together. The memory of the
poet who could only die after correcting a mispronunciation returns to
Malte who announces with approval: 'Er war ein Dichter und haßte
das Ungefähre'.[53]

Malte observes, remembers and reads. He recalls the deaths of
Charles the Bold and Charles the Sixth of France: the face of the
former split, crushed and frozen in the ice, the body of the latter
putrefying into the very bedclothes which enfolded it. He reads of
Pope John the Twenty-second who expounded the doctrine of the
beatific vision, yet who recanted, and demonstrated papal fallibility
and uncertainty. Yet the psalms and lamentations of the prophets, the
music of Beethoven and the greatness of Ibsen are hailed as supreme
moments of the human spirit, and the greatness of the unrequited
lovers is also extolled. Poised between affirmation and despair,
assailed by dread from all sides, Malte almost — yet not quite —
achieves the destined strength: 'Oh, es fehlt nur ein kleines, und ich
könnte das alles begreifen und gutheißen. Nur ein Schritt, und mein
tiefes Elend würde Seligkeit sein. Aber ich kann diesen Schritt nicht
tun, ich bin gefallen, und kann mich nicht mehr aufheben, weil ich
zerbrochen bin . . .'.[54] It would seem that the tasks of reappraisal and
affirmation proved too much for him, that he had been unable to
endure to that point of suffering which would, miraculously, turn into
ineffable joy, that he had, in fact, remained an aesthete rather than a

true artist. Yet practically every statement concerning this fascinating book must be qualified, for to equate Malte with aestheticism, to see him as a typical *fin-de-siècle* littérateur is an over-simplification: Malte is not a Detlev Spinell, nor is he trapped within a solipsistic play of mirrors and reflections, as was Narcissus, for he looks outwards, away from the self and sees an alien otherness which he attempts to portray. And is it ultimately true that he does *not* succeed? Perhaps Rilke was as baffled as his readers, for, in yet another letter, he admits:

> Und mit einemmal (und zum ersten) begreife ich das Schicksal des Malte Laurids. Ist es nicht das, daß diese *Prüfung* ihn übersteig, so daß er sie am Wirklichen *nicht bestand*, obwohl er in der Idee von ihrer Notwendigkeit überzeugt war, so sehr, daß er sie so lange instinktiv aufsuchte, bis sie sich an ihn hängte und ihn nicht mehr verließ? Das Buch von Malte Laurids, wenn es einmal geschrieben sein wird, wird nichts als das Buch dieser Einsicht sein, erwiesen an einem, für den sie zu ungeheuer war. Vielleicht *bestand* er ja auch, denn er schrieb den Tod des Kammerherrn: aber wie ein Raskolnokow blieb er, von seiner Tat aufgebraucht, zurück, nicht weiterhandelnd im Moment, wo das *Handeln* erst beginnen mußte, so daß die neue errungene Freiheit sich gegen ihn wandte und ihn, den Wehrlosen, zerriß.[55]

In his review of *Die Aufzeichnungen des Malte Laurids Brigge* Stephen Spender complained of the 'lack of narrative foreground' in the work. The remark is surely unjustified, for Rilke was not concerned with the portrayal of 'character' but with the presentation of a certain consciousness. In *Malte Laurids Brigge* and, indeed, in most of the important novels of the twentieth century, the traditional narrative technique has been replaced by a new, more tentative style, the tenuous nature of which is better suited to convey the uncertainties of the hero's experiences. The inherited forms of belief, together with yesterday's forms of expression, seem no longer valid: like Lord Chandos, Malte had wished to dissociate himself from his former work. The narrative technique in *Malte Laurids Brigge* springs from the conviction that all 'finished' forms of literature impose a false order on their account of what 'happened': there can be no omniscient narrator in a work which is a fragmentary expression of one man's individual vision. Malte's consciousness is presented directly; no other perspectives are given. The result may be solipsistic, but is also a highly effective way of conveying isolation.

The traditional narrative forms of the nineteenth century bestowed a sense of coherence and confidence; after the turn of the century a technique was sought to convey uncertainty and doubt, for language, it was sensed, was an inadequate tool. 'Damals zuerst fiel es mir auf, daß man von einer Frau nichts sagen könne', Malte admits,[56] and also acknowledges the inadequacy of his attempt to describe the death of Grischa Otrepjow, and calls for 'einen Erzähler, einen Erzähler'. In a letter to Lou Andreas-Salomé Rilke admits: 'Ich aber, Lou, Dein irgendwie verlorener Sohn; ich kann noch lange, lange noch kein Erzählender sein, kein Wahr-Sager meines Wegs, kein Beschreiber meines gewesenen Schicksals'.[57] Seven years after this letter Franz Kafka confided to Felice Bauer (on 16 June 1913): 'Ich kann auch nicht eigentlich erzählen, ja fast nicht einmal reden; wenn ich erzähle, habe ich meistens ein Gefühl, wie es kleine Kinder haben könnten, die die ersten Gehversuche machen'.[58] A linear narrative seems impossible to the modern writer, whose faith in the established tradition no longer remains, whose language is unable to grasp the meaning of things and who, often in intense loneliness, is cast back upon himself, with the sole hope that he might transform his own anguish into some separate, independent entity. The original versions of *Malte Laurids Brigge*, incorporating a narrator, and the third person singular, were rejected by Rilke, who preferred the subjectivity of the 'Ich'-form, thereby anticipating the lyrical novel of modern fiction, or, rather, the fusion between lyric and epic, which Kurt Martens noticed in his review of the work. The interest in plot has given way to the play of associations and repetitions more reminiscent of rhythmical qualities: the undeniable tendency at the beginning of the century to turn prose into poetry is certainly found here. The lack of fixed qualities which characterises Malte is similar to the condition shared by Robert Musil's Törless, as well as his later, more famous creation; he feels himself to be a nullity, much as Franz Kafka did. Yet Malte's passivity and openness, as well as making him vulnerable at all points, and intensifying his loneliness, enables him to absorb *all* things more readily, and becomes something positive and valuable, much as Kafka's 'Nichtigkeit', as he explains in the *Brief an den Vater*, becomes 'ein in anderer Hinsicht allerdings auch edles und fruchtbares Gefühl'.[59] The Prodigal Son, who feared the obliteration of the self in the demands of the family, could well be a creation of Kafka's, who also realised the fruitfulness of isolation. The importance of childhood, the reluctance to substitute 'chronological' time for 'psychological' time, and the concept of the artist as the true explorer of reality link these two writers again, as does the emphasis on the apparently trivial and commonplace (a button, for example), which links them both with Hofmannsthal's Lord Chandos. *Die Aufzeichnungen des Malte Laurids Brigge* has been rightly hailed as 'jenes Werk, das zu Beginn des zwanzigsten Jahrhunderts sowohl vom Inhalt als auch von der Form her wohl als das lehrreichste Beispiel moderner Erzählung von der Entwicklung, das heißt hier von der Selbstfindung eines Menschen',[60] and its author as being the initiator of an eminently modern narrative technique: 'Von ihm [Rilke] war nur noch ein kleiner Schritt zur extremen und konsequenten Romankunst unserer Zeit'.[61]

The work of Rilke in the decade preceding the First World War is remarkable in that it demonstrates on the one hand a unique ability to create perfect art forms — the sonnets of the *Neue Gedichte* — and yet also a reluctance to use the traditional form of the novel, and the preference for a fragmentary, more tenuous and modern form of narration. Rilke's keen interest in Shakespeare's *The Tempest*, particularly in Prospero's foreswearing of magic, his restlessness and uncertainty about his poetic task (Hans Carossa describes a meeting with Rilke and Lou Salomé when Rilke even declared art to be superfluous and considered being a country doctor[62]) betray a profound psychic disturbance; the precise creation of perfect images must yield to a more passionate, less exclusive attitude to reality. From this time dates the following confession:

> Uns verwirrt es, die wir seiend heißen
> immer so zu leben: nur von Bildern;
> und wir möchten manchesmal mit wildern
> Griffen Wirklichkeiten in uns reißen
> Stücke, Abzufühlendes, ein Sein . . .[63]

and also the famous poem 'Wendung', with its knowledge that seeing must now give way to 'heart-work', not self-indulgence, but an openness to the great questions confronting human existence. The problems which Malte Laurids Brigge faced — the meaning of love and death, and the relationship between life and art — haunted Rilke after the completion of that book (or, rather, the termination of the notebooks). And that which Rilke realised as his own was nothing more than a radical reinterpretation of existence, a poetic reappraisal of traditional concepts and ways of feeling; Rilke's poetry after 1912 is 'modern' because it can no longer rely upon a traditional, universally held picture of reality; it creates its own world, trusting that the reader, if not

immediately comprehending, will be moved by the power and
sincerity of the poet's incantation and come to an independent
discovery of the new ways of thought and feeling. The poet's task
becomes enormous; he has to explore an unknown realm and dare to
leave behind all traditional evaluations:

> Von allen großgewagten Existenzen
> kann eine glühender und kühner sein?
> Wir stehn und stemmen uns an unsre Grenzen
> und reißen ein Unkenntliches herein.[64]

The 'Unkenntliches', the mystery of human existence in its poignant
vulnerability, assails the poet who must, nevertheless, stand fast. What
Hölderlin (a poet who, after the Norberth von Hellingrath edition,
would be of considerable importance for Rilke) described as the
'hochherstürzenden Stürmen des Geists' which the heart, 'tieferschüt-
tert' must survive,[65] became for Rilke the fearful advent of the Angel
and the rush of inspiration which resulted in the *Duineser Elegien.*
At Duino, in the early days of 1912, the poet claimed that he was
summoned (much as Nietzsche claimed for his *Also sprach Zarathustra*),
that he had no choice. There is no deliberately self-willed work
process such as Rilke had admired in Cézanne and Rodin, but a rush of
lyrical intensity, a hymn-like pathos far removed from the 'French'
perfection of the *Neue Gedichte*, and resembling more the confessional
poetry of Klopstock and Hölderlin. Yet the *Duineser Elegien* are
also a modern document, a portrayal not only of man's ontological
insufficiency but also of a crisis wrought by inauthentic living,
thoughtless technology and the vulgarisation and Babel of the modern
Vanity Fair. It is an interesting coincidence that the *Duineser Elegien*
were completed in the year in which *The Waste Land* was published.

The very first line of the first elegy immediately places the reader
in a sphere which is remote and strange. Who, or what, is this Angel
who appears terrible to man? From the start it must be made clear
that Rilke's Angel has nothing to do with the Christian concept. Rilke
will become more and more opposed to Christianity, whose emphasis
on an after-life cannot, in his opinion, but deny and destroy earthly
significance. (The *Brief des jungen Arbeiters* written after the elegies,
states the objection very clearly: 'Welcher Wahnsinn, uns nach einem
Jenseits abzulenken, wo wir hier von Aufgaben und Erwartungen und
Zukünften umstellt sind . . .'[66]) Rilke continued to arrogate certain
Christian figures and situations, but uses them purely as aesthetic

symbols; the vapid, nebulous religiosity of his earlier work has certainly been rejected by 1912, but certain symbols or ciphers remain, the Angel being one of them. What Rilke is concerned with here is a radical reinterpretation of human existence without transcendent sanctions, and Erich Heller has forcefully demonstrated the similarity between Nietzsche's *Übermensch* and Rilke's Angel, both being creatures which, in their own way, replace the Christian God and exemplify an immanent, aesthetic, religious-yet-pagan attitude to existence.[67] The Angel may also be looked upon as an ideal, a cosmic extension of what Rilke considered the true artist to be: it is that being which has achieved a godless, 'aesthetic' view of existence, who blesses, accepts and assimilates all. The Angel is to succeed, where Malte failed, in executing a radical *Umwertung*: the traditionally held distinctions between life and death, pain and joy, presence and parting are transcended in his gaze. Yet there is nothing static in Rilke's poetic vision. The *Duineser Elegien* are just as tentative, as hesitant as *Malte Laurids Brigge* in their positing and their reservations. The relation between man and Angel is not fixed; if the Angel is a yard-stick against which man measures his achievements, then the scale is a sliding one. Trapped within the flux and turmoil of transient phenomena, it seems that man cannot embrace and accept all: he differentiates between the positive and the negative, the darkness and the light. But there are certain moments of human existence, Rilke knows, that have such a greatness of integrity that the Angel must needs be aware of them. The position is not wholly one of lament, and man's position *vis-à-vis* the Angel vacillates according to Rilke's prevailing attitudes. It should be remembered that the elegies were conceived and written over a period of ten years, during which time the First World War totally destroyed the fabric of that European civilisation of which Rilke felt himself to be a scion, perhaps one of the last.

The first elegy may be seen as an overture, where all the main themes are stated. The Angel is fearful to man because it is seen as an absolute, or as an exemplification of pure being, against which fragmentary human existence is paltry indeed. Man is 'not at home' in his interpreted world: this experience of existential homelessness anticipates much of the writing of Martin Heidegger and, indeed, became endemic amongst the avant-garde writers of modern Europe. The animal world, which is to play a most important role in this cycle of poems, has an integrity which man does not possess: the problem of self-consciousness is adumbrated here, to be analysed at great depth in the eighth elegy. It is at night that human existence is most vulnerable, exposed and threatened, unable to seek support from the habits of day: the great theme of the lovers is introduced early in this first elegy, and the poet feels that all too often this most intense moment of human existence is betrayed by man's inadequacy, his weakness and lassitude. The fault lies entirely with man himself: the created world around him continues to give and enthrall yet man, preoccupied and distant, fails to respond to the beauty of that which he arrogantly rejects as insignificant. Here Rilke touches upon certain aspects of Kafka's work — the knowledge that it is man himself who blocks the path towards beauty and truth by his own arrogance. But the themes of the unrequited lovers, and the young dead, are very much Rilke's own. That which links them is the fact that they have not spent their spiritual energy upon an opposite, upon the particular partner or moment: the unrequited lovers, Rilke feels, are able to turn their love outwards towards the whole of existence, rather than waste this love in trivial habit, as those who have died young have passed into the 'anderen Bezug' inviolate and pure. It is here that Rilke's poetry proves a stumbling block for many readers, who sense in this praise of the unrequited lovers, those who transcend the need for a partner, not so much sublimity, but a shrinking inability to consummate a relationship. The cult of the young dead, likewise, seems to derive from earlier, neo-romantic attitudes, but Rilke wished to stress the need for a more subtle distinction between life and death which the memory of the young dead may bring about. The elegy ends with the beautiful image of the death of Linos, whose departure caused the air to oscillate, and music was born, music as a threnody, but a lament so beautiful that joy and solace prevailed.

The first two elegies were completed in the winter of 1912. The second elegy puts forward the belief that isolation and lack of integrity were not always the lot of man, that there was once a time when man and Angel walked together. Rilke here uses symbolism from the apocryphal book of Tobias to portray the Fall of man into time and transience; in his invocation of the angelic orders he uses vocabulary and imagery greatly reminiscent of Klopstock and Hölderlin. Yet such is Rilke's poetic range that he can also use the homely image of the heat rising from a warm meal to describe the passing of man's essence, and the picture of the vague expression in the face of a pregnant woman. Again the lovers are hailed, those who apparently experience moments of true joy, of pure being, but the inevitable disillusionment is also acknowledged. In the turmoil of passion man seeks to find the greatest confirmation of his existence, yet seeks, ultimately, in vain. The Greeks, Rilke knew, had immense restraint, and admitted the boundaries of human possession, leaving the rest to the gods; without such faith modern man seeks in sexual love a revelation which will never come. The elegy ends with an invocation of stone (permanence) and water (transience), between which a quiet abode may be sought for the human spirit, but this serenity is threatened by man's inordinate restlessness and lack of orientation.

The third elegy was likewise started in Duino in 1912, and was continued the following year in Paris. It takes up the notion of sexual love which was touched upon in the second elegy and carries it to a fearful extreme. It dismisses the view that man's lost integrity may be regained by sexual passion, and portrays primeval lust as something unspeakably horrible. The imagery is powerful and thrusting; the portrayal of the dark gods of the blood is reminiscent of D.H. Lawrence, whilst the description of the choking, rank jungle of lust is closely related to Gustav von Aschenbach's nightmare version. The poem is an injunction to the young girl to save the youth from the Dionysian jungle and to lead him into the ordered garden, but Rilke is also remorseless in his portrayal of the dark, powerful springs of lust which well up within the youth: the whole history of the human race, the ancient terrors and desires of mankind, precede the young girl's influence, who merely triggers off the sexual longing which is not directed towards a personality, but purely to a sexual release. The vision is worthy of Schopenhauer, but this is no *Tristan and Isolde*, and Rilke knows that integrity cannot be found in this obliteration of individuality during the sexual act. Both Rilke and Lawrence may have learnt much from emancipated German (or Russo-German) ladies who were steeped in the erotic movement in Germany at the beginning of the century, but Rilke, although always remarkably frank in sexual matters (the unfinished *Sieben Gedichte* of 1915 are quite overt in their praise of the erect phallus), dismissed the concept of the orgasm as panacea. Lou Salomé introduced him to Freud's work in 1913, at the time when this elegy was completed, but the idea of psychoanalysis was repellent to him.

The outbreak of the hostilities in 1914 found Rilke in Germany: on 1 August he arrived in Munich to consult the neurologist Dr von Stauffenberg. The tumults of patriotic jubilation impressed him: here, at last, were 'Ergriffene' who submerged their narrow interests in the common dedication. The *Fünf Gesänge* begin with lines very reminiscent of Hölderlin, and were written, in fact, in Norbert von Hellingrath's edition of Hölderlin's poetry: the description of the advent of the 'Kriegsgott', his awesome presence and apocalyptic destiny bear Hölderlin's undeniable stamp. But Rilke was soon to withdraw from the tide of chauvinism and belligerence: it is not war, but pain which is greeted and affirmed. Six years before he had written that famous line: 'Wer spricht von Siegen? Überstehn ist alles', words which, as has been mentioned, would have an even greater meaning in 1945. 'Das schwere, schlagende Schmerztuch'[68] can be hailed: it is the ability to bear suffering which betokens greatness. The testing time was at hand for whole peoples, not simply for the sensitive individual. Stefan George had, likewise, seen through the unthinking patriotic fervour: like Rilke he was too cosmopolitan in his outlook to revile his country's enemies. 'Er kann nicht schwärmen/Von heimischer tugend und von welscher tücke' proclaimed the seer of George's 'Der Krieg' (1917), who also knows 'Zu jubeln ziemt nicht: kein triumf wird sein/Nur viele untergänge ohne würde'.[69] In a line almost expressionistic in its elemental power – 'Erkrankte welten fiebern sich zu ende' – George, commonly held to be totally lacking in historical and political awareness, saw more clearly than many the rottenness and imminent collapse of the old order in Europe. Rilke, alone in Munich (apart from a brief period of service in the War Archives in Vienna), wrote down in November 1915 the bitterest of all the elegies, the fourth, which, in iambic pentameters, differs stylistically from the hymn-like tone of the other three.

The poem echoes the traditional lament for man's inability to participate in the rhythmical processes of nature, his exaggerated attempts to act in accordance with them and his inevitable failure. His actions are blighted by inauthenticity and lack of direction, his emotional life is distorted by petty apprehension and selfishness. The concept of the 'opposite', so skilfully expressed in the eighth elegy is touched upon here, that 'Grund von Gegenteil',[70] that sense of limitation which prevents pure, open experience: Rilke is precise and economical in his description of complex psychological states. Human existence, the roles that men assume and act, is seen as a shabby performance, executed, as it were, by inferior actors against makeshift scenery. Human half-heartedness and lack of profound emotional commitment become important themes for Rilke at this time, failure to respond in love above all. The lovers fail, as do the adults who force the child to conform to preconceived categories of behaviour. Doll and Angel, that is, total lack of consciousness on the one hand and absolute being on the other, have an integrity which man, fatally flawed by his self-consciousness, cannot achieve. The mood of the elegy darkens:

the child is extolled as enjoying that openness and unselfconsciousness which the adult lacks, but the precarious nature of childhood is recognised, the vulnerability and exposure of the child to destructive powers. The death of the child is, for the poet, *unbeschreiblich*: here the Nietzschean process of praise, of exultation, is severely threatened, even invalidated.

In his copy of *Les fleurs du mal* Rilke once wrote the following words:

Der Dichter einzig hat die Welt geeinigt,
die weit in jedem auseinanderfällt.
Das Schöne hat er unerhört bescheinigt,
doch da er selbst noch feiert, was ihn peinigt,
hat er unendlich den Ruin gereinigt:

und auch noch das Vernichtende wird Welt.[71]

Yet the war years in Munich gave rise to profound doubts concerning the validity of art: could it praise the negative and the destructive? Was it not superfluous, an unparalleled self-indulgence? Carossa's description of Rilke dates from this time, as does the bitter poem 'Der Tod', which describes death not in the early manner (as a dark fruit within the human psyche, waiting for release), but as a bluish decoction within a dusty, broken cup. The stark, unalterable facts of human life bring his poetry almost to a halt; those poems which would later become the sixth, ninth and tenth elegies, begun at Duino, are left incomplete. 'Ergreife/ein Seiendes'[72] − this injunction from a late poem emphasises the almost existential awareness of the need for a valid human life, for a reverential appreciation of that which truly *is*. (The word *Sein*, and its verbal forms, becomes of crucial importance to Rilke in both the *Duineser Elegien* and the *Sonette an Orpheus*.) Rilke's Nietzscheanism has been refined and made subtle to an incomparable degree, and although the long war years rendered facile affirmation impossible, and almost prevented any more poetry being written, the old idea of the *Umschlag*, of survival and patience and, ultimately, a transformation of pain into joy, sustained Rilke and enabled him to create again. Nietzsche's individualism, his emphasis upon self-fulfilment, became in Rilke a desire to preserve man's essential core against the depredations wrought by human failings. After the end of the war, in the little Swiss castle of Muzot, the task of completing the elegies after the apparently endless hiatus was

renewed; 'ein Orkan im Geiste',[73] an upsurge of creative energy, seized
the poet as it had in Duino: the sixth, ninth and tenth elegies were
completed, and the seventh, eighth and most of the fifth were
written. The *Sonette an Orpheus* also presented themselves, totally
unexpectedly: other important poems were completed. It is an
interesting paradox that these late works of Rilke, which deal with the
existential situation of man in an essentially modern idiom, should
have been written in a rush of what can only be described as inspiration,
a term not in frequent use in the twentieth century, and one which
would earlier have been rejected by the author of the *Neue Gedichte*.

The sixth elegy links the hero with the young dead, with those who
have not dissipated their lives in a meaningless sham existence, but
reached fulfilment and passed into the 'other realm' untarnished:
Rilke's concept of death as the unilluminated side of human existence
may seem alien to the modern reader, but it is best viewed as a device
to preserve the oneness of things, to preserve the meaning and
memory of the dead and to reject Christian belief in a transcendent
after-life. Rilke's interest in spiritualism was never deep, and the
more eccentric manifestations of such beliefs were to be later rejected
in the *Sonette an Orpheus*: his desire to treat of the concept of death
as a valid seed-bed for living receptivity, for human interpretative
faculties, is surely not as esoteric as is sometimes held. The idea of a
personal death was severely undermined by Rilke's Parisian
experiences, and the death of the child was felt to be beyond his
descriptive powers in the fourth elegy; yet as the Angels refuse to
differentiate, so the poet should likewise attempt to experience all
things as being somehow eternally present. The great themes of praise,
acceptance and passionate 'in-seeing' of all things come into the open
in the seventh elegy, the most positive, optimistic and defiant of them
all. The praise of the rising bird in spring and the all-embracing joy
which greets summer, evening, night and the dead is unique in Rilke:
once more the lovers are called, and their emotional ecstasy is
greeted without reservation. For the poet proclaims, with Nietzschean
fervour, that 'Hiersein ist herrlich'; the wonders of the natural world,
the intense raptures of human emotion far outweigh, in this elegy, the
dross and hypocrisy of human existence. But there is no false
optimism here: Rilke is aware of a threat to human creativity and
stresses the need to reinstate the spiritual and emotional achievements
of man within an inner dimension: 'Nirgends, Geliebte, wird Welt sein
als innen. Unser/Leben geht hin mit Verwandlung'.[74]

The concept of an inner, invisible dimension where the things of the

world may be retained and even carried across into that other realm
of death, found here and in the ninth elegy, is an esoteric one, but is
best understood as a realm of emotional and spiritual receptivity
capable of receiving and preserving the outward manifestations of
human creativity, a faculty of empathy and naive wonder able to grasp,
hold and admire. For the seventh elegy describes the dangers of abstract
intellectualism, of mass-production and the obliteration of the
individual. The anti-human bias of technology has resulted in an
impoverishment of the outer vessels for human emotional creativity:
Rilke saw that his own generation had been given the task of 'saving'
the works of spiritual splendour by praising, blessing and loving them,
by cultivating a sensitivity so intense as to allow the impact of an
indelible impression. The works of artistic greatness, the sphinx, and
the cathedral at Chartres, for example, as well as the emotional
intensity of love, must be hailed and recalled: even the Angel must
admit their glory. Transience can be conquered, the poet continues in
the ninth elegy, by this act of blessing and of transformation: one life
alone is given to man, and in this brief span he must praise not only the
sublime manifestations, but also the humble examples of human
creativity. The ecstatic tone of the seventh gives way in the ninth to a
more modest task: to 'say', that is, to understand and respect the
simple things, 'Tor, Krug, Obstbaum, Fenster', and not merely the great
excesses of the human spirit. A new image describes the 'Tun ohne
Bild',[75] the image-less activity of so much modern life, the dichotomy
between outer action and inner response. This praise of the simple
and unassuming artefact is surely one that the modern reader would
understand and appreciate, however estranged he may possibly be from
Rilke's insistence on synthesising life and death, and seeing both realms
as participating in the process of transformation.

The elegies do not, however, move unequivocally from lament to
eulogy: the eighth is a most subtle and moving account of the human
predicament, and quietly conveys a mood of melancholic acceptance.
The problem of self-consciousness is felt to be a central one, and man's
inability to see 'das Offene', to gaze out into the pristine clarity of
existence is felt to be a basic defect. Conceptualisation necessarily
creates a barrier between subject and object; interpretations of the
world prevent a sense of infinite being, that experience almost beyond
description, yet described by Rilke as the 'Nirgends ohne Nicht'.
Childhood, he claims, and the point of death, are two moments of
human life where such a sense of openness and oneness might be
experienced; it is, however, the animal world, not cursed with an

awareness of self, which truly *is*, and which has no sense of alienation. Rilke's portrayal of this animal experience is precise: the higher mammals are shown as possessing memory which causes possible dissatisfaction with the present: the less developed the animal world is, the closer it adheres to oneness and wholeness. This theme of regression links Rilke with the otherwise so different Gottfried Benn, whose praise of the 'Klümpchen Schleim in einem warmen Moor'[76] sprang from a rejection of the burden of cerebral sophistication; the theme of atavistic primitivism is, of course, common to much modern poetry, but the German expressionists, as chapter 6 will show, made much of this idea. The eighth elegy ends on a lament for human failings, for man's inadequacy in establishing personal relationships and his homelessness in his rigidly interpreted world. This poem, of all those written at Muzot, bears most poignant witness to the human destiny, trapped within forms of understanding which obstruct rather than clarify.

The tenth elegy, begun at Duino and completed at Muzot, opens in hymn-like grandeur, with a heroic determination to praise, and to bless pain as a source of joy. Juxtaposed with this stoical acceptance is the Vanity Fair of specious modern existence, where man (greatly reminiscent of Zarathustra's 'letzte Menschen') flees from an acceptance of love and pain into a cheap and tawdry world of comfort. Rilke's tone is frequently ironic here, as it is in the fifth, the last elegy written, but the satirical tone gives way to a portrayal of the death-land itself, a moonlit realm whose topographical and mytho-logical elements bear the mark of Rilke's Egyptian journey. The strange mingling of the senses in this realm demonstrates Rilke's need to reinterpret and suggest new nuances of feeling; the emphasis is again on the positive nature of pain, and the need to see in a downward, swooning movement not defeat and abnegation, but a fructifying preparation for ascension and praise. This idea is now central to Rilke's literary (and epistolary) output and is constantly reiterated: as Nietzsche strove to reassess the traditional dichotomy between good and evil, so Rilke attempts a readjustment of man's traditional distinction between pain and joy. The *Requiem für Wolf Graf von Kalckreuth* and certain of the passages from *Malte Laurids Brigge* prepared the way: the artist does not reject and despair, but accepts and praises. But in the elegy which Rilke wrote last, the fifth, he puts forward a surprising and devastating idea: that it is not the artist who necessarily has these superhuman qualities, but a humble boy who manages to smile in spite of pain and loneliness. Formal perfection is deemed to be arid: if the third elegy rejected Dionysus, then the fifth rejects Apollo.

The external impetus was provided by Picasso's painting 'Les Saltimbanques', a picture which Rilke knew intimately after his stay in Frau Hertha König's house in Munich, where it was hanging. But the poem also marks the climax of his doubts concerning the validity of his calling, which had beset him ever since the inception of *Malte Laurids Brigge*: doubts not only about his own art, but about art itself. The tone of the elegy is light and ironic; the issues, however, are profound. The acrobats leap and twist, they dazzle by their virtuosity, but the very first words of the poem question their existence — 'Wer aber *sind* sie, sag mir . . .?'.[77] They are even more transient than the rest of mankind, they jump and land on the carpet which becomes thinner and thinner, and throw up a dust which is not pollen (here Rilke puns on the meaning of 'Staub') to fructify the spectators, but which is dust purely and simply, which produces weariness and dissatisfaction. Here surely is a perfect portrayal of the arid meaninglessness of artistic expertise, an empty charade, a stubborn urge to describe life rather than live it and, in the process, an exploitation and 'wearing out' of the fabric of human existence, and all to no avail — a situation well known to a writer like Franz Kafka. At best art is described as being like a toy given to a sick child, at worst it is a destructive process which, in its labyrinthine complexity, resolves, like a mathematical equation, ultimately to zero, to nothingness. It is human emotion, human life in all its vulnerability that the Angel must preserve and admire here — the boy who smiles through his tears and the 'wahrhaft lächelnde Paar'; artistic cleverness cannot compete with this. Rilke did not abjure, as did Prospero, the 'magic' of the word, but rejects here sterile aestheticism; the praise of the artefact rather than the work of art itself seems again a demonstration of Rilke's determination to use his art not predominantly in the creation of beauty, but in the exploration of the realm of human emotion and the sheer mystery of human existence.

Rilke's famous letter to his Polish translator of November 1925 describes the great task of reinterpretation which he attempted in the elegies, and also portrays the advent of the *Sonette an Orpheus*, stressing the similar concerns and preoccupations shared by the two cycles. It would seem that Orpheus, or, rather, the Orphic principle, that identification of artistic subjectivity and objective reality, is utterly remote from the existential turmoil of the elegies, and that Rilke had reached a serenity which ultimately lacked conviction.

But as early as the third sonnet the fundamental question arises: is man capable of such an Orphic, godlike experience of existence? 'Gesang ist Dasein. Für den Gott ein Leichtes./Wann aber *sind* wir?'[78] Pure unity between man and world is not possible; it would seem that at no one moment can man enjoy pure being. The eleventh sonnet hails the stars, creates new symbols for new modes of experience and expresses the belief that the two realms, human and infinite, are one. But immediately the question arises: 'Aber *sind* sie's? Oder meinen beide/ nicht den Weg, den sie zusammentun?'.[79] Orpheus praises both the dark and the light, receiving and accepting all facets of being; he experiences all in a timeless state of intensity. This man cannot achieve: the last lines of the fifth sonnet of the second part of the cycle ask: 'Aber *wann*, in welchem aller Leben,/sind wir endlich offen und Empfänger?'.[80] The tone of lament is undeniable in these apparently most radiant utterances: 'Wehe, wo sind wir?' (twenty-six), and the cry '*Was* war wirklich im All' (eight) issue from a poet by no means at home in an Orphic vision. The light, pagan, Mediterranean atmosphere is troubled by existential difficulties and strained injunctions: the line 'Sei – und wisse zugleich des Nicht-Seins Bedingung'[81] does not reflect ease and acceptance. More appropriate to Heidegger's writing, it seems to stem from a desperate desire to partake of a superhuman, Angelic, Orphic vision of life, whereas the awareness of limitations and vulnerability make the poetry more acceptable and more memorable. The testament of the last poems of all – 'Auch ich bin dort, wo die Wege nicht gehn,/im Schwaden, den manche mied',[82] and the despairing cry 'O Magier, halt aus, halt aus, halt aus!'[83] show that the Orphic powers are too remote, and that the vulnerable poet, moving into the darkness, paradoxically achieves greatness where he is most aware of fragmentation.

The poetry of Georg Trakl bears certain similarities to that of Rilke – the preoccupation with death, the figure of Orpheus and, above all, a transition from *fin-de-siècle* lassitude towards a more modern style of writing. His *oeuvre* is slender beside Rilke's, yet contains much that is fascinating, particularly a form of imagism which prepares the way for certain expressionist devices. Trakl's mature style (it must, however, be remembered that he was only twenty-seven years old when he committed suicide) is elusive and haunting: the use of parataxis, unusual topoi and above all of compressed, laconic imagery create a decidedly original tone. The problem of the metaphor is a crucial one in Trakl, for his poetry exemplifies a gradual movement away from the conventional use of metaphor towards a more tenuous and immaterial form of comparison. The associative images linked to a particular situation come to exist in their own right, apparently only very loosely connected with the original idea; the very indefiniteness of the relation between the original situation and that to which it is compared sets up a host of complex reactions, makes the familiar seem strange and thereby 'poeticises' and strangely transforms the natural world. It is, of course, a characteristic of modern poetry as a whole that the metaphor has become more complex in that the link or point of comparison has become less transparent, more personal, laconic and esoteric. The tendency for a metaphor to become more and more independent and 'absolute' is one of the hallmarks of poetry written since, roughly, 1910.

In Trakl's work metaphors are used in which the original situation, the experience which should call to mind the comparison, no longer exists: the concrete situation fades behind a weight of metaphorical associations, the noun, as it were, being lost behind its attributive adjectives. The metaphor tends to exist in its own right as an image, often juxtaposed with other images to create a world remote from the real, elusive and frequently bizarre. The metaphor (or image) then becomes expressive rather than imitative, and exists as an autonomous figure of speech from which radiates a host of evocative meanings. It may be argued that in Trakl's late poetry there are no direct metaphors or unambiguous images: the 'weißes Tier' of 'In den Nachmittag geflüstert', for example, points to nothing directly, but rather hints at a whole mass of associations, all concerned with the idea of vulnerability. The conventional simile is certainly found in Trakl (in 'Die Raben' and 'Verfall' for instance), and other poems use a comparative form where the 'wie' is understood, although not written. But even a comparatively early poem such as 'Im roten Laubwerk voll Guitarren' contains a bold metaphor (the sun as a carriage) while 'An den Knaben Elis' uses a complex extended metaphor (those who think of the boy resemble a monk who turns the pages of a holy book). 'Drei Blicke in einen Opal' is a good example of a poem which, in its entirety, is to be looked upon as one long metaphor, where each part points to a shadowy existence beyond the immediate situation: the mass of impressions are linked to the iridescent, shifting light associated with that stone. The poem 'Sebastian im Traum' is more recondite with its line 'Mutter trug das Kindlein im weißen Mond'.[84] The mother's nature is such that her embrace is felt to have the coldness and whiteness of the moon; feelings of remoteness, coldness and a child's pain are hinted at here. These metaphors are, in fact, becoming remarkable

images, which radiate an evocative power of their own. Most disturbing
are the lines from 'Die Verfluchten': 'Ein Nest von scharlachfarbnen
Schlangen bäumt/Sich träg in ihren aufgewühlten Schoß',[85] where the
sexual act is associated with horror, evil and a sense of debilitating loss;
the poem 'Anif' contains the metaphoric expression which links
memory with seagulls against a dark sky: memories, as they rise from a
dark subconscious, resemble seagulls against a sombre background.

An absolute, or autotelic, metaphor may then be called an image,
an image being defined as a simile, metaphor or figure of speech
objectifying or re-enacting an inner experience. In modern poetry
images become autotelic in the sense that they become increasingly
divorced from the object and exist as a powerfully evocative nucleus.
That which makes Trakl's poetry so elusive is that the same image may
be used for different purposes, sometimes merely descriptive, but
sometimes symbolic. The colour epithets are of interest here, for they
sometimes have a symbolic extension, but at other times simply express
an evocative synaesthesia. The chief difficulty in interpreting Trakl's
poetry is to know to what extent an image may be a symbol
(related possibly to a religious preoccupation), or whether it exists
purely in its own right. The predominance of the image, with frequently
symbolic overtones, is a characteristic feature of expressionist poetry,
expressionism being a movement in which the writer feels driven to
use images not merely as a mirror of external reality but as vital nuclei,
impulses to the reader's imagination, or catalysts to his reactions.
Both image and symbol express an inner world of meaning and are
abstracted from common experience: image-as-metaphor and image-
as-symbol move beyond mimesis and accumulate heightened meanings
in a reinterpretation of the world.

Only the most detailed cross-reference can demonstrate the extent
to which the persistence of an image in Trakl's poetry suggests a
symbolic meaning. It is obviously false to impose a rigid symbolism on
such essentially imagist poetry, as certain Catholic interpreters were
wont to do, before the more recent Trakl criticism, but the reader
should also be ready to appreciate the symbolic extension of certain
images, particularly such elemental ones as fire, water and rock, and
such overtly Christian ones as shepherd, dove and cross. The symbols
may be personal and dreamlike (in the form of obsessive images) or
universal (bread and wine); Elis may be a poetic cipher for the
vulnerability of the poet, or partake of Christian attributes, and,
similarly, Helian may be an oblique reference to Verlaine or to the
Christian saviour. The same is true of the colour adjectives: there is

no key to an understanding of them, and the reader must not attempt to impose an inflexible framework, but must accept the unorthodox way in which they may be used and feel the emotional meaning that the poet means to convey. The colours within an abstract painting may be successful if they stand in an aesthetically pleasing relationship with one another, their 'meaning' being immanent within the work, and yet, in Trakl, the colour values are not always private: some concession is made to conventional usage, and this leads to an atmosphere of uncertainty and half-familiarity to his work. The poem 'Jahr' from *Sebastian im Traum* may be cited as a good example of his mature style:

> Dunkle Stille der Kindheit. Unter grünenden Eschen
> Weidet die Sanftmut bläulichen Blickes; goldene Ruh.
> Ein Dunkles entzückt der Duft der Veilchen; schwankende Ähren
> Im Abend, Samen und die goldenen Schatten der Schwermut.
> Balken behaut der Zimmerman; im dämmernden Grund
> Mahlt die Mühle; im Hasellaub wölbt sich ein purpurner Mund,
> Männliches rot über schweigende Wasser geneigt.
> Leise ist der Herbst, der Geist des Waldes; goldene Wolke
> Folgt dem Einsamen, der schwarze Schatten des Enkels.
> Neige in steinernem Zimmer; unter alten Zypressen
> Sind der Tränen nächtige Bilder zum Quell versammelt;
> Goldenes Auge des Anbeginns, dunkle Geduld des Endes.[86]

Trakl has been called the literary equivalent of Kandinsky: his autonomous images are compared with Kandinsky's colours and lines, although painters like Van Gogh and Franz Marc, who do not reject the representational object, seem closer to his work.

In Trakl's poetry the substantive frequently (although not always) disappears behind the qualifying adjectives, as the colours in an expressionist canvas seem to absorb the body to which they are attached. But the most distinctive use of independent metaphor at this time is found in the work of Franz Kafka (1883–1924): Walter Sokel's discussion of *Die Verwandlung* stresses the way in which the metaphor describing Samsa's existence has *become* his existence.[87] This chapter must now finish with a brief discussion of Kafka, a writer both fascinating and infuriating, compelling and insufferable. He has somehow become the spokesman of modern Europe, and his private agonies have become part of the stock-in-trade of every sensitive devotee of literature. In the case of Kafka, more so than with Rilke,

Thomas Mann and Robert Musil, the student of literature is faced with an intrepid task: a massive forest of rank literary criticism must be cut down before the palace containing the Sleeping Beauty is glimpsed, let alone entered; the fruitful encounter between the explorer and the imaginative quick of the writer rarely ensues. The besetting sin of literary criticism is to force the text to conform to a set of pre-conceived notions or beliefs, be they religious, philosophic, political or psychological, and Kafka has provided a happy hunting-ground for those eager to claim him as their own. It is imperative in the case of Kafka to have the courage to stay close to the surface of the text; only occasionally does he indulge in mystification for its own sake. It is also important to remember the different emphases and pre-occupations of his work: to consider him as a writer wholly bound up in a labyrinthine portrayal of *Angst* is an oversimplification, for in the two decades which his writing spanned different problems presented themselves to him, some purely personal, others of a more universal nature.

Much has been made of Kafka's Prague background, his sense of alienation as a non-orthodox Jew living within the German-speaking minority of the Czech capital in the kingdom of Bohemia. The problem of language would be of importance here; Fritz Mauthner wrote: 'Der Deutsche im Innern von Böhmen, umgeben von einer tschechischen Landbevölkerung, spricht ein papiernes Deutsch, es mangelt an Fülle des erdgewachsenen Ausdrucks, es mangelt an Fülle der mundartlichen Formen. Die Sprache ist arm'.[88] The resulting overcompensation is seen in the predilection of many Prague writers for the grotesque and the inflated: Franz Werfel and Gustav Meyrink are good examples here. But Kafka chose to cultivate a cool, sober and elegant prose, where his legal training (and possibly also his Jewish exegetical practice) could be used to good purpose. As early as 1902, in the year of the publication of Hofmannsthal's *Ein Brief*, Kafka wrote in a letter to Oskar Pollak of the difficulty of communica-tion and his desire to attempt a form of writing 'ohne Schnörkel und Schleier und Warzen',[89] that is, without the convolutions and excrescences of much of the writing examined in the previous chapters of this book.

Through Max Brod Kafka made contact with the *literati* of the Café Arco (lampooned by Kraus as the 'Arconauten'): his first publications were eight small vignettes under the title *Betrachtungen* appearing in 1908 in *Hyperion*, a journal edited by Franz Blei (1871–1942), and, in its first year, by Carl Sternheim (1878–1942). Franz

Blei had not only encouraged Carl Sternheim but also Carl Einstein (1885–1940) as well as Kafka, and took pains to point out that Kafka was not a pseudonym for Robert Walser but 'ein junger Mann in Prag, der so heißt'.[90] (The work of Carl Einstein will be discussed in the next chapter: suffice it to say here that his *Verwandlungen* also appeared in *Hyperion* in 1908 and resembled Kafka in their portrayal of the gulf between mind and world; *Bebuquin* (1912), a remarkable novel which was greatly admired by Ernst Stadler and Gottfried Benn, shares with Kafka's early writing a capricious awareness of the absurd and the grotesque.) The impressionistic quality of these eight small pieces has been described as a 'poor man's Hofmannsthal';[91] the dramatic fragment *Der Gruftwächter* is similarly indebted to Viennese neo-romanticism. Kafka's prose has not yet found that pellucid quality which would be its distinguishing feature: the descriptions of aeroplanes, however (*Die Aeroplane in Brescia*) which appeared in the newspaper *Bohemia* in 1909 and the account of the safety regulations for the prevention of mangled limbs in his insurance work demonstrated a greater precision and sobriety. It was only with extreme reluctance that Kafka, encouraged by Max Brod, let the *Betrachtungen*, albeit in an extended and more disciplined form, be published by Ernst Rowohlt; his increasing fastidiousness and high literary standards prevented the rush into print of so many younger writers. For literature, as Kafka came more and more to realise, should not be a self-indulgence, but a self-discipline: in giving form to inner realities it represented control and exploration and became, in fact, the highest task of which man was capable. The famous statement 'Ein Buch muß die Axt sein für das gefrorene Meer in uns'[92] demonstrates the earnestness of the would-be writer and the esteem in which he held the highest manifestations of literature.

The section 'Kleider' of *Betrachtung* greatly resembles the descriptions of clothes, faces and mirrors found in *Malte Laurids Brigge*; 'Der Fahrgast' is a sober portrayal of the difference between human and the animal; 'Die Bäume', with its comparison between the trees standing in the snow and human life in general, is a good example of Kafka's tendency to state, qualify and suggest a further, more disquieting, situation. But is is 'Das Unglück des Junggesellen' that is of interest because it is an expression, at this early stage of Kafka's life and work, of a crucial concern: the desirability or disadvantages of remaining single. For it is linked to the whole problem of the isolation imposed by literature as opposed to the normality of marriage, children and responsibility. It is not surprising that we learn that one of Kafka's favourite books was Thomas Mann's *Tonio Kröger*, and that he was an avid reader of memoirs and descriptions of the lives of such men as Flaubert and Grillparzer. On 13 August 1912, Kafka met Felice Bauer at Max Brod's house, and what had been an abstract problem now became acutely real. Kafka's literary breakthrough in 1912 was the direct result of his meeting with Felice Bauer and the emotional difficulties surrounding the relationship with her and also with his own father, who seemed to be all that his son was not. If the woman represented a temptation and a threat, then the father represented a challenge, and both provided material for the artist's imagination. The story *Das Urteil*, written six weeks later, during the night of 22 to 23 September, amazed Kafka by its force, precision and mystery: 'Nur so kann geschrieben werden, nur in einem solchen Zusammenhang, mit solcher vollständiger Öffnung des Leibes und der Seele'.[93] The protagonist Bendemann is sent to his death or, rather, acquiesces in his death: both father and friend triumph. The friend represents the lonely, introvert idealist whose unusual way of life immediately provokes the outburst from Frieda Brandenfeld: 'Wenn du solche Freunde hast, Georg, hättest du dich überhaupt nicht verloben sollen'.[94] Kafka himself described the friend thus: 'Der Freund ist kaum eine wirkliche Person, er ist vielleicht eher das, was dem Vater und Georg gemeinsam ist. Die Geschichte ist vielleicht ein Rundgang um Vater und Sohn, und die wechselnde Gestalt des Freundes ist vielleicht der perspektivische Wechsel der Beziehungen zwischen Vater und Sohn'.[95] Before the giant form of the father and the vital, disturbing memory of the friend, Bendemann succumbs: thoughts of marriage are as nothing before Kafka's determination to devote his life to literature, and the forbidding shadow of his own father, Hermann Kafka.

Kafka's *Briefe an Felice* have been recently published (the later *Briefe an Milena* are already well known); for five years Kafka corresponded with her until his tuberculosis provided him with the perfect excuse to terminate his engagement, or, rather, his second engagement to her. The difference between the letters and Kafka's literary output is most marked: against the precision and lucidity of his published work the letters' torrents of self-pity and remorse make very difficult reading. The egoism is extreme, and ultimately barren, whereas that which is art satisfies by its objectivity and allowance for mystery. To demand that a man be in his private letters what he is in his artistic achievements is excessive, however; the letters, if nothing else, provide biographical data which may, or may not, be of interest. The letters to Felice are frequently unreadable because there is a posturing on his part; Kafka's stories, on the other hand, are often masterpieces because they have sublimated and formalised the personal. The letters certainly help to understand certain aspects of *Das Urteil*, also of *Der Prozess*, but the elusive qualities of these works derive from the particular quality of art which is always *more* than the sum of its different parts. Kafka knew Hebbel's diaries, where the following statement is found:

> Die höchste Wirkung der Kunst tritt nur dann ein, wenn sie nicht *fertig* wird; ein Geheimnis muß immer übrig bleiben . . . Im Lyrischen ist das offenbar; was ist eine Romanze, ein Gedicht, wenn es nicht unermeßlich ist, wenn nicht aus jeder Auflösung des Rätsels ein neues Rätsel hervorgeht? Eben deshalb gehört das Didaktische . . . nicht hinein, weil es nichts gebären kann, als sich selbst. Aber auch in der Novelle und Erzählung finde ich zu viel Licht bedenklich.[96]

In the letters to Felice (and Milena) the spotlight is too harsh, and the masochism, self-exculpation and self-reproach are given full reign; the reader would do well to eschew these letters and turn to the stories themselves.

Hebbel had also written: 'Als die Aufgabe meines Lebens betrachte ich die Symbolisierung meines Innern'.[97] In his diary on 6 August 1914 Kafka confessed: 'Von der Literatur aus gesehen ist mein Schicksal sehr einfach. Der Sinn für die Darstellung meines traumhaften innern Lebens hat alles andere ins Nebensächliche gerückt'.[98] Since the end of 1912 he had been working at a novel to be called *Der Verschollene* (which would be published posthumously as *Amerika*), but sensed that the longer form of prose fiction was not conducive to him, a realisation well borne out when *Der Prozeß* and *Das Schloß* are considered, works which are flawed and not infrequently tedious. The first scene, *Der Heizer*, was published by Kurt Wolff in 1913: Kafka also announced the forthcoming story *Die Verwandlung* at that time, and suggested that *Das Urteil, Die Verwandlung* and *Der Heizer* might be published together under the title *Die Söhne*. In writing his *Der Verschollene* Kafka could well have had in mind Robert Walser's *Jakob von Gunten*, published in 1909 and which portrayed, in notebook form, the life of a 'guileless fool' who rejects the conventional interpretations of life, its arrogant assumptions and ideologies, and withdraws from the roles which society persists in imposing. Kafka was a great admirer of Walser's limpid prose; Walser's portrayal of the boy's experiences in a school for servants run by the brother and sister Benjamenta may well have been in Kafka's mind at the inception of his new work. The arrival of the innocent Karl Rossmann in New York (where the Statue of Liberty holds a sword and not a torch) has a charm and freshness not often found in later Kafka: the symbolic associations of the depths of the ship and the large country house are hinted at but not forced. The work published by Max Brod, *Amerika*, with the laboured allegory of the Oklahoma Nature Theatre, is of inferior quality and had been discarded by Kafka; the episode with the two tramps Robinson and Delamarche anticipates Beckett by forty years, and the description of the rubbish in Brunelda's room certainly calls to mind Harold Pinter. The portrayal in the chapter 'Hotel Occident' of the death of Theresa's mother shows Kafka's ability to write of unemployment, poverty, hopelessness and death in an entirely 'realistic' manner: the ruthlessness of American capitalism here finds its most powerful indictment, yet Kafka had more pressing concerns.

Die Verwandlung is an acknowledged masterpiece, probably one of the greatest short stories in the German language. Kafka had read, and indeed reviewed, Kleist's work: the precision and economy of his finest writing is certainly reminiscent of Kleist's prose fiction. (Tucholsky called him 'ein Großsohn von Kleist' and added 'Er schreibt die klarste und schönste Prosa, die zur Zeit in deutscher Sprache geschaffen wird'.[99]) First published in René Schickele's *Die weißen Blätter* in 1915, it appeared in Kurt Wolff's collection 'Der jüngste Tag' in the same year with a title-page drawing by Ottomar Starke. Kafka insisted that the insect should not be drawn: to delineate would be to limit and define, which ran counter to his purpose, and description enough was given in the first paragraph. This paragraph is the most famous in modern German literature, equalled possibly solely by the opening of *Der Prozeß*: the situation was already adumbrated in Kafka's earlier prose sketches *Hochzeitsvorbereitungen auf dem Lande*, dating from 1907. Raban's wish that he might remain in bed in the form of an insect has here become reality: in Walter Sokel's words, the metaphor is treated here as an actual fact, and no explanation is given, simply the image. The reader's reaction is one of shock, bafflement and — when he reminds himself of what he is reading and talking about — amusement. But serious issues are also involved. Samsa is shown *vis-à-vis* his job, his family and his own self: he has become literally what he essentially is — something inhuman and insect-like. His degradation is somehow logical: his ant-like industry, his total lack of valid human relationships, his servile acceptance of the impositions of professional and family life are now objectified, externalised in his insect shape. He has now no choice but to experience tangibly, physically, what he had so far chosen to neglect. The reader is tempted to think of the relationship between Kafka and his own family, or of the position of the artist in society; the peculiar predicament may indeed have prompted the initial premise, but the story, one of degradation, has a wider significance. The refusal to *live*, in the fullest sense, is the greatest sin of all. It is surely wrong to see a growth of sensitivity in Samsa: his reactions to music are bestial and aggressive. And yet the reader should not overlook the *Galgenhumor*, which plays an important part in the story, the sheer lack of commensuration between situation and response: the absurd, even farcical nature of talking all too earnestly about such a fantastic situation should always be admitted.

The outbreak of the war in 1914 passed practically unnoticed by the writer who was concerned above all with the possibility of objectifying into satisfactory images his inner preoccupations: the diary simply records 'Neid und Haß gegen die Kämpfenden, denen ich mit Leidenschaft alles Böse wünsche'.[100] References to the military machine may be sought in *In der Strafkolonie*, but this sombre story would seem to be the expression more of a need for self-immolation, for punishment which a more 'liberal' mentality fails to comprehend. The problematic nature of his relationship with Felice Bauer preoccupied him. He had enjoyed a few days intimacy with her in Marienbad in 1916, but sensed the impossibility of continuing the engagement, which had once been broken off; his novel *Der Prozeß* may well have started as an examination of Kafka's feelings of guilt surrounding the affair, but becomes also a more universal statement. Elias Canetti has said:

> Zwei entscheidende Ereignisse in Kafkas Leben, die er sich nach seiner Art besonders privat gewünscht hätte, hatten sich in peinlichster Öffentlichkeit abgespielt: die offizielle Verlobung in der Wohnung der Familie Bauer am 1. Juni und sechs Wochen danach am 12. Juni 1914 das 'Gericht' im Askanischen Hof, das zur Entlobung führte. Es läßt sich zeigen, daß der emotionelle Gehalt beider Ereignisse unmittelbar in den *Prozeß* einging, mit dessen Niederschrift er im August begann. Die Verlobung ist zur Verhaftung des ersten Kapitels geworden, das 'Gericht' findet

sich als Exekution im letzten.[101]

This is indeed possible, but Kafka's novel, unfinished, unpolished and with its undeniable longueurs, is best approached as an explanation of those human failings which prevent man from living an authentic, fulfilled existence.

The thirty-year-old protagonist (Kafka's own age when he started writing the novel, and traditionally the age at which a man must take stock of himself and his life) is 'arrested' by those aspects of himself which he had hitherto ignored, by externalisations of certain tendencies which achieve an independent life. His involvement in a legal battle is, in fact, his obsession with his own ratiocination: his undoubted intellect, his arrogance and his furtive sexuality assert themselves and prevent the emergence of a loving, generous character. Josef K. is his own enemy; occasionally a glimpse of the truth dawns on him, and he almost is ready to admit his guilt, but selfishness invariably prevails. He turns to Huld, to Leni, to Titorelli in his attempts at self-exculpation; it is the prison chaplain who advises self-scrutiny. The famous parable *Vor dem Gesetz* demonstrates that it is man who prevents himself from reaching the truth, that man is not thwarted by malevolent demons, but by that which is human, all-too-human. Josef K.'s rejection of Huld, who represents excessive, labyrinthine ratiocination, and Leni's sexuality is a progressive step, but Kafka is ruthless: the execution is as meaningless and as embarrassing as Josef K.'s life had been. The 'highest judges', the figure at the window glimpsed at the point of death? It may be possible to admit of the existence of a divine realm, but Kafka's Gnostic meditations on man's shortcomings did not allow him to believe in an impingement of the divine on human existence: it is man's own attempts — and his failure — to achieve love and unselfishness in this world which is his ultimate concern. Kafka's analysis of man's tragic failure in love may have been nurtured by the Felice Bauer experience, but the biography is not of ultimate importance: *Der Prozeß* stands as a tortured attempt to show how man, after being given a chance to justify himself, fails, and has only himself to blame.

Kafka wished to have this novel, as well as *Das Schloß* and other works, destroyed. His fastidious craftsmanship prevented him from allowing anything to be published which he felt was in any way unsatisfactory: Max Brod felt unable to carry out his wishes. The situation concerning Kafka's 'will' is confused, but it is obvious that Kafka saw the shortcomings of attempts at the more extended forms of prose. *Das Schloß* is likewise unfinished, and shares many of the faults of *Der Prozeß* — tedium, an inability to translate an inner state into sustained external narration, labyrinthine self-obsession lit only infrequently by shafts of humour. As regards *Das Schloß*, certain images, clear, disquieting and redolent of menace, remain in the mind: the castle itself (or rather a huddle of broken buildings) surrounded by crows, the road that gets nowhere, the snow-bound wastes — a certain plasticity of imaginative power is undeniable here. (Kafka's reading of Dickens is well-known, and the cramped, sub-human world of Dickens is frequently alluded to, especially with reference to *Der Prozeß*; it is obvious, however, that Kafka had neither the sweep nor the sustaining power of the English novelist.) *Das Schloß* is concerned with the attempt to break the citadel of the ego, to come to terms with the self; it is a portrayal of self-knowledge similar to *Der Prozeß*. The land-surveyor K. has to map out, or define, the boundaries of self and his relationship to the claims of the emotions: his assistants are grotesque parodies of his own preoccupations and desires. His abasement is necessary: he 'goes to school' in an attempt to know himself and 'be accepted', that is, to find the meaning of his own life. The novel is a stunted *Bildungsroman*: unfinished and perhaps unfinishable it shows the reader a real world of bureaucratic confusion and telephone exchanges, insolent officials and dulled, ignorant villagers against a background now precise, now blurred, for it is an extension once more of the self of the protagonist who, perhaps more readily than Josef K., is willing to learn and submit. The Castle, resembling more and more an obsessed, deranged mind, is ultimately unimportant: K. attempts to live, and does not entirely fail. Had the novel been completed he may have been accepted into life; the rest is mere speculation.

In an aphorism of the year 1917 Kafka wrote: 'Die Sprache kann für alles außerhalb der sinnlichen Welt nur andeutungsweise, aber niemals auch nur annähernd vergleichsweise gebraucht werden'.[102] One Kafka scholar has stressed a movement in Kafka away from the use of comparison, simile and metaphor towards the symbol, which is ambiguous in its extension, and which puzzles the reader by its elusive qualities.[103] A castle may symbolise impregnability and power: the link 'castle-self' may well appear tenuous, but by dint of frequent reading and knowledge of other works by Kafka a pattern emerges in which crows are crows, yet bring to mind grackles and jackdaws (the Czech version of Kafka's own name), in which wintry desolate fields invoke loneliness, in which a bridge 'becomes' a transition, and in which 'surveying' becomes defining and learning. The dissenting reader, not convinced of Kafka's merit, may be unwilling to study an *oeuvre* that apparently is obsessed with guilt, failure, *Angst* and bleak isolation; if the novels do not satisfy, however, then the short stories and parables do convince by this artist's excellence and the wider vision that informs them. And Kafka's professed intention, 'die Welt ins Reine, Wahre, Unveränderliche [zu] heben'[104] must surely command respect and admiration: writing, through its intensity and purity, reaches an almost religious incantation, a re-enactment and elevation of existence to the status of myth and symbol.

The *Brief an den Vater* occasioned by Kafka's abortive engagement to Julie Wohryzek in 1919, is Kafka's final statement concerning the father-son tension which many critics have overrated: with his tuberculosis confirmed, and a greater objectivity achieved, Kafka, ensconced in his loneliness, was able to meditate on the position of the artist (in *Josefine die Sängerin oder das Volk der Mäuse* and *Der Hungerkünstler*) and, with irony, on the dubious nature of artistic histrionics, very much as Rilke had done in the Fifth Duino elegy. As a Jewish writer he defined the position of the writer *vis-à-vis* the race (*Josefine*); he also questions the springs of the artist's creative impulse in a way very similar to Thomas Mann (*Der Hungerkünstler*). In the remarkable *Forschungen eines Hundes* (again, Kafka derives humour and ironic alienation by using the animal world) he takes stock of his own intellectual development and the position he had reached (in 1920): he recalls the effect made upon him by the Jewish theatrical troupe (the 'seven dogs'), his initial admiration and ensuing reservations, his subsequent investigations into the history of his race and his ultimate loneliness (and the amusing description of the 'alter Hund' − Max Brod? − whom he tolerates). The dog's attitudes to the 'Lufthunde', the aesthetes, are dealt with in great precision, as is his decision to meditate in utter isolation on the truth and its representation; his sickness, in bloody vomit, is not spared, neither is the vision of the hunter − surely a vision of death − which rises before him. The ultimate story, *Der Bau*, written during the last year of Kafka's life, is a harrowing self-analysis, referring specifically to his own work, his own labyrinthine self as a burrow where the enemy − death − lurks to destroy at any time: it also, by extension, is an apt portrayal of that human tendency to create an ophidian intellectual construction or system to prevent an existential encounter with the ultimate truth of the self, and how this must needs fail.

Much that Kafka wrote is too obsessively personal to be exemplary: his published letters, as has been said, are often embarrassing in their self-indulgent enjoyment of misery. He fails as a novelist because he is not a great organiser of experience – his work seems to have gained notoriety because of the excuse it gives to the critic for the working out of an *idée fixe*. Some see in his work an uncanny anticipation of arrest, torture, irrationality and bestial degradation (his three sisters died in Auschwitz); W.H. Auden has proclaimed him as the spokesman of the modern world, the Age of Anxiety. But it would seem that the time has come for a reappraisal of his work: he may well have known best when he asked Brod to destroy much of it. A few short stories and fables earn the title of minor modern classics: although Edmund Wilson's comment that 'What he has left us is the half-expressed gasp of a self-doubting soul trampled under. I do not see how one can possibly take him for either a great artist or a moral guide'[105] is a little severe (he neglects Kafka's humour, for instance), it may be preferable to the inflated claims of those who compare him to Joyce, Proust and even Dante, and this, after all, was what he sensed himself. To open men's eyes to the puzzling and the elusive qualities of life, to the truth, in fact, is all that the story-teller can do; it may even help if he were a little less able to live than his fellows:

> Eine Nuß aufknacken ist wahraftig keine Kunst, deshalb wird
> es auch niemand wagen, ein Publikum zusammenzurufen und
> vor ihm, um es zu unterhalten, Nüsse knacken. Tut er es dennoch
> und gelingt seine Absicht, dann kann es sich eben doch nicht nur
> um bloßes Nüsseknacken handeln. Oder es handelt sich um
> Nüsseknacken, aber es stellt sich heraus, daß wir über diese Kunst
> hinweggesehen haben, weil wir sie glatt beherrschten und daß uns
> dieser neue Nußknacker erst ihr eigentliches Wesen zeigt, wobei
> es dann für die Wirkung sogar nützlich sein könnte, wenn er etwas
> weniger tüchtig im Nüsseknacken ist als die Mehrzahl von uns.[106]

This chapter has sought to examine certain German works to determine their 'modernity' and their European status; whereas chapter 4 dealt with the visionaries, this present one has looked at the crisis of language which was experienced at the turn of the century (particularly by the Jewish writers who, forbidden the use of other media, were acutely aware of language as an instrument of revelation and sensitive to its disastrous debasement),[107] the new poetic worlds of Rilke and Trakl, and the unique position of Franz Kafka. It is now time for an analysis of expressionism: Kafka's writing ran parallel to that movement and touched upon it at certain points, in spite of his strictures and reservations. A remarkable novel by Ernst Weiss (1882–1940), friend of Kafka at the time of his diengagement from Felice Bauer, *Der Aristokrat*, seems to link the world of Kafka with that of certain writers of expressionist prose; Robert Walser's influence may also be detected in the portrayal of the Belgian boarding school for aristocrats. It has been claimed that expressionism is the form that modernism took in Germany, although this is a possibly unsubtle view. Expressionism is a complex phenomenon, which chapter 6 will attempt to examine in detail.

Notes

1.   See Toulmin and Janik, *Wittgenstein's Vienna*, London, 1973.
2.   Nietzsche, I, 453.
3.   Ibid., II, 960.
4.   Hölderlin, *Werke*, Große Stuttgarter Ausgabe, II, 234.
5.   Hofmannsthal, *Gesammelte Werke, Prosa*, I, 7.
6.   Ibid., 7-8.
7.   Ibid., 12.
8.   Thomas Mann, *Werke*, VIII, 64-65.
9.   Hofmannsthal, 14.
10. Ibid., 22.
11. Quoted in Paul Schick, *Karl Kraus in Selbstzeugnissen und Bilddokumenten*, Reinbek, 1965, 151.
12. See Gabriel Josipovici, 'The Abstraction of the Voice' (*TLS*, October 1972).
13. Mann, *Werke*, VI, 75.
14. W. Berghahn, *Robert Musil in Selbstzeugnissen und Bilddokumenten*, Reinbek, 1963, 33.
15. Musil, *Sämtliche Erzählungen*, Hamburg, 1968, 9.
16. Ibid., 25.
17. Ibid., 48.
18. Pascal, *From Naturalism to Expressionism*, 225.
19. Musil, 134.
20. Ibid., 112.
21. Ibid., 113.
22. Toulmin and Janik, *Wittgenstein's Vienna*, 197.
23. Musil, *Der Mann ohne Eigenschaften*, 1,611.
24. Walter Benjamin, *Illuminationen*, Frankfurt/Main, 1961, 285.
25. Quoted Schick, 153.
26. Letter to Schnitzler, March, 1893, quoted in Schick, 29.
27. *Literatur und Lüge*, 'Der Fall Kerr', *Werke*, Munich, 1952–1967, VI, 187.
28. Ibid., 69.
29. *Worte in Versen*, VII, 259.
30. *Literatur und Lüge*, 14.
31. Wedekind, *Gesammelte Werke*, Munich and Leipzig, 1919, III, 187.
32. *Beim Wort genommen*, 351.
33. Ibid., 348.

34. *Widerschein der Fackel*, Munich, 1956, 404.
35. Toulmin and Janik, *Wittgenstein's Vienna*, 87.
36. Karl Kraus, *Briefe an Sidonie Nadherny von Borutin* (16 May 1936), Munich, 1974, I, 687.
37. *Die letzten Tage der Menschheit* (Vorwort), *Werke*, V, 9.
38. Benjamin, *Illuminationen*, 388.
39. *Die dritte Walpurgisnacht*, I, 9.
40. Georg Trakl, *Dichtungen und Briefe*, I, 123.
41. T.S. Eliot, *The Four Quartets*, 'East Coker', Lines 180-182.
42. Rilke, *Werke*, I, 663.
43. T.S. Eliot, *Selected Essays*, London, 1934, 21.
44. Rilke, 557.
45. Ibid., 609-610.
46. See Walter Kaufmann, *Rilke: Nirvana or Creation* (*TLS*, December 1975).
47. Rilke, VI, 724.
48. Rilke, *Briefe aus den Jahren 1907–1914*, Leipzig, 1933, 197.
49. Ibid., 95.
50. Rilke, *Werke*, VI, 727.
51. Ibid., 749-751.
52. Ibid., 775.
53. Ibid., 863.
54. Ibid., 756.
55. *Briefe aus den Jahren 1906–1907*, Leipzig, 1930, 394-395.
56. *Werke*, VI, 785.
57. *Rainer Maria Rilke–Lou Andreas-Salomé Briefwechsel*, Zurich, 1952, 126.
58. Kafka, *Gesammelte Werke. Briefe an Felice* (ed. Heller and Born), 1967, 400.
59. Kafka, *Gesammelte Werke* (ed. Brod), *Hochzeitsvorbereitungen auf dem Lande*, 1953, 167.
60. W. Welzig, *Der deutsche Roman im 20. Jahrhundert*, Stuttgart, 1967, 21.
61. W. Emrich, *Protest und Verheißung*, Frankfurt/Main and Bonn, 1960, 182.
62. Hans Carossa, *Führung und Geleit*, Leipzig, 1936, 105-106.
63. Rilke, II, 352.
64. Ibid., 411.
65. Hölderlin, *Große Stuttgarter Ausgabe*, II, 210.
66. Rilke, VI, 1,114.
67. Heller, *The Disinherited Mind*: see the essay on 'Nietzsche and Rilke'.
68. Rilke, II, 86-92.
69. Stefan George, *Das neue Reich*, 30.
70. Rilke, I, 697.
71. Ibid, II, 246.
72. Ibid., 209.
73. *Briefe aus Muzot (1921–1926)*, Leipzig, 1937, 114.
74. Rilke, I, 711.
75. Ibid., 718.
76. Gottfried Benn, *Gesammelte Werke in 8 Bänden*, Wiesbaden, 1960, I, 25.
77. Rilke, I, 701.
78. Ibid., 732.
79. Ibid., 738.
80. Ibid., 754.
81. Ibid., 759.
82. Ibid., II, 157.

83.   Ibid., 150.
84.   Georg Trakl, *Dichtungen und Briefe*, I, 88.
85.   Ibid., 104.
86.   Ibid., 138.
87.   Walter Sokel, *The Writer in Extremis*, Stanford, 1959, 46-49.
88.   Fritz Mauthner, *Erinnerungen, I*, Munich, 1918, 51.
89.   Kafka, *Gesammelte Werke. Briefe, 1902–1924*, 1968, 10.
90.   Quoted *Kafka Symposium*, Munich, 1965, 7.
91.   Politzer, *Franz Kafka. Parable and Paradox*, New York, 1966, 24.
92.   Kafka, *Briefe*, 28.
93.   Kafka, *Gesammelte Werke. Tagebücher 1910–1923*, 294.
94.   Kafka, *Erzählungen und kleine Prosa*, Berlin, 1935, 56.
95.   *Briefe an Felice*, 396-397.
96.   Quoted Pasley, *Franz Kafka. Der Heizer. In der Strafkolonie. Der Bau*, Cambridge, 1966, 22.
97.   Ibid., 15.
98.   *Tagebücher*, 420.
99.   Quoted in K. Wagenbach, *Kafka in Selbstzeugnissen und Bilddokumenten*, Reinbek, 1964, 143.
100. *Tagebücher*, 420.
101. Elias Canetti, *Der andere Prozeß*, Munich, 1969, 68.
102. *Hochzeitsvorbereitungen auf dem Lande* (ed. Brod), 1966, 45.
103. Pasley, *Franz Kafka, Short Stories*, Oxford, 1963, 14.
104. *Tagebücher*, 534.
105. See *Franz Kafka* (ed. Gray), Englewood Cliffs, 1962, 97.
106. Kafka, *Erzählungen und kleine Prosa*, 242-243.
107. Martin Swales, *Arthur Schnitzler. A critical study*, Oxford, 1971, 153-154.

6 THE PROBLEM OF EXPRESSIONISM

The quotation from *Der Mann ohne Eigenschaften,* with which this book opened, ironically described the confusion of different artistic styles which characterised the transition from the nineteenth to the twentieth centuries. The naturalist-impressionist tendency, which concentrated upon surface realities, or social and political problems, and the aesthetic or neo-romantic attitude, which was one of flight from the world towards the creation of artificial paradises, both failed to satisfy on a profound level. The former tendency remained too close to the surface of things, and, in its emphasis on social amelioration, was felt to be stultifying and drab; the latter tendency, in its emphasis on the rarefied and the refined, became ultra-precious, decadent and jejune. The naturalist's description of social conditions gave way to the expression of a subjective vision regardless of mimesis, and the concern for human life, for man crushed by pitiless machinery and ruthless cities, became far more intense than mere social reporting; likewise the emphasis upon inner vision, and on the fertile powers of the imagination, would far exceed the symbolist cult of the soul. More vital emotions, more dynamic powers of description were extolled, as was an intense subjectivity which had no reluctance in destroying the conventional picture of reality in order that the expression be more powerful. And if distortion and aggressive expression of emotion were found in earlier works of art, then these were extolled as being forerunners of the new outlook, which was given the name 'expressionism'.

The term, derived from painting, has never been used with precision. Associated with intensity of expression is the tendency to dissolve conventional form, to abstract both colours and metaphors and use various anti-naturalist devices, and hence the word 'expressionist' was also used to describe modernist techniques in general; not unlike imagism, the word was used to denote an anti-mimetic employment of autotelic metaphors. The movement towards modern techniques, such as simultaneity, collage-effects and startling, even absurd, imagery, may have little to do with fervour and passion, but the word 'expressionist' has had to describe both phenomena. In Germany particularly the sense of revolt implied in the new movement was associated with a vitalism which often found political manifestations on both the Left and the Right; the word 'expressionist' came to be applied to a desire to alter radically the

161

meaning of art, man, and society: a spiritual regeneration was frequently adumbrated. It is no wonder that the word has been increasingly modified, qualified and rejected because of its lack of precision: to group such writers as Jakob van Hoddis (1887–1942), Franz Werfel (1890–1945), Georg Kaiser (1878–1945), and Hanns Johst (b. 1890) under this blanket term is hardly satisfactory, and when the names Carl Sternheim, Frank Wedekind and even Alfred Mombert are claimed as being 'expressionist', then the critic is inclined to make objections to its use.

A further problem concerns the applicability of the term 'expressionist' to writers not necessarily German, that is, the desirability of using the word to describe authors such as Strindberg, Dostoevski, Whitman and others who expressed with passionate intensity extreme subjective states. Playwrights such as Sorge (1892–1916) and Hasenclever (1890–1940) learned much from Strindberg's 'Stationendramen', with their pseudo-religious portrayal of purification and resurrection. Zola's letter of 14 December 1889 to Strindberg, lamenting the schematic nature of his characters, is an interesting reaction to Strindberg's rejection of naturalism and his development towards what could be called more expressionist themes, of which *To Damascus* is the finest example. Both the dramatic technique used by Strindberg (the characters as emanations of one soul) and the ultimate message (the need for self-transcendence) will later dominate the German stage: Strindberg is of great importance to any study concerning the roots of those anti-naturalistic tendencies which appeared at the turn of the century. The predilection for extreme psychic states, ecstatic or desperate, came to be identified with these tendencies and also termed expressionistic; here Dostoevski is of importance. The naturalists had admired him for his portrayal of poverty and social outcasts (particularly in *Crime and Punishment*), but the new generation extolled him as the explorer of pathological conditions, and the psychologist of crime: here Moeller van den Bruck found the perfect mouthpiece for his own reactionary pronouncements. Dostoevski's portrayal of suffering and passion, from which a spiritual rebirth might ensue, fascinated readers who had grown tired of both the mechanical nature of naturalism and of sterile aestheticism.

What might be called the rhapsodic utopianism of much German expressionist writing was already present in the work of Walt Whitman, a poet whose writing had a profound effect upon the young writers in Germany. Arno Holz's *Revolution der Lyrik* was as nothing compared with Whitman's power and force, his hymnlike grandeur which Johannes

Schlaf propagated and translated. (The dithyrambic ecstasies of
Whitman were also possibly surprisingly, hailed by a writer like Arthur
Holitscher, the model for Detlev Spinell described in chapter 3, in an
equally dithyrambic eulogy.[1]) The Belgian Emil Verhaeren was greeted
in a similar manner by Schlaf and also Stefan Zweig, who praised
particularly the collection *Les forces tumultueuses* (1902) with its
motto: 'Toute la vie est dans l'essor'. Dostoevski's *From the House of
the Dead* seems close in spirit to Whitman's 'You felons on trial in
courts'; Whitman's praise of the creative potential of the New World
also strikingly anticipates the emphasis on the modern which played
an important part in the new outlook, and would reach its extreme
climax in Marinetti's *Futurist Manifesto* of 1909, which extolled in
rhapsodic utterances the age of the machine, the destruction of museums
and art-galleries, and the need to 'murder the moonlight', the need, in
fact, to wage war on the old and the moribund.

It is obvious that the movement away from naturalism and
symbolism, towards a more intense subjectivity, and the rejection of
mimesis in favour of abstraction and distortion is a European
phenomenon: its manifestations are seen in such disparate works as
Strindberg's late plays, Dostoevski's novels, Whitman's poetry,
Marinetti's manifestoes, and in the canvases of Van Gogh and the other
French painters known as 'les fauves'. A disturbing vitalism broke to
the surface, basically apolitical, but later to be associated with an
anarchic rejection of social norms and, as an aftermath of the First
World War, tending towards radical political extremes. Vitalism and
rejection of the established order — any account of expressionism must
consider the importance of Nietzsche, whose dithyrambic ecstasies
reverberated throughout German literature during the first quarter of
the twentieth century. Gottfried Benn explained:

> Eigentlich hat alles, was meine Generation diskutierte, innerlich
> sich auseinanderdachte, man kann sagen: erlitt, man kann auch sagen:
> breittrat — alles das hatte sich bereits bei Nietzsche ausgesprochen
> und erschöpft, definitive Formulierung gefunden, alles Weitere war
> Exegese. Seine gefährliche stürmische blitzende Art, seine ruhelose
> Diktion, sein Sich-Versagen jeden Idylls, und jeden allgemeinen
> Grundes, seine Aufstellung der Triebpsychologie, des
> Konstitutionellen als Motiv, der Physiologie als Dialektik —
> 'Erkenntnis als Affekt', die ganze Psychoanalyse, der ganze
> Existentialismus, alles dies ist seine Tat. Er ist, wie sich immer
> deutlicher zeigt, der weitreichende Gigant der nachgoetheschen

Epoche.[2]

Benn here stresses the daring pathos of Nietzsche's thought, also the profundity of his psychological insights (Nietzsche, incidentally, had applauded the subtleties of Dostoevski, 'des einzigen Psychologen, anbei gesagt, von dem ich etwas zu lernen hatte'[3]); others would find, as was mentioned in chapter 4, the rhapsodic fervour of *Also sprach Zarathustra* a most powerful stimulus. The provocative imagery of this work, the often hectic emphasis on heroism, individualism, and the destruction of the moribund inspired a whole generation: the praise of creative frenzy and unbridled energy seemed to herald a new beginning, a new epoch. 'Wo ist doch der Blitz, der euch mit seiner Zunge lecke? Wo ist der Wahnsinn, mit dem ihr geimpft werden müßtet?'[4] — these utterances could not fail to enthrall. The naturalists had applauded Nietzsche's attack on bourgeois complacency, and the aesthetes had derived much from his aphorisms on art; the new generation, however, that which may be called the expressionist generation, saw in his daring apostasy and imperious gestures, his emphasis on idealism and passionate ecstasy a necessary defiance. The New Man, an ideal frequently upheld by the expressionists, often bore a striking resemblance to Zarathustra.

The inflated hyperbole of much expressionist writing may well result from an unsuccessful attempt to emulate the style of *Also sprach Zarathustra:* Nietzsche's own lapses into bathos became grossly magnified by lesser writers who strove to embrace the cosmos in their writing or to exult in an emotional pantheism in the manner of Whitman. But that which has been called expressionism is a complex mentality, and the description has to cover not only swirling rodomontade but also clipped, paratactic compression not far removed from Anglo-Saxon imagism. Certain writers expressed the fervour of their vision in language derived from Nietzsche and from the cosmic poets described in chapter 4; others reduced language to a minimum, to the limits of intelligibility to express not an outer reality, but an inner state, frequently one of foreboding, or the nonchalant acceptance of absurdity. Absurdity, together with anti-bourgeois attitudes, is not far from the surface of expressionism: both fervour and the reduction to essentials lead towards an alienation from conventionally held reality and the language of normal usage, and Dada is the ultimate consequence. Some of the worst excesses, and the boldest experiments, of expressionism are found in the lyric (although as chapter 1 had hinted, the impressionist's dissolution of reality had led the way); the bombast of Werfel and Becher (1891–1958), together with the extreme concentration of

Stramm (1874–1915) and the montage effects of van Hoddis and
Lichtenstein (1889–1914), provided the finest examples in German
of the movement's basic features. It may safely be claimed that early
expressionism (that is, the new work in the years leading up to the First
World War) was inner-directed and found in the lyric the most suitable
vehicle for expression: Stefan Zweig's influential essay 'Das neue Pathos',
first published in 1907, stressed the power of the lyric to convey inner
states and the 'new pathos'.[5] But the theatre in Germany also broke new
ground in these years; prose fiction however took longer to break with
nineteenth-century models.

Johannes R. Becher described in the following passage the sense of
excitement and expectation prevailing in Berlin at the beginning of the
century:

> Wir waren leidenschaftlich unserer Sache ergeben, einzig und allein
> von ihr erfüllt, ja, wir waren wie Besessene. In Cafés, auf den Straßen
> und Plätzen, in den Ateliers, Tag und Nacht, waren wir 'auf dem
> Marsch', setzten uns selbst in rasante Bewegung, um das
> Unergründliche zu ergründen und um, als Dichter, Maler, Musiker
> vereint, die 'Kunst des Jahrhunderts' zu schaffen, die unvergleichliche,
> die alle Künste aller vergangenen Jahrhunderte zeitlos überragende.
> Wir – Unsere Zeit – das Zwanzigste Jahrhundert! So traten wir vor
> das Forum der Jahrhunderte hin, sie zum Wettkampf herausfordernd.
> Und – 'es ist eine Lust zu leben' – so 'heilig ergriffen' von dieser
> Lebenslust waren wir, daß wir keinen Augenblick gezögert hätten,
> uns dieses herrlichen Lebensaufgangs wegen eine Kugel durch den
> Kopf zu jagen, als Zeichen, daß wir, wenn dieses *unser* Leben uns
> nicht lebensmöglich ist, auf jedes andere 'Am-Leben-Sein'
> verzichteten.[6]

This passage is interesting in that it describes a vitalism so extreme that
it paradoxically is akin to a death-wish: the motto of Hanns Johst's
play *Der junge Mensch. Ein ekstatisches Szenarium* proclaims 'Es ist
eine rasende Wollust, jung sein und um die Verzückung des Todes
wissen',[7] thus betraying a similarly exaggerated sense of passionate
intensity which is potentially destructive at the same time. The
Nietzschean element is undeniable here, similarly a dynamic, Faustian
desire to seize all or perish in the attempt; Georg von der Vring
(1889–1968) later described the power wielded by *Faust* and *Also
sprach Zarathustra* on the young minds at this time.[8] Becher also
describes the importance of the cafés, particularly in Berlin: whereas

the older, more conservative writers would gather at the home of the publisher Samuel Fischer (Otto Flake (1880–1963) describes meeting Gerhart Hauptmann, Thomas Mann, Arthur Schnitzler and Hugo von Hofmannsthal there, as well as politicians such as Walther Rathenau[9]), the younger writers would prefer the cafés, the most important being the Café des Westens (or Café Grössenwahn), where the most influential journals *Der Sturm* (1910–1932) and *Die Aktion* (1911–1932) were founded.

Chapter 3 described the group associated with the 'Zum schwarzen Ferkel': this included Strindberg, Przybyszewski and Edvard Munch, who, in certain respects, anticipated expressionism, also Bierbaum and Hartleben, who were closer to literary *Jugendstil;* at the beginning of the century the Hart brothers moved to Berlin-Schlachtensee to form *Die neue Gemeinschaft,* an anarchist circle whose members included Erich Mühsam (1878–1934), Peter Hille (1854–1904), Gustav Landauer (1870–1919) and Else Lasker-Schüler (1876–1945). In 1909 Kurt Hiller and Erich Loewensohn founded *Der neue Club* and the 'Neopathetisches Cabaret' associated with it, and Loewensohn wrote in a letter to Frank Wedekind (24 April 1910) that this club was 'eine Vereinigung von Studenten und jungen Künstlern, die sich verschworen haben, den Blasphemien dieser Zeit nicht länger untätig zuzusehen und ihren Ekel vor allem Commishaften im Kunst- und Wissenschaftsbetrieb und ihre Bewunderung der Einzelgeister kundzutun'.[10] This manifesto was pinned to the noticeboard in the Friedrich-Wilhelm university in Berlin: a line from Hofmannsthal was also appended: 'Merkt auf! merkt auf! Die Zeit ist sonderbar'. Jakob van Hoddis – that is, Hans Davidsohn (1884–1942), – joined the group and read his poem 'Weltende' at one of the gatherings; it was published in Pfemfert's *Der Demokrat* on 11 January 1911:

Dem Bürger fliegt vom spitzen Kopf der Hut,
In allen Lüften hallt es wie Geschrei,
Dachdecker stürzen ab und gehn entzwei
Und an den Küsten – liest man – steigt die Flut.

Der Sturm ist da, die wilden Meere hupfen
An Land, um dicke Dämme zu zerdrücken.
Die meisten Menschen haben einen Schnupfen.
Die Eisenbahnen fallen von den Brücken.[11]

The collage effect, the juxtaposition and concatenation of bizarre images,

presents a picture, but above all *expresses* the poet's sense of vulnerability and disharmony in the world; formally quite conventional, it
nevertheless conveys a disturbing sense of malaise which borders on
the grotesque; the tension between regular metre and irregular vision
is most effective. (The poem may, incidentally, be an ironic reference
to the 'effect' caused by Halley's comet in May 1910,[12] but, nevertheless,
was felt to be itself prophetic of the end of 'sense' both in art and in
the bourgeois world.) With characteristic hyperbole J.R. Becher again
describes the impact that this poem made:

> Meine poetische Kraft reicht nicht aus, um die Wirkung jenes
> Gedichtes wiederherzustellen, von dem ich jetzt sprechen will. Auch
> die kühnste Phantasie meiner Leser würde ich überanstrengen bei
> dem Versuch, ihnen die Zauberhaftigkeit zu schildern, wie sie dieses
> Gedicht 'Weltende' von J. v. Hoddis für uns in sich barg. Diese zwei
> Strophen, o diese acht Zeilen schienen uns in andere Menschen
> verwandelt zu haben ... wir sangen sie, wir summten sie, wir murmelten
> sie, wir pfiffen sie vor uns hin, wir gingen mit diesen acht Zeilen auf
> den Lippen in die Kirchen, und wir saßen, sie vor uns hinflüsternd,
> mit ihnen beim Radrennen. Wir riefen sie uns gegenseitig über die
> Straße hinweg zu wie Losungen, wir saßen mit diesen acht Zeilen,
> beieinander, frierend und hungernd, und sprachen sie gegenseitig vor
> uns hin, und Hunger und Kälte waren nicht mehr.[13]

Becher's reactions to the poem may seem extreme; the impact made by
its modernity at that time must have been, however, considerable. Other
memorable evenings at the 'Neopathetisches Cabaret' included Max
Brod's reading of Franz Werfel's poetry; Georg Heym (1887–1912) was
also introduced to the Club after submitting his play *Die Hochzeit des
Bartolomeo Ruggieri*. Whereas Werfel's poetry exemplifies the
Whitmanesque, utopian-pantheist elements of expressionism, Heym's
came more and more to manifest a sense of disaster: his portrayal of the
grotesque horror of cities, and his sombre, chiliastic presentiments of
doom express a mythological awareness of human destiny. As a
student Heym had used Zarathustrian imagery in his 'Versuch einer
Religion', a longing for the disruptive chaos of elemental forces; the
desire for violence found in his diaries (and also in the Novelle *Der
fünfte Oktober)* springs from an urgent need to wipe out the moribund
and the stagnant aspects he saw in the society around him. Heym was
killed in a skating accident in 1912; the poem 'Der Krieg', to be found
in most anthologies of modern German poetry, combines a sense of

dread with a feeling of awe for that fearful god of war who arises from chthonic depths:

> Aufgestanden ist er, welcher lange schlief,
> Aufgestanden unten aus Gewölben tief.
> In der Dämmrung steht er, groß und unbekannt
> Und den Mond zerdrückt er in der schwarzen Hand.[14]

This poem exemplifies that expressionist tendency to see through the surface of things to behold a mythical, archetypal vision; Kasimir Edschmid (that is, Eduard Schmid), reading his famous essay 'Expressionismus in der Dichtung', before the *Deutsche Gesellschaft 1914* in 1917 stressed the fact that although the expressionist may take the same themes as the naturalist, there is a vast difference between the two methods of description: 'So wird der Raum des expressionistischen Künstlers Vision. Er sieht nicht, er schaut. Er schildert nicht, er erlebt. Er gibt nicht wieder, er gestaltet. Er nimmt nicht, er sucht. Nun gibt es nicht mehr die Kette der Tatsachen: Fabriken, Häuser, Krankheit, Huren, Geschrei und Hunger. Nun gibt es die Vision davon'.[15]

The group which gathered at Herwarth Walden's table in the Café des Westens formed *Der Sturm,* a periodical at the very centre of the expressionist development. Walden (1878–1941) had been dismissed from the journals *Das Theater* and *Der neue Weg* for his radical views, and seeing the need for a reorientation of thought and language he formed his own journal: Else Lasker-Schüler suggested the title. The avant-garde of Berlin and elsewhere flocked to Walden: Alfred Döblin (1878–1957), Carl Einstein and Mynona (Salomon Friedländer) contributed, as did August Stramm, who sought to reduce language and syntax to an absolute minimum. For Walden Stramm's work seemed to provide the literary equivalent of futurist and cubist paintings: subjective, inner states are expressed in a form of words which approximate to an abstract picture, where neologisms intensify the sense of alienation from conventional descriptive poetry. The poem 'Sturmangriff' is a good example of his work:

> Aus allen Winkeln gellen Fürchte Wollen
> Kreisch
> Peitscht
> Das Leben
> Vor

Sich
Her
Den keuchen Tod
Die Himmel fetzen.
Blinde schlächtert wildum das Entsetzen.[16]

In spite of the extreme compression of this poem there is nothing static, as there is in much imagist work: each word is charged with an intense energy which contains a latent explosiveness. In his need to convey absolute essences Stramm rejects adjectives and visual images (there is only one in the above poem) in favour of verbs and nouns juxtaposed in a staccato pattern. Stramm's plays likewise reduce utterance to dramatic essentials; at the end of 1913 Stramm sent Walden his *Sancta Susanna,* which received its first performance at the *Sturm-Bühne* in October 1918. Walden also arranged a memorial evening for Stramm, who was killed on the Russian front, one year after his death, on 1 September 1916. (Stramm's letters from the front show that other side to expressionism, a mysticism which merges into a pantheistic vision of oneness.)

Walden's rival in Berlin was Franz Pfemfert, who started publishing *Die Aktion* in 1911. Pfemfert had first published in the literary-anarchist journal *Kampf,* founded and edited by Senna Hoy (Johannes Holzmann): he went on to edit *Der Demokrat* before launching *Die Aktion.* His circle included Kurt Hiller (1885–1973), Ludwig Rubiner (1881–1920), Gustav Landauer, Carl Sternheim and Alfred Lichtenstein: his approach was more pragmatic than Walden's, and his political objections were more sharply defined (Walden's interest in Communism was a comparatively late development). Pfemfert fought for the release of Otto Gross, the admirer of Freud who had been committed to a mental home by his father: he was frequently in touch with Karl Liebknecht and Rosa Luxemburg and sought to identify himself with the radical Left far earlier than did Walden. In 1916 Pfemfert launched his 'Aktions-Bücher der Aeternisten', whose first spokesman, Ferdinand Hardekopf (Stefan Wronski) proclaimed the overtly anti-bourgeois attitudes and extolled the extremist, anti-traditional forms of art:

Hier wird, auf einem Kap, Extremes geformt. Unsere Bücher werden euch unfaßlich sein, Bürger . . . Durchwühlt haben wir die Eingeweide der Millionenstädte und phosphoreszierender Seelen . . . In uns ist alle Vergangenheit Gegenwart Zukunft . . . Unsere Psychologie wird euch skandalisieren. Unsere Syntax wird euch asphyxiieren. Wir werden eure großen Konfusionen belächeln, abstrakt und augurisch.

Erhabene Konjunktive werden zerstäuben, Futura exacta
narkotisch verdampfen, und je-m'enfichistisch zergehen schaumige
Duftbälle von Quintessenz . . .[17]

Pfemfert also planned a private theatre, based on Walden's *Sturm-Bühne,*
to produce the most recent plays, but the plan was not realised.

Other important Berlin journals included Alfred Richard Meyer's
Lyrische Flugblätter and *Die Bücherei Maiandros:* his most important
publication was Gottfried Benn's *Morgue und andere Gedichte* (1912).
Benn (1886–1956), a military doctor, recalled the course in dissection
he had undertaken in the Berlin Moabit hospital, and the *Morgue* poems
shocked by their nonchalant cynicism, for here was no poeticising of
death such as the young Rilke indulged in, but a clinical awareness of
disease and anonymous dying. 'Schöne Jugend' is a flippant variation on
the Ophelia theme, but there is nothing pre-Raphaelite about the nest
of rats beneath the diaphragm: 'Kreislauf' gives an amusing deviation from
the theme of 'dust to dust'. A poet such as Ernst Stadler (1883–1914)
spoke highly of Benn's poems in his *Cahiers Alsaciens* (1912): the
worthy anonymous reviewer of the *Augsburger Abendzeitung,* however,
reacted with horror and disgust, and doubtless voiced the opinions of
the middle-class reading public: 'Pfui Teufel! Welch eine zügellose, von
jeglicher Herrschaft geistiger Sauberkeit bare Phantasie entblößt sich
da: welche abstoßende Lust am abgründig Häßlichen, welches hämische
Vergnügen, Dinge, die nun einmal nicht zu ändern sind, ans Licht zu
ziehen'.[18] After the publication of the *Morgue* poems Benn's work
appeared in the *Sturm* as well as the *Aktion* and the *Weiße Blätter,*
edited by René Schickele (1883–1940), which appeared in 1913 in
Leipzig and during the war transferred to Switzerland. In 1914 Benn
published in Schickele's journal his *Ithaka,* a short sketch which
extolled youth, myth and violence as opposed to petrified academic
pedantry; this anticipates Benn's later preoccupation with atavistic
mythologies and 'thinking with the blood'. Before the First World War
Benn was very much part of the expressionist activity in Berlin;
admired by both Sternheim and Stadler, as well as being a military
doctor, he was a keen observer of the new tendencies in the arts. In the
same year as the *Morgue* poems Pfemfert published in instalments Carl
Einstein's *Bebuquin oder die Dilettanten des Wunders,* and Benn
greatly admired the 'absolute prose' of Einstein's novel, a concept which,
together with that of the absolute poem, would come to preoccupy
him.

Mention has been made of Ernst Stadler, a poet whose work perfectly exemplifies the movement away from neo-romantic and *Jugendstil* elements towards what may be called predominantly expressionist poetry. The collection *Praeludien* (1904) is clearly indebted to Hofmannsthal, with many references to 'Abendgold', 'Schönheit' and 'Zauber': 'Freundinnen' is dedicated to that poet, but the perverse nature of the love described inevitably brings George to mind. Yet the poem 'Incipit vita nova' rejects sterile aestheticism in favour of something eternal and natural, remote from 'den smaragdenen Grüften . . . den betörenden Düften';[19] the poem 'Der Zug ins Leben' portrays a Dionysian intoxication with life in topoi derived from Dehmel, but also betrays a vitalist involvement in life more in tune with the expressionist mentality. Stadler's review of Heym's *Der ewige Tag* and *Umbra Vitae* made him aware that the time of the 'Wiener Kulturlyrik' was passed, and that a more positive, affirmative, expressive form of poetry was necessary to convey the 'new pathos'. Kurt Hiller's anthology of early expressionist verse, *Der Kondor,* met with his full approval: it was Gottfried Benn, Stadler acknowledged, who had finally dispatched the 'Blaublümeleinritter' and boldly presented something new and startling with profundity and precision. Most striking in its Nietzschean terminology is Stadler's contribution to the journal *Neuland,* which conveys a rejection of the past in an uncompromisingly iconoclastic fashion: 'Und dies sei fortan das höchste Ziel des Künstlers, vom Bestehenden zu sagen: "Es war" und darüber hinwegzuschreiten zu dem Neuen. Und dies sei euer Gesetz, ihr Künstler und Dichter: nicht länger "rückwärts schauende Propheten" zu sein. Seht vorwärts! Seht in Morgensonnen! Zerschmettert die alten Tafeln und schreibt euch euer eigen Gesetz aus eurem Eigen-Willen!'[20] The late poem 'Leoncita' continues the praise of energy and vital powers, and portrays the 'wild beast' which will destroy utterly the jejune and the lacklustre:

> Auf! Reiße dich empor! Die Barrikade steht!
> Der Himmel ist von tausend Freiheitsfackeln aufgehellt —
> Brich aus, Raubtier,
> Stürme an ihren erstarrten Reihen,
> Aufgerissnen Mäulern, schreckerstickten Schreien
> Vorbei
> In deine Welt!
> Brich aus, Raubtier!
> Brich aus![21]

In 1913 Kurt Wolff published Stadler's mature work in the 'Verlag der

weißen Blätter'; the title Stadler gave to it, *Der Aufbruch,* shows that
the world of the *Praeludien* has been left far behind. The famous 'Form
ist Wollust' contains *in nucleo* the expressionist desire to burst the
bonds of social convention and reach out in a universal embrace; it is
interesting that *formally* the poem is quite conventional (as, in fact,
were many of the poems included by Kurt Pinthus in his anthology
Menschheitsdämmerung[22]). Stadler's excellent craftsmanship is
apparent in this poem, as also in his masterly 'Fahrt über die Kölner
Rheinbrücke bei Nacht', which preserves the dynamic sweep of the
poem from formlessness. Rhymes are used, albeit delayed ones, and the
ecstatic acceptance of 'Wollust', 'Gebet', 'Meer' and 'Untergang', the
symbolic extension of the night journey itself, is held in a taut and
quivering bow. Similarly the poem 'Anrede', with its Nietzschean
imagery (flame, thirst, scream and fire) does not become bathetic, as it
might easily have done in the hands of a lesser poet: the excesses of
J.R. Becher are not to be found in Stadler, whose poem 'Der Spruch'
contains the injunction very dear to the heart of the expressionist
generation, the motto from Angelus Silesius: 'Mensch, werde
wesentlich!' (The Silesian poet was also quoted by Georg Simmel in
his *Der Konflikt der modernen Seele;* Simmel's lecture on 'Deutschlands
innere Wandlung', delivered in Stadler's home town of Strasbourg in
November 1914, shortly after his death at Ypres, prophesied a New Man
with vitalistic, mystical qualities.) Had Stadler lived he would doubtless
have joined those expressionists who hailed this new and transfigured
image of man, but the Nietzschean accents would certainly have been
tempered by his experiences amongst the poor in the East End of
London, and with a Werfel-like desire for communion with all.

Franz Werfel, born in Prague, that 'Retortenexperiment moderner
Entfremdung',[23] faced similar problems to those which Franz Kafka
experienced. As a German and as a Jew the sense of isolation, of
alienation from the surrounding culture, was acute, and the need to
break through to a passionate, universal awareness of community and
brotherhood most keenly felt. The cosmic symbolism of the Czech poet
Otokar Březina (Václav Ignác Jebavý), who was one of Alfred
Mombert's associates, together with the social themes presented in the
poetry of Petr Bezruč (Vladimír Vasek) – particularly the *Slezské
cislo* of 1903, with its fervent portrayal of the plight of the miners and
peasants in the Beskids – quickened Werfel's social awareness; Rilke's
pantheistic cult of 'die Dinge', his Franciscanism and quietism also
played a part in moulding Werfel's poetic premisses. The sultry
decadence of Paul Leppin (1878–1941) and the weird mysticism of

Jewish Prague could not satisfy Werfel, neither could the 'Indifferentismus' of Max Brod's *Schloß Nornepygge*. And yet Brod's hero, in his alienation and his cosmic, impersonal stance is not entirely remote from Werfel's position; before his death Walder Nornepygge envisages a dissolution into the cosmos in a manner which certain expressionists could condone:

Ja ich bin die eifrige selbstlose sehnsüchtige Kälte, die Kälte voll Glut und Lebensdrang, das, was es noch nie gegeben hat . . . die All-Liebe, die All-Bewunderung . . . Dinge der Welt, kommt nur, kommt an mein Herz. Willkommen, tausendmal willkommen . . . Ein Strahlenkranz umgibt mich, die Visionen in Haufen, Sternennebel, Milchstraßen . . . In meinen Augen kreisen Sonnensysteme. Ich bin das Weltall . . . das Weltall.[24]

The influence of Whitman, later acknowledged by Werfel in America, is also undeniable; Dostoevski and Nietzsche also play their part. But fervour and sincerity do not necessarily produce great poetry: the 'prophetischen Umarmungsrufen' with the 'weltlichen Hosiannas und den Cafégeiger-Gebärden' criticised by Edschmid,[25] and the attack launched by Karl Kraus are not entirely without justification. But the appearance of *Der Weltfreund* towards the end of 1911 (and Max Brod's reading of 'An den Leser') made an enormous impact: the four thousand copies of the first edition were sold within a matter of weeks, and Werfel's success was such that it was frequently claimed that the expressionist movement began with him and with these poems.

'An den Leser', the last poem of the collection, frequently appears in collections of expressionist verse, representing, as it does, the declamatory, rhetorical aspect of that movement. Walder Nornepygge had greeted the 'Dandys, Knopfagenten, Bergwerksbesitzer, Sozialistenführer, Beamten, Abenteurer, Tramwaykondukteure, Hochstapler, Familienväter, Redakteure, Rentner, Spiritisten, Markensammler, Errichter von Arbeiterwohnhäusern, Gewürzkrämer, Friedenker, Klerikale, Vereinsvorstände, Alpinisten, Wagnerianer, Bohémiens, Bakteriologen, Buzeranten . . .'[26] with a bemused detachment; Werfel, however, is more intense in his desire for involvement:

Mein einziger Wunsch ist, Dir, o Mensch, verwandt zu sein!
Bist Du Neger, Akrobat, oder ruhst Du noch in tiefer Mutterhut,
Klingt Dein Mädchenlied über den Hof, lenkst Du Dein Floß im

Abendschein,
Bist Du Soldat oder Aviatiker voll Ausdauer und Mut . . .

Ich lebte im Walde, hatte ein Bahnhofsamt,
Saß gebeugt über Kassabücher und bediente ungeduldige Gäste.
Als Heizer stand ich vor Kesseln, das Antlitz grell überflammt,
Und als Kuli aß ich Abfall und Küchenreste.

So gehöre ich Dir und allen!
Wollt mir, bitte, nicht widerstehn!
O, könnte es einmal geschehn,
Das wir uns, Bruder, in die Arme fallen![27]

It is difficult not to think of Whitman here, particularly his 'Salut au
Monde!' from the *Leaves of Grass,* which Johannes Schlaf emulated in
'Frühling' and had met with Dehmel's enthusiastic praise. The grotesque
sonnet 'Pompe funèbre' in the second part of *Der Weltfreund* is
reminiscent of Heym (between October 1910 and May 1911 Werfel was
in Berlin, and Heym's contacts with the New Club have already been
mentioned), while 'Schmerz, Erzeuger Du der Gefühle und Urgott'
seems to derive from Klopstock. The attempt at sublimity is most marked
in Werfel's second collection of poems, entitled *Wir sind,* whose ecstatic
tone is difficult to respond to at length. The 'O Mensch!' pathos cannot
be sustained on a high level; although Werfel's name is invariably linked
with this utterance he is not the first to essay it: Dehmel's *Zwei
Menschen* with its exclamation 'Wir Welt!' at the end of the 'Leit-lied'
is equally ecstatic. Rapturous fervour sinks all too readily into the
bathetic, especially when the poet expects a response from tables and
chairs ('Mystisch beginnen schon alle Möbel zu tönen'[28]); the obligatory
trumpets and trombones blaze forth in 'Der Feind':

Nun braust der Himmel als Posaunenmeer,
Triumphtrompeten schnellen drunterher.
Aus mir stürzt Liebe, Lieb', Weltsinn, der dunkel lag.
Und golden durch mich donnert jüngster Tag![29]

Kafka's references in his diary (23 December 1911) to the effects of
reading too much of Werfel's poetry are perceptive: 'Durch Werfels
Gedichte hatte ich in den ganzen gestrigen Vormittag den Kopf wie von
Dampf erfüllt'[30]: the clouds of cosmic steam, emanating from
somewhere half-way between cosmos and coffee-house generate dense

obfuscation. The third collection, *Einander*, does, however, contain two of Werfel's most successful poems, 'Lächeln Atmen Schreiten', with its debt to Lao-tse, and 'Veni creator spiritus', a variation on the famous medieval hymn which Mahler had already used in his Eighth Symphony, first performed in Munich in 1910.

It is, however, not Werfel, but Johannes R. Becher who is guilty of the worst excess and lapses of taste in his poetry, a descent into abysmal bathos and a flight into grotesque hyperbole. For Becher it was tumult and cacophony that are the poet's milieu, and disruption is his task:

> Der Dichter meidet strahlende Akkorde.
> Er stößt durch Tuben, peitscht die Trommel schrill.
> Er reißt das Volk auf mit gehackten Sätzen.[31]

For Becher, future Minister of Culture in the German Democratic Republic, political commitment was indispensable; this would seem to result in the complete abnegation of critical acumen. The turbulence of 'Mensch stehe auf' can indeed be called farcical:

> Verfluchtes Jahrhundert! Chaotisch! Gesanglos! Ausgehängt du
> Mensch, magerster der Köder, zwischen Qual Nebel-Wahn Blitz.
> Geblendet. Ein Knecht. Durchfurcht. Tobsüchtig. Aussatz und Säure.
> Mit entzündetem Aug. Tollwut im Eckzahn. Pfeifenden Fieberhorns.
> Aber
> Über dem Kreuz im Genick wogt mild unendlicher Äther.
> Heraus aus Gräben Betrieben Asylen Kloaken, der höllischen
>   Spelunke!
> Sonnen-Chöre rufen hymnisch auf die Höhlen-Blinden.
> Und
> Über der blutigen Untiefe der Schlachtengewässer
> Sprüht ewig unwandelbar Gottes magischer Stern.[32]

The 'Hymne an Rosa Luxemburg' represents, however, the most extreme depths of pretentious absurdity into which expressionistic rapture can collapse: after such earnest ecstasy the nihilistic antics of the Dadaists are welcome indeed:

> Notschrei Jeremias
> Ekstatischer Auftakt
> Gewitter-Sätze versammelt in dir.

Blanke unschuldsvolle
Reine jungfrauweiße
Taube Glaubens-Saft
Ob Tribünen-Altar schwebend Hostie hoch . . .
Durch die Welten rase ich —:
Den geschundenen Leib
Abnehmend vom Kreuz,
In weichste Linnen ihn hüllend
Triumph dir durch die Welten blase ich:
Dir, Einzige!! Die, Heilige!! O Weib!!![33]

To subsume the collage-effects of a van Hoddis poem and the hymnic
fervour of Werfel and Becher under the heading 'expressionist verse'
is perhaps unsatisfactory: discussions concerning the use of abstract
metaphor, autotelic images, simultaneity and parataxis are relevant
to certain areas yet are inapplicable to others. The broadest common
denominator would seem to be the desire to express a subjective
insight, whether it be in terse, urban images or in rhapsodic, cosmic
metaphors. Van Hoddis and Lichtenstein convey an almost flippant
sense of urban malaise, bordering on the bizarre, in poems whose
syntactical compression represent one pole of the movement; the
vision with Heym is mythological and frequently eschatological; with
Stadler it is vitalistic yet also humane. The desire to express from
within, regardless of mimesis, is the most characteristic urge of the
times, and the lyric provides the most appropriate art-form for an
intense, and often bizarre, expressiveness.

The links between the arts at this time are a fascinating source of study:
as well as being an important innovator in painting, Kandinsky (1866–
1944) also wrote poems and 'abstract plays'. *Der gelbe Klang* is a work
written for music, speech, dance and coloured lights, and *Violett* is
a study in synaesthesia similar to the experiments of Scriabin, a
composer whose work was discussed in the almanac of *Der blaue
Reiter*, the Munich school of painters of whom Kandinsky was the
mouthpiece. The music of Schönberg was also admired by
Kandinsky who included three of Schönberg's paintings in
the first *Blauer Reiter* exhibition, and devoted a large part
of the almanac to his ideas, including his essay *Das Verhältnis
zum Text* and also the score of his 'Herzgewächsse' song. Kandinsky
had read a pre-publication extract from Schönberg's *Harmonielehre*
whilst writing his own *Über das Geistige in der Kunst*, a work of
seminal importance for any study of expressionism. Both Schönberg

and Kandinsky were developing upon similar lines, insisting on the need for an *inner necessity*, and for all the arts to progress towards the abstract status of music, which relates to nothing outside itself, but is pure expression. Kandinsky's work particularly had a receptive audience at this time: 'Blind gegen "erkannte" oder "unerkannte" Form, taub gegen Lehren und Wünsche der Zeit soll der Künstler sein. Sein offenes Auge soll auf sein inneres Leben gerichtet werden und sein Ohr soll dem Munde der inneren Notwendgkeit stets gerichtet sein . . . Dieses ist der einzige Weg, das Mystischnotwendige zum Ausdruck zu bringen'.[34] Another important essay dating from this time which, in fact, predates Kandinsky, is Wilhelm Worringer's *Abstraktion und Einfühlung* (1908), which explored the movement in the arts away from realism and representation towards the non-naturalistic and the abstract, the art, in fact, of expressionism, where subjective vision (or *Geist*) abstracted itself from nature and created in a purely autonomous manner. Worringer detected that the new art emerged in a time of crisis, where the mind, no longer at home in the inherited world, imposes its own will upon phenomena in a Nietzschean act of defiance: 'Einfühlung', or sympathetic representation, gives way to 'Abstraktion' and modernism.

A discussion of modern theatrical techniques is now necessary and another painter, Oskar Kokoschka, prepared the way for a new intensity. In 1909 Herwarth Walden visited Vienna to discuss publishing a Berlin edition of Kraus's *Die Fackel*: Adolf Loos showed Walden some drawings that Kokoschka had done for his short psychodrama of violent sexual urges, *Mörder Hoffnung der Frauen*, which Kokoschka had put on a year earlier and which had led to a riot, a caution by the police and his dismissal from the *Kunstgewerbschule* at the insistence of the Ministry of Education. It was Walden who saw Kokoschka's true genius after the latter later fled Vienna and went to Berlin; *Der Sturm* benefited greatly from his work (his illustrations of *Mörder Hoffnung der Frauen* appeared on the front page in 1910). Although Kokoschka's plays do not possess the same importance in his output as those of Barlach, they are nevertheless related organically to his painting at this period and anticipate some characteristic aspects of expressionist drama. His first lyrical monologue, entitled *Die träumenden Knaben*, is a typical piece of Vienna *Secession à la* Klimt; *Mörder Hoffnung der Frauen* is a far more sombre, violent portrayal of the gulf between the sexes. (It was written in 1907, after an important Van Gogh exhibition in Vienna and a performance there of Strindberg's *Dance of Death*.) The presentation of the action is febrile and nightmarish in its intensity; the work is basically a sequence of highly charged utterances from the subconscious minds of the two antagonists, Man and Woman. There can be no talk of plot here; it is a psychodrama, predominantly irrational, full of surging and ebbing emotions, and the murderous combat between hero and heroine brings to mind Heinrich von Kleist's *Penthesilea*, with contributions by Nietzsche, Strindberg and Freud. The sexual imagery is quite transparent: the Man and his followers are 'Bestürmer verschlossener Festungen', while the Woman exults 'Mit meinen Atem erflackert die blonde Scheibe der Sonne'. Sexual images of futile, senseless 'whirling' predominate as the Man chants: 'Sinnlose Begehr von Grauen zu Grauen, unstillbares Kreisen im Leeren. Gebären ohne Geburt, Sonnensturz, wankender Raum'. And the Woman's followers proclaim: 'Der Streit ist unverständlich und dauert eine Ewigkeit'.[35] The Woman is finally killed by the Man in an outburst of furious violence. There are anticipations here of Schönberg's *Erwartung* (1909), a feverish monodrama of presentiment, fear, dread and cruel knowledge, raised to a plane of hectic exaggeration, and also of his *Die Glückliche Hand*, a less extreme work but one with a similar theme, the apparent impossibility of true communion between man and woman. Schönberg was his own librettist here, and regarded the lighting and other scenic effects to be of equal importance as the music. (He also planned to have the short opera filmed with Kokoschka and Kandinsky as designers and with a colour organ to provide the music and the play of coloured lights *à la* Scriabin.) Other works which push hectic musical expressiveness to an unheard-of intensity, and which are also preoccupied with the expression of psychic disturbance and sexual violence are Alban Berg's *Wozzeck* and his *Lulu*, works which did not appear until the 1920s and 1930s but which had fascinated Berg for many years. He had seen Wedekind's *Die Büchse der Pandora* in 1905: that same year saw Richard Strauss's *Salome* in Dresden, followed four years later by *Elektra*, an unparalleled musical portrayal of frenzy, hysteria and obsession.

Kokoschka's *Sphinx und Strohmann* is a diverting curiosum, written in the same year as *Mörder Hoffnung der Frauen*, but which anticipates the Dadaist antics of the war years and was, in fact, staged by them in 1917: the fears of Strindberg's captain in *The Dance of Death* are transposed here into the absurd. On a far profounder level Kokoschka's illustration of Bach's Cantata *O Ewigkeit, du Donnerwort* shows once more his obsession with the gulf between antithetical powers, without hope of harmony or reconciliation. The gulf is still evident in the famous painting *Die Windsbraut* of 1914; there is once more the whirling turmoil, the woman and man who lie close, yet separated by immeasurable distances, the woman serene, the man tense, pre-occupied and remote. Georg Trakl saw and admired this canvas; he resorted to the mystical notion of androgyny in certain of his poems to resolve the tension, but Kokoschka is unable to follow him here.

Any discussion of the problematic relationship between the sexes in early expressionist drama must needs include the name of Frank Wedekind. Julius Bab's assessment of him is without doubt the shrewdest: 'Er ist kein Künstler, der ein Werk durch Jahre und Tage bildet, aber ein tragischer Pierrot, ein Gehirnerotiker, ein mathe-matischer Phantast, der auf Augenblicke genial ist';[36] Wedekind's eccentric talent, verging at times on the grotesque, seems more appropriate to cabaret and Grand Guignol than the theatre itself. His contributions to *Simplicissmus* and, later, his appearances in the *Elf Scharfrichter* cabaret in Munich, with his scandalous and amusing ballads ('Herr von der Heydte', for example, to be sung to a guitar, suggests that *Minna von Barnhelm* be performed in the nude to avoid the charge of perversion[37]) anticipated Brecht's early poetry: 'Ich habe meine Tante geschlachtet' is a fore-runner of 'Jakob Apfelböck'. Wedekind's stance, however, is unlike Brecht's in that he is utterly asocial: his world consists of roués, outsiders, cynics, prostitutes and swindlers, all motivated by a monstrous egoism. Wedekind's attack on bourgeois morality is frequently bracketed with that of later expressionist dramatists, but his cult of vitalism has strange advocates, ranging from 'der vermummte Herr' of *Frühlings-Erwachen*, through Lulu and the Marquis von Keith to Bismarck. Obsessed by sensuality and egoism, Wedekind cannot possibly share the inflated ideals of later dramatists; Brecht, who will later denounce the hollow rhetoric of 'O Mensch Dramen' again resembles Wedekind here. But Wedekind shares with many of the expressionist dramatists a refusal to comply with naturalist canons and a predilection for the grotesque; whereas Max Halbe's *Jugend* (1893), with its psychology of adolescent love, has certain things in common with *Frühlings-Erwachen*, which appeared in book form in 1891, Wedekind's play, with the absurd names of the teachers, the headless ghost of the last act and the personification of 'life', belongs very much in the new camp. It is this play which is probably Wedekind's best: the torments and confusion of the young people, as well as the hypocrisy and pusillanimous deviousness of the older generation, are portrayed with sympathy and precision. The imagery derived from the natural world, so rare in Wedekind, anticipates that of Brecht's first play *Baal*:

Melchior's utterance 'Der Tauwind fegt über die Berge. Jetzt möchte ich droben im Wald eine junge Dryade sein, die sich die ganze lange Nacht in den höchsten Wipfeln wiegen und schaukeln läßt'[38] prefigures Baal's more powerful arboreal fantasies. Max Reinhardt produced the play in 1906 in Berlin, but the censor objected to the outspoken discussion of sexual problems and the directness of certain scenes (the torment of Melchior, for whom the whole world seemed to resolve around 'P – und V –!'[39] and the masturbatory fantasies of Hänschen Rylow in his lavatory). Wedekind's protracted battle with the censor over this and other works, and his insistence on the absolute freedom of the creative artist endeared him to the avant-garde and greatly enhanced his reputation as a *Bürgerschreck*.

Wedekind greeted the new century in prison on a charge of *lèse-majesté* after the publication (under the pseudonym 'Hieronymus Jobs') in *Simplicissimus* of his poem 'Im Heiligen Land', a lampoon on the Kaiser's visit to Jerusalem. (Th. Th. Heine, who provided the satirical drawings, was also arrested.) During his imprisonment he wrote *Mine Haha oder Über die körperliche Erziehung der jungen Mädchen*, an erotic fantasy which delighted in describing the limbs of young girls and their costumes: 'Um die schmale, schlanke Brust und feinen Schultern trug sie ein enganliegendes Netzwerk aus dicken, dunkelgrünen Glasperlen, in der Art eines Mieders, das aber ihre zarten Brüste vollkommen frei ließ, indem es beide mit großen Ringen einfaßte, deren Perlen um einiges dicker waren als die des übrigen Netzes'.[40] This short, preposterous work is of interest in that the physical is paramount: the mental, intellectual powers are ignored in the girls' establishment. The body is trained to perfection here, not for any sinister, political purpose but for pleasure and sexual accomplishment. This is the world of Effie in *Schloß Wetterstein*, but it inevitably brings to mind Wedekind's most notorious creation. His stays in Paris (1891–1892) and London (1894) sharpened his observations of the pimps, swindlers, perverts and prostitutes, as well as of the dark London streets, haunted by Jack the Ripper; the painting Bohême of Munich, the corruption of Parisian society and the sordid wretchedness of Whitechapel provided the world through which Lulu moved with disdain and a curious naiveté.

The prologue to *Erdgeist* uses a circus technique, later to be endorsed by Bert Brecht: the lion tamer, with whip and pistol, announces that he will provide the true, wild, beautiful animal, and derides the so-called 'heroes' of the German theatre. Wedekind is, in fact, attacking the art of Gerhart Hauptmann; Hauptmann's use, in

Das Friedensfest, of certain facts relating to the Wedekind household
in Zurich incensed the self-appointed *Bürgerschreck*, who also
detected a certain shallowness in the ease with which Hauptmann
wrote. (His *Die junge Welt* of 1881 is an obvious parody of
Hauptmann's work.) In contrast to Hauptmann's ineffective heroes the
lion-tamer announces that he will provide a heroine who is full of vital
energy and passion:

> Der eine Held kann keinen Schnaps vertragen,
> Der andre zweifelt, ob er richtig liebt,
> Den dritten hört ihr an der Welt verzagen,
> Fünf Akte lang hört ihr ihn sich beklagen,
> Und niemand, der den Gnadenstoß ihm gibt. –
> Das *wahre* Tier, das *wilde, schöne* Tier,
> Das – meine Damen – sehn Sie nur bei mir.[41]

Lulu is both fascinating and revolting, and personifies a type of woman
which both Strindberg and Nietzsche would have endorsed, tempting,
cunning, cruel and destructive. Yet her courage and ultimate integrity
must be admired: she remains true to herself throughout *Erdgeist* and
throughout most of *Die Büchse der Pandora*; it is only when she resorts
to prostitution that she is betraying her own integrity, and is finally
destroyed at the hands of Jack the Ripper. The men in these two plays
call her by different names – Nellie, Mignon and Eva – it is only
Schigolch (almost an anagram of 'logisch') who knows her true origins
and her destiny. In *Die Büchse der Pandora* the Countess Geschwitz
ousts Lulu from the centre of interest: her lesbianism is portrayed by
Wedekind with sympathy and compassion. This play is marred by
discursive longueurs and a tendency to exhibitionism in Wedekind,
which is seen at its most flagrant in *Die Zensur*: *Erdgeist* is more
successful in its curious mixture of Feydeau farce and Victorian
melodrama.

Wedekind never tired of describing the charlatan, the impostor, the
swindler who cynically moves through society and demonstrates his
superiority by furtive ruse and dubious method: the Parisian art-
swindler Willy Grétor (to whom *Erdgeist* is dedicated) amazed him and
inspired the *Marquis von Keith*, published in book form in 1901 with
the subtitle 'Münchner Szenen'. Wedekind himself called the play 'das
Wechselspiel zwischen einem Don Quijote des Lebensgenusses und
einem Don Quijote der Moral',[42] an interchange, that is, between
Keith and Ernst Scholz. Thomas Mann, who saw the play in Munich,

singled out the final scene between Keith and Scholz for particular
praise, that scene where Scholz, a broken man, attempts to lure Keith
into a private mental home, with obvious lack of success. Keith, after
the collapse of his enterprises, contemplates suicide, but, grinning, puts
the revolver to one side. 'Wedekind hat Größeres, Krasseres, äußerlich
Kühneres entworfen, das ist sicher. Aber in meinen Augen ist die
letzte Szene zwischen Scholz und Keith das Schrecklichste, Rührendste
und Tiefste, was dieser tiefe, gequälte Mensch geschrieben hat.'[43]
Thomas Mann's praise may seem excessive: he saw the play but once,
with Wedekind acting the part of Keith, and may have been impressed
by the performance rather than the play itself. *Der Marquis von Keith*,
with the two Lulu plays and *Frühlings-Erwachen*, has kept its place in
the standard repertoire, whereas the later plays, including *Schloß
Wetterstein* and *Franziska*, the 'female Faust', have failed; Wedekind's
talents, eccentric and one-sided, did not develop or mature, and the
'Gehirnerotiker' remains a flawed and freakish example in modern
German drama.

Thomas Mann's Wedekind essay refers to conversations with
Wedekind in which the writer Oskar Panizza and his frenzied antics
(dancing clad only in a shirt on the streets in Munich) were
discussed. Panizza, who died insane in 1921 was called by Kurt
Tucholsky 'den geistreichsten und revolutionärsten Propheten seines
Landes'.[44] In 1891 Panizza read before the *Gesellschaft* circle in
Munich his paper on *Genie und Wahnsinn*; three years later his
notorious *Das Liebeskonzil* appeared in Zurich. A storm of protest
greeted this gigantic blasphemy, and Panizza was imprisoned for one
year. Other writings include the *Psichopatia criminalis* and the five-
act tragedy *Nero* (1898): paranoia and other mental disorders clouded
much of his later work. Panizza's writing, like Wedekind's, is included
in this discussion of expressionism because of its attack against the
established order (in this case exemplified by the church) and the
grotesque hyperbole of much of the writing. *Das Liebeskonzil* tells of
Pope Alexander VI and his corrupt court, to which the devil brings
syphilis through woman; a drooling, senile God, an ineffective Jesus
and a flirtatious Mary are powerless to resist. The Pope, infected by
the devil's daughter, spreads the poison through his concubines;
cardinals and bishops and finally the whole of society becomes rotten
and putrescent. As so often before, it was Theodor Fontane who
raised his voice in defence of this new and controversial work; his
letter (12 July 1895) to Maximilian Harden calls the work a
significant one, and in a further letter (8 September 1895) Fontane

explains that any attempt to make him an orthodox believer would be enough to drive him into Panizza's camp. Panizza's work could be said to exemplify the iconoclastic tendencies associated with expressionism, but as an extreme outsider, fanatic and apostate he can scarcely be regarded as exemplary.

A name which invariably arises when the precursors of expressionist drama are considered is that of Carl Sternheim. Sternheim wrote over thirty plays, but, like Wedekind, his reputation rests largely on a handful of works written in his early years, the famous cycle *Aus dem bürgerlichen Heldenleben*. The attack against red plush, potted palms and *bric à brac* is heightened and sharpened to ruthless precision in these plays, and a satirical attack is launched against the 'juste milieu', the pusillanimous conformity of the bourgeoisie, who are unable to cast aside the weight of received ideas, jargon and attitudes provided by the press above all and the literati of the day. If Wedekind may be called the cynical moralist, then Sternheim, the 'modern Molière', is a satirist, aloof and quite merciless: that which he shares with Wedekind is the anti-naturalistic tendency, seen in the frequency with which Sternheim reduces his characters to types, and the deliberate artificiality of the language. He strove to cut through the 'genteel' in the German language, to expunge sentimentality and platitudes; the foreshortening of language and syntax is highly effective. This 'Telegrammstil' could be called an anticipation of the 'Neue Sachlichkeit' tendencies of the 1920s, but can also be called expressionist as it tends towards concentration, abstraction and extreme intensity. Synthetic curtness is much to the fore in the plays of Georg Kaiser: in Sternheim it does not have the steely quality to be found in that quintessentially expressionistic dramatist, but rather the deliberate quirkiness and unreality which alienate and yet fascinate the reader.

The deliberate flouting of Wilhelmine taboos is seen in the very title of the play *Die Hose*, whose hero, Theobald Maske, a monster of selfishness, derives advantage from the embarrassment caused when his wife loses that garment before the reigning prince. It may be appropriate here to mention the difficulties that Sternheim encountered with the censorship, for the changing of the play's title reveals Sternheim's ambiguous attitude towards his Maske. Traugott von Jagow, the Chief of Police and censor of Berlin, had closely watched the activities of Alfred Kerr and Paul Cassierer, editors of the journal *Pan*, and had banned the issue of 16 January 1910 for its publication of selections of Flaubert's diaries. Kerr had attacked Jagow

in satirical poems, and had caused much bitterness. At the end of
1910 Cassierer published *Die Hose*, which Max Reinhardt produced.
Jagow initially banned the play, but Sternheim and Cassierer invited
him to a dress rehearsal at which the actress Tilla Durieux was to
distract him by her charms and certain possibly affectionate movements. The ruse succeeded — Jagow lifted his ban on the play after
demanding a change in title; the play became *Der Riese*. The title may
be ironic, but the vitalism of Maske and his heirs is surely a positive
quality: the lodgers, pusillanimous and prurient, cut very sorry figures
indeed. Maske achieves his aims and realises his true, brutal self — that
self-interest which Sternheim called his 'Nuance'; the fight for survival
is portrayed by Sternheim not with contempt, but with undeniable
admiration. In the second play, *Der Snob*, Maske is outwitted by his
own son, who besmirches his mother's honour in his desire for social
advancement; proclaiming a French aristocrat to be his father, his
ruthless selfishness knows no bounds as he achieves that position of
eminence that Theobald Maske never dreamed of. The third play,
1913, shows the merciless battle between Christian Maske and his
own daughter Sophie: Sternheim's work here assumes political and
moral dimensions, for the ruthless battle of capitalist big business is
enacted against a world moving inexorably towards disaster. Greed and
stupidity rule triumphant: the vicious battle within the family is acted
out to the strains of Schumann's *Mondnacht*, a totally incongruous
juxtaposition of romantic 'Schwärmerei' and financial machinations.
The children, effete, or brutal, or opportunist, blindly pursue their
aims on the very edge of the abyss: Christian Maske's vital powers,
inherited by the more brutal of the children, ultimately destroy
themselves (the foppish Philip Ernst has inherited his father's
snobbishness, if nothing else). 'Nach uns Zusammenbruch! Wir sind
reif!'[45] — this is Christian Maske's final knowledge as the stage is left
in darkness, the curtains blowing in the wind.

Sternheim reveals his satirical method in the famous essay on
Molière (1917): 'Ein Dichter wie Molière ist Arzt am Leib seiner
Zeit. Des Menschen sämtliche, ihm von seinem Schöpfer gegebene
Eigenschaften blank und strahlend zu erhalten, ist ihm unabweisbare
Pflicht'.[46] Similarities to Molière are indisputable (*Der Snob* and
Tartuffe, Die Kassette and *L'Avare*, for instance); the pose of the
dandy, in which Sternheim indulged, brings Oscar Wilde to mind, and
his castle and liveried servants show an aloofness hardly commensurate
with the view of Sternheim as a champion of the Left. There is no
expressionist fervour in his work: can Count Ago von Bohna, the

aristocrat-cum-communist of *Das Fossil* be the 'New Man' so dear to many expressionist dramatists? In November 1918 Sternheim launched an attack in *Die Aktion* (and later in book form under the title *Berlin oder Juste Milieu*) against the military machine which had wrought such havoc in Germany, but also against the Social Democrats and Communists themselves. Thoroughly non-aligned, and basically remote from any such ideals as brotherhood or Utopia, Sternheim remains an outsider whose position is ambiguous and whose 'comedy of manners' is unique in German literature.

It is time to leave the outsiders and look at those remarkable works which appeared on the German stage immediately preceding and during the First World War and which portray, with increasing violence, the emergence of a new type of man. This vision will later become fused with a Utopian ideal, but in the plays of Hasenclever, Johst, Sorge and Kornfeld is found a desire for self-expression and vital release which must stem from Nietzsche rather than from any other source. If it was the problem of sex which loomed large in Wedekind and Kokoschka, then the theme of the conflict between father and son becomes now of prime importance. The younger German playwrights, between 1900 and the war years, portrayed with incredible intensity and violence the clash between generations, where incest and murder played a significant role. The father-figure becomes a symbol for authority in many of these plays, and the rebellion against this image reached febrile and strident proportions. Reinhard Sorge's work is a perfect example of ecstatic expressionism: fascinated by Nietzsche, he composed his own *Zarathustra* in 1911, in which the writer arrogated to himself the right to create and destroy at will. He shoots an invalid, yet a vision of Nietzsche appears before him and utters a gnomic pronouncement: 'Du hast töricht getan, Fremder, aber nun nicht auch gut? Sieh selbst zu!'[47] *Der Antichrist*, which dates from the same year, attempts a fusion of Zarathustra and Christ, a union which fascinated so many German minds at this time, and is even attempted by the eponymous hero of Josef Goebbels's novel *Michael*. But Sorge's most famous work is his *Der Bettler*, published in 1912 and performed five years later; the protagonist is a poet, an incarnation of pure feeling, who pioneers a new drama which will sweep away outmoded conventions and bring spiritual illumination to the masses. The poet strides through various stations and experiences, including the murder of his father: the conflict between father and son is here caused by the former's insanity and monstrous astronomical-technological visions ('Der ganze Mars brannte sich förmlich in mein Gehirn ein. Und mein Gehirn war wie eine riesige Spinne, die den Mars umklammerte, und denn tauchte sie ihren Rüssel in ihn, einen spitzen Stachel, und sog ihm seine Geheimnisse aus . . .'[48]). The scientific interpretation of life, of which the father's insane vision is somehow an inevitable climax, is rejected and superseded by the struggle towards spiritual regeneration; the poet finally reaches an awareness, ecstatic and yet desperate, of the meaning of his life, his love and his mission:

> Laß sinnen . . . sinnen . . . (Jäh empor, mit Händen aufwärts)
>   O Trost des
> Blitzes . . . Erleuchtung . . . Schwerttrost des Blitzes . . .
> *Symbole der Ewigkeit . . .*
> Ende! Ende! Ziel und Ende! . . .
> *Durch Symbole der Ewigkeit zu reden* . . .[49]

The form of this play owes much to Strindberg: the characters are nameless, the scene with the pilots and the prostitutes verges on a grotesque nightmare. The chorus-like chanting, the harsh spotlighting and grouping of characters deliberately stresses the movement away from naturalism towards the expression of a fervent, if somewhat confused, ideal. Sorge's publisher, S. Fischer, showed no interest in Sorge's mystical works written after *Der Bettler* (*Werden der Seele*, *Metanoete* and *Mystische Zwiesprache*); he prepared himself for the priesthood, but was killed at the battle of the Somme in 1916.

But the play which became the central expression of revolt in the theatre was Hasenclever's *Der Sohn*, written after Sorge's play but performed one year earlier in the Deutsches Landestheater in Prague. Hasenclever's play is constructed formally along traditional lines, but the mixture of dramatic prose and blank verse reflects an intensely held vision, an emphasis upon fervour and hyperbole. Again the characters are not named: there is the Son, who is tyrannised by the Father, the Friend, who lures him into life, and the Governess who watches his revolt with trepidation and hope. 'Man lebt ja nur in der Ekstase, die Wirklichkeit würde einen verlegen machen!'[50] cries the young man, full of Nietzschean ecstasy and Faustian desires; rescued by his friends (to the strains of Beethoven's Ninth Symphony) he joins a revolutionary organisation demanding the death of fathers, the brutilisation of the ego and a Dionysian frenzy. The Friend gives him a revolver to commit parricide: the final confrontation between father and son is one of extreme tension, but the actual murder is pre-empted by the father's heart attack. In another play, however, *Vatermord* by Arnolt Bronnen (1895–1959), written in 1915 and performed in uproar in 1922, the act of murder is perpetrated in a paroxysm of hatred; the son kills his father yet also rejects the incestuous advances of the mother. Violence and sexual bestiality prevail in Bronnen's work at this time: his *Die Exzesse* (1923) contains the notorious scene where the woman, Hildegard, embraces a goat in place of her lover. A play by Alfred Brust, *Die Wölfe* (1921), culminates in the longings of a parson's wife to be raped by a wolf before the dreadful act itself is committed; the work of Hans Henny Jahnn (1894–1959), dating from the same time, contains similar fantasies, which result from the dichotomy between matter and spirit (Pastor Ephraim Magnus, in the play of the same name, which was adapted by Brecht and produced by Bronnen in 1923, undergoes castration and crucifixion). Further violence is rife in Paul Kornfeld's play *Die Verführung* which was written in 1913 and shows, in exalted prose, how the rebellious young man murders a man he has never met before, simply because he seems to embody the oppressive spirit of the age. The intensity of revolt is also found in Hanns Johst's play *Der junge Mensch. Ein ekstatisches Szenarium*, with the motto which has already been quoted. Much influenced by Hasenclever's play is Anton Wildgans's *Dies Irae* (1918) which culminates in the suicide of the young hero, whose fatal conflict with his father finally destroys his life; Act 5, the 'Actus quintus fantasticus', consists of a 'chorus puerorum et adolescentum' where a Friend, the 'choragetes', summons the father to a final judgement. The hymn-like rapture comes to a frenzied climax: 'O, die den Menschen zeugen/Nicht um des *Menschen* willen,/Ihrer die Schuld!!/ Weh! Weh! Weh!'; the 'vox patris e tenebris infimis' proclaims 'Posaunen! – Posaunen – Posaunen!' and 'voces apokalypticae de coelis cantantes' declaim the 'Dies irae'.[51]

In so many of these plays the father represents authority, discipline and order, an order which is stultifying and ultimately destructive, for it stifles the passionate life of the young man who longs to burst forth in an act of self-affirmation. Criticism of parental authority implied also criticism of military academies and educational establishments: Gottfried Benn's short play *Ithaka* has already been mentioned, which reaches its climax where the students, sick of pedantry, seize the professor, beat him about the head and proclaim: 'Wir wollen den Traum. Wir wollen den Rausch. Wir rufen Dionysos und Ithaka!'[52] But the revolt portrayed in so many of these works has virtually no constructive motives: it is pure self-expression. This fervent desire for life is not far removed from an intoxication with death, for vitalism is not necessarily a sign of health, but can spring from deep uncertainty, even neuroses. There is an undeniable atavism about much of this attitude, a primitivism and a dangerous instability which was to become increasingly apparent in German history. (Kafka's contention, à propos a discussion of Hasenclever's *Der Sohn*, that the father-son conflict should be treated as comedy as Synge had done in *The Playboy of the Western World*[53] comes like a breath of sanity; his views on such writers as Ehrenstein (1886–1950) and Becher are similarly down to earth and pertinent.) As well as irrational violence and sexuality there is also in many of the works of this time an atmosphere of religious fervour, seen for example at the end of *Dies Irae* and also in Kornfeld's *Himmel und Hölle*, an operatic drama where the temptations of nihilism are overcome by a vision of love and self-sacrifice for humanity. An element of mysticism emerges, which characterises those aspects of expressionism which derive from the need for subjectivity and vision; this religious quality is seen at its purest in the plays of Ernst Barlach referred to in chapter 4. *Der tote Tag* is of interest in that the Father-principle is divine, and it is the mother who must be rejected; Ernst Weiss's novel *Der Aristokrat* is also unusual in its portrayal of the great love between father and son.

An unusually prescient play is *Der Krieg*, by Carl Hauptmann (1858–1921), written in 1913: it contains many anti-naturalist devices, visionary and grotesque elements and the typically expressionist themes of the clash between the generations (Enoch Kail and his father) and the birth of the New Man out of chaos and destruction. The desire for *Blutrausch*, for total abandonment to violence and the toppling of reason is ubiquitous: the desire for *Aufbruch*, for action and change at all costs, pervaded German art and life. In the same year as the Hauptmann play the anarchist Erich Mühsam proclaimed:

> Alle Revolution ist aktiv, singulär, plötzlich und ihre Ursachen entwurzelnd . . . Einige Formen der Revolution: Tyrannenmord, Absetzung einer Herrschergestalt, Etablierung einer Religion, Zerbrechen alter Tafeln (in Konvention und Kunst), Schaffen eines Kunstwerks, der Geschlechtsakt.
>
> Einige Synonyma für Revolution: Gott, Leben, Brunst, Rausch, Chaos.
>
> Laßt uns chaotisch sein![54]

This incandescent fervour had not yet achieved an overtly political direction: in 1914, however, Kurt Hiller, Alfred Wolfenstein (1883–1945) and Rudolf Kayser (1881–1964) adopted the term 'Aktivismus' to demonstrate a need for involvement in political life and a concern for social amelioration. Looking to Heinrich Mann, particularly his essays *Geist und Tat* and *Voltaire und Goethe*, they strove to give a political, left-wing orientated lead to the men of letters around them in defiance of Imperial Germany which was now at war. But the most famous German expressionist playwright, Georg Kaiser, in his vision of the New Man, preferred an Utopian, even mystical portrayal of *Aufbruch* and apocalypse, of regeneration and love. Kaiser was utterly obsessed by his task, or mission, as a dramatist: his intense energy and logical schematisation derive from a passionately-held vision – the regeneration of man. The lucid, mathematical precision of his plays contains a zealous fervour, and the staccato *Telegramm-stil* becomes the perfect tool to describe the clash of concepts and the dialectical vitality of the resolution. In 1918 he wrote of this vision:

> Gefährlich versucht die Vision: – Leidenschaft stachelt sie –
> die erstickt die Stimme, die reden soll, um gehört zu sein.
> Furchtbar schwingt dieser Kampf zwischen Schrei und Stimme.
> Im Schrei will es sich aus dem Munde reißen – Aufschrei aus
> Entsetzen und Zorn! – zur Stimme muß er herabsinken, um
> wirkend zu werden. Kühle Rede rollt leidenschaftlicher Bewegtheit
> entgegen – das Heißflüssige muß in Form starr werden! – und
> härter und kälter die Sprache, je flutend-überflutender
> Empfindung bedrängt.
> Von welcher Art ist die Vision?
> Es gibt nur eine: die von der Erneuerung des Menschen.[55]

In Kaiser the idea of social reform is only of secondary importance: a Nietzschean self-overcoming, a spiritual regeneration must be achieved before society can be changed. It is false to refer Kaiser's plays solely to the conditions prevailing in Germany during and immediately after the war, as his idealism is universally valid, but a certain relevance is undeniable. *Die Bürger von Calais* was written in 1913 and published in the following year; it is an argued condemnation of war, and received its first performance in 1917. (Between 1917 and 1923 no fewer than twenty-four plays by Kaiser were performed on the German-speaking stage.) The clash between Duguesclins, Constable of France, who demands resistance to the English, the salvation

of honour and the fight to the death, and Eustache de Saint-Pierre,
who sees that surrender and the resultant preservation of the work of
generations is far more valuable, has a fascinating dramatic impetus:
thesis and argument are rigidly controlled and the white-heat of
intellectual passion is compressed and concentrated until an intolerable
tension is achieved. Eustache de Saint-Pierre demands an absolute self-
purification, a dedication to the noblest vision — self-sacrifice and the
preservation of the city with its new harbour. Military glory, he
explains, is a worthless ideal, and he who longs for it is as debased as
the enemy: acquiescence must always be preferred to armed
resistance. Seven citizens come forward (this is Kaiser's original
alteration of the traditional account); six are needed to humiliate
themselves before the English king and sacrifice themselves. Eustache
de Saint-Pierre knows that they are not yet ready for the deed of
self-sacrifice, that they will each yearn to draw the lot which will
determine who shall be spared. He ruthlessly admonishes them to
transcend human weakness, and the final scene of act two is a strange
fusion of Christian communion and Nietzschean imperiousness:

> Seid ihr reif — für eure neue Tat? . . . Ihr buhlt um diese Tat — vor ihr
> streift ihr eure Schuhe und Gewänder ab. Sie fordert euch nackt
> und neu. Um sie klirrt kein Streit — schwillt kein Brand — gellt
> kein Schrei. An euerer Brunst und wütenden Begierde entzündet
> ihr sie nicht. Eine klare Flamme ohne Rauch brennt sie — kalt in
> ihrer Hitze — milde in ihrem Blenden. So ragt sie hinaus — so
> geht ihr den Gang — so nimmt sie euch an: — ohne Halt und ohne
> Hast — kühl und hell in euch — ihr froh ohne Rausch — ihr kühn
> ohne Taumel — ihr willig ohne Wut — ihr neue Täter der neuen
> Tat![56]

In the final act Eustache de Saint-Pierre commits suicide that he may
go on before the six into death and show the way: his father brings the
body and speaks as a prophet to the waiting citizens: 'Ich komm aus
dieser Nacht — und gehe in keine Nacht mehr. Meine Augen sind offen
— ich schließe sie nicht mehr. Meine blinden Augen sind gut, um es
nicht mehr zu verlieren: — ich habe den neuen Menschen gesehen —
in dieser Nacht ist er gerboren!'[57] The body of his son is carried into
the church and laid against the altar, so that the English king, who has
spared the lives of the six because of the birth of his son, and who
wishes to give thanks to God, must kneel before his spiritual
conqueror. The final tableau, assisted by lighting, emphasises the

Christ-like sublimity of the moral victor, showing resurrection and ascension.

Three months later, in the same year, Kaiser's most famous play, *Von morgens bis mitternachts*, was staged in Munich (it was, in fact, his thirtieth play, written in 1912, shortly before *Die Bürger von Calais*). It is this play more than any other which seems to represent the quintessence of German expressionism, and made Kaiser's name and method famous outside Germany, particularly the deliberate unreality of the play, its jerkiness, frenzy, self-laceration and almost flippant awareness of the worthlessness of life. A nameless bank-cashier passes through several stations in a process of self-exploration: he revolts against the meaninglessness of life, steals sixty thousand marks and sets off ('bricht auf') in search of frenzied excitement. The concentration is extreme: the opening scene in the bank has a deliberately mechanical quality, as though the actors were, in fact, puppets, and in each 'station' the grotesque element becomes more and more apparent. The action becomes barely causal; the cashier indulges in sensual pleasures in a scene very similar to the prostitute scene in *Der Bettler*, and with an undeniable sadism he exults in the febrile excitement of a six-day cycle race. Finally, in a Salvation Army Hall he comes to realise the worthlessness of money and hurls it amongst the audience, who madly fight for it; betrayed by the Girl he shoots himself before a crucifix, his dying words sounding like 'Ecce Homo'. He had hoped to live life to the full, but was corrupted from the start by his crime; reliance on capitalist gain was not the premise for a process of self-purification. It is obvious from the start that Kaiser does not attempt to create rounded characters of flesh and blood: psychological naturalism was of no interest to him. The characters are stripped to bare essentials, they are frequently little more than abstractions. The Salvation Army penitents seem to be emanations from the protagonist's mind as in Strindberg: the symbol of death, the skeleton in the wintry trees and also in the wires holding the chandelier, is a warning and a projection of the cashier's dread. The blasts on the trumpet which intersperse his final peroration seem to herald a last judgement.

After *Die Bürger von Calais* and *Von morgens bis mitternachts* it is the *Gas* trilogy which established Kaiser's reputation. The first part, *Die Koralle*, was staged in 1917; in it Kaiser shows himself to be highly critical of capitalist ruthlessness, for although the Millionaire dominates the play both his son and daughter reject his world. His son defies him, and joins the workers; it is he who will be the hero of the

next play, *Gas I*. Connected with the idea of regeneration is a theme
which is common in Kaiser, that of the exchange of a man's identity
to gain a new lease of life: this the Millionaire attempts to do by
assuming the role of his murdered secretary, and living vicariously
through his son. *Gas I* made Kaiser a European name: it was
performed a few days after the armistice and, with its idea of the
regeneration of society at large, it seemed again, like *Die Bürger von
Calais*, to have a meaning especially relevant to the German situation
at that time. Gas becomes the symbol for the driving force behind all
modern machinery; at the factory which produces it the Millionaire's
Son rules with a devoted idealism, but he cannot prevent the
immense explosion which reduces the factory to rubble. (A Strindberg-
ian touch is 'der weiße Herr', who is an embodiment of a premonition
of disaster, the white terror – gas – which obliterates all.) After the
catastrophe the Millionaire's Son sees the chance for a new life: he will
resettle his workers on the land and restore them to health and joy.
But he has not reckoned with the Engineer, who represents ruthless
technology; Act 4 consists of a brilliant dialectical exchange between
the two *Weltanschauungen*, one pastoral-idyllic, the other materialist-
scientific: the workers themselves are swayed to and fro between the
opposing theses. In spite of his genuine idealism the Millionaire's
Son cannot prevent the workers from pouring back into the
demolished factory after the Engineer: the vision of the Millionaire's
Son has not been realised. At the end of the play representatives of
big business as well as the army seize the works to ensure the
production of gas: egoism and brutal mechanisation have won the day.
But the Millionaire's Son cannot forget his ideal, and the daughter
kneels before him, full of the knowledge of her new mission:

> Sage es mir: wo ist der Mensch? Wann tritt er auf – und ruft sich
> mit Namen: – Mensch? . . . Muß er nicht ankommen – morgen
> und morgen – und in stündlicher Frist? – Bin ich nicht Zeuge für
> ihn – und für seine Herkunft und Ankunft? – ist er mir nicht
> bekannt mit starkem Gesicht?! Soll ich noch zweifeln?!!
> TOCHTER (*nieder in Knie*): Ich will ihn gebären![58]

Gas I ends on a note of optimism, but *Gas II*, performed two years
later, is a portrayal of apocalyptic doom. The Millionaire's grandson
remained true to humanitarian ideals: he is now the Millionaire-
Worker. His antagonist is the Engineer, now Chief-Engineer, who is
virtually an automaton: the mechanical regularity of his movements

mirrors the machinery around him, and the total abstract soullessness of modern technology. Gas is in even greater demand since the outbreak of war, and the workers are practically reduced to machinery themselves; the Millionaire-Worker, however, suggests that the workers should unite with their fellow-men on the enemy's side, that a call for peace be broadcast across the world. But he is greeted only with silence and with the destructive savagery of the Chief-Engineer, who tells of the production of a poison-gas which eats away the living flesh. In a climax of horror the Millionaire-Worker sees that his ideal of brotherly love is unrealisable, and, in bitterness and disillusionment, he smashes the glass of poison-gas on the floor, while the enemy bombardment starts outside. A Yellow Figure, one of the enemy soldiers, sees the shattered building, the concrete slabs lying on top of each other like gravestones, beneath which are lying the skeletons of those whose flesh the gas has destroyed. He reports back to his troops, crazed and demented, for he has seen the Day of Judgement: 'Kehrt die Geschütze gegen euch und vernichtet euch – die Toten drängen aus den Gräbern – jüngster Tag – dies irae – solvet – in favil – –. (er zerschießt den Rest in den Mund)'.[59] In this startling work Kaiser shows what war means in an age which can produce weapons of mass destruction; he sees how the demagogue seizes power over others and how, finally, man can destroy himself in a paroxysm of self-hatred. It would seem that man devoted his energies ultimately to suicide, and that the self-annihilation of civilisation was at hand.

What, then, of the New Man? Would the potential in man for goodness and love be realised, or is he bent on destroying the world and himself? A play written between *Gas I* and *Gas II, Hölle Weg Erde*, describes in almost religious terms a journey made by 'Spazierer' out of the hell of modern capitalism to the heaven-on-earth of universal brotherhood: light floods the stage at the end as men struggle towards true communion. But is it achieved? And the question must be asked: is there not in Kaiser a ruthless, almost cruel element, a narcissistic sense of power which contradicts the altruism of the vision of the New Man? The hectic selfishness of the Bank-Clerk in *Von morgens bis mitternachts*, the deliberate, almost sadistic prolongation of suffering deemed necessary in *Die Bürger von Calais*, the violence found in *Kanzlist Krehler, Zweimal Oliver* and *Rosamunde Floris*, the hideous carnage of *Gas II*, are remembered here, as is Kaiser's statement to the Landgericht in Munich in 1921, where, accused of theft, he declared that he regarded himself as an exceptional man beyond the jurisdiction of the law. ('Ich halte mich für einen exorbitanten

Ausnahmefall. Auf mich ist das Gesetz nicht anwendbar . . . Wer viel geleistet hat, ist a priori straffrei'.[60]) The obsession of Kaiser with certain themes, the almost monomaniacal dedication of many of his characters, the reduction of men to automata, the abstract stage settings, the steel constructions and harsh lighting seem to reflect a predisposition towards cruelty and bleakness which is not altogether dispelled by an ideal which, in any case, seems frequently Nietzschean rather than Christian. It must, however, be remembered that the plays Kaiser wrote between 1917 and 1923 were created while Germany was in the grip of defeat, collapse, disillusion and revolution; the country was tremulous with hopes for the future, yet shot through with brutality and civil strife.

Before the end of the fighting in 1918 two further plays appeared on the German stage (albeit in restricted performances) which showed the senselessness of war and its brutalising effect upon men: Fritz von Unruh's *Ein Geschlecht* and Reinhard Goering's *Seeschlacht*. (This latter play was staged by Max Reinhardt in his theatre 'Das junge Deutschland', which had been established towards the end of the war for the production of modern plays for invited guests only; Sorge's *Der Bettler* had opened the season.) Fritz von Unruh (1885–1970) was a Prussian officer, formerly a page at the Imperial Court, who had devoted himself to literature, modelling himself upon Heinrich von Kleist. His earlier play *Prinz Louis Ferdinand von Preußen* had extolled the Prussian military traditions, and was full of patriotic fervour and panache, yet *Offiziere*, produced by Max Reinhardt in 1912, had expressed certain doubts about the wisdom of a military career. Direct experience in the fighting of 1914 convinced von Unruh of the horror and degradation of modern warfare: his dramatic poem *Vor der Entscheidung* described his change of heart, the rejection of Heinrich von Kleist with his hectic and morbid nationalism, and the debt to Shakespeare, the writer who loved life in all its forms. Kleist may tempt to a glorious death, but von Unruh does not heed him: he recognises and abominates the life-destroying cult of militarism and glory and turns his back upon his birth, upbringing and traditions. *Ein Geschlecht* was written in 1916: its blank verse is taken from that of Kleist, and the lofty grandeur of the language looks back to Schiller, but the violence and the extremity of the emotions expressed place von Unruh very much within the expressionist fold.

The play has as its setting a nocturnal cemetery, where the Mother, Daughter and Youngest Son have buried a favourite son who died as a hero in battle. The two remaining sons are brought in chains,

one guilty of conwardice, the other of brutal insubordination. This
latter is the Eldest Son who is the protagonist, a figure exemplifying
amoral energy and radical nihilism. Brutalised by the war, he turns his
violence against the Mother and Daughter, his sexual urges directed
towards an incestuous relationship with his sister. Von Unruh sees that
nationalism and war encourage violent aggressiveness which they
cannot ultimately control, and yet which they obtusely expect to
keep within limits (the Eldest Son had been found guilty of rape);
frustrated and racked with searing torment the Eldest Son curses the
Mother for giving him life which contains death within it:

> Ohnmacht in euch, wenn fette Würmer schleichen,
> und sich in Augen Eurer Leibesfrucht
> Nachtpilz und Molch mit aller Fäulnis Wurzeln
> einnisten wie in Kot! O Mütter, Weiber:
> Ihr tragt das Grab in Eurem feuchten Schloß,
> was ihr gebärt, ist Tod und nichts als Tod![61]

He cannot control these murderous impulses which were formerly
condoned: his vitalism, perverted, turns to self-destruction, and he leaps
from the cemetery wall. The Mother, spritually transformed, calls
upon the mothers of the world to stop the madness of war, and
proclaims the message of peace and love. Although she is killed by the
Commander, the Youngest Son is inspired by her vision and leads
the soldiers to rebellion; the dawn proclaims a new day for mankind.

Von Unruh's play is a concentrated expression of explosive powers:
it is basically anti-war in that the Mother seizes the staff of power and
calls for a halt to the killing. But the work also touches upon the theme
of the proximity of lust and violence, and also contains a deep
conviction of the absurdity of life: the Eldest Son condemns all
conception as harbouring future decomposition within it. It is
quintessentially expressionistic in that it is an outburst (albeit in
traditional verse-form) of pent-up, lava-like emotions; it combines an
optimistic humanitarian ideal with a shrill, hectic sadism which is only
just dispelled.

Reinhard Goering (1887–1936) wrote his play in a Davos sanatorium
during convalescence: although not as powerful as *Ein Geschlecht* and
more closely linked to a particular situation (the Battle of Jutland) it
has a gripping, fatalistic quality at times reminiscent of ancient tragedy.
The action takes place in the gun-turret of a battleship, dominated by
a huge gun; the seven sailors are nameless and, after donning their

gasmasks, faceless. The language is clipped and jagged, but swells at times to a rhythmic pathos: memories and visions give way to a sombre and fervent ecstasy. The battle commences, and the final explosion kills all: the fifth sailor, the most rebellious, recognises before his death that dedication finally conquered the thought of insurrection. But Goering is not simply a 'patriotic' playwright here: he portrays men under stress, going ineluctably to their doom and reacting with expressive intensity to their predicament. His *Scapa Flow*, which appeared in the following year, is a much more conventional and less distinguished work; *Die Retter*, however, is a remarkable anticipation of Samuel Beckett in its expression of the futile monologues of two old, dying men.

The collapse of Germany, the establishment under enormous difficulties of the Weimar Republic, the turmoil of violence unleashed upon the streets during the fighting between extremist factions, the hectic optimism and the strident call for brotherhood created an atmosphere without parallel anywhere else in Europe. Hopes for the emergence of the New Man, for a spiritual transfiguration of mankind, alternated with a sense of frustration and disillusionment; in his famous anthology of many of the younger poets already discussed, *Menschheitsdämmerung*, the editor Kurt Pinthus wrote: 'Und immer wieder muß gesagt werden, daß die Qualität dieser Dichtung in ihrer Intensität beruht. Niemals in der Weltdichtung erscholl so laut, zerreißend und aufrüttelnd Schrei, Sturz und Sehnsucht einer Zeit, wie aus dem wilden Zug dieser Vorläufer und Märtyrer'.[62] The supreme example in the theatre of this fervent expression of hope for the transfiguration and redemption of man is Ernst Toller's *Die Wandlung*, performed in Berlin in 1919 and perhaps the greatest product of the German theatre at this time. Toller (1893–1939) had joined the army in 1914; at the front line he underwent a complete transformation and suffered a spiritual and physical collapse. In Munich he joined the extreme Left and was imprisoned for his pacifist views; there, in prison, he wrote *Die Wandlung. Das Ringen eines Menschen*, a *Stationen-drama* moving on two planes, one realistic, the other symbolic, which describe the hero's conversion from an unthinking patriot to a fervent revolutionary leader.

A nightmare vision opens the play, where skeletons climb from graves and roll their heads by numbers: a universal death prevails. The first station shows the hero, Friedrich, in opposition to his parental home (a situation well known from Hasenclever); he longs to join the army and fight in the colonies. The realistic scenes alternate with dream-like episodes which could be interpreted as the workings of his subconscious mind and are also frequently anticipations of what the realistic pictures later bring. The train carrying soldiers to their death precedes his awareness of the futility of war; the ghastly scene of the skeletons crawling from the barbed wire entanglements is a premonition of his own wounding and convalescence. (A debt to Büchner, particularly *Woyzeck*, is evident in the scene with the medical Professor and the hideously mutilated patients.) After the war Friedrich, now a sculptor, works on a colossal statue of Victory, but the sight of two wretched war invalids overwhelms him; he shatters the statue and strides forth, after a mental crisis bordering upon suicide, to join the masses. His task is to move among men and inspire them with his ideal of brotherhood and peace: he sees the wretchedness of slums, the sufferings of the oppressed and the indifference and cruelty of the authorities. He attends a political gathering and clashes with the agitator who preaches revolution and yet has no love in his soul; he foretells the new hope, the new vision in radiant imagery:

> Nun öffnet sich, aus Weltenschoß geboren,
> Das hochgewölbte Tor der Menschheitskathedrale.
> Die Jugend aller Völker schreitet flammend
> Zum nachtgeahnten Schrein aus leuchtendem Kristall.
> Gewaltig schau ich strahlende Visionen.
> Kein Elend mehr, nicht Krieg, nicht Haß,
> Die Mütter kränzen ihre lichten Knaben
> Zum frohen Spiel und fruchtgeweihtem Tanz.
> Du Jugend schreite, ewig dich gebärend,
> Erstarrtes ewig du zerstörend,
> So schaffe Leben gluterfüllt von Geist.[63]

The *Zarathustra* imagery intensifies: Friedrich becomes Leader, *Führer*, and, in the symbolic mountain scene, leaves the friend who cannot follow. Finally, on the market-place, he preaches a message of love which stresses the godlike qualities of man and calls for a realisation of man's highest potentialities. The prerequisite for this is revolution, glorious yet bloodless; the workers join hands and stride forth with Friedrich, proclaiming with an almost religious ecstasy the advent of the New Millennium.

This play represents an outstanding example of what might be called expressionist political activism: the revolt and aggressive egotism of the writers of the pre-war years have been channelled into an overtly political direction. But the idealism and spiritual foundation of Toller's political commitment was of such an intensity that disillusionment was perhaps inevitable. The Soviet Republic set up in Munich in the winter of 1918–1919 seemed to Toller the promise of a new world, but the acts of outrage committed by both the Left and the Right (the brutal murder of Gustav Landauer could be mentioned here) profoundly disillusioned him. His next play *Masse Mensch* (1919) is the working out of a conflict between the intellectual and the mob who are not yet ripe for ultimate comprehension: the situation is obviously Toller's own. His further imprisonment for having taken part in the Munich venture lasted five years, and forced him to take stock of his situation and that of his country, together with the whole problem of political activism; his next play, *Hinkemann*, shows in a way very similar to *Woyzeck* the hard core of suffering at the base of existence which no social amelioration can improve. The hero of *Hinkemann*, emasculated during the war, returns home to humiliation and degradation; reduced to earning his living by eating live mice, he sees his wife seduced and hears himself ridiculed. In one section reality is transcended and the contemporary world is shown in a series of nightmare pictures which are reminiscent of the newspaper reading scene of *Der Bettler*; Hinkemann, deranged, hangs himself after the suicide of his wife. The play *Hoppla, wir leben* of 1927 again contains Toller's bitter awareness of the futility of political activity: the hero, closely modelled on Toller himself, sees the fading of the old ideals and the re-emergence in Germany of powerful and reactionary forces. The influence of Erwin Piscator was seen in the production in the use of film-shots and documentary elucidation of contemporary history; the suicide of the hero seemed a sombre anticipation of Toller's own.

Messianic fervour and passionate intellectualism, grotesque violence and radiant transfiguration, apocalyptic splendour and incestuous bestiality — the German stage between 1906 and 1925 contained expressionistic excesses undreamt of in any other European country. It is probably true to say that it was the theatre (as well as painting) which made the movement known throughout Europe and even the world. The New York stage of the early 1920s was aware of German expressionism as a theatrical force and emulated many of its achievements: short scenes took the place of longer ones, the dialogue became staccato, symbolic characters replaced naturalistic ones, the sets became starkly abstract and lighting was used to create an atmosphere of unreality. The most extreme of the German plays on the

New York stage was Hasenclever's *Jenseits*, a highly subjective
expression, with nebulous and hallucinatory effects, of the meaning of
life and death. As well as Toller's *Masse Mensch* and Wedekind's
Erdgeist, Werfel's *Bocksgesang* and his *Spiegelmensch* trilogy were
also performed. If the American stage was more open to German
expressionism than the British, then at least Sean O'Casey's *The Silver
Tassie* should be mentioned which, particularly in the second act,
uses certain techniques which bear the mark of their German originals,
Reinhard Goering particularly.

The *Spiegelmensch* trilogy of Werfel deserves wider recognition: in it
Werfel demonstrates the dangers of expressionist idealism which is
frequently nothing more than monstrous self-delusion or self-obsession.
The figure of Thamal represents those messianic figures who apparently
stand for altruism and universal love, but who are in fact inspired by
megalomania: he is taught that men see not the world but themselves
when they gaze outwards, for solipsism is the inevitable consequence of
human pride. Men must battle against that mirror-image, the Self,
before the mirror becomes a true window, but Thamal, in his
impatience to shatter the mirror image, releases instead the Self which,
liberated, achieves independent life and seduces him. Thamal's inflated
activism leads to neurotic self-aggrandisement: he kills his father and
demands the death of his unborn child in his arrogant egomania.
The second part of the trilogy brilliantly conveys the chaos of beliefs
associated with the expressionist years — religious longing fused with
political activism, primitivism, quietism, Buddhism and theosophy:

> Eucharistisch und tomistisch,
> Doch daneben auch marxistisch,
> Theosophisch, kommunistisch,
> Gotisch kleinstadt-dombau-mystisich,
> Aktivisitisch, erzbuddhistisch,
> Überöstlich taoistisch,
> Rettung aus der Zeit-Schlamastik
> Suchend in der Negerplastik,
> Wort- und Barrikaden wälzend,
> Gott und Foxtrot fesch verschmelzend.[64]

Walter Sokel writes: 'Beneath the surface inconsistencies and paradoxes
of Expressionism — its fusion of God and foxtrot, of mystic
religiosity and left-wing politics — Werfel sees its basic and fatal
hypocrisy in its blasphemous deification of mankind, which serves as

a disguise for the deification of self. Thamal, in pretending to establish Utopia, and proclaiming himself God, sins not only against God but also against reality. In the blasphemous deification of man lies the archsin of expressionism and the cause of its ruin'.[65] It is only Thamal's willingness to die which saves him from the Mirror-man; the mirror becomes a true window on to reality after the self has been conquered. This work, written in 1920 and performed the following year, should be read as a salutary antidote against the grandiloquent claims of those expressionists who arrogated to themselves exorbitant powers.

If the theatre and the lyric were in the foreground of avant-garde expressionism, then prose fiction seemed to lag behind, apparently lacking the potentiality for immediate, ecstatic expression. But a closer examination would show that the discursive prose form also underwent drastic modification in the early years of this century: parataxis, dislocation, simultaneity and ellipsis characterise the work of many writers, and the rejection of naturalist psychology, rational plot and objectivity, together with a predilection for the grotesque is certainly found in the prose of Carl Einstein, Alfred Döblin, Franz Jung (1888–1963) and Curt Corrinth (1894–1960) and, to a lesser extent, in Otto Flake, Kasimir Edschmid and Klabund, that is, Alfred Henschke (1890–1928). The attack against bourgeois society, although not necessarily couched in radically experimental prose, should also be considered here, and is certainly found in the work of Heinrich Mann and Jakob Wassermann (1873–1934). The former's *Das Kaiserreich* trilogy contains the novel *Der Untertan* (1918) with its brilliant portrayal of the arrogant and pusillanimous vanity of Dietrich Hessling; Wassermann's *Caspar Hauser oder die Trägheit des Herzens* (1908) attacked the torpor and indifference of German provincial society when faced with the miraculous foundling, and *Das Gänsemännchen* (1913) gives again a most perceptive picture of the narrowness of a small German town in which the musician, Daniel Nothafft, is driven into a shrill and bitter self-assertion. Again, the term 'expressionism' is unsatisfactory, for it must cover not only the stylistic innovators but also other writers whose style was conventional, yet who sought changes elsewhere. The common desire seems to be for radical change, in art and society, and this characterised the most disparate writers, the radical nature of whose work derives not from any naturalist 'modernity' but from far more radical sources, for example Italian futurism.

Marinetti has already been mentioned: his novel *Mafarka le futuriste* (1909) with its cult of speed, turbulence and toughness had a far-reaching effect on the style of many of the new German writers, in whose work extreme concentration, simultaneity of action and various montage effects became increasingly apparent. Grotesque effects were also noticeable in Marinetti: the decapitation of a thousand women in *Le Monoplan du Pape* and Mafarka's aeroplane-shaped son, produced without any female aid, are two notable examples. D'Annunzio likewise, with his flamboyant sexual and political life, together with the drastic violence in many of his stories (the murder of a cripple to make way for the Superman, for instance) was a most potent inspiration.[66] Gigantic figures, outsiders, amoral heroes dominate early expressionist fiction: Jakob Wassermann's *Alexander in Babylon* (1905) is a good example here: the 'New Man' of expressionist political activism has not yet appeared, but the man of monstrous energy has. A link undeniably exists between the more extreme products of the decadents and the predilection for grotesque cruelty which is found in much early (and not so early) expressionist prose: Döblin's *Berge Meere und Giganten* demonstrates the delight in portraying cosmic uproar and violent confusion; the novel by Bernhard Kellerman (1879–1951), *Der Tunnel*, the film of which, incidentally, greatly impressed Adolf Hitler, similarly delights in the description of monstrous catastrophes, and cruelty and torture abound in Heinrich Mann's *Die Göttinnen*. A delight in barbaric, particularly African, scenes predominates, something far more extreme than the Orientalism of Max Dauthendey (1867–1918) or Lafcadio Hearn (1850–1904); Klabund's story *Der Neger* revels in a portrayal of sexual prowess. The eccentric perversion of the decadents, combined with the futurist's cult of speed and power, produced an atmosphere of instability, both fascinating and disturbing.

Max Brod's *Tod den Todten!* (published 1906) is a story which well exemplifies the atavistic, iconoclastic aspect of the new tendency: the disused theatre, full of works of art, is to be dynamited in a manner which smacks of Marinetti's vision of destruction; his *Schloß Norne-pygge* (1908), already mentioned, is a fascinating novel in its portrayal of Walder Nornepygge's indulgence in decadent practices (the orgies in the castle, and the ball in the open-cast mine, where the resentment of the proletariat is meant to heighten the pleasure of the participants) and his involvement in anarchy and other destructive movements. Marinetti is recalled in the references to armoured cars and dirigible air-ships; the total amorality of Guachen is a debased Nietzscheanism, whereas the hero's *Indifferentismus*, his inability to assume any role — debauchee, anarchist, hermit, husband or revolutionary — reminds the reader forcibly of Robert Musil's hero. In that long tirade before his death he also comments ironically on those writers who had become identified with a particular stereotype (himself included):

> George muß hieratisch-ernsthaft bleiben, Rilke katholisch, Bierbaum gesund-graziös-lustig . . . Und warum schildert Schaukal nur Aristokraten, Meyrink nur Magier, Blei nur galante Frauen, Scheffel nur Alkohol und blaue Augen, Laforgue nur den Mond, Oskar Wilde nur schöne Lasterhafte, Brod nur nachdenkliche Jünglinge, Frenssen nur gutmütige Idioten, Hesse nur Schüchterne, Hamsun nur Ungeschickte, Heinrich Mann nur von Leidenschaften Zerwalkte, Flaubert nur Enttäuschte, Erbärmlich![67]

Brod's novel is of great importance as it perfectly mirrors the transition between decadence and early expressionism; an equally significant novel is Carl Einstein's *Bebuquin oder die Dilettanten des Wunders* (1912) which derives from nothing in German literature (rather from André Gide), and anticipates the 'nonsense' utterances of the Dadaists. Einstein's short novel is 'logical', but his logic is utterly divorced from any recognisable reality, and is more in the nature of Flaubert's 'livre sur rien, un livre sans attache extérieure, qui se tiendtrait de lui-même par la force interne de son style'.[68] The hyper-cerebral and the logic of unreason exist side by side with the ironic in *Bebuquin*: the parody of the Eleanora Duse-D'Annunzio affair, for instance, is highly entertaining: 'Durch die regengepeitschte Nacht fuhr in ihrem Auto die Schauspielerin Fredegonde Perlenblick . . . Auf dem Dache des Kupees war ein Kintopp angebracht, der den verschlafenen Bürgern zeigte, wie die Schauspielerin Fredegonde Perlenblick sich auszog, badete und zu Bett ging'.[69] The inflated nimiety of a Döblin or a Jahnn, the cerebral precision of an Einstein and a Mynona, the grotesque excesses of Franz Jung's *Das Trottelbuch* (1912) and his story *Dagne* (with its thinly-veiled account of the murder or suicide of Przybyszewski's wife) or Curt Corrinth's *Trieb* are all normally held to belong to expressionism, although the elements in common are often difficult to define.

As far as links with the theatre are concerned, Werfel's *Nicht der Mörder, der Ermordete ist schuldig* is of interest; the following statement could well have been spoken by a young protagonist contemplating parricide: 'Die *patria potestas*, die Autorität, ist eine Unnatur, das verderbliche Prinzip an sich. Sie ist der Ursprung aller Morde, Kriege, Untaten, Verbrechen, Haßlaster und Verdammnisse, gleichwie das Sohntum der Ursprung aller hemmenden Sklaveninstinkte ist, das scheußliche Aas, das in den Grundstein aller historischen Staatenbildung eingemauert wurde'.[70] Jakob Wassermann, in his *Christian Wahnschaffe* (1919), is close to Kaiser in his portrayal of the young man who rejects his father's industrial wealth and goes to join the poor, exclaiming:

> Sohn bin ich, du bist Vater. Heißt das Knecht und Herr sein? Ich bin nicht mehr von deiner Welt. Deine Welt macht mich zu deinem Widersacher, Sohn und Widersacher, anders kann deine Welt nicht anders werden. Gehorsam ohne Überzeugung, was ist das denn? Die Wurzel von allem Übel. Du kannst mich nicht sehen; der Vater sieht nicht den Sohn. Die Welt der Söhne muß sich gegen die Welt der Väter erheben, anders kann es nicht anders werden.[71]

A writer like Heinrich Mann stressed the social task of the novel and condemned self-indulgence in the arts, as did Werfel in his *Verdi* novel, where Wagner is rejected for hysteria and excess, yet he also prided himself on being, with the dramatists Frank Wedekind and Carl Sternheim, one of the precursors and teachers of the modern generation of writers. His novel *Der Kopf* (1925), with its use of slang, its dislocation of syntax and extreme concentration of language, seems to be more modern than he would admit, and similarly the Novelle *Kobes* (1923) has a strange jerkiness and reduction to essentials characteristic of Kaiser. It is probably in his plays, however, that the new techniques are most apparent: *Brabach* is reminiscent of *Von morgens bis mitternachts* and *Das gastliche Haus* is not far removed from the world of Carl Sternheim.

The common denominator of all the works mentioned in this chapter in the lyric, the drama and in prose fiction is an attitude of revolt, sometimes political or mystical, sometimes eccentric and grotesque. The revolt is seen either in the subject matter (defiance of authority, frequently with sexual motives) or in stylistic experimentation. Naturalistic description of man trapped in the labyrinth of cities gives way to a vision of the New Man, who transcends the dross of poverty and depravity; the decadent flirtation with extreme situations gives way to a grotesque dislocation and distortion, sometimes desperate, but frequently flippant. It may be claimed that expressionism, with its emphasis on frenzied hyperbole, absurdity, distortion and revolt carried the seeds of its own destruction within itself. It is true to say that the three main tendencies which superseded expressionism – Dada, *Neue Sachlichkeit* and surrealism – were unthinkable without it.

The links with Dada were particularly close. Hugo Ball and Richard Huelsenbeck, as early as 1912, met in the Café Stephanie in Munich to discuss the new ideas in literature; Huelsenback, after their move to Berlin, explained in a letter:

> Ball und ich haben uns für nichts als für den Expressionismus interessiert, hauptsächlich Ball . . . Wir huren hier herum, um die Tauentziehenstraße, wir trinken, auch sitzen wir manchmal in den Tavernen und Liqueurstuben zwei Tage lang, bis uns die Polizei hinauswirft. Wir halten das alles für Expressionismus . . . Sexualität, haben wir herausgefunden, ist eine spielerische Lebensform und dem Expressionismus sehr verwandt.[72]

Huelsenbeck stresses the 'playful' aspects of expressionism, the flirtation with the absurd; later, in his famous 'Dada-Rede' on 18 February 1918 he stressed the total, anarchic irrationality of Dada that, as a movement, it was basically *nothing*: 'Dada wollte mehr sein als Kultur und es wollte weniger sein, es wußte nicht recht, was es sein wollte. Deswegen, wenn Sie mich fragen, was Dada ist, würde ich sagen, es war nichts und wollte nichts'.[73] The designation Dada ('hobbyhorse') was deliberately chosen for its meaninglessness; during the war, at the Café Voltaire in the Spiegelgasse in Zurich, Hugo Ball, Tristan Tzara, Hans Arp and others staged chaotic performances and pushed language into total incomprehensibility; reason and order were deemed bourgeois and Dada, an 'anti-art', imitated the physical battles raging outside Switzerland. If the bourgeois world, so proud of its civilised institutions, had condoned the war, then art could follow that civilisation and become likewise atavistic and absurd. Towards the end of the war a Club Dada was founded in Berlin, consisting of Huelsenbeck, Raoul Hausmann, Georg Grosz and Helmut Herzfelde (or John Heartfield), founder of the Malik Verlag, which was named after a novel by Else Lasker-Schüler and whose book jackets were decorated with a very effective style of photomontage.[74] An interesting variation on Dada was Kurt Schwitters's 'Merz'; Schwitters, like many other artists associated with expressionism and Dada, worked in different media and desired likewise to ignore the difference between what was deemed 'art' and what was not. As the Merz columns were composed of *objets trouvés*, so his poems and prose are full of fragmentary utterances, platitudes and advertisement jargon, which were all embedded in the text: artistic pretentiousness was to be avoided at all cost. Schwitters's short stories, some of which were published in *Der Sturm*, are bizarre and obviously idiosyncratic: *Die Zwiebel* and *Frau Müllers Drahtfrühling* are both farcical and satirical; if the Revolution could not shake the bourgeois out of his petrified respectability, then perhaps the devotee of Dada or Merz might stand a better chance.

Dada, basically anarchic, still maintained its irreverence after the move to Berlin and the affiliations with the Communist party, for Bolshevism was felt to be the channel through which a new life would flow into society. On 16 November the 'Oberdada', Joannes Baader (1875–1955), shouted obscenities in Berlin Cathedral during a sermon by the Court Preacher and later managed to interrupt a meeting of the National Assembly in Weimar at the official declaration of the foundation of the Republic. Political and sexual reform was demanded; in the spring of 1919 a march through Berlin was organised to sell the journal *Jedermann sein eigener Fußball*, which contained contributions by Mynona, Wieland Herzfelde and his brother, and Georg Grosz (the journal was, in fact, banned for 'obscenities' after only one number). The Berlin Dadaists were not to know that that party, which they believed would guarantee freedom in all spheres, would utterly condemn both their antics and the bold experiments of the expressionists as being decadent and somehow symptomatic of a bourgeois culture.

Like futurism, from which it inherited several ideas, including that of public provocation, Dada was not a new set of artistic premisses, but rather a mood or state of mind which became a form of intellectual emergency. The anarchy of the Zurich days, the wholesale rejection of bourgeois norms, the political direction and the urge to shock and offend are also expressionist preoccupations: Stramm's extreme concentration is not far from Hugo Ball, and his play *Erwachen*, with its roaring and its disintegration, could well have been acted by Ball, Tzara and Emmy Hennings (who did, in fact, put on a chaotic performance of Kokoschka's *Sphinx und Strohmann*). Iwan Goll's *Methusalem* is reminiscent of Sternheim in its ambiguous attitude towards the *Urbürger* of the same name, and is akin to Dada in its cast of super-ego, id, joke-box, monkey and cuckoo; his one act play *Der Ungestorbene* (with Dr Golfstrom, several *Litfaßsäulen* and a student who hurls his brain at the audience) is even closer to the antics perpetrated in Zurich. It is interesting that Goll (1891–1950) equated the demise of expressionism with the failure of the German revolution; as early as 1921 he could write: 'Expressionismus war eine schöne, große, gute Sache. Solidarität der Geistigen. Aufmarsch der Wahrhaftigen. Aber das Resultat ist leider, und ohne Schuld der Expressionisten, die deutsche Republik 1920 . . . Der "gute Mensch", mit einer verzweifelten Verbeugung, begibt sich in die Kulisse'.[75] In Goll's view expressionism was equated with revolt and the need for a new society: the more settled conditions prevailing in Germany as the turbulence of the early 1920s receded did not seem conducive to experimental excess, hyperbole or visionary Utopias.

It is false, however, to see *Neue Sachlichkeit* as a total antidote to expressionism: the deliberate modernity and big-city terminology is found in Marinetti and Gottfried Benn as well as in Bertolt Brecht and other poets writing in the late 1920s. Much of the poetry of van Hoddis and Alfred Lichtenstein is far closer to the poetry of the writers of *Neue Sachlichkeit* than they are to the declamatory forms of expressionism. With surrealism the links are apparent – the emphasis on *expressing*, on liberation from realities, on deliberate distortion: the poet Guillaume Apollinaire, who invented the term surrealism, was in close contact with the literary expressionism of the *Sturm*-circle. It is also false to assume that expressionism came to an abrupt end with National Socialism. Goebbels's novel *Michael*, with its rejection of the stultifying intellect, its praise of Van Gogh and Dostoevski, its worship of energy and its Zarathustra imagery displays obvious expressionist features; the experiments with the *Thing-Spiel* were very close to certain manifestations of the expressionist dance, and Hitler's demand for a New Man was not entirely dissimilar to the hopes of Kaiser and others. The perverted vitalism of both National Socialism and Fascism (in Italy Mussolini had learned much from Marinetti and D'Annunzio) sprang from certain premises shared with expressionism which neither the burning of the books nor the Degenerate Art exhibition could quite conceal.

Notes

1. *Die Aktion* (Kraus reprint), 1914, Spalte 617.
2. Gottfried Benn, *Gesammelte Werke in 8 Bänden*, Wiesbaden, 1962, IV, 1,046.
3. Nietzsche, *Werke*, II, 1,021.
4. Ibid., 281.
5. See Raabe, *Expressionismus. Der Kampf um eine literarische Bewegung*, Munich, 1965, 15-22.
6. J.R. Becher, *Gesammelte Werke*, Berlin, 1969, XII, 495.

7.   Hanns Johst, *Der junge Mensch*, Munich, 1919.
8.   Georg von der Vring, *Soldat Suhren*, Berlin, 1928, 244.
9.   Otto Flake, *Es wird Abend. Bericht aus einem langen Leben*, Gütersloh, 1960, 192.
10.   See Martens, *Vitalismus und Expressionismus*, 189.
11.   Jakob van Hoddis, *Gesammelte Dichtungen*, Zurich, 1958, 28.
12.   See Arnold, *Prosa des Expressionismus*, Stuttgart, 1972, 108.
13.   J.R. Becher, XIV, 339-340.
14.   Georg Heym, *Dichtungen und Schriften*, Hamburg/Munich, 1964, I, 346.
15.   See Raabe, *Expressionismus*, 96.
16.   August Stramm, *Das Werk*, Wiesbaden, 1963, 73.
17.   See Zeller (ed), *Expressionismus: Literatur und Kunst 1910–1923. Eine Ausstellung des deutschen Literaturarchivs im Schiller-Nationalmuseum*, Marbach, 1960, 124-125.
18.   Gottfried Benn, *Lyrik und Prosa. Briefe und Dokumente*, Wiesbaden, 1962, 11.
19.   Ernst Stadler, *Dichtungen*, Hamburg, 1964, II, 198.
20.   Ibid., II, 10.
21.   Ibid., I, 200.
22.   See Robert Newton, *Form in the 'Menschheitsdämmerung'*, The Hague, 1971.
23.   K. Wagenbach, *Franz Kafka. Eine Biographie seiner Jugend*, Berne, 1958, 77.
24.   Max Brod, *Schloß Nornepygge*, Leipzig, 1918, 502.
25.   Kasimir Edschmid, *Lebendiger Expressionismus*, Munich, 1961, 100.
26.   Max Brod, *Schloß Nornepygge*, 497.
27.   Franz Werfel, *Das lyrische Werk*, Frankfurt/Main, 1967, 62-63.
28.   Ibid., 80.
29.   Ibid., 99-100.
30.   Kafka, *Tagebücher 1910–1923*, 202.
31.   J.R. Becher, *Werke in 3 Bänden*, Berlin, 1971, I, 30.
32.   Becher, *Gesammelte Werke*, Berlin, II, 57-62.
33.   Ibid., 30-33.
34.   W. Kandinsky, *Über das Geistige in der Kunst*, 8th ed., Berne, 1965, 84.
35.   O. Kokoschka, *Das schriftliche Werk*, Hamburg, 1973, I, 49.
36.   Julius Bab, *Über den Tag hinaus*, Heidelberg, 1960, 202.
37.   Frank Wedekind, *Gesammelte Werke*, Munich, 1919, VIII, 153.
38.   Ibid., II, 100.
39.   Ibid., II, 123.
40.   Ibid., I, 340.
41.   Ibid., III, 8.
42.   *Prosa. Dramen. Verse*, Munich, 1954, 947.
43.   Th. Mann, X, 70-76.
44.   Quoted in *Oskar Panizza. Das Liebeskonzil und andere Schriften*, Neuwied/Rhein, 1964, 248.
45.   Carl Sternheim, *Das Gesamtwerk*, Neuwied/Rhein, 1963, I, 285.
46.   Ibid., VI, 31.
47.   Reinhold Sorge, *Werke in 3 Bänden*, Nuremberg, I, 325.
48.   Ibid., II, 53.
49.   Ibid., II, 88-89.
50.   Walter Hasenclever, *Gedichte. Dramen. Prosa*, Hamburg, 1963, 103.
51.   Anton Wildgans, *Dies Irae*, Leipzig, 1918, 210.
52.   Gottfried Benn, *Gesammelte Werke*, VI, 1,497.
53.   Franz Kafka, *Gespräche mit Janouch*, Frankfurt/Main, 1961, 38.

54.   Erich Mühsam, quoted in the first number of *Revolution* (ed. Jung and Leybold), Munich, 1913, reprinted 1969.
55.   Georg Kaiser, *Werke*, Frankfurt/Berlin/Vienna, 1971, IV, 548-549.
56.   Ibid., 561-562.
57.   Ibid., 577.
58.   Ibid., II, 57-58.
59.   Ibid., 88.
60.   Ibid., IV, 562.
61.   Fritz von Unruh, *Sämtliche Werke*, Berlin, 1973, *Dramen*, II, 36.
62.   Kurt Pinthus in *Menschheitsdämmerung*, Berlin, 1919, xv.
63.   Ernst Toller, *Die Wandlung*, Potsdam, 1922, 77.
64.   Franz Werfel, *Spiegelmensch. Magische Trilogie*, Munich, 1920, 130.
65.   Walter Sokel, *The Writer in Extremis*, Stanford, 1958, 216.
66.   See Arnold, *Prosa des Expressionismus*, Stuttgart, 1972, 31-32.
67.   Max Brod, *Schloß Nornepygge*, 497.
68.   Flaubert, *Oeuvres complètes. Correspondance (1847–1852)*, Paris, 1926, 345.
69.   *Die Aktion*, August, 1912, 1,011.
70.   Franz Werfel, *Nicht der Mörder, der Ermordete ist schuldig*, Munich, 1920, 101.
71.   Jakob Wassermann, *Christian Wahnschaffe*, Berlin, 1919, II, 441.
72.   Kasimir Edschmid (ed.), *Briefe der Expressionisten*, Frankfurt/Main, 1964, 68-69.
73.   Richard Huelsenbeck, *Dada. Eine literarische Dokumentation*, Reinbek/Hamburg, 1964, 30.
74.   Walter Mehring, *Berlin Dada. Eine Chronik mit Photos und Dokumenten*, Zurich, 1959, 67-70.
75.   Iwan Goll, quoted in Raabe, *Expressionismus*, 180-181.

7 THE 1920s AND 1930s

It has frequently been held that the period of the Weimar Republic coincided with the triumph of the avant-garde in Germany, that 'Weimar culture' meant a radical break with the past and a hectic experimentalism in the arts which was terminated by the Nazis in 1933. Attempts have been made, however, to show that the revolution in poetry, the theatre and also the novel occurred in the years immediately preceding the First World War, that certain aspects of early expressionism anticipated the techniques of *Neue Sachlichkeit* and that the cynical, nonchalant *Großstadtlyrik*, associated with writers such as Bertolt Brecht, was already to be found as early as 1910 in the poetry of Gottfried Benn. It should also be remembered that figures such as Hugo von Hofmannsthal, Stefan George, Gerhart Hauptmann, Robert Musil, Thomas Mann and Hermann Hesse were writing throughout the Weimar period, that Rilke completed his *Duineser Elegien* in the same year that Brecht saw his first play on the stage, and that Franz Kafka's *Das Schloß* was published by Max Brod in the same year as Hans Grimm's enormously popular *Volk ohne Raum*. A recent study has quite rightly seen that it is pointless to limit 'Weimar culture' chronologically, even geographically: writing the history of art in the age of Stresemann is acknowledged to be a curious occupation.[1] The legends created by the Weimar period, and particularly those centring on Berlin, may be fascinating, yet the student of modern German literature should be wary of them: 'Weimar culture' is as much Hofmannsthal's *Der Turm*, Thomas Mann's *Der Zauberberg* (picked out by his son Golo as being *the* representative novel of the whole Stresemann era), and Hermann Hesse's *Steppenwolf* as well as the Brecht-Weill *Dreigroschenoper*. Before 1933 Robert Musil had published part one of *Der Mann ohne Eigenschaften* and Hermann Broch his trilogy *Die Schlafwandler*: as well as being an era of epic theatre, this is also the period of the monumental novel. Before looking at Brecht, Klabund, Fallada and Tucholsky, and others whose names are inseparably linked with the 1920s, it is appropriate to look at the writers of the older generation, who also lent Weimar its flavour, and indeed its greatness.

Hofmannsthal's lyric poetry and early drama were discussed in chapter 2; the note of frenzy associated with expressionism, apparently so alien to the Viennese poet, was noticed in *Elektra* and may also be found in his *Das gerettete Venedig* (1905). His collaboration with Richard Strauss reached its climax in *Der Rosenkavalier* (1911) and *Die Frau ohne Schatten* (1919); his increasing awareness of his debt to the Austrian theatrical tradition, and the need to establish a bridge to the widest possible audience led to the formation of the Salzburger Festspiele, but the international Babel *à la* Bayreuth could not have been welcomed by this most fastidious of men. The collapse of Austro-Hungary was a profound shock to Hofmannsthal, who nevertheless strove to reassert cultural and spiritual values, and to extol the great figures of Austrian literature in the face of a threatening world. Those works above all were greeted by Hofmannsthal which, in their irony and their refinement, seemed to be quintessentially Austrian rather than German: the tendency towards humourless nimiety, which he observed in German culture, became increasingly alien to him. It is Hofmannsthal's *Der Schwierige* (1921) which portrays upper-class Austrian society at its finest, with as memorable a representative as Robert Musil's Ulrich — Hans-Karl Bühl: the humour, occasionally wry, always urbane, and never forced, circumvents or disposes with the darker problems besetting the age. (Both this play and Lessing's *Minna von Bernhelm* exemplify Novalis's profound contention that, after lost wars, it is comedy that is needed, not simply as light relief, but as a genre more able to comprehend and even forgive the foibles of the human condition.) In Hofmannsthal's portrayal of Hans-Karl's charm and irony there is much of Oscar Wilde, even Evelyn Waugh, particularly in Act 2, where the fearfully earnest Edine Merenberg commits one *faux pas* after another in her endeavours to impress, and Hans-Karl is right to prefer the antics of the clown Furlani to these frightful soirées, where that lady is reported to have once 'beim ersten Löffel Suppe ihren Tischnachbar interpelliert, ob er an die Seelenwanderung glaubt'.[2] The truly civilising values, Hofmannsthal sees here, are those of tolerance, respect for the elusive nature of truth and the refusal to pass a heavy-handed judgement: Hans-Karl's inability to come to a decision may be infuriating, but springs from an undeniable intelligence and humanity.

But weariness and resignation characterise much of Hofmannsthal's work in the twentieth century, in spite of *Der Schwierige* and its statement of human values: the correspondence with C.J. Burkhardt is full of disillusionment and foreboding when the European situation is considered. (The unfinished Bildungsroman *Andreas*, called by Jakob Wassermann 'einen österreichischen *Wilhelm Meister*'[3] and

which was published posthumously, is a work more reminiscent of the
first decade of this century than of the second, and its Venetian setting,
its juxtaposition of flux and stability bring to mind the water-and-rock
imagery of Thomas Mann and Rilke.) It is *Der Turm* which is
Hofmannsthal's most profound statement concerning the nihilistic
forces of his time, and the second version particularly, without the
intoxicated language of the first, is a work of undeniable power. The
turmoil and confusion within the realm of Basilius is very similar to
that prevailing in Europe at the time of the First World War; it is a
situation which Sigismund, brought up within his tower remote from
life, can scarcely begin to understand.[4] The first version particularly
stresses the links between Sigismund's education and Hofmannsthal's
early neo-romanticism, the period of the *Magier*-poet in his enchanted
world of inwardness; it is this aesthetic state of 'pre-existence'
which Hofmannsthal now criticises for its lack of any ethical core.
Sigismund must emerge from his tower, but he is not equal to the
demands of practical life and perishes, but not before the appearance
of the *Kinderkönig*, who symbolises the ultimate regeneration of man.
It is to Hofmannsthal's credit that he realises the weakness of this quasi-
operatic ending – the second version eschews such facile visions of
hope and is far more taut, tense and dramatic, rather than effusively
lyrical. Utopian solutions are always suspect, yet Sigismund glimpses
a moment of Rilkean 'Ursprung', of Alpine simplicity, before his death
at the hands of Olivier's henchmen. It is questionable whether the
episode of the slaughtered pig essentially denotes an awareness of
nihilistic brutality and its ultimate triumph; Sigismund's reflections
seem to show that he has transcended fear and anguish and has
achieved a martyrdom beyond nihilism: 'Der Bauer hatte ein
Schwein geschlachtet, das war aufgehangen neben meiner Kammertür,
und die Morgensonne fiel ins Innere, das war dunkel; denn die Seele
war abgerufen und anderswo geflogen. Es sind freudige Zeichen, aber
inwiefern, das kann ich euch nicht erklären'.[5] It would be false to
conclude that Hofmannsthal's final statement is a dark one; in 1927,
two years before his death, he asserted once more in his Munich
address 'Das Schrifttum als geistiger Raum der Nation' his faith in the
triumph of civilised values and his hope for a conservative revolution,
a transformation of German life away from the irrational and the
musical towards order, lucidity and tolerance.

'Das unverantwortliche Spekulative . . . das unverantwortliche
Musikalische' – the dangers of these German tendencies Thomas Mann
will choose in *Doktor Faustus* twenty years later to characterise the

roots of the German disaster. But if Hofmannsthal saw these dangers in his Munich address, then Thomas Mann, in the early 1920s, cannot but acknowledge his indebtedness to the speculative and the musical and created, in Hans Castorp, the embodiment of these German qualities, which he never ceased to admire. In 1924 appeared *Der Zauberberg*, begun in 1912 as a result of a visit to Davos with his wife, and originally intended as a grotesque *Satyrspiel*, a humorous parody of *Der Tod in Venedig*. (There are obvious parallels between the works, as a recent study of Thomas Mann has demonstrated: the removal of both heroes to an unfamiliar sphere and an interruption of their ordered lives by strange influences, their passion for an exotic, in both cases Slav, beloved, an exhilaration experienced by their indulgences in forbidden adventures and the proximity of knowledge and disease.[6]) But this was not to be: the war and Thomas Mann's attitudes during the hostilities were crystallised in the *Betrachtungen eines Unpolitischen* (1918), which brought to the surface a complex fabric of ideas, beliefs and situations. The work on *Der Zauberberg* now grew to become a vast reappraisal, couched in exquisite irony, of Thomas Mann's own intellectual heritage: the speculations of the *Betrachtungen* brought into a sharper focus those ideas and attitudes which *Der Zauberberg* embodied. The very title smacks of German romanticism, whose glories and whose dangers Thomas Mann must assess: music, love and disease are here, yet also medical science, x-rays, thermometers and the daily treatment of patients. In a wholly articulate and well-organised fashion a symbolic world rises imperceptibly from the realistic: Hans Castorp, the *Sorgenkind des Lebens*, spends seven years in the sanatorium, a hermetic resort where those potentialities which lay dormant within him are realised. This Hamburg engineer is not so unremarkable as he may have appeared at the beginning of the novel: he learns to give to as well as take from his two mentors, Settembrini and Naphta, and rises above his love for Clawdia Chauchat, the slack and fascinating woman with the Kirghiz eyes. A discussion of this vast novel, however brief, must refer at the start to Thomas Mann's views expressed in the *Betrachtungen*; that which had become an intellectual feud between two brothers assumed in *Der Zauberberg* a paradoxical resolution.

In January 1911 the journal *Pan* had published Heinrich Mann's most famous essay, *Geist und Tat*, in which he sought to enlist the support of the intellectual in the fight for justice and humanity. The German intellectual, notorious for his arrogant isolation from political matters, should look, Heinrich Mann explained, to France as a model, to Rousseau and above all Zola, who embodied the 'ratio militans'. 'Die Zeit verlangt und ihre Ehre will, daß sie [die Literaten] endlich, endlich auch in diesem Lande dem Geist die Erfüllung seiner Forderungen sichern, daß sie Agitatoren werden, sich dem Volk verbünden gegen die Macht, daß sie die ganze Kraft des Wortes seinem Kampf schenken, der auch der Kampf des Geistes ist'.[7] To Thomas Mann, however, the issues were not so simple: his conservative stance, his Germanness and also his depth of perception prevented the acceptance of his brother's position: platitudinous and unthinking liberalism may not always be able to satisfy the spiritual yearnings of man. The German intellectual belongs, Thomas Mann believed, in a different tradition, one richer and more profound, also potentially more dangerous, than his French counterpart. After the outbreak of war Thomas Mann published his essay *Friedrich und die große Koalition*, written in December 1914; by no means chauvinist in any vulgar sense, this essay attempted to understand (and presumably thereby excuse) the violation by Frederick of Saxon neutrality – the parallels with the German advances in 1914 were apparent. Thomas Mann's letter of April 1915 to the *Svenska Dagbladet* repeated and stressed the rightness of Germany's cause: the ideal of 'das dritte Reich', culled from Bertram, Bondi and Moeller van den Bruck, a synthesis of power and the spirit, became the visionary goal to which Germany aspired. Heinrich Mann responded with his essay *Zola*, printed in *Die weißen Blätter* in November 1915, which was an impassioned attack on Germany and that war which Germany, in Heinrich Mann's eyes, was launching against humanity. But also against the spirit? Thomas Mann produced, in the *Betrachtungen eines Unpolitischen*, a defence of his country's position, a reply to Heinrich Mann and also to other European intellectuals such as Romain Rolland, who were appalled at Thomas Mann's attitudes. He argued that the spirit, or *Geist*, was incommensurate with the shallow ideals of Western democracy, and that the German contribution to world culture – metaphysics and music – had nothing in common with belles-lettres and the ideals of the French revolution. (At its most extreme formulation the war could be described, he claimed, as a struggle between the Prelude to *Lohengrin* on the one side and the sophistication of international society on the other: given such a choice he had no alternative.) Belief in the progressive happiness of the human race could not satisfy on the profoundest level: social amelioration was a watchword frequently used without discrimination. In having the courage to remain conservative and German, Thomas

Mann must surely be admired, as must his magnanimity of spirit in admitting, later in life, that those powers which he had formerly worshipped and adored had led directly to Germany's disaster. (It should also be remembered that a host of writers and intellectuals had welcomed the war in terms far cruder than those which Thomas Mann had used in trying to understand its premisses: a look at *Die neue Rundschau II* of 1914 shows that men like Alfed Kerr, Oskar Bie and Juilius Meier-Graefe saw something salutary and heroic in the struggle, and that poets like R.A. Schröder (1878–1967), Dehmel, Hermann Stehr (1864–1940) and even Rilke had responded with admiration.) In 1914 Thomas Mann believed that an artist must accept the primitive and the vital: he must seek the purifying element of war and not shirk from extolling suffering and harshness. After 1918 there is not simply a *volte-face*, but a sincere realisation on his part of the dangers of the German flirtation with the irrational. The murder of Walther Rathenau shocked him deeply: his address in memory of Rathenau acknowledged the need for vigilance and political awareness, and his Berlin oration of the previous year, *Von deutscher Republik* (although hardly understood by the politicians and trade-unions with its curious admixture of Novalis and Walt Whitman) had given the new Republic his blessing and emphasised his intention to support it in whichever way he could. It is possible that Thomas Mann simplified the complex issue of the times and supported the Weimar Republic in spite of his original aversion to democracy and his reservations regarding worth political activism; the shock of Rathenau's death certainly impressed upon him the need for humanism and political vigilance. At such a time no responsible writer could be 'interesting' rather than morally correct. He became one of the few intellectuals to give such open support to the Republic; Tucholsky, apparently the more politically conscious, attacked the social democrats in virulent terms, Becher, Rubiner and Brecht would take up positions to the extreme Left, whereas Johst, Bronnen and Benn would assume right-wing attitudes.[8] All the problems and tensions of the time came together at the writing of *Der Zauberberg*, and in that novel the worthy and possibly shallow views on democracy, enlightenment and progress are put into the mouth of Settembrini, whereas the more conservative reactionary views of Naphta, although frequently profound and fascinating, are portrayed as basically perverse: Naphta's suicide demonstrates the self-destruction of those doctrines of mysticism, discipline and terror.

Der Zauberberg is a rich fabric of many strands, the most important of which being the education of Castorp-Germany. Madame Chauchat fascinates the *Sorgenkind*: another embodiment of the Slav world (as was the figure of Vuic in Hofmannsthal's *Reitergeschichte*), she incorporates the thrill of dissolution and of dubious sexuality. The rationalism of the 'Drehorgelmann' Settembrini on the one hand and the lure of Madame Chauchat – what is the true destiny of Castorp and of Germany? The distinction, however, seems unsubtle, for it is the fascination that Madame Chauchat's body exerts which directs Hans Castorp to the apparently 'humanistic' interest in the sciences; love of a diseased object becomes transmuted into a desire for more and more knowledge in an act of erotic sublimation. He is given time – seven years – to learn and develop and change, to let those potentialities dormant within him come to full fruition. In true romantic fashion Thomas Mann knows that the proximity of death enhances the meaning of life: death, as Novalis knew, is the minus sign which translates into the positive all that precedes it. Hans Castorp explains to Madame Chauchat that there are two ways to life: 'der eine ist der gewöhnliche, direkte und brave. Der andere ist schlimm, er führt über den Tod und das ist der geniale Weg!'[9] In a letter written as early as 1915 Thomas Mann had described his novel thus: 'Der Geist des Ganzen ist humoristisch-nihilistisch und eher schwankt die Tendenz nach der Seite der Sympathie mit dem Tode';[10] later, however, he took stock of this fascination with death, and also ironically contemplates his earlier belief that the sick were somehow more interesting, more aristocratic and more intelligent than the healthy. The inmates of Berghof are vain, petty, vulgar and often ludicrously ignorant (Frau Stöhr's enthusiasm for Beethoven's 'Erotica' symphony is a good example of this); it soon becomes apparent that the atmosphere in which they live is indicative of that of European society before the outbreak of war. A late-comer on the scene is Mynheer Peeperkorn, apparently a Titan, but a man flawed and pathetic, in spite of his grandiose poses before the natural Alpine scenery: Gerhart Hauptmann acted as model here, whose *Der Ketzer von Soanna*, which appeared in 1918, had not entirely convinced Thomas Mann. As so often before, he took the external features of a writer – this time Hauptmann – to use as an impetus for the imagination: it is the cult of Dionysian vitalism, which Thomas Mann found in Hauptmann's work at this time, which is parodied, not the figure of Hauptmann himself. The vogue which the work of Whitman was enjoying in Germany is also parodied in Hans Castorp's remarkable effusions (in French!) in the 'Walpurgisnacht' chapter: the

fulsome praise of the opulent voluptuousness of the female body is
satirised, as is the romantic elevation of love, sickness and death above
life.

Hans Castorp must finally pass through the carnage of Armageddon
but not before having learned in a vision at the point of death itself
that 'Der Mensch soll um der Güte und Liebe willen dem Tode keine
Herrschaft einräumen über seine Gedanken'.[11] To acknowledge that
which is life-enhancing even in the realm of sickness, to bestow a
Nietzschean affirmation (albeit tinged with ironic awareness and self-
awareness) on all things – this is surely the lesson learnt from this
profound, complex and highly entertaining novel, to find a balance
between facile humanism and the temptations of pessimism,
between utilitarianism and the romantic abyss. In a letter to Josef
Ponten, dated 5 February 1925, Thomas Mann explains that man may
indeed be 'zu vornehm für das Leben', and aware of the fascination of
death, yet he also adds 'Aber namentlich ist er zu vornehm für den Tod
und darum sei er frei und gütig in seinen Gedanken'.[12] In the words of
T.J. Reed:

> The elevation of the Mountain, sometime symbol for pure art, is
> now the symbol of that divorcing of art from realities which has
> been the chief social characteristic of German art since the age of
> Weimar Classicism. 'Aestheticism' is the word for both, but the
> valuation has changed. It is a radical change. By locating the
> 'hopelessness' and 'lack of prospects' of pre-1914 Europe in
> aestheticism, Thomas Mann had come fully round to his brother's
> view and stated it in identical terms.[13]

'Ich sehe die Welt als Künstler an und glaube zwar demokratisch zu
denken, fühle aber durchaus aristokratisch, das heißt, ich vermag
jede Art von Qualität zu lieben, nicht aber die Quantität.'[14] These
sentiments may have been entertained by Mann at a certain time, but
they would never have been expressed with such lack of subtlety.
The writer is Hermann Hesse, who achieved fame with a series of works
dating from the time immediately following the end of the war. The
melancholy lyricism of the *Romantische Lieder* (1898) and the rather
pallid 'Bildungsroman' *Peter Camenzind* (1904) appealed to those who
cared little for modernism and preferred a diluted romanticism
(Hugo Ball described Hesse as 'der letzte Ritter aus dem glanzvollen
Zug der Romantik'[15]); the works after the war, apparently more
sophisticated and problematic, achieved popularity because of their

pretentious mysticism (*Demian*), orientalism (*Siddharta*) and nature-worship. *Eine Kinderseele*, a portrayal once more of the relationship between child and parental authority lacks the nervous subtlety of Kafka's *Brief an den Vater*, written in the same year (1919); *Klein und Wagner*, which tells of a flight to the south, away from order and discipline into turbulence and ultimate dissolution ('sich fallen lassen'), seems a poor imitation of *Der Tod in Venedig*. Hesse's move to his house at Montagnola, his awareness of the south, and its profusion of colours and forms is reflected in *Klingsors letzter Sommer*, where the feast of sensual pleasure indulged in by the poet is another variation on the theme of sensual abandonment, the dissolving of all order and the merging of the self into the oneness of nature which is so frequently found in German literature. It was, however, *Der Steppenwolf* (1927) which endeared Hesse to countless readers who saw in him the psychologist most able to analyse the problems of the fragmented self. The romantic alienation and transcendent illumination which Hesse seemed to guarantee to a later generation are already adumbrated here: the 'outsider' Harry Haller and his various psychic adventures possess little of originality, for German literature has been haunted by outsiders ever since Anton Reiser; the pseudo-psychology, superficially impressive, fails to satisfy at a later reading. The mawkish sentimentality of *Narziß und Goldmund*, brilliantly criticised by Karlheinz Deschner, confirms the suspicion that Hesse rarely succeeds in shaking off the elegiac *Schwärmerei* of his youth (Ernst Stadler commented shrewdly on his lack of incision and passion[16]); a scarcely understood Nietzscheanism and a predilection for psychological platitudes brought but little respect from writers of a tougher, more incisive temperament.

Hesse's fame derived basically from his popularisation of doctrines derived from the psychology and anti-materialism of his day: his work is easy to assimilate, and the preference for subjectivity, flux and fluid forces, for synthesis rather than analysis gained wide acceptance among a reading public who preferred the nebulous to the precise. Hesse's 'theology' need not be discussed here; the belief in a 'unity' or 'oneness' beyond conventional morality is derived from such disparate sources as Nietzsche, Christianity and Buddhism, and the poem 'Besinnung' (1933) describes the position in somewhat portentous terms. In *Mein Glaube* Hesse elucidates this poem, stressing the ultimate unity beyond all phenomena and, in *Ein Stückchen Theologie* discusses the movement towards the third realm of the spirit; such doctrines, however, have as little originality as the narrative descriptions have vitality and power.

To affirm all in a pantheistic embrace is also the way of Baal, the central figure in the first play of Bertolt Brecht (1898–1956); the differences between the two men are, however, immense. *Baal* was written when Brecht was merely twenty, but it speaks with an indisputable originality of tone and forcefulness of language. Written in 1918 it demonstrated without doubt that Brecht was a better playwright than Hanns Johst, to whose *Der Einsame. Ein Menschenuntergang* the play *Baal* was meant as a reply. Whereas Johst had used the stock-in-trade of expressionism in his portrayal of the anti-hero, Brecht savagely gave his audience a portrayal of Baal which eschewed pathos and hyperbole: Baal's amorality and brutishness have the power of a natural force, overwhelming, repellent and fascinating at the same time. In the first version of the play Brecht, through Baal, ridiculed two poems, one by Stramm, the other by the worker-poet Nowotny, whose socialism Brecht obviously cared little about at this stage of his writing; Wedekind is brought to mind in Baal's obscene ballads, and the portrayal of the wanderings of Baal and Eckart and their indulgence in sexual promiscuity, both heterosexual and homosexual, reminds the reader of Rimbaud and Verlaine. The theme of drifting, of openness to all experience, is akin to the central theme of Rimbaud's *Le bâteau ivre*, whose splendid rhetoric, masterful coinage of imagery and sense of revolt openly appealed to Brecht. The self is merged into the natural processes of birth and decay: totally at the mercy of his sexual urges, Baal experiences and expresses all, and his poems are the ultimate expression of his attitude to life, particularly 'Vom ertrunkenen Mädchen', with the description of the gradual dissolving of the girl's body in the water. Brecht later deplored the 'lack of wisdom' of his first play, but he could not have disapproved of its vital images:

> Und die Liebe ist, wie wenn man seinen nackten Arm in Teichwasser schwimmen läßt, mit Tang zwischen den Fingern; wie die Qual, vor der der trunkene Baum knarzend zu singen anhebt, auf dem der wilde Wind reitet; wie ein schlürfendes Ersaufen im Wein an einem heißen Tag, und ihr Leib dringt einem wie sehr kühler Wein in alle Hautfalten . . .[17]

The 'Choral vom großen Baal', with its remarkable colour imagery, is likewise impressive in its brutal vigour.

Brecht was one of a group of young dramatists who emerged in the early years of the Weimar Republic and their works, frequently awarded the Kleist Prize, created theatrical scandals by their fearless outspokenness. After a *succès de scandale* many faded into obscurity: Marieluise Fleisser (1901–1974) is a good example here, whose *Fegefeuer in Ingolstadt* (1926) and *Pioniere in Ingolstadt* (1929), promoted and encouraged by Brecht, provoked scandalised discussion, but which lapsed from the repertoire. But Brecht, through collaboration (with Feuchtwanger and others), cunning and undeniable talent, kept abreast of the modern techniques of a man like Piscator, and produced a corpus of work which was to mark a watershed in theatrical history. The *enfant terrible* of Berlin, abrasive, cynical, witty and nonchalant in turns, deliberately rejected all the manifestations of bourgeois culture, particularly the 'well-made play', but also rejected much of expressionism, in particular its rodomontade, formlessness and pretentiousness. The hero with a vision was ousted by the cynical Kragler of *Trommeln in der Nacht*; the expressionist *Stationendrama* gave way to a balladesque, almost flippant, structure and the baleful moon, which, in many expressionist plays, presaged doom or sombre self-destruction, falls from the wings, an obvious stage prop. 'Glotzt nicht so romantisch!'[18] — this exhortation to the audience was a deliberate attempt to return to an older form of theatre, medieval and also oriental, which felt no need to create an atmosphere of illusion; Brecht's later, rather more subtle *Verfremdungseffekte* should not be flaunted for their own sake, but assessed as attempts to liberate the critical faculties of the audience. Piscator, Brecht later believed, carried the use of anti-illusory devices to excess: their use must be judicious and telling. Novalis's aphorism 'Die Kunst, auf eine angenehme Art zu befremden, einen Gegenstand fremd zu machen und doch bekannt und anziehend, das ist die romantische Poetik'[19] claims that romanticism 'alienates' to make the object more fascinating; for Brecht the purpose entailed the stimulation of critical thought. Leaving behind those plays which extolled individuality above all else and which portrayed struggles to communicate in a hostile and absurd world (such as *Im Dickicht der Städte*, with its obvious echoes of Upton Sinclair's novel of Chicago life *The Jungle*, and his adaptation, with Feuchtwanger, of Marlowe's *Life of Edward II of England*), Brecht turned towards a Marxist interpretation of human life: the loss of a certain exuberance, particularly at the end of the 1920s, was the price he had to pay for a growth in ideological commitment. It is surprising that Arnold Zweig's *Der Streit um den Sergeanten Grischa* was of little interest to him; Rilke, less surprisingly, is rejected, as is the 'aristocratic' Gottfried Benn. In Kafka Brecht detected several *Verfremdungseffekte* which pleased him: Kafka's lucidity and precision would also have appealed to him.

Brecht's greatest success was the *Dreigroschenoper*, which was first
performed on 31 August 1928 in the Theater am Schiffbauerdamm:
this play, together with Carl Zuckmayer's rustic comedy *Der fröhliche
Weinberg* (which anticipates Brecht's *Herr Puntila und sein Knecht
Matti*, particularly with the scene of the four engagements) was *the*
theatrical event of the 1920s. This adaptation of John Gay's *The Beggar's
Opera* of 1728, plus ballads derived from Kipling and Villon, owed
much of its success to Kurt Weill's music, but the grotesque *Moritat*,
with its cheeky equation of capitalism with criminality, has an
undeniably comic element. It was after the enormous success of this
work, which the audience seemed bent on enjoying at all costs, that
Brecht tended to the extremes of dogmatism which he felt necessary to
convey his social message — the need for a new society free of exploitation and privilege. Fortunately, however, this period was a transient
one, and the well-rounded, plausible, deeply human characters which
his dramatic flair never tired of creating asserted themselves after the
cardboard sterility of *Der Jasager* and *Der Neinsager*. What makes
Mahagony, Mann ist Mann and *Die Dreigroschenoper* such excellent
entertainment is the plenitude of ebullient characters, rooted in a
fantastic Anglo-American (or Anglo-Indian) world never found in
reality but culled from the legends of the Roaring Twenties or the
heyday of the British Raj; Brecht never ceased to admire the world
of boxers, lumberjacks, colonial soldiers and gamblers, which may
partly be derived from the expressionist cult of vital, atavistic forces.
The theme of survival, likewise, is a central one, from *Baal* right
through to *Galileo*: tragic inevitability was totally alien to Brecht, for
whom metamorphosis, development and change precluded dramatic
clash, and 'Epic' theatre, with its working out of a particular fable, was
seen as being a far more satisfactory mode of portrayal than conventional drama.

Brecht's name is frequently linked with the movement inaugurated
in the mid-1920s under the name *Neue Sachlichkeit*. In 1925 G.H.
Hartlaub organised an exhibition in Mannheim of pictures by
Beckmann, Dix, Grosz and Schlichter which was characterised by an
objectivity and nonchalant modernity which were far more akin to the
forms of social life at that time than expressionism had ever been. At
the same time the music of Hindemith and Weill, and, in literature,
the trend towards documentary *Reportage*, reflected a new sobriety or
matter-of-factness; flippancy and deadpan humour were also very
much the order of the day. The light verse of Erich Kästner (b. 1904),

Joachim Ringelnatz (that is, Hans Bötticher, 1883–1934) and Kurt
Tucholsky (1890–1935) became extremely popular; Hans Fallada
(that is, Rudolf Ditzen, 1893–1947), who assumed the pseudonym
after the martyred horse Falada of the Grimm fairy tale whose head,
after being cut off, still spoke the truth to a world sadly in need of it,
was an acute observer of the plight of the underdog and achieved world
fame with his novel *Kleiner Mann, was nun?* Brecht's first book of
poems *Die Hauspostille* reflects the movement away from the nature-
imagery *à la* Baal towards the theme of the city, the modern, the
sachlich and the political; his original use of strange images, mixed
with colloquialisms, to produce a 'realism' which is nevertheless
bizarre, lends a very distinctive tone to his poetry at this time. Both
Brecht and Benn, with their big-city poetry, seem part of the movement
which, as was mentioned in chapter 6, may be seen as an offshoot of
expressionism rather than as a reaction to it. Yet its unheroic
materialism and cynicism are utterly remote from expressionist rapture,
which is closer if anything to the National Socialist emphasis on energy
and idealism.

Brecht needed the stimulus of collaboration, which stemmed rather
from a sincere desire to discuss and learn rather than from paucity
of invention, as Alfred Kerr claimed when gleefully discovering what
he denounced as plagiarism. In the decade from 1918 onwards Brecht
and Klabund worked extremely closely; Klabund subsequently married
Carola Neher, who played the part of Polly Peachum in the film version
of the *Dreigroschenoper*, and was later murdered in the Soviet Union.
(He had met Brecht in the Wedekind seminar, run by Arthur Kutscher,
at Munich University in 1917.) Klabund's poetry is similar to that of
Heine's in its mixture of lyricism and satire; in the 1920s his novels
(*Borgia, Pjotr* and *Bracke*) were extremely popular, and the grotesque
anecdote *Der Mann in der Maske* is, as Walter Sokel has pointed out, a
classic example of expressionistic 'vampirism' where the hideously
deformed writer, concealing his disease-ridden face behind the mask,
sits like a spider in a café and waits for life to provide vicarious enjoyment. The novel *Moreus: Roman eines Soldaten*, written in
marked parataxis, shows great similarity to film technique
(Klabund did work on a film script for *Rasputin*); his *Spuk*,
'geschrieben im Fieber einer Krankheit',[20] is a sombre exploration of
madness and hallucination, the mental-home providing a distorting-
mirror image of society. Klabund's eclecticism, his virtuosity and
facility in writing tend to the journalistic; his plays have not been
successful, although *Der Kreidekreis* formed the basis of Brecht's better

known work.

The literary verve, satirical skill and humanitarian concerns of Ringelnatz, Kästner, Tucholsky, Fallada and Klabund give pleasant relief from the ponderous earnestness of much German writing. It is, of course, axiomatic that the great names are not always the most popular: in the decade immediately preceding Hitler's coming to power the most widely read author in the German language was Stefan Zweig (1882–1942), who was certainly the most widely translated, not only into English and French, but also into Italian, Hungarian, Bulgarian, Russian, Chinese, Japanese and even Georgian. The early poems, typically *Jugendstil*, and the monographs on Verhaeren and Rolland had appeared before 1919, and brought success, but between 1925 and 1933 Zweig's Novellen, essays, dramas and, above all, the biographies and historical miniatures, particularly the *Sternstunden der Menschheit* (1927), brought enormous prestige. His polished style may well appear too facile, his Maugham-like stories too superficial to be ultimately satisfying, but it cannot be denied that the German language achieved great suppleness and smoothness in his hands. Zweig's work for the theatre is not so well known, but the range is impressive, from the anti-war dramatic poem *Jeremias*, produced in Zurich in 1917, to his greatest stage success *Volpone*, freely adapted from Ben Johnson, and his libretto for Strauss's *Die schweigsame Frau*. Another Austrian novelist, Josef Roth (1894–1939), is a light-weight who nevertheless achieved great acclaim with his *Hiob* (1930) and *Radetzkymarsch* (1932), a completely unsentimental portrayal of the decline of the Dual-Monarchy which is not without a sense of the melancholy absurdity of all things. The moral dissolution of Lieutenant von Trotta, grandson of the 'hero of Salferino', in the remote Eastern provinces, his lassitude and helplessness seem symptomatic of a wider malaise, yet Roth writes with a lightness of touch and lack of pretension that are wholly admirable. There is nothing theatrical in the portrayal of the old Emperor, nothing written with the obvious advantage of hindsight which mars so many historical novels. It is false to describe Roth as hankering for the days prior to 1914: his articles for *Der neue Tag*, written in and about the Vienna of 1919 and Berlin 1921–1924 (Roth also contributed to the left-wing *Vorwärts*), show a hard-headed realisation of the obvious failings of both Habsburg and Hohenzollern: the past was only glorified ironically, yet the future was feared – the successor to *Radetskymarsch, Die Kapuzinergruft*, ends in the darkness of the *Anschluss*.

The most impressive achievements of the later Weimar period are, however, the complex and weighty novels by Döblin, Musil, Broch (1896–1951) and, later, Canetti (b. 1905), scarcely popular, but literary accomplishments of the first order, which leave far behind the conventional war novels of Renn (b. 1889) and Remarque (1898–1970), and the worthy yet simplistic stories of the women writers: *Die Letzte am Schafott* by Gertrud von Le Fort (1876–1971), *Der Aufstand der Fischer von St Barbara* by Anna Seghers (b. 1900), and the novels of Ina Seidel (1885–1974). It is obvious that the prose-form is more suitable to the 'matter-of-fact' writers, but it is only Döblin who might partially qualify for inclusion in a discussion of *Neue Sachlichkeit*: as the 1920s came to an end the novel form achieved a symphonic, even cosmic stature which left the realm of the merely factual. As far as the theatre is concerned it is Brecht who dominates the scene, but Zuckmayer (1896–1977) and Ödön von Horváth (1901–1938) were names of comparable stature at that time. *Der fröhliche Weinberg* had been second only to *Die Dreigroschenoper* in its popularity, and had been taken up instantly by over one hundred theatres in Germany; Zuckmayer had, under Brecht's influence, begun by writing a 'Wild-West' play called *Pankraz erwacht*, but after this had failed he left the aggressively avant-garde and turned to the *Volks-stück*, rooted in the soil of his native Rhineland. Here is *Volkstum* without any of its Nazi implications, a robust sense of the rightness of the natural order, which reflected Zuckmayer's love of folk diction and the folk-song (like Brecht he excelled at singing ballads). *Der Haupt-mann von Köpenick* (1931) consolidated Zuckmayer's reputation as a leading dramatist after a series of realistic didactic plays; propounding no new theory of drama or stage production, Zuckmayer remained within the tradition of naturalist theatre, with distinctly romantic overtones. Far more abrasive, and closer to Brecht, was Ödön von Horváth, grotesquely killed by a falling branch during a thunderstorm in Paris. Horváth, who did not write his first German sentence until the age of fourteen, was awarded the Kleist Prize at the age of thirty on Zuck-mayer's recommendation: his *Volksstücke* look back to Raimund, Nestroy and Anzengruber but, as in the case of Brecht, Büchner and Lenz seem to be the direct ancestors. His most famous play, *Geschichten aus dem Wienerwald* (1931), has a cutting edge which is certainly reminiscent of much in Brecht, who knew his work intimately, and often obtained copies of even the unpublished plays. In the general iconoclasm Horváth was concerned above all with self-delusion, particularly the linguistic masks that men use unknowingly to conceal their true motives. After his exile he took to short stories and novels: *Ein Kind unserer Zeit* (1938) demonstrates the senselessness of patriotic gestures and jargon ('All die hohlen Phrasen, unverschämt und überheblich, nachgeplappert und nachgebetet . . .'[21]), and lets the disillusioned hero freeze to death on a park bench.

The lyric, as has been stated, found expression in light satirical verse which had none of the intensity of the expressionistic experiments: Brecht's *Die Hauspostille* collection (1927), with echoes of Wedekind, Rimbaud, Kipling and Villon, parodies the bible and the German classics and is frequently diverting in its mock-didactic tone. The exception to the meagreness of the lyric is the poetry of Gottfried Benn. The *enfant terrible* of the *Morgue* poems had seen active service in Belgium; he attended, as a medical officer, the execution of Nurse Edith Cavell and later, in Brussels, enjoyed the intellectual companion-ship of Otto Flake, Carl Einstein, and Carl Sternheim, who was living in exile at La Hulpe. In 1917 his collection *Fleisch* appeared, containing most of his earlier poetry; the stories, under the collective title *Gehirne* had appeared in 1916 in an expressionist series *Der jüngste Tag*, edited by Franz Werfel. In the 1920s Benn, established as a doctor in Berlin, was very much *au fait* with the literary scene, and had, in fact, appeared in court as a witness in the case of the Dadaist journal *Jedermann sein eigener Fußball* which, as was mentioned in chapter 6, was prosecuted for obscenity. The poetry which Benn wrote in the 1920s is a combination of deliberately modern, urbane phrasing, of medical scientific terms which are deliberately 'unpoetic', and intense, fre-quently irrational longings: a hallmark of his poetry is an accumulation of nouns which insist upon an essential, static meaning. The concept of the 'absolute poem' is emerging in his work: in an incomprehensible universe meaning is only achieved through the poetic act, the mysterious fusion of disparate parts — Broadway, inter-stellar space, the Parthenon, the cervical cortex. The poem 'Der Sänger' (1925) is a statement of the poet's position and task: poetry now, a purely cerebral experience, moulds the chaotic mass of impressions and concepts into a form of absolute experience, expressing the void and the senselessness of which the poet is all too aware, yet paradoxically transcending meaninglessness in that very act. Brecht's esteem for Benn's modernity (if not for his aloofness) led him to present a signed copy of *Die Hauspostille* to him; Brecht also saw in Döblin a colleague who was achieving in the novel what he, Brecht, had done for the theatre and the lyric, a man who dared to get away from a purely 'literary' language and who was toughly realistic without slavishly 'imitating' reality.

Berlin Alexanderplatz has been called the most radically modernist novel of the twenties: the themes of passivity and action, adumbrated in *Die drei Sprünge des Wang-lun* (1915) and *Wallenstein* (1920), are updated and transposed to Berlin: a sense of reality is achieved which is yet somehow also oblique to the real. The book is as soaked in reality as *Manhattan Transfer*, but comparisons have also been made with Joyce's *Ulysses* (Julius Bab, Hans Henny Jahnn and others referred in their reviews of the book to the Irish novelist): interior monologue, collage and montage convey the density as well as the fragmentary and elusive quality of life. There is *Sachlichkeit*, yet also a deliberate alienation *à la* Brecht: the novel is an enormous *Moritat*, and the motto given at the beginning of the book could have been taken directly from the *Dreigroschenoper*: 'Hier im Beginn verläßt Franz Biberkopf das Gefängnis Tegel, in das ihn ein früheres sinnloses Leben geführt hat. Er faßt in Berlin schwer wieder Fuß, aber schließlich gelingt es ihm doch, worüber er sich freut, und er tut nun den Schwur, anständig zu sein'.[22] Descriptions of Franz Biberkopf's passage through the roaring city alternate with medical reports on certain sexual difficulties, excerpts from the municipal transport timetable, cuttings from the sports pages, and with weather reports and stockmarket information, which carry a sense of absolute immediacy. Yet Döblin also precludes too close an involvement in the fate of Franz Biberkopf by describing his actions, as does Joyce with those of Leopold Bloom, in terms of physical laws: a description of the murder, a crime for which Biberkopf served four years' prison sentence before the novel opens, is transformed into the ludicrous. There is no attempt at naturalism as in *Die Familie Selicke*, but a fusion of Joyce and Brecht; a fragmented mass of impressions is moulded into an epic account, using several alienating techniques, of the forces acting upon Franz Biberkopf. In Herbert Ihering's words, 'Es ist das Thema *Mann ist Mann* in der Sphäre eines Berlinischen *Dreigroschenepos*'.[23]

Biberkopf, within the space of one year, passes through the jungle of the city and is dealt violent blows in the battle 'mit etwas, das von außen kommt, das unberechenbar ist und wie ein Schicksal aussieht . . . Es stößt und schlägt ihn mit einer Gemeinheit. Er kann sich schon schwer erheben, er wird schon faßt ausgezählt. Zuletzt torpediert es ihn mit einer ungeheuerlichen äußersten Roheit'.[24] Obstinate, yet good-humoured, naive, sentimental and at times violent he sinks from one stage of degradation to another, is deceived, becomes involved in criminal activities, is hurled from a car travelling at high speed, is crushed between the wheels of a second car, loses an arm, yet finds

brief respite in a love affair with a prostitute who is brutally murdered.
He loses his sanity, yet is finally restored to life and finds work in a
factory. The author tells us:

> Das furchtbare Ding, das sein Leben war, bekommt einen Sinn. Es ist
> eine Gewaltkur mit Franz Biberkopf vollzogen. Wir sehen am Schluß
> den Mann wieder am Alexanderplatz stehen, sehr verändert, rampon-
> iert, aber doch zurechtgebogen. Dies zu betrachten und zu hören
> wird sich für viele lohnen, die wie Franz Biberkopf in einer
> Menschenhaut wohnen und denen es passiert wie diesem Franz
> Biberkopf, nämlich vom Leben mehr zu verlangen als das
> Butterbrot.[25]

Visions of Job, of 'die große Hure Babylon' and, finally, 'der singende
Tod', accompany this tale of one who is no longer blind, but has gained
insight: he cannot live for himself, but only as part of the teeming
multitude: 'Viel Unglück kommt davon, wenn man allein geht . . . Ein
Schiff liegt nicht fest ohne großen Anker, und ein Mensch kann nicht
sein ohne viele andere Menschen. Was wahr und falsch ist, werde ich
jetzt besser wissen'.[26] Some of the quietism of *Wang Lun* has been
achieved here, and his question at the end of *Die drei Sprünge* answered
affirmatively. *Babylonische Wandrung*, published in Amsterdam in
1934, continues to curse the sin of pride, and portrays with grotesque
humour the passage of Konrad through the Babylon of Western
Civilisation in a journey of self-exploration and expiation. The fusion of
mythology, history, modern events, statistical facts and popular songs
may be rejected as formless, but an inexhaustible richness cannot be
denied.

Franz Blei, writing in *Das Tagebuch 2* in 1921, praised Döblin's
Wallenstein highly, especially the psychological precision of its
handling of both individuals and masses. Blei called it 'ein Werk größten
Stiles . . . in allem Romanhaften der Deutschen dieser letzten
Jahrzehnte ein einziges Mal noch, von Musil in *den Verwirrungen*
erreicht',[27] and Döblin himself, writing in the *Berliner Tagblatt* (3
February 1924) insisted that: 'Es wird dem deutschen, sehr in Gefühlen
schlampenden Lesepublikum gut tun, sich mit dem hellen, elastischen
Geist Musils zu befassen'[28] (it was Döblin who recommended Musil
for the Kleist Prize in 1923 for his play *Die Schwärmer*). It was the
precision and elegance of Musil's style which Döblin admired, its
psychological finesse and intellectual vigour; Musil was, as was pointed
out in chapter 3, a man of letters who had first studied engineering.

It is interesting that Hermann Broch, leading member of the *Öster-reichischer Industriellenverband*, should have seriously considered becoming a mathematician, that Elias Canetti should be a scientist by academic training, and that Hans Henny Jahnn should devote much energy to biological studies; it would seem that the analysis of a particular individual, or of a disintegrating social system needed the skill of a writer with scientific training as well as the sensitivity of the traditional artist: the 'undisciplined squads of emotion' of much expressionism, and the wincing sensitivity of aestheticism were rejected in favour of precise statement, frequently tempered with irony.

In 1930 Robert Musil published the first volume of his *Der Mann ohne Eigenschaften*; he had been working on this for the best part of a decade (although the idea for the work was found as early as 1901), and the rest of his life would be spent on the task of writing (or rather failing to write) this enormous narrative discourse. Certain themes of the work are also adumbrated in the *Drei Frauen* stories which Musil published in 1924: the passivity of the women and the journey of self-realisation that the men undertake are reminiscent of the relationship between Ulrich and Agathe; the theme of 'der andere Zustand', that sphere of mystical reality beyond reason, is also hinted at in *Tonka*. Similarly the hero of the short play *Vinzenz* oder *die Freundin bedeutender Männer*, first published in Berlin in 1923, shares with Ulrich the reluctance to 'take on a quality', to turn the potential into reality, for fear that the result would be trivial and absurd. Musil's unfinished *monstrum*, left incomplete at his death in 1942 and whose final shape is still the subject of acrimonious debate, is called by its detractors muddled and chaotic, rambling and infuriating in its ironic detachment and a typical product of a decaying, over-sophisticated society; its defenders claim that it certainly holds a mirror to Austro-Hungary, or Kakania (and, indeed, is a brilliant portrayal of that Empire on the point of collapse), but that Musil's insights into human behaviour have a universal applica-tion. Far from being formless, the work betrays the organic principle of growth and complexity which is life itself, and its irony, resulting from an unwillingness to simplify and pronounce moral disapprobation, to fix and locate, is a virtue; in Musil's epic novel are freshness, charm and intellectual curiosity unequalled anywhere in twentieth-century German literature.

Der Mann ohne Eigenschaften was originally planned in four parts, volume one to contain part one (*Eine Art Einleitung*) and part two (*Seinesgleichen geschieht*), and volume two would have contained part

three (*Die Verbrecher*) and part four (*Eine Art Ende*). The first volume
was published, as has been noted, in 1930; a second volume, containing
part three, and now entitled *Ins tausendjährige Reich*, was published in
1933; a third volume, which remained unfinished, was published
privately in Switzerland after Musil's death: it included the unrevised
chapters. This unfinished work of over one thousand five hundred
pages concerns a 'man without qualities', a man who, rather, has many
qualities, some remarkably good ones, but who is not defined by them,
who does not settle down amongst them, who moves away from
fixities and rigid definitions, from ideologies and attitudinising. He
'takes a year off life', and moves with elegance, intelligence and irony
through Viennese society: the year is 1913—1914. Opportunities for
delicious satire abound: the Imperial and Royal, imperial-royal Dual
Monarchy of Austro-Hungary is not scourged in the manner of Karl
Kraus, but its shortcomings are wittily observed. Robert Musil was
familiar with the idiosyncrasies of his native land; his studies in Berlin
had likewise made him aware of the nature of Prussian ambitions.
But this book is not basically concerned with Kakanian velleities:
profounder, more universal issues are involved. A 'journey into a
millennium' is proposed, a movement beyond rationalism; as society
moves towards disintegration a mystical transfiguration is posited and
mythical archetypes emerge.

Ulrich (originally called Robert) resembles his author in many ways,
and similarities exist between characters in this book and people whom
Musil met and more often than not disliked. Arnheim the industrialist
is based on Walther Rathenau, and the irrationalist philosopher Ludwig
Klages, whose work was discussed in chapter 4, is seen in the 'prophet'
Meingast; the poet Feuermaul is a parody of Franz Werfel, and the
Swedish essayist Ellen Key seems to have provided the model for
Diotima. But this is not simply a *roman à clef*: the characters are
singled out because they seem to exemplify a malaise which is endemic
not only in Kakania and Germany, but which relates to mankind as a
whole. Ulrich starts his intellectual journey by visiting his cousin, Frau
Ermelinde Tuzzi (or Diotima), where he learns that great plans are
afoot: the year 1918 would mark the seventieth anniversary of the
accession to the throne of the Emperor Franz Josef, as well as the
thirtieth anniversary of the upstart Hohenzollern: to prevent the
Prussian Empire from capturing the world's imagination a vast 'World-
Austrian-Year' is planned, a year in which Austria would lead the
world in high ideals. Diotima invites to her house the leading figures
of Viennese society to plan the campaign, the conception of a crowning

Austrian idea for world civilisation. Committees are set up to deal with
the various categories of opinion, the wheels of Kakanian bureaucracy
(which Franz Kafka knew well) are set in motion, commercial concerns
begin to associate themselves with the patriotic movement, representa-
tions are received on behalf of orphans' homes and birdwatching, the
Öhl shorthand system and vegetable culture, physical education and the
abolition of open salt-cellars in public restaurants, the society for
the care and protection of domestic cats, the Emperor Franz Josef
Jubilee Year Soup Kitchen and a thousand more. And Ulrich looks on
with dispassionate irony. He sees attitudes being struck, millions and
millions of words being written and circulated, an eternal revolving
round a vacuum which threatens to become a vortex. The industrialist
Arnheim appears to be altruistic, yet the overheated idealism displayed
in Diotima's salon conceals a tangle of selfish ambitions. Far less
sinister is General Stumm von Bordwehr, seconded by the Ministry of
War to study the civilian mind; baffled in his attempt to understand the
'great idea' he withdraws, pleading the need for modern artillery.

As well as frequenting his cousin's home Ulrich visits his friend Leo
Fischel, a Jewish banker at whose home have gathered a group of
pan-German racialists and Christian idealists, exemplified by one Hans
Sepp, opponent of science and the intellect, champion of the 'symbol',
and highly critical of his time. Discussing the group Musil writes:

> Ihr Hauptlehrstück war das 'Symbol'; soweit Ulrich folgen
> konnte, und er hatte ja einiges Verständnis für derlei Dinge, nannten
> sie Symbol die großen Gebilde der Gnade, durch die das Verwirrte
> und Verzwergte des Lebens, wie Hans Sepp sagte, klar und groß
> wird, die den Lärm der Sinne verdrängen und die Stirn in den
> Strömen der Jenseitigkeit netzen . . . und was ein Symbol, in
> nüchternen Worten ausgedrückt, sei, das sagten sie nicht, erstens,
> weil sich Symbole in nüchternen Worten nicht ausdrücken lassen,
> zweitens weil Arier nicht nüchtern sein dürfen.[29]

Musil's tone is light, yet his insights are trenchant: the leather-shorts,
boy-scout attitudes of Sepp and his followers have not yet acquired
the demonic qualities that they would in another ten or twenty years.
But here again is endless discussion and a hardening of attitudes, while
reality, strangely elusive, evades all attempt at formalisation. Ulrich
plays the devil's advocate — he counters and parries, yet remains
mercifully uncommitted. But the second sphere of action in the book
is not the Fischel home, interesting though this may be, but the circle

around Ulrich's friends Walter and Clarisse, and here the book touches
upon themes that are sombre and fascinating – the themes of genius,
crime and madness, the concept of an 'Einbruch von unten' of
murderous forces which links Musil with other such Austrian writers as
Broch, Heimito von Doderer and, to a lesser extent, Elias Canetti.
The eruptive forces threaten from below, but Musil also knows that
civilisation is threatened when respectable men, jaded with the bland
and worthy attitudes of the civilised, long pruriently for contact with
the chthonic and the brutal.

The characterisation of Walter is sympathetic: the passage quoted
at the beginning of this book described the intellectual *pot pourri*
which he and Ulrich had tasted, and Walter's dilettantism may partly
be seen as being caused by such a confusion. When all seems propitious
for the creation of an art work Walter has to realise that his life is
barren: he consequently blames the times in which he lives and declares
that the pure artist must abstain from creation in such a degenerate age.
But his wife Clarisse is determined that he should become a genius:
fired with Nietzschean ideas she refuses him a child until he is worthy
of it, for she rightly suspects that Walter's main reason for wanting a
family is to occupy her and make their home a little less like
Zarathustra's cave. There is something highly entertaining in Musil's
description of her quoting Zarathustra to Walter as he is attempting to
assert conjugal rights, yet also very disturbing: Walter's description of
'das unselig Genialische in Clarissa, die geheime Kaverne, wo etwas
Unheilvolles an Ketten riß, die eines Tages nachlassen konnten'[30] shows
that with Clarisse there lurks a morbid interest in the irrational and the
violent: in Musil's novel it is Christian Moosbrugger who exemplifies
these dark forces, a carpenter on trial for multiple sexual murder.
Not only Clarisse, but the whole of Viennese society is fascinated by
Moosbrugger, and by the descriptions of the fearful wounds inflicted on
the prostitute's body: the prurient desire to read the details of the case
and to feel vicarious pleasure is well understood by Musil, who
nevertheless avoids the earnest platitude by a sense of humour which
delights in imagining the possibility 'daß in diesen Tagen beim Zubett-
gehen ein korrekter Herr Sektionschef oder ein Bankprokurist zu seiner
schläfrigen Gattin sagte: "Was würdest du jetzt anfangen, wenn ich ein
Moosbrugger wäre . . ." '.[31] Even Ulrich cannot dispel the thought
'Wenn die Menschheit als Ganzes träumen könnte, mußte Moosbrugger
entstehn'.[32] The theme of dreaming and sleep-walking will achieve
greater significance in Hermann Broch's *Die Schlafwandler*, where
Huguenau particularly, in an almost somnambulistic trance, obeys the

command of the irrational with dreadful consequences. Even Diotima herself is very interested in Moosbrugger: her salon seems all too ready to discuss him, the sex murderer. With consummate skill Musil shows how the rarefied idealism of the salon turns more and more to themes that hardly touch on the soul, how talk of beauty, truth, goodness becomes talk of ugliness, evil, and deception; questions regarding the meaning of truth become more concerned with untruth and crime, while questions concerning beauty become more and more obsessed with the sexual. Clarisse's suggestion that 1918 should be a Nietzsche-Year, even a Moosbrugger-Year, is palpably absurd, but the interest shown by civilised and refined people in the brutal and the lubricious is a phenomenon Musil saw clearly. Like the dreadful creature in Dostoevski's *Notes from the Underground* Moosbrugger lurks beneath the floorboards of modern civilisation, a black shadow of evil which calls into doubt all man's talk of moral perfection and enlightenment.

Clarisse's Nietzschean histrionics are a source of embarrassment to Ulrich, and he grows increasingly estranged from her and from Walter, as he does from Leo Fischel and his cousin's dramatic gestures. The Collateral Campaign is becoming a monstrous absurdity, and the Nietzsche-Meingast-Moosbrugger atmosphere intolerable. The year of absence from life has seemed to be a failure, yet he has learned much, and seen with astonishment the attitudes and beliefs of his fellow men. He feels the need to take stock of himself, to see if belief and love were possible, or if a boundless solipsism were all that he was doomed to experience. It is the death of his father which, paradoxically, involves him in the activities of life once more: he leaves Vienna for the town of his youth, which is to become the scene of his second birth. Ulrich sets out on a road which will lead him, and the novel as a whole, to a new dimension: against a background of social concern is silhouetted a new and visionary world of possibilities, a journey into the millennium, a mystical transfiguration of reality. But is it appropriate to use these terms? Ulrich is portrayed as having a highly developed intellect, his mind is incisive, his thinking is lucid — and yet he has sensed that there was a reality beyond scientific exactitude; he had longed to synthesise the objective, factual terms of science with the subjective, emotional states of poetry. Talking to Graf Leinsdorf he had described a Secretariat for Exactitude and the Soul, in terms not dis-similar to those used by his cousin; she, however, like many others, leapt from the super-rational to the subrational, thereby anticipating attitudes which, less than two decades later, would crystallise into a

national creed. Ulrich sought clarity and mystery, he longed to look
clearly at phenomena and at the same time to see that other side of
reality, 'den anderen Zustand'. It is his sister Agathe who enables him
to break through his hitherto cerebral approach to a vision of synthesis
and transfiguration, where clarity and revelation are one. ' "Ich habe
nicht gewußt, daß wir Zwillinge sind!" sagte Agathe, und ihr Gesicht
leuchtete erheitert auf'.[33] Both she and Ulrich wear, on the night of
their arrival at their father's house, a sort of pierrot costume, and
Musil embarks upon the themes of similarity, identity and oneness.
The concept of the hermaphrodite frequently crops up in the conversations between these two; Musil is by no means the only modern
author to touch upon it, for his fellow countrymen and contemporaries
Rilke and Trakl knew of it also. The hermaphrodite seems to become
more and more of an ideal (together with the theme of the incestuous
brother-sister relationship) in an age whose literature stresses the
ultimate loneliness of the individual, the impossibility of significant
human relationships and the almost inevitable disillusionment of sexual
love. Together with Narcissus and the symbol of the mirror, the theme
of the androgyne plays a role which is by no means insignificant within
the modern literary mythology.[34] While all around them move towards
disintegration, Ulrich and his sister, the identical pair, move towards
an ever-increasing intimacy. All around them people chase feverishly
from one attitude to another, throwing themselves into aesthetics,
athleticism, vitalism, pacifism and racialism – they are reformers,
antisemites, bankers, patriots, statesmen, authors, and harden
their attitudes into ludicrous and dangerous postures. Yet Ulrich and
Agathe embark upon a fascinating journey of exploration, in which all
becomes fluid, living and dynamic. Many, many pages follow brother
and sister into an ever-profounder intimacy, both of body and mind.
They think, move and develop, and Musil gives essay after essay,
treatise after treatise to convey the ever-scintillating incandescence of
their love, pages which are difficult to follow for any reader not
enthralled by the sheer fascination of living. The essay form preferred
by Musil cannot be seen simply as deriving from an inability to sustain
a coherent narrative thread; an 'essayistic' life style, with its perspectiv-
ism and open-mindedness had seemed to Ulrich to be the most
suitable: 'Ungefähr wie ein Essay in der Folge seiner Abschnitte ein
Ding von vielen Seiten nimmt, ohne es ganz zu erfassen – denn ein
ganz erfaßtes Ding verliert mit einem Male seinen Umfang und
schmilzt zu einem Begriff ein – glaubte er, Welt und eigenes Leben
am richtigsten ansehen und behandeln zu können'.[35] The essay, in

its combination of precision and reticence, does not abuse reality by inordinate demands and a too rigid method of interpretation.

Agathe, trapped in an unsatisfactory marriage, had been accused by her husband, the arid educational theorist Hagauer, of lacking community spirit. She shares much of Ulrich's creative passivity and, like him, is unable to assume the roles that the world expects of her. Her intimacy with her brother saves her, particularly the endless conversations that lead nowhere, prove nothing, and yet are captivatingly exhilarating. The journey to the South, to the glittering silver of the Mediterranean becomes a return to a world of mythical archetypes and to an earlier memory of Ulrich's of a mystical island where a wrapt communication with all the world became possible again. Yet Musil is mercilessly precise in his analysis of this love. He did not finish the novel, yet it became obvious that he realised that Ulrich and Agathe could not remain static in their love or their defiance of the world. The vision of paradise, the myth of Utopia is as old as the human race, and the love between brother and sister has indeed dispelled the dross and trivia of life, but no permanence can be assumed; indeed, the state of perfection itself may be a petrified and ultimately sterile condition. The ascent into the mythical has given a luminous meaning to their lives, but the charge of self-indulgence (even an arid, narcissistic selfishness) can be levelled at this love: flight and defiance may be ultimately self-defeating. The blazing days of heat do not last — rain and a feeling akin to boredom supersede the ecstasy of the beginning. Musil knows that timeless perfection is the greatest illusion of all, that life, to be tolerable, must have variety, an essential compound of good and bad, happiness and despair, toil and leisure. Their lives immeasurably enriched, they return to Vienna — but it is the summer of 1914.

The book gathers momentum. The Collateral Campaign, as may be expected, moves towards fiasco. A rumour appears in the capitals of Europe that in the autumn a peace conference is to be held in Vienna: in great embarrassment the government agrees to take over the political aspects, and leaves the festivities to Diotima. She is forced to give up her study of 'erogenous zones' and prepares the costume procession. The government gradually takes over more and more of the organisation, whilst the Ministry of Education leaves her hardly any more work to do than decide if, in the procession, a group called 'Wiener Schnitzel' should have precedence over 'Rostbratl mit Nockerln'.[36] She attempts to save her pride by calling the campaign a 'pan-erotic human experience', but it is brought to a ridiculous conclusion. The fragmentary notes ('Gartenfest') describe Diotima as a Napoleonic officer at a masked ball in Vienna: she is intoxicated, a pathetic figure who can no longer control her lascivious inclinations for any man who may come along, even a man without qualities. The other idealists, after their endless, high-flown rhetoric, reap material benefits: Arnheim increases his capital at the outbreak of war, General Stumm is gratified that the civilians are behind the army in times of crisis, and Graf Leinsdorf, totally unable to comprehend the situation, is convinced that the upstart Serbs would be crushed within weeks. Leo Fischel speculates to great advantage, whilst Hans Sepp, the pan-German idealist and seeker after glory, commits suicide, unable to bear the roughness of barrack life. Clarisse's case is most poignant: deranged, she journeys south, to Rome and Venice, in Nietzsche's footsteps, awaiting the Messiah and, like Nietzsche, she is brought back to the North, to sink into apathy and silence. The collapse of society, of the Collateral Campaign, of Austria and of Europe provide an appropriate background to the collapse of her mind.

The question arises: has anything been learned by Musil's characters as they move towards the holocaust? Is the outcome of this immense novel purely negative? Many doctrines and ideologies were put forward to give shape to life – Arnheim's fusion of heroism and industry, Sepp's demand for a powerful symbol, Meingast's desire for will and force, and Schmeisser's call for revolution. These ideas, Musil insists, have one thing in common: they all attempt total solutions, are schematic and singularly inept when faced with the quick of growth and life. Ulrich sees that these *Weltanschauungen* lack clarity and imagination: he sees that basically man fears to live, and clings instead to the dead husks of past beliefs rather than act out a new and living code. He rejects these rigid constructs which are arid and pretentious; his love for Agathe teaches him that man must forget ideologies, prejudices, outmoded loyalties and dogmatic beliefs; he must start from the facts, but facts transfigured by love, a 'heilige Nüchternheit'. The idealists run like Gadarene swine downwards towards destruction; the ironic 'man without qualities' moves towards a higher integrity – not a suspect Utopia, but a respect for life in all its manifold richness, both of the intellect and of the emotions. It is the hegemony of the *idée fixe,* the obsession with plans and jargon which obfuscated the mind of statesmen, soldiers and many intellectuals in the years leading up to 1914 and Musil, dying in loneliness and deprivation in 1942, saw that the lesson had not been learned, and that the *terribles simplificateurs* had imposed an even more brutal and irrational system upon life.

At the same time as the publication of volume one of *Der Mann ohne Eigenschaften* there appeared Hermann Broch's trilogy *Die Schlafwandler*. The similarities between Musil and Broch are striking: both embarked upon novels which would encompass the problem of the age, and would radically break with the traditional novel form, both combined rationalism and mysticism (Broch regarded his mathematical gifts as paramount), both suffered from lack of readers, and both died in exile, scarcely understood. Musil feared that Broch may have plagiarised his ideas — the charge is unfounded, for the similar backgrounds and dedication to the task in hand must needs have resulted in a natural affinity. Broch's ponderous earnestness lacks the humour and relativising irony which saves Musil's masterpiece; the concern with the social and the metaphysical and, ultimately, the question concerning the validity of art itself makes Broch's work a daunting yet stimulating experience. The *Schlafwandler* trilogy, encyclopaedic and 'poly-historical' novels, have as their central concern the disintegration of values and the decay of European civilisation, and cover the period 1888 to 1918. The first, *1888: Pasenow oder die Romantik*, has been compared with the work of Fontane, but the secure ground of the nineteenth century has been left far behind: the security of Joachim von Pasenow, Prussian officer, is severely undermined. For support and meaning he clings to the symbol of the uniform; he also seeks to convince himself that romantic love may also be found in marriage, stubbornly preferring the idea to the intransigent demands of harsher realities. The second novel of the trilogy, *1903: Esch oder die Anarchie* portrays the confusion of values of the small bookkeeper Wilhelm Esch, who neither escapes from Europe nor comes to any true understanding or acceptance of his life; the total insubstantiality of his existence is strikingly conveyed in the description: 'oft war es, als ob das Getane und das Gesprochene und Geschehene nichts wäre als ein Vorgang auf mattbeleuchteter Bühne, eine Darbietung, die vergessern wird und nie vorhanden war, Gewesenes, an das niemand sich klammern kann, ohne das irdische Leid zu vergrößern'.[37] The third novel, *1918: Huguenau oder die Sachlichkeit*, is the most sombre and dramatic of the trilogy in its portrayal of the dark, anarchic forces which threaten and finally destroy the social fabric. Broch, and later Doderer, describes the sinister forces as coming from below, just as Moosbrugger, from the lower regions, exerted his evil fascination; in *Huguenau* it is the Hanna Wendling episode which clearly demonstrates this. Hanna Wendling, trapped within a narcissistic circle of arid self-reflection and sterile, masturbatory fantasies, longs, much as Clarisse does, for violent realities:

more and more she becomes obsessed with the concept of the
'Einbruch von Unten' – a term used initially to describe the Bolshevist
revolution – and yearns for a catastrophe to liberate her from her
abnormal isolation.[38] Her death is indirectly caused by the mutiny of
local soldiers and the escape of several prisoners from military prison
in November 1918: the explosion which she hears seems to herald the
long-awaited catastrophe and, fatally attracted to one of the escaped
convicts, she goes towards the intruder in the night air, to the
detriment of her health. The Huguenau strand identifies Huguenau
with anarchic violence, beyond all moral categories, who murders
and deceives and deliberately joins the mutineers to exult in
destruction; it is he who murders Esch by stabbing him in the back
with a bayonet. The series of theoretical chapters on the 'Zerfall der
Werte' emphasises Huguenau's amorality; later writing by Broch,
particularly the work on *Massenpsychologie*, assumes that the 'Einbruch von Unten' is indubitably to be associated with Communism.

Broch dispenses with the traditional narrative form in his trilogy:
different perspectives are given, theoretical essays introduced as well as
a 'Geschichte des Heilsarmeemädchens in Berlin', which leaves prose
altogether for the more emotional vehicle of blank verse, sublime in its
intensity:

> Wie im Keime künft'ger Spiegelmeere
> ruhn im Regenbogensilberschaum,
> Odem über feuchtem Raum,
> zitternd Bündel goldner Sonnenspeere
> und an jenem fernsten Saum,
> wo der Himmel, daß er sich gebäre,
> selber Spiegel einem Spiegelmeere
> niedersinkt in Aphroditens Traum . . .[39]

The fusion of prose and poetry at certain points of this novel anticipates the technique used in the second of Broch's published novels,
Der Tod des Vergil (1945); this is essentially a prose-poem described by
Broch as 'nichts als ein ausgewalztes lyrisches Gedicht',[40] and it has
also been acclaimed as being the only advance beyond Joyce in the
matter of technical form. (Broch claimed that, had he been able to read
a German translation of *Ulysses* a few years earlier he would have
abstained from writing *Die Schlafwandler*: it was the intervention of
Joyce and others that released him from Nazi imprisonment in 1938.)
The description of the arrival of the dying Virgil at Brindisi is a perfect

example of Broch's skill in the creation of beautifully modulated sentences, sentences which are also paragraphs in themselves, which combine epic breadth with lyrical intensity. (The second sentence particularly is most effective in the juxtaposition of majestic pomp and fatal disease, of power and the spirit.) The novel is essentially a vast interior monologue of the dying Virgil, whose essential meaning concerns the relevance of art in a time of crisis. The whole problem of aestheticism and the ethical task of the artist achieves in this book its most luminous and wrapt portrayal: the poet who seeks beauty above all is 'dämonisch der Schönheit verhaftet, dämonisch trotz seiner göttlichen Gabe, ein Rauschbringer, doch nicht ein Heilsbringer der Menschen'.[41] Like Aschenbach shortly before his death, Broch's Virgil questions the claim of the artist to be a lawgiver and seer: in times of turbulence the poet has little wisdom to offer. The self-consciousness and doubt of so much modern German literature reaches its apogee here — ironically the visionary beauty of the work belies the doubts incorporated within it, for it is undoubtedly Broch's masterpiece, and a more eloquent abnegation of the word would be difficult to find. The artist dedicated to beauty, who, in Platen's words, is 'dem Tode schon anheimgegeben',[42] admits the vital powers of the man of action, before whose accomplishments all writings seem purposeless. Yet this is not simply a resigned awareness of the power of the *vita activa* over the *vita contemplativa*; there is also contained in it a realisation of the helplessness of the word when faced with the unspeakable, a problem which will haunt the German writer of the Nazi and post-Nazi era.

The third novel, *Die Schuldlosen*, is similar to *Die Schlafwandler* in its treatment of twentieth-century themes and the use of dates (1913, 1923 and 1933) to establish significant stages in a historical process of barbarism. The novel is not overtly political but, rather, shows how the unpolitical *Bürger*, in his evasion of responsibility and commitment, enables the unscrupulous to push to the fore. Andreas's attempt to find self-fulfilment implies an indifference towards the suffering of others; his escapism is seen as a form of solipsism which, too late, he regrets, and it is questionable whether or not his suicide is a meaningful act of expiation.

Broch's last novel, *Der Versucher*, published posthumously, attempts a parabolic description of the evil of National Socialism: the pseudo-mystical demagogue Marius Ratti who tempts the inhabitants of a mountain village to savagery and sacrificial murder is an obvious portrayal of Adolf Hitler. The work is ultimately unsatisfactory, however, in the portrayal of Mutter

Gisson and her Demeter-like qualities: the book is uncomfortably
suspended between political allegory and romantic myth. The
landscape descriptions do not have the power and weight
of those of Hans Henny Jahnn, but do possess a sensitive
precision, an intellectual, more transparent quality than is found in
Jahnn's depiction of Norway, and betray the mathematician rather than
the biologist. The description of mass psychology is however
masterful; Broch depicts with precision and subtlety man's surrender
to the blandishments of the irrational; the speculative study on *Massenpsychologie*, already mentioned, stands along with Elias Canetti's
Masse und Macht as being one of the most perceptive analyses of the
relationship between the individual self and the corporate whole.

Broch twice refers to his inability to understand Canetti's *Die
Blendung*, a novel which appeared in 1935 and is a grotesque study of
idées fixes and manic encapsulation. His confession is curious:
Canetti, like Broch in his *Schlafwandler* trilogy, is concerned with
paranoia and the individual's reaction to power. The protagonist of
Die Blendung, Peter Kien, exemplifies that extreme of paranoia which
becomes utter self-delusion; dedicated scholar and distinguished sinolo-
gist, Kien is obsessed by his enormous private library in a room whose
wide windows have been bricked up. When threatened by the outer
world, he withdraws into a shell of solipsism where, rigid and inflexible,
he is ultimately destroyed by fire, ancient source and symbol of
transformation. The other characters of the novel, Therese Krumbholz,
later to become Kien's wife, Benedikt Pfaff and Leo Fischerle become
lunatic rulers in their own realms, utterly self-centred and convinced of
their importance and their power. Theresa's reaction on finding Kien
unconscious on the floor is typical: her thoughts revolve around the
general inconvenience that his fall, with resultant bloodstains, would
cause. The hideous dwarf Fischerle, with monstrous hump, dreams of
becoming chessmaster of the world; before being murdered and
mutilated he imagines a reception in New York, organised for him
alone:

Von der Dachrinne tropfte es in den Hof. Alle Tropfen fließen
in den Ozean. Auf einem Ozeanriesen schifft sich Dr Fischer nach
Amerika ein. New York besitzt zehn Millionen Einwohner. Die
Bevölkerung ist in einem Freudentaumel. Auf der Straße küssen
sich die Menschen und schrein; Hoch! Hoch! Hoch! Hundert
Millionen Taschentücher wehen zum Empfang, an jeden Finger
bindet sich jeder Einwohner ein Stück. Die Einwanderungsbehörde

verduftet. Was soll sie viel fragen? Eine Deputation der New Yorker Huren legt ihm ihre Himmel zu Füßen. Das gibt es dort auch. Er bedankt sich. Er hat studiert. Flugzeuge malen DR. FISCHER in die Luft. Warum soll man für ihn keine Reklame machen? Er ist mehr wert als Persil. Tausende fallen für ihn ins Wasser. Mann soll sie retten, befiehlt er, er hat ein weiches Herz . . . Von einem Wolkenkratzer schießen die Kanonen. Der Präsident der Vereinigten Staaten reicht ihm die Hand.[43]

The manic brutality of Benedikt Pfaff, staring out from his peep-hole in the door, and waiting to leap at the throat of any who attempted to enter the house, has obviously amusing qualities; grotesquely disturbing, however, is his treatment of wife and daughter and the assumption of his innate value and indispensability. Solipsism, power-seeking and obsessions — these play an important part likewise in the work of Franz Kafka, an author whose work Canetti has studied deeply. Monomania and arid misconceptions abound in both Kafka's and Canetti's work: it was in the Vienna of the 1920s that Canetti observed the dangerous growth of extreme and uncompromising attitudes. The idea for *Die Blendung* came in 1927, the year which contained that fateful 15 July, when the Palace of Justice was burned to the ground and ninety people were killed, all political stability being lost. The novel, although not overtly political, echoes with the violence of the times and *Masse und Macht*, the first volume of a projected study of crowd psychology, analyses both the paranoia of the ruler and the delusion of the mob. Although the work of Heimito von Doderer falls outside the scope of this book, his *Dämonen* could be quoted as a novel which likewise is concerned with the rioting that led to the conflagration of 15 July: Doderer portrays, as did Broch, the irruption of irrational powers from the underworld, this time in the figure of Meisgeier, who lurks in the sewers beneath the city.[44] The 'Einbruch von Unten' — in the form of Meisgeier, Moos-brugger, Huguenau and, possibly, Fischerle — is a preoccupation of these Austrian novelists whose work, ironic, prophetic or grotesque, shows an awareness of destructive powers, frequently associated with a criminal or totalitarian menace about to be unleashed on a frail and corruptible civilisation. Doderer, of course, enjoyed the benefit of hindsight (*Die Dämonen* was published in 1956), but the awareness of extreme and violent tendencies is an undeniable element of the work of Musil, Broch and Canetti: the Austrian novelists were certainly not isolated in the 1930s from threatening realities.

Turning from Austria to Germany, a most remarkable phenomenon is the work of Hans Henny Jahnn, whose *Das Holzschiff*, the first part of the vast trilogy *Fluß ohne Ufer*, was begun in 1934. Jahnn made his name in the 1920s with expressionist plays which outraged the theatre-going public (*Pastor Ephraim Magnus* was mentioned in chapter 6): the obsession with castration and crucifixion, with testicles and nipples (albeit male), together with a spiritual longing associated with music (Jahnn founded the musical publishing house Ugrino in 1921, and repaired and built several organs), produced a unique and fascinating *oeuvre*. In the 1930s Jahnn settled on the Danish island of Bornholm and ran a stud farm: the gulf between flesh and the spirit, between the biological and the musical, became an obsessive preoccupation. Jahnn abjured the violent tensions of expressionist drama and turned to the epic form: the experimental novel *Perrudja* appeared in 1929. The elemental force and vitality of his nature-descriptions, particularly of Norway, where he lived from 1914 to 1918, is unparalleled in modern German literature, as is the ability to communicate the essence and consciousness of the animal world. *Perrudja*, with its cascade of nouns, its parataxis and merging of fact and vision, is very much of the expressionist mould; *Das Holzschiff*, however, is more restrained, and lacks the obsessive and psychological probing of the earlier novel. The ship may be seen as a symbol for the human self; the limits of human reason are acknowledged, together with the inadequacies of a narrowly rational approach to life, but a surrender to totally irrational forces is also deplored. The hero, Gustav Anias Horn, comes to terms with his developing sexuality and, on the high seas, encounters mysteries which his reason cannot solve. The labyrinthine vessel, with its secret doors, corridors and compartments, exerts a fearful fascination: the loss and murder of Ellena, the captain's daughter and Gustav's betrothed, is the price which Gustav must pay for initiation into the mysteries of life. The supercargo, Georg Lauffer, in his unwillingness to accept the diversity of human nature, his abhorrent vivisection and furtive sexuality, represents an inimical force; his hidden microphones betray a reliance on arid technology. The storm at sea is a release of natural, violent energy which threatens to destroy the vessel, and Gustav learns that the sails, like human reason, can, if properly adjusted, give power and progress, taking advantage of the natural conditions. The ship, however, sinks, destroyed not by the elements without, but by violence within: Jahnn sees that greed and irrationalism, when unchecked, overthrow the mind and destroy all order.

This is a novel which can be read as one of the few great German novels of the sea: it can be compared with Conrad and Melville, yet also brings to mind Edgar Allan Poe's *The Narrative of Arthur Gordon Pym* and, at times, Kafka's *Der Heizer* fragment. *Das Holzschiff* is a self-contained narrative, but should also be looked upon as being an introduction to the *Fluß ohne Ufer*, whose main section, *Die Niederschrift des Gustav Anias Horn, nachdem er neunundvierzig Jahre alt geworden war*, appeared after the Second World War; the last section, a fragmentary *Epilog*, was published posthumously. The work reverts to the vastness of *Perrudja*, and even exceeds it: it is unique in German literature in its fusion of the biological and the musical, the elemental and the symphonic. The enormous 'shoreless river' of life carries Gustav Anias Horn and Alfred Tutein, murderer of Ellena, into manifold experiences and ever-increasing intensity of relationship: the love of man for man, and man for beast (Gustav and his mare Ilok) is described with strength and delicacy against the magnificent background of Norwegian scenery. In his landscape descriptions Jahnn combines precision with vital, emotional empathy; Karlheinz Deschner has praised the 'totale Kommunikation des Ich mit der Welt, die Jahnn immer wieder so sinnfähig und wie selbstverständlich zu vollziehen weiß'.[45] The seasons have never been described with such immediacy and fervour: the following passage, which depicts the sheets of torrential rain, is a good example of his art:

Es ist, als ob alle grauen Tage der vergangenen Woche mit ihrer Nässe, die den Schnee zerlöste, und den Boden in Morast verwandelte, nur eine Vorstufe der Feuchtigkeit gewesen, und daß erst diese Nacht und dieser Tag eine Belehrung darüber bringt, was es bedeutet, daß die Wolken aus Wasser gemacht sind. Daß es in der Luft schwimmende Meere gibt, einen unfaßbaren Verstoß gegen die Kräfte der Anziehung. Von jeder einzelnen Ziegelrinne strömt ein kleiner Bach und ergießt sich durch die Luft in einem Wasserfall zur Erde. Vor meinen Fenstern hängt ein Gitterwerk aus zerperlendem Wasser. Und die Landschaft, weiter hinaus, ist verschleiert durch unablässig fallende, dicke, unzählbare Regentropfen. Es ist wie eine unbegrenzte, stillestehende Brandung, wie ein Ozean zu neun Zehnteln aus Luft, zu einem Zehntel aus Wasser. Die Landschaft der Erde verwandelt sich schnell. In einer Nacht sind all die Quellflüsse entstanden, die den Boden überströmen, die Tümpel, die die noch undeutlichen Wiesen ausfüllen, die aus Gräben und Bächen hervorwachsen und die Äcker mit graublanken Spiegeln durchsetzen. Ich bin an diesem Morgen in den Wald hinausgegangen,

um das Steigen des Wassers, das Hervorsickern aus Moosen und
Gräsern, die Strudel und Gießbäche in den Senkungen und
Tälern zu sehen. Ein Gurgeln und Rauschen von überall her.
Blank gewaschener Steinschotter auf allen abschüssigen Wegen.
Ein eintöniger trübbrausender Gesang.[46]

Frost and winter are likewise invoked, the vast elemental forces against
which the love of the two men is most movingly depicted, this love
which embraces the whole of the natural world; Gustav explains:

Gehe ich durch das feuchte Gras einer Wiese, beginnen unzählige
voreilige Eindrücke in mir zu lispeln. Die Regenbogenfarben in einem
Tautropfen scheinen so wichtig wie der müde Käfer am Rande eines
Wegerichblattes. Ich nehme das Entzücken wahr, das von der Summe
tausend gelber Blumen ausgeht; mein Verstand bestaunt den Bau
einer einzelnen Blüte . . . Ein Hase, der sich aufrichtet und mich
verwundert betrachtet, wie sehr liebe ich ihn![47]

This cosmic love for all natural things is conveyed in epic prose which
transcends the conventional novel form, as did the work of Musil and
Broch (Jahnn knew the work of Joyce, reviewed Döblin's *Berlin
Alexanderplatz* with this writer in mind, and greatly admired John
Cowper Powys's *Wolf Solent*): long digressions on music are given,
together with extracts from the work of Samuel Scheidt and Vincent
Lübeck, and also Horn's own work (his compositions, we are told,
include a symphony 'Mein Leben mit Ilok'); quotations from
Klopstock's *Messias* also emphasise the cosmic scale of the novel. The
climax of the work, weird, possibly repulsive, and yet immensely
moving, is the description of Gustav's attempt to arrest putrefaction by
injecting Tutein's corpse with formaldehyde.[48] Many readers may feel
that Jahnn has overstepped the bounds of the acceptable and has
become grotesque and morbid, but the sincerity of the love between
the two men raises the work above the charge of mere sensationalism.
Jahnn's work is life-enhancing in its almost pagan openness to nature
in all its manifestations, its evocation of powerful emotions and the
sweetness of flesh, of music and the very rhythm of creation itself;
he is essentially a writer of health and vitality, not of perversion. His
later concern, after the Second World War, at the development of
nuclear weapons is a natural development of his life-long preoccupation
with the vulnerability, beauty and transience of the organic world.

Hermann Broch depicts a world prey to the eruption of irrational forces from below and also to the tempter from the mountains: his Virgil finds in art no answer, and only in death a mystical transfiguration. Robert Musil describes a world of gestures and ideologies which are unable to express the true meaning of life: the figure of Moosbrugger represents those elements that appal and fascinate, while Ulrich and Agathe flee to their Utopia, only to realise that perfection is a state as sterile as the every-day ritual. Canetti portrays the dangers of solipsistic paranoia — all three writers show man blinded to reality by his infinite powers of self-delusion. Jahnn sees the need for humility *vis-à-vis* natural phenomena and for a synthesis between biological and artistic life, a mighty river of blood to fructify the petrified intellect. These are novels of crisis: they are experimental, daring, and difficult of access, but seek a simplicity beyond the meaningless dross of deluded living. Another important novel written during the 1930s and which also deals with man's attitude to Utopia is Hermann Hesse's *Das Glasperlenspiel*, part of which appeared as early as 1934 in *Die neue Rundschau* and also in the periodical *Corona*. After the portrayal of isolation and neurosis in *Der Steppenwolf*, Hesse shifted his emphasis to the world of spiritual ideas and communion in his *Morgenlandfahrt* (1932): the movement towards the establishment of a communal Utopia, where man's ideals and responsibilities are closely interwoven, reached its culmination in Castalia, that ideal realm posited in *Das Glasperlenspiel*. The time is the year 2400: a narrator reconstructs the life of Josef Knecht, erstwhile musical prodigy educated in Castalia according to the highest intellectual ideals, and finally the Magister Ludi of the Order itself. The Glass Bead Game is an intellectual game with all the contents and values of culture — analogies with the playing of the organist upon his pedals and manuals are deliberate. The vast ideal is one of harmony, a synthesising of art, nature and spirit: devotion and exclusivity are axiomatic and unquestioned, for here is a Utopian realm of pure ideals. But Knecht does question them, and feels a need to leave the Order to remain true to his intellectual principles; he had sensed a growing emptiness and aridity in the aesthetic manipulation of concepts. He realises that the restless flux of the world, with its disorder and confusion, was vaster and richer than Castalia; he rejects Castalian aestheticism and satisfies an emotional as well as an intellectual need in his decision to leave and become a tutor to the son of an old friend. Knecht longs to fulfil his true vocation, that of teacher; a few days after leaving the Order he dies after plunging after the boy into an icy mountain lake.

Knecht's death is ambiguous: is it a sacrificial act, which would
have exemplary consequences for his pupil ('Die drei Lebensläufe',
appended to the book, do deal with different degrees of sacrificial
service), or is it a warning, an admonition not to leave the static serenity
of Utopia for the icy flux of life? Musil's lovers rejected their paradise
to return, albeit transfigured, to normality; Knecht's plunge into the
waters may be exemplary or wasteful, for the Order survives without
him and his death did not cause fundamental changes in Castalia.
Hesse's study of Eastern religions (the book is dedicated to 'den
Morgenlandfahrern') may have influenced him in his emphasis on the
lack of importance of the individual, whose only meaning lies in his
transference of spiritual values to his pupil; the rarefied atmosphere of
Castalia is not troubled by Knecht's defiance, but it is possible that his
pupil will bear his precepts in mind and learn from his sacrifice. Hesse's
novel does not have the stature of those of Broch, Musil, Canetti or
Jahnn: remoteness from experience, persistent dwelling on harmony,
synthesis and flux, and the ambiguity of the ending, exasperating rather
than fertile, detract from its merit. Hesse lacked the intellectual prowess of Broch and Musil, and the emotional weight and intensity of
Jahnn: the schematic juxtaposition of order and flux, rock and water
(so many of Hesse's heroes feel the obligatory lure of that element),
mathematics and music is self-conscious and lacking in organic
spontaneity. Certain poems by Knecht are appended at the end of the
book, for example 'Klage':

> Uns ist kein Sein vergönnt. Wir sind nur Strom,
> Wir fließen willig allen Formen ein:
> Dem Tag, der Nacht, der Höhle und dem Dom,
> Wir gehn hindurch, uns treibt der Durst nach Sein.[49]

and 'Zu einer Toccata von Bach':

> Urschweigen starrt . . . Es waltet Finsternis . . .
> Da bricht ein Strahl aus zackigem Wolkenriß,
> Greift Weltentiefen aus dem blinden Nichtsein . . .[50]

whose imagery, pretentious and lacking in immediacy, betrays the
essentially undistinguished nature of Hesse's writing.

Das Glasperlenspiel is a contemplative work, a crystallisation of
Hesse's meditations upon human life and culture; the tensions of the
fifty-year old Harry Haller (and Hermann Hesse) seem far behind, yet

that novel had appeared only seven years before Hesse published part of his later book in the *Neue Rundschau*. As was stated before, he also contributed to the conservative journal *Corona*, where he found himself in the company of such writers as Rudolf Alexander Schröder, author of the *Deutsche Oden* and the *Geistliche Lieder*, Rudolf Borchardt and Hans Carossa, who deliberately avoided the strident modernism of the expressionists, the flippant cynicism of much *Neue Sachlichkeit* writing and the almost symphonic vastness of Broch, Musil and Jahnn. Such writers are scarcely considered when the literature of the Weimar period is discussed, but this chapter has attempted to show that it is superficial to claim a particular ambience for the literature between 1918 and 1933 and a particular locus, Berlin. Conservative tendencies were as much a part of that period as jarring modernist techniques: that which could be called a neo-classical revival was attempted by such writers as Schröder and Borchardt: the latter discussed a 'schöpferische Restauration' in a famous speech in 1927, as did Hofmannsthal in his essay 'Das Schrifttum als geistiger Raum der Nation' of the same year. It would seem that, in the face of disquieting political developments and an increasing complexity of artistic expression which rejected outmoded form, a 'conservative revolution' was posited, to uphold and preserve those ideals of humanity and moderation which the brief age of German Classicism had striven to uphold. The constitution of the Weimar Republic had been formulated in the town with which Goethe's name was inextricably linked, and politicians were exhorted to remember those ideals which Goethe and Schiller had extolled. A writer like Hans Carossa (1878–1956) likewise modelled his work on that of Germany's greatest literary figure, and deliberately eschewed the new techniques. Like Gottfried Benn, Carossa was a doctor, but the *Sektionslyrik* of the Berliner was utterly repugnant to him; he owed much to Hesse's early novels *Unterm Rad* and *Peter Camenzind*, both derivative and insipid works, and in Munich had associated with Karl Wolfskehl and had met Richard Dehmel. It was Hofmannsthal who asked Carossa to contribute poems to a new journal, and who recommended his poetry for publication in 1910. The great popularity of Carossa (*Eine Kindheit*, 1922, and *Der Arzt Gion*, 1913), also of Werner Bergengruen (1892–1962), is due to the fact that both authors made little demand on the reader, possessed the ability to tell a good story, and remained firmly within the nineteenth-century tradition of narrative fiction. Similarly Jakob Wassermann, with his detective novel *Der Fall Maurizius* (1928) and its sequels *Etzel Andergast* (1931) and *Joseph Kerkhovens*

dritte Existenz (1932) and Lion Feuchtwanger (1884–1958) with his
Jud Süß (1925) provided fiction of high quality for a discriminating
middle-class public.

The literature of the period under discussion is rich and varied,
comprising expressionism and *Neue Sachlichkeit*, Brechtian theatre
and experimental novels, satirical verse and cosmic utopias. Although
a discussion of the cinema falls outside the scope of this book, it
should be noted that many talented writers contributed to it as a new
genre, and that any discussion of the cultural situation of the 1920s
inevitably includes references to Fritz Lang's *Metropolis* (1926) with
its obvious debt to Kaiser's *Gas* trilogy (the clash between father and
son, and the fearful 'Moloch' scene). The foundation of the 'Bauhaus'
in Weimar by Gropius, Feininger, Itten and Marcks (1919), the
appearance of Oswald Spengler's *Der Untergang des Abendlandes*
(1922) and Heidegger's *Sein und Zeit* (1927) and the performance of
Alban Berg's opera *Wozzeck* in Berlin (1925) are achievements in other
fields which gave that period its characteristic flavour. But the fragile
Republic, under attack from so many quarters and buffeted by
economic recession, failed to survive: more radical creeds held promise
of a deeper, more passionate involvement and quest.

In 1932, the centenary year of Goethe's death, Gerhart Hauptmann
greeted the spirit of Goethe in the following way:

> Die Welt wird weder mit Gold noch durch Gewalttat erlöst, sondern
> allein durch Menschlichkeit, durch Menschenachtung, durch
> Humanität ... Nicht Revolutionen bringen die Fortschritte, aber
> eine immerwährende, wie das Leben selber gegenwärtige, stille
> Reformation. Es wäre verlockend, einen Vergleich anzustellen
> zwischen der, die mit dem Namen Luthers und unserer, die mit
> dem Namen Goethes verbunden ist. Ich kenne nur einen Unter-
> schied: keine Art Fanatismus, keine Art Geistesknechtung, keine
> Art Menschenfeindschaft, keine Art Verfolgung kann in der
> neuen einen Platz finden.[51]

No fanaticism, no enmity or persecution – these were the watchwords
associated with the new Goethean spirit which, Hauptmann fervently
hoped, would inspire a new Germany. (His play *Vor Sonnenuntergang*
dates from this year and shows that Hauptmann's apparent optimism
was short-lived: it portrays the decline of the Goethean values before
the onslaughts of a ruthless and tenacious younger generation.) One
year later it was precisely those sinister tendencies which Hauptmann

had condemned which triumphed in Germany: in May 1933 that which was best in German literature was consigned to the flames with the blessing of the authorities in the presence of a vast and jubilant crowd. The Nazi victory represented a victory of the vicious and the banausic, yet, also, perversely, the triumph of certain tendencies which had hitherto remained but latent and peripheral within the literary tradition. Nietzsche's provocative imagery, derived frequently from war, the violence of the Futurists, the atavistic shrill-ness of much expressionism, the tendency towards myth and Wagnerian grandeur rather than practical realities found in National Socialism a possibly appropriate conclusion. Weimar culture, with its cosmo-politanism and large Jewish contribution was wiped from the European scene, dispatched into diaspora and, a few years later, into ultimate liquidation.

Notes

1. See Walter Laqueur, *Weimar: A Cultural History 1918–1933*, London, 1974.
2. Hofmannsthal, *Lustspiele*, II, 1948, 337.
3. In the first edition, Berlin, 1932, 175.
4. R.T. Llewellyn, 'Hofmannsthal's Nihilism', *MLR*, April 1966, Vol. LXI, No. 2.
5. Hofmannsthal, *Dramen*, IV, 1958, 460.
6. T.J. Reed, *Thomas Mann. The Uses of Tradition*, Oxford, 1974, 229.
7. Heinrich Mann, *Essays*, East Berlin, 1960, 14.
8. See article by Gordon Craig, 'Engagement and Neutrality in Weimar Germany', and by Harry Pross, 'On Thomas Mann's Political Career', *Journal of Contemporary History*, Vol. II, No. 2, 1967.
9. Thomas Mann, III, 827.
10. Thomas Mann, *Briefe an Paul Amann 1915–1952*, Lübeck, 1959, 29.
11. Thomas Mann, III, 686.
12. Thomas Mann, *Briefe 1889–1936*, Frankfurt/Main, 1962, 232.
13. T.J. Reed, 272.
14. Hermann Hesse, *Betrachtungen und Briefe, Gesammelte Schriften VII*, Frankfurt/Main, 1952, 774.
15. See *Hermann Hesse. Sein Leben und sein Werk*, Berlin and Frankfurt/Main, 1956, 23.
16. Stadler, II, 39.
17. Brecht, *Gesammelte Werke in 20 Bänden*, Frankfurt/Main, 1967, I, 12.
18. Brecht, ibid., 70.
19. Novalis, *Werke in einem Band*, Hamburg, no date, 418.
20. See S. Gilman, *Form und Funktion. Eine strukturelle Untersuchung der Romane Klabunds*, Frankfurt/Main, 1971, 98.
21. Ödön von Horváth, *Gesammelte Werke*, Frankfurt/Main, 1975, III, 507.
22. Döblin, *Berlin Alexanderplatz*, Berlin, 1929, motto to Book One.
23. *Döblin im Spiegel der Kritik*, Berne, 1973, 227.

24.   *Berlin Alexanderplatz*, introduction.
25.   Ibid.
26.   Ibid., 527-528.
27.   *Döblin im Spiegel der Kritik*, 90.
28.   Quoted in Berghahn, *Robert Musil in Selbstzeugnissen*, 162.
29.   Musil, *Der Mann ohne Eigenschaften*, 313.
30.   Ibid., 147.
31.   Ibid., 69.
32.   See R.H. Watt, ' "Der Einbruch von Unten": an Austrian syndrome of the interwar years?', *GLL*, July 1974, Vol. XXVII, No. 4.
33.   Musil, 676.
34.   See R.S. Furness, 'The androgynous ideal: its significance in German literature', *MLR*, 1965.
35.   Musil, 250.
36.   Ibid., 1,248.
37.   Hermann Broch, *Die Schlafwandler*, Zurich, 1931–1932, 364.
38.   See R.H. Watt, 316.
39.   Broch, 503.
40.   Broch, *Briefe 1921–1931*, Zurich, 1957, 416.
41.   Broch, *Gesammelte Werke*, III, 150.
42.   Platen, *Sämtliche Werke*, Kildesheim, 1969, II, 94.
43.   Canetti, *Die Blendung*, Munich, 1963, 399.
44.   R.H. Watt, 319.
45.   Karlheinz Deschner, *Kitsch, Kunst und Konvention*, Munich, 1961, 34.
46.   Jahnn, *Werke und Tagebücher*, Hamburg, 1974, *Romane*, II, 624.
47.   Ibid., *Romane*, III, 412.
48.   Ibid., 120-140.
49.   Hesse, *Gesammelte Dichtungen*, VI, 544.
50.   Ibid., 548.
51.   Hauptmann, *Sämtliche Werke*, VI, 855.

BARBARISM, EXILE AND RETURN

It may safely be claimed that the rapid decline of the Austro-Hungarian
Empire was accompanied by the release of a nervous intellectual and
artistic energy which formulated or anticipated those cultural
premises commonly accepted as part of the heritage of modern
European thought: the names of Freud, Wittgenstein, Mauthner and
Mach, of Hofmannsthal, Kraus and Weininger, of Mahler and
Schönberg have been mentioned in this book. The remarkable
efflorescence of cultural life, associated particularly with Vienna, set
up as reaction a heightened anti-Semitism and a lower-middle-class
resentment, which gathered momentum: Adolf Hitler was as much a
product of the Habsburg monarchy in decline as Otto Weininger.[1]
The dark fantasies of Kraus and Broch, the prophetic torture-visions of
Kafka, the uneasy awareness of the growing impossibility of using
language in the quest for clarity and humanity which haunted so many
writers, and above all the death-wish sensed by Freud to rest at the
heart of civilisation, may all be seen as anticipations of what would
come to pass within the twelve years of Hitler's dictatorial rule.
To destroy root and branch any cultural manifestations which were in
any way modernist, experimental or cosmopolitan was Hitler's aim:
'das zersetzende Schrifttum' was destroyed by fire and a 'Schreibverbot'
was imposed upon those who dared to place civilised artistic values
before narrowly patriotic propaganda. More predisposed to passing
his *petit-bourgeois* criteria upon architecture and the visual arts, Hitler
allowed Josef Goebbels free hand with the manipulation of the written
word: a *Reichsschrifttumskammer*, under the direction of the
erstwhile expressionist Hanns Johst (now an SS Gruppenführer) was
formed to impose an Aryan or *völkisch* ideology upon all German
literature. Johst's play *Schlageter*, dedicated to Adolf Hitler in 'lie-
bender Verehrung und unwandelbarer Treue', received its first
performance on 20 April 1933, and became a national sensation; it is
now only remembered for the notorious line 'Wenn ich Kultur höre,
entsichere ich meinen Browning'.[2] Before such brutish ineptitudes
men of discrimination and taste could not but despair; the diary of
Oskar Loerke gives an excellent description of the triumph of the
third-rate chauvinist writers inside the 'Dichterakademie', and the
sense of impotence felt by all sensitive and civilised men before

the Nazi victory.

Josef Goebbels's novel *Michael. Ein deutsches Schicksal in Tagebuch-blättern* was briefly mentioned in chapter 6. Published in 1933, it rejected the 'modern', that is, the culture of the cosmopolitan cities, and longed for the essential 'German' virtues. 'Während ein ganzes Volk im Sterben liegt, proklamiert seine angefaulte Intelligenz, was modern ist: Film, Monokel, Bubikopf und Garçonne. Ich danke!'[3] As in the case of Hitler, the artist-manqué vented his spleen upon the avant-garde who had no interest in *Blut und Boden* or the triumph of Nordic man: 'Dieses Schwabing muß einmal ausgeräuchert werden. Es ist die Brutstätte der zersetzenden Tendenzen; und dabei hat es mit dem eigentlichen München gar nichts zu tun . . .'[4] The rejection of modern developments in the arts, however, does not prevent Goebbels from allowing his hero to betray undeniably expressionistic sentiments — the enthusiastic admiration for Van Gogh, Nietzsche, and Dostoevski, the rejection of the intellect, the flight into the elemental and such utterances as: 'Mir ist, als lebte ich nicht mehr in dieser Welt. Ich rase im Rausch, im Traum, im Zorn. Ich ahne neue Welten. Ferne wächst in mir. Gib mir, o Gott, zu sagen was ich leide!'[5] together with the following invocation of the mining areas of the Ruhr: 'Grauer Nebel! Rauch! Lärm! Kreischen! Ächzen! Flammen schlagen auf gegen den Himmel! Symphonie der Arbeit! Grandioses Werk aus Menschenhand!'[6] This pretentious novel, with its wooden characterisation and lapses into bathetic verse, does demonstrate the links between certain aspects of expressionism and the Nazi creed; Michael himself puts forward the following rather unsubtle definition of that movement:

> Impressionismus ist Eindruck, Expressionismus ist Ausdruck. Impressionismus ist Eindrucks-, Expressionismus ist Ausdrucks-kunst. Das ist das ganze Geheimnis. Unser Jahrzehnt ist in seiner inneren Struktur durchaus expressionistisch. Das hat mit dem Modeschlagwort nichts zu tun. Wir heutigen sind alle Expressionisten. Menschen, die von innen heraus die Welt draußen gestalten wollen. Der Expressionist baut in sich eine neue Welt. Sein Geheimnis und seine Macht ist die Inbrunst.[7]

Definite similarities exist between *Michael* and the short novel by Gustav Sack, *Ein verbummelter Student*, which appeared in 1917; Sack's hero yearned likewise for action, energy and 'life': 'Sollte vielleicht das, was ich meine blaue Sehnsucht nenne, die versteckte Wut nach lautem Leben sein? Soll erst dann meine Willenskraft aufwachen, wenn ihm etwas Gewaltiges entgegentritt, und nicht dieser elende Mikrokrimskrams von Bücherstaub und Tiftelei – Kampf und Krieg, ein lohendes Glück, ein mich niederschmetterndes, buchstäblich mich mit Füßen tretendes Leid: brausendes, riesenfäustiges Leben? '[8] The yearning for Iceland and the North, the cries of 'Ich bin das X, bin Gott, All, ich bin die Welt!'[9] of *Ein verbummelter Student* and the descriptions of the industrial landscape of the Ruhr are reproduced in *Michael* almost to the point of plagiarism: Josef Goebbels found it all too easy to slip into the more excessive diatribes of expressionistic prose. It is also of interest that Goebbels's later admiration for the painter Nolde caused the party much embarrassment; to claim that expressionism was a typically 'Nordic' phenomenon did not entirely resolve the difficulty.

Goebbels's hero meets his death in the depths of the mine: inspired by Van Gogh's example, he sought fulfilment in work, having rejected his university studies at Heidelberg and Munich. His apotheosis is achieved in an urban, rather than an agricultural, milieu (this is reminiscent of expressionist *Arbeiterdichtung*), but attempts were also made to describe the Frisian Islands and the Bavarian Alps, the storm-girt and the elemental, which were regarded as external correlations to the power of the German soul. Obligatory *Heimatdichtung* is detected here, the praise of the German landscape as being somehow superior to all other, and the German man and woman, close to the natural rhythms of the earth, are extolled as archetypal heroes, radiant with health and a sense of earnest dedication. Goebbels and other National Socialist writers could look back on a long tradition of nationalist literature: Julius Langbehn's *Rembrandt als Erzieher*, published in 1898, and which reached over one hundred editions in the space of a few years, did much to encourage the cult of closeness to the soil, a mystical communion with the earth within a specifically German landscape. Langbehn had written: 'Eine gesunde und vollsaftige Lebenslust, wie sie Rembrandt eigen ist, wäre der blasierten und bildungsmüden, geistig und allzu häufig auch körperlich kahlköpfigen deutschen Jugend von heute sehr zu wünschen: an niederdeutscher Fülle, Derbheit und Frische, Ruhe und Gedrungenheit der Existenz fehlt es gar sehr'.[10] It is the peasant (or 'Bauer') who is endowed with almost mystical qualities in many of the works of the chauvinist writers, and Langbehn himself explained: 'Im Bauer begegnet sich das irdische mit dem himmlischen, das äußere mit dem inneren Leben des Menschen, der König mit dem Künstler . . . Die Kontinuität des Volkslebens zu wahren, darauf kommt alles an. Nicht Menschenrechte

vom Himmel zu holen, wie man es einstmals wollte, sondern
Volksrechte aus der Erde zu graben, ist die Aufgabe der Gegenwart'.[11]

The problem of *Heimatdichtung* was much discussed at the turn
of the century: the influence of Zola, Ibsen and Tolstoi was resented,
and the themes preferred by the naturalists rejected in favour of
healthier, more 'German' topics. The Berlin 'Dramaturg', Ernst Wachler,
in his *Die Läuterung deutscher Dichtkunst im Volksgeiste* demanded
'*eine volkstümliche Poesie*, eine solche, die in der *Art, Eigenheit und
Geschichte unseres Landes und Stammes wurzelt, die dem Geiste und
der Größe der geeinten deutschen Nation entspricht*'.[12] Wachler
praised Hauptmann's *Die versunkene Glocke*, yet with reservations:
similarly Friedrich Lienhard, in his *Die Vorherrschaft Berlins.
Literarische Anregungen* (1900) criticised both Hauptmann and Max
Halbe for having taken too much from foreign sources. It was 'Los
von Berlin!' that was his most famous rallying cry, and the emphasis
on the provincial, the conservative and the traditional met a responsive,
ready public. There is, indeed, nothing sinister in *Heimatdichtung* at
this stage: Rilke enthusiastically reviewed Gustav Frenssen's *Jörn Uhl*,
and praised its 'Frische, Kraft und Menschlichkeit',[13] while the novels
of Clara Viebig, particularly *Die Wacht am Rhein* (1902) and *Die
Kinder der Eifel* appealed to a civilised public. It should be noted,
however, that Frenssen's *Der Glaube der Nordmark*, with its praise of
Nordic man and a new religion, led by a charismatic leader, exemplified
well the transition from *Heimatdichtung* to something far more
ominous; its central thesis is disturbing in the extreme:

> ... weil der Führer und seine Bewegung ihr Werk aus der tiefsten Tiefe
> der germanischen Seele holten, so erscheint, ohne ihr Zutun und ihr
> Wollen, hinter ihr, in ihrem Hintergrund, und deutlicher als jemals
> in der deutschen Geschichte, der uralte, urgermanische Glaube. Und
> diese Bewegung wird sich nicht wieder aufhören. Ja, sie wird wachsen
> und sich ausbreiten ... Der christliche Glaube ist alt und welk
> geworden. Die Zeit ist erfüllt.[14]

It was the sense of belligerent superiority in the years leading up to
the outbreak of the First World War, combined with an awareness of
vulnerability *vis-à-vis* both West and East that lent a note of shrillness
and abnormal intensity to German nationalism and its literary
manifestations: Hermann Burte's *Wiltfeber, der ewige Deutsche* (1912)
and Artur Dinter's *Die Sünde wider das Blut* (1918) push anti-Semitism
and truculent nationalism to an intolerable extreme. The collapse of

Germany, the turmoil of the early years of the Weimar Republic, the sense of betrayal and the vindictive desire to assert an inherent superiority once again encouraged an anti-democratic, nationalistic form of writing which infected the public imagination and played straight into the hands of the Nazis.

It has been quite rightly claimed that 'notwithstanding many claims to the contrary, National Socialism was not accompanied or supported by a vigorous literary movement. Blood and soil literature is in content merely the offshoot of an older regional nationalism; still less did the political upheaval create a literary style of its own'.[15] The peasant in earlier writing may have been harassed by impending industrialisation: later it became the Jew who threatened the 'Erbhof', and who came to represent an invidious poison in the otherwise healthy veins of the community. Lienhard's 'Los von Berlin' was again heard, for Berlin and other great cities exemplified modernism in the arts, cosmopolitanism and an undeniable Jewish presence — everything, in short, that was 'artfremd', 'zersetzend' and contrary to the 'arteigene Volksgemeinschaft'. Writers like Agnes Miegel (1879–1964) could, and did, extol the peasant, the earth and the blood after 1933 as they had done before: Agnes Miegel became more and more associated with her East Prussian background, and published in *Ostland* (1940) a poem 'An den Führer', with the obligatory genuflexions. Both she and Lulu von Strauss und Torney (1873–1956) had been associated with the 'Göttinger Kreis' of Börries, Freiherr von Münchhausen (1874–1945); in 1916 Lulu von Strauss und Torney married Eugen Dietrichs, who had started as a publisher of neo-romantic literature (particularly its more religious manifestations), and who went on to cultivate works that were above all German and anti-rational. The cult of 'deutsches Volkstum', also his interest in the German Youth Movement, led to an increasingly reactionary stance on Dietrichs' part; his collaboration with Houston Stewart Chamberlain, Wagner's son-in-law, and Adolf Bartels, the most anti-Semitic of all German literary historians, emphasised the dangerous, albeit fascinating, concoction of *Volk*, myth, romanticism and anti-enlightenment which helped to feed the Nazi *Weltanschauung*.

Dietrichs died in 1930, but perverted romanticism and aggressive *Heimatdichtung*, exacerbated by the loss of territory suffered after 1918, which he had encouraged and published, gathered momentum. Four years before his death his wife reviewed a book by Hans Grimm (1875–1959) which enjoyed enormous popularity, and which provided Nazism with one of its watch-words — *Volk ohne Raum*.

Grimm's novel sold half a million copies before the Second World War
(and by 1964 more than seven hundred thousand), and exercised a
powerful influence, particularly on the young and all those unable to
come to terms with the Treaty of Versailles. Lulu von Strauss und
Torney hailed the book as being 'nicht erdichtet, sondern erlebt – und
erlitten . . . Hans Grimms Buch *Volk ohne Raum* ist nicht Literatur
im Sinne von Wortkunst, es ist eine Tat und ein deutsches, geistiges
Ereignis. Es ist ein Weckruf . . .'[16] The terminology used here, the
fusion of the spiritual and the military, is typical of the chauvinist
groups who refused to acknowledge Germany's defeat and sought a
revivification of national life through the cultivation of specifically
'Germanic' values. Grimm's vast novel, well over one thousand two
hundred pages, is blatantly propagandist: his hero, Cornelius
Friebott, is forced to leave his farm by the Weser and, rejecting life
in a Bochum steel works, emigrates to South Africa, where he
volunteers for the Boer War and, after imprisonment by the British on
St Helena, settles in South-West Africa. After the German collapse in
1918 he escapes to Portuguese Angola and, in the early 1920s, returns
to Germany and awakens his countrymen to their lack of space, and the
need for room to expand. It is only the novelist Hans Grimm (who
figures as a character in the novel) who understands the true import of
his message, and is determined that Friebott, killed by a political enemy,
shall not have died in vain. The readers of *Volk ohne Raum* were told
that they were 'das reinlichste und anständigste und ehrlichste und
tüchtigste und fleißigste Volk der Erde';[17] even a non-German, a
Portuguese officer, can explain: 'Der Welt ist ein ungeheures Unglück
geschehen durch die Erwürgung Deutschlands. Als die deutschen
Kriegsschiffe noch fuhren mit der leuchtenden Fahne, und als es noch
ein deutsches Heer und einen deutschen Kaiser gab, da hatte die Freiheit
unter den Völkern eine Stütze'.[18] It is British perfidy which is
responsible, Grimm writes, for German confinement and lack of
opportunity: the collusion between the British and the social-democrats
is repeatedly emphasised. The Jew is likewise singled out for attack:
a German officer serving in South-West Africa discusses the scabrous
attacks made upon Germany and describes those responsible thus:

> das Schlimmste aber ist, daß der Stoff zu dem frechen Märchen
> vom bösen Deutschen seit sehr vielen Jahren von gebürtigen
> Deutschen geliefert wird . . . Bei Marx und bei Moses Hess und bei
> Engels und bei Liebknecht und bei Jacoby und bei Pfau, wenn
> Sie die Namen alle noch kennen, bis hin zu Harden können Sie es

lesen, was die Hetzer in der Welt gegen uns nachschwätzen; und
früher hieß es Preußen, und dann hieß es das verpreußte Deutschland und der Kaiser.[19]

Hans Grimm's book has little literary merit: the characterisation
lacks subtlety, the landscape descriptions are slackly written, and the
epic breadth is sustained almost solely by the tedious nationalistic message.
But literary taste became utterly subservient to political obedience;
after 1933 the Prussian Academy of Arts, which had contained such
writers as Thomas Mann and Heinrich Mann, Alfred Mombert, Alfred
Döblin and Max Halbe, was purged, and Germany's literary élite fled
abroad, or withdrew into 'inner emigration'; the 'Abteilung für
Dichtung', responsible to the *Reichsschrifttumskammer*, contained
now as its 'Dichterakademie' the names of Agnes Miegel, Hanns
Johst, Emil Strauss (1866–1960), Rudolf Binding (1867–1938),
Börries von Münchhausen, Erwin Guido Kolbenheyer (1878–1962),
Wilhelm Schäfer (1968–1952) and Hans Grimm, hardly names to
inspire confidence in the new regime's intellectual and artistic standards.
The diary of Oskar Lorke (1884–1941) may be quoted as a testimony
of the reaction of the sincere and dedicated poet to the new *literati*
and to the obligatory denunciations and genuflexions, to that sense of
spiritual desolation above all:

> Hegelschauer, als ich in den Garten hinaustrat. Einsamkeit. Die
> Freunde fast alle tot, fern, verschollen. Verboten zu denken,
> Menschen menschlich aufzufassen . . . Mittwoch vormittag
> konstituierende Sitzung der 'Dichter'-Akademieabteilung . . . Die
> guten Alten triumphieren. Emil Strauss, Hermann Stehr, sie fühlen
> sich jetzt würdig und wichtig. Man hat ihnen auch Senatstellen
> gegeben. Im übrigen waren die Herren Nationalisten sehr unter sich.
> Schäfer, immer zu hysterischen Wutausbrüchen neigend, brüllend,
> schwarzer Alberich. Das tückische aufgeblasene breiige Nichts
> Kolbenheyer stundenlang redend . . . Die alten Mitglieder wurden
> absolut ausgeschaltet, außer mir: Stucken, Molo, Scholz, Benn,
> Seidel, Halbe.[20]

The triumph of the mediocre had been achieved, and ruthless measures
were to be taken against those whose work was deemed to be 'artfremd',
experimental and outside the purely nationalistic; the infamous burning
of the fruits of German culture was accompanied by the ritual
proclamation:

Gegen Klassenkampf und Materialismus, für Volksgemeinschaft und
idealistische Lebenshaltung! . . . Gegen Dekadenz und moralischen
Verfall! Für Zucht und Sitte in Familie und Staat! Gegen
seelenzerfasernde Überschätzung des Trieblebens, für den Adel
der menschlichen Seele! Gegen Verfälschung unserer Geschichte
und Herabwürdigung ihrer großen Gestalten, für Ehrfurcht vor
unserer Vergangenheit! . . . Gegen volksfremden Journalismus
demokratisch-jüdischer Prägung, für verantwortungsbewußte
Mitarbeit am Werk des nationalen Aufbaus! . . . Gegen literarischen
Verrat am Soldatenleben des Weltkrieges, für Erziehung des Volkes
im Geist der Wahrhaftigkeit! . . . Gegen dünkelhafte Verhunzung der
deutschen Sprache, für Pflege des kostbarsten Gutes unseres Volkes!
Gegen Frechheit und Anmaßung, für Achtung und Ehrfurcht vor
dem unsterblichen deutschen Volksgeist![21]

The shameful *auto-da-fé* consumed the work of Thomas and Heinrich
Mann, Bertolt Brecht, Franz Kafka, Erich Maria Remarque, Kurt
Tucholsky, Leonhard Frank, Alfred Döblin, Jakob Wassermann,
Franz Werfel, Robert Musil, Arnold Zweig, Stefan Zweig, René
Schickele, Fritz von Unruh, Lion Feuchtwanger and such non-literary
writers as Marx, Kautsky and Freud. The burning became, in fact, an
accolade of excellence: to have been accepted by the régime became
the highest insult, and Oskar Maria Graf (1894–1967), mistaken by
the Nazis as a nationalist writer because of his description of Bavarian
peasant life demanded, from the safety of exile, that his work be
burned along with the writings of the great; to have been spared
was an intolerable insult. 'Vergebens frage ich mich, womit
ich diese Schmach verdient habe . . . Nach meinem ganzen
Leben und nach meinem ganzen Schreiben habe ich das
Recht, zu verlangen, daß meine Bücher der reinen Flamme
des Scheiterhaufens überantwortet werden und nicht in die blutigen
Hände und die verdorbenen Hirne der braunen Mordbanden
gelangen.'[22] To be associated with the 'Dichterakademie' was
impossible for men of good faith and high artistic standards, and so
the flood of German emigrés swelled monthly; some two thousand
were in exile by 1938.

Gottfried Benn, however, remained and enthusiastically greeted
the Nazi rise to power. This was by no means an aberration, but a
natural development of certain tendencies which characterised his
poetry from the expressionist period. His primitivism and rejection of
Zivilisation, his suspicion of reason and fascination with the 'blood',

led him to sympathise with the irrationalism and atavistic vitalism
of Nazism: his standpoint was quite clearly put forward in *Der neue
Staat und die Intellektuellen* of 1933. Of great interest in this
context is his *Antwort an die literarischen Emigranten*, dating from the
same year, and written in reply to Klaus Mann's letter demanding an
explanation for his acceptance of Hitler and the new Reich; Benn's
thinking is characteristically apolitical, and he can only see the historical events *sub specie aeternitatis* and from an almost mystical
dimension:

> ... die Geschichte ... kennt ja Ihre Demokratie nicht, auch nicht
> Ihren vielleicht mühsam hochgehaltenen Rationalismus, sie hat
> keine andere Methode, sie hat ja keinen anderen Stil, als an ihren
> Wendepunkten einen neuen menschlichen Typ aus dem uner-
> schöpflichen Schoß der Rasse zu schicken, der sich durchkämpfen
> muß, der die Idee seiner Generation und seiner Art in den Stoff der
> Zeit bauen muß, nicht weichend, handelnd und leidend wie das
> Gesetz des Lebens es befiehlt ... Verstehen Sie doch endlich dort
> an Ihrem lateinischen Meer, daß es sich bei den Vorgängen in
> Deutschland gar nicht um politische Kniffe handelt, die man in der
> bekannten dialektischen Manier verdrehen und zerreden könnte,
> sondern es handelt sich um das Hervortreten eines neuen
> biologischen Typs.[23]

The letter, surprisingly for Benn, rejects 'Großstadt' and extols 'die
Ebene, die Weite, Jahreszeiten, Erde, einfache Worte —: Volk' and ends
with quotations from Nietzsche, Fichte and Burckhardt in a rejection
of utilitarianism and democratic platitudes. This essay was widely
broadcast by Goebbels, but tensions between Benn and the *Reichsschrifttumskammer* were inevitable: Benn had been one of the
foremost expressionist poets, and the movement was pronounced
degenerate, in spite of the close links already discussed. In his
Bekenntnis zum Expressionismus, written at the end of 1933, Benn
strove to defend the movement, seeking antecedents in Kleist's
frenzied *Penthesilea* and Nietzsche's dithyrambs, but the attacks upon
him increased in volume and in venom: the SS journal *Das Schwarze
Korps* rejected Benn's *Ausgewählte Gedichte* as being the product of a
'Selbsterreger', and the polemic is on a level of ignorance and crudeness
typical of a vulgar and rapacious mentality. 'Aber Herr Benn wühlt
seinen Stift nicht nur in stinkende Wunden, er macht auch in Erotik,
und wie er das macht, das befähigt ihn glatt zum Nachfolger jener, die

man wegen ihrer widernatürlichen Schweinereien aus dem Haus
jagte'.[24] This was in 1936; in the following year the notorious
Entartete Kunst exhibition in Munich decried the modernist canvases
and the expressionist mentality in brutal terms: 'Gequälte Leinwand –
seelische Verwesung – Krankhafte Phantasie – Geisteskranke
Nichtskönner'[25] and in so doing destroyed what was probably
Germany's most original contribution.to the arts for decades. Benn,
who represented in the eyes of the party a suspect affinity with
modernism and expressionism, in spite of his emphasis on the meaninglessness of western civilisation, withdrew into the 'aristocratic'
form of inner emigration: he rejoined the army and concentrated on a
definition of poetry as being an act of defiance in the face of absurdity
and nihilism. The concept of the absolute poem, created *ex nihilo*,
became of increasing importance for Benn during the Second World
War; the poem 'Ein Wort', written in 1943 and published in the
Statische Gedichte of 1948, emphasises the impact, yet also the
transience, of articulate utterance:

> Ein Wort, ein Satz–: aus Chiffren steigen
> erkanntes Leben, jäher Sinn,
> die Sonne steht, die Sphären schweigen
> und alles ballt sich zu ihm hin.
>
> Ein Wort –, ein Glanz, ein Flug, ein Feuer,
> ein Flammenwurf, ein Sternenstrich –,
> und wieder Dunkel, ungeheuer,
> im leeren Raum um Welt und Ich.[26]

A word, a phrase, the aesthetic incantation, the successful manipulation
by the poet of this word and this phrase gives meaning and form, and
it becomes an act of such intensity that even cosmic processes
register it. The word becomes the reality, and blazes forth, yet is
transient, and is swallowed up by the ubiquitous darkness, a darkness
which, however, is made more fearful by the absence of the brief light.
This, Benn believed, is all that the poet can do: to create, even in the
face of darkness. His mentor is Nietzsche here, also George, who, in a
late poem, realised that the word creates even in the midst of absurdity,
and that there is indeed only meaninglessness without the poetic act:
'Kein ding sei wo das wort gebricht'.[27] Benn's poem 'Leben – niederer
Wahn' repeats this awareness in the apodictic statement: 'Form nur ist
Glaube und Tat' – to freeze the flux of incomprehensible impressions

into an articulate utterance is the highest that can be achieved. It is the static quality of perfect form that Benn praises, the Ptolemaic principle rather than the Heraclitean, and his last collection of prose writings, *Der Ptolemäer* (1949) portrays the situation prevailing in Berlin at the end of the Second World War in a series of associative fragments, which do not reflect a recognisable situation but respond to the total collapse of meaningful reality.

> It was Benn's vain hope that Nazism would liberate him from his isolation as an intellectual by founding a new world on the principle of energy – an energy at once biological and artistic; and his error to be far less aware than Nietzsche of the difference between the energy and the power-principle of men whose only concern was to harness every kind of energy to their personal needs.[28]

Benn's essentially apolitical mentality and his blindness to the true nature of Nazism was by no means unique but typical rather of a generation of German writers and thinkers, some of whom have been discussed in this book, who preferred the mythological to the historical, the utopian to the pragmatic and who cherished an instinctive reluctance to consider the realm of politics as being anything more than peripheral and superficial. A writer of similar calibre is Ernst Jünger (b. 1895) who, like Benn, stayed in Germany and re-entered the army. During the First World War Jünger had been wounded fourteen times and had been decorated with the highest military honour *Pour le mérite*: after the war he described his experiences in *In Stahlgewittern* (1920), which went through many revised editions and was reissued during the Second World War in 1942 under the title *Ein Kriegstagebuch*. In contrast to Ludwig Renn's *Der Krieg* (1928), Erich Maria Remarque's *Im Westen nichts Neues* (1929) and Arnold Zweig's *Der Streit um den Sergeanten Grischa* (a novel, incidentally, which demonstrates an impressive ability to come to terms with the complex economic and social factors which led to the war, and juxtaposes with great effect the code of honour of Exzellenz von Lychow and the purely pragmatic criteria of General Schieffenzahn), Ernst Jünger's book, apart from random descriptions of dirt and boredom, applauded the excitement and vitalism of war and greeted the heroism and valour gained in the face of death. Pain was to be accepted again in a Nietzschean act of will, and Jünger likewise emulates Nietzsche in his attempt to experience existence aesthetically, imposing no moral categories. With clarity and a fastidious exhilaration Jünger describes the death and carnage of war; he nowhere indulges in expressionist histrionics or pacifist platitudes. In *Der Kampf als inneres Erlebnis* (1922) and *Feuer und Blut* (1926) Jünger continued to extol the heroism and tumult of war, the sense of dedication and courage which conflict bestowed and the transcendence of the merely personal in times of need; the *furor teutonicus* is greeted and acclaimed as a cleansing force, ready to do battle with a suspicious and inimical world.

Jünger envisaged a worker-state where the military virtues held absolute sway; not unlike Goebbels in *Michael* Jünger saw that worker and soldier were basically the same, and that the Leader is first worker, first soldier and also servant of the state. It is tempting to speculate upon Jünger's entymological interests here: his study of ant and beetle life, particularly the *genus coleoptera*, seems to have entered his view of human society. Total mobilisation in the interest of the state is recommended in *Die totale Mobilmachung* of 1931; in *Der Arbeiter. Herrschaft und Gestalt*, 1932, the following disquieting lines are found:

> Man wird eine Eigenschaft, die man vor allen anderen für das Kennzeichen des Deutschen hält, nämlich die Ordnung, immer zu gering einschätzen, wenn man nicht in ihr das stählerne Spiegelbild der Freiheit zu erkennen vermag. Gehorsam, das ist die Kunst zu hören, und die Ordnung ist die Bereitschaft für das Wort, die Bereitschaft für den Befehl, der wie ein Blitzstrahl vom Gipfel bis in die Wurzeln fährt. Jeder und jedes steht in der Lebensordnung, und der Führer wird daran erkannt, daß er der erste Diener, der erste Soldat, der erste Arbeiter ist. Daher beziehen sich sowohl Freiheit wie Ordnung nicht auf die Gesellschaft, sondern auf den Staat, und das Muster jeder Gliederung ist die Heeresgliederung, nicht aber der Gesellschaftsvertrag. Daher ist der Zustand unserer äußersten Stärke erreicht, wenn über Führung und Gefolgschaft kein Zweifel besteht.[29]

Jünger's nationalism and militarism would seem to have made him an enthusiastic supporter of National Socialism, but Jünger, unlike Benn, felt unable to throw in his lot with the new regime. His letter of 16 November 1933 explains the reasons for his inability to join the 'Dichterakademie'; he also refused to contribute to the *Völkischer Beobachter*. The vulgarity of Hitler offended him, and he saw in Hitler the ignorant criminal who never understood the metaphysics of power and service. The allegorical novel *Auf den Marmorklippen* (1939) meditates upon the relationship between power and resistance, and advocated a 'heroic resistance'; this work, as the later *Heliopolis* (1949) fails as literature because of Jünger's lack of imaginative feeling: the detailed landscape descriptions have a clarity and a precision, but also an inherent coldness, and cannot begin to equal those of Jahnn for sheer vitalism and empathy. The theme of resistance in *Auf den Marmorklippen* was a dangerous one at that time, but the remoteness and intellectual abstraction of the author's discussion preclude any assumption concerning Jünger's rejection of Hitlerism. A good example of Jünger's aestheticism, élitism, essential neutrality and fatalism *vis-à-vis* developments in the Nazi Reich are provided by his war diaries *Strahlungen*, published in 1949. The neutral stance adopted by Jünger in Paris seems either to spring from an admirable objectivity or an offensive lack of contact with, or understanding of, a world of human suffering: the description of lobster and oysters at Pruniers, the feeling of the binding of old books, the conversation with the Princesse de Sixte-Bourbon and the bottle of Chambertin 1904 (with its art-nouveau label) alternates with a clinical account of the execution of a young deserter, where the black flies in the bullet holes in the tree become of equal, even greater, interest for him. An undeniable lack of humanity characterises Jünger's writing: his correctness and good breeding betoken a lack of imagination rather than classical imperturbability.

Fastidiousness, élitism and aesthetic aloofness – these terms are conventionally used during a discussion of the work of Stefan George. His last collection of poems, *Das neue Reich*, appeared in 1928; earlier in this book George's cosmopolitan outlook was stressed, as was his detachment from, although by no means ignorance of, the world around him. The concept of the *Reich*, however spiritual in content, could not but have appeared to many to coincide with that millennial yearning of those who despised the Weimar Republic and all that it stood for. Josef Goebbels had studied under Gundolf in Heidelberg and, like many other devoted National Socialists, felt that George, author of 'An die toten' and 'Einem jungen führer im Ersten Weltkrieg' and herald of a new and powerful vision, was worthy of adulation and veneration. George's metaphors did, as Nietzsche's, approximate to those favoured by the Nazi mentality, and the following lines from *Das neue Reich* seem unambiguous to the blinkered fanatic:

Und wenn im schlimmsten jammer lezte hoffnung
Zu löschen droht: so sichtet schon sein aug
Die lichtere zukunft. Ihm wuchs schon heran
Unangetastet von dem geilen markt
Von dünnem hirngeweb und giftigem flitter
Gestählt im banne der verruchten jahre
Ein jung geschlecht das wieder mensch und ding
Mit echten maassen misst, das schön und ernst
Froh seiner einzigkeit, vor Fremden stolz,
Sich gleich entfernt von klippen dreisten dünkels
Wie seichtem sumpf erlogner brüderei
Das von sich spie was mürb und feig und lau
Das aus geweihtem träumen tun und dulden
Den einzigen der hilft den Mann gebiert . . .
Der sprengt die ketten, fegt auf trümmerstätten
Die ordnung, geisselt die verlaufnen heim
Ins ewige recht wo grosses wiederum gross ist
Herr wiederum herr, zucht wiederum zucht, er heftet
Das wahre sinnbild auf das völkische banner
Er führt durch sturm und grausige signale
Des frührots seiner treuen schar zum werk
Des wachen tags und pflanzt das Neue Reich.[30]

Yet George refused candidature as the new president of the
'Dichterakademie'; he emigrated to Switzerland in 1933 and remained
deaf to Goebbels's entreaties. The idealism and visionary fervour of
the new Germany, with its emphasis on youth, hardness and dedication,
were qualities which George may well have admired; the brutishness
and banausic vulgarity were, of course, abhorrent to him.

Even the most pedestrian writing is enhanced by the hysterical
nationalist outbursts which surround it; the undistinguished but
respectable work done in Nazi Germany has a value, in that it provided
an alternative to the general freakishness and mediocrity. Bergengruen's
Der Großtyrann und das Gericht (1935) looks back to C.F. Meyer in
many ways, yet also could be said to contain a veiled reference to
Hitler in the portrayal of the tyrant who, himself guilty, corrupts a
whole society and spreads fear and panic everywhere. Bergengruen
was expelled from the 'Dichterakademie' in 1937 after having had the
courage to insist upon an essentially neutral position. The writer
Edzard Schaper (b. 1908) also warrants attention here, whose historical
novels, particularly *Die sterbende Kirche* (1935), with their portrayals

of stoicism and the need for religious faith, may also be seen as referring obliquely to the dark times in which they were written. But a writer of far greater stature remained, adamantly refusing to leave the Silesian land which he loved because of a vindictive and criminal regime: this was Gerhart Hauptmann, Nobel Prize Winner like Thomas Mann and a writer, who, like Mann, had been seen in the role of *praeceptor Germaniae*, even as a possible President of the Weimar Republic. But, as Michael Hamburger has pointed out, Hauptmann was singularly unsuited to such a role: his essential naiveté and inability to provide 'a more sophisticated, more intellectualized kind of writing'[31] led to a decline of his earlier fame and the subsequent cultivation of a 'Goethean' classicism. (In Sorge's *Der Bettler* the 'Dritter Kritiker' had explained: 'Wir warten auf einen, der uns unser Schicksal neu deutet, den nenne ich Dramatiker und stark. Unser Haupt-Mann, sehen Sie, ist groß als Künstler, aber als Deuter befangen'.[32] An age which sought prophets would, mercifully, be at a loss when confronted with his work.) But the reluctance (and inability) to comprehend the more extreme forms of modernism, and the assumption of an apparently Olympian detachment, did not in any way invalidate Hauptmann's remarkable powers of compassion and his awareness of human suffering. To suffer and give shape to the suffering were the task of the dramatist, not to formulate novel-sounding theories; Hauptmann's intuitive understanding of the human predicament and his all-pervading humanity, his aversion to dogma and ideology, to any hardening of the human heart into sterile attitudinising never left him. The *Dom* fragment, at which Hauptmann was working intermittently in the 1930s and during the war, with its prophetic stage directions – a shattered cathedral tower on which a canon is mounted, and its 'Folterkammer' scene – explains: 'Nur was der Mensch den Menschen zufügt und was der Mensch vom Menschen erleidet, kommt hier in Betracht'.[33] The translation of the scene of suffering in Hauptmann's last works from the realistic to the mystical and the mythical is not a symptom of waning powers, but an indication of Hauptmann's realisation of the universal problem of human anguish; it was also prudent, after 1933 to prefer the allusive reference to the unambiguous statement.

The outward signs of acquiescence (the flying of the swastika flag upon his house[34]) did not preserve Hauptmann from Nazi criticism and innuendo. The writer of *Florian Geyer* was also the writer of *Die Weber*, essentially not a revolutionary play, in spite of the Kaiser's fears, but one which could be exploited for political purposes (at the end of the war the Russians who entered Silesia were, in fact, to greet

Hauptmann primarily as the writer of that play). Hauptmann was
attacked for his former allegiance to 'der meinungsmachenden jüdischen
Literaturklique um Sami Fischer' and was given the following advice:
'Wer einst der Weimarer Republik gefeiertster Poet gewesen ist, dem
steht es wohl an, die verstimmte Leier hinterm Ofen zu bergen und
sich in bescheidener Zurückgezogenheit die Wohltat des Vergessen-
werdens zu erwerben'.[35] But Hauptmann, in ever-increasing isolation
and advancing age (his eightieth birthday was grudgingly noticed in
1942), refused to refrain from writing: his remarkable play *Die
Finsternisse*, dating from 1937 and first published ten years later,
was a moving requiem to his Jewish friend Max Pinkus, Silesian patriot
and benefactor, who had died in 1934 and been buried at night. This
sombre play moves on two planes, realistic and mythical: the dead
Joel, transfigured by death, is greeted by Elijah, John the Baptist and
Ahasuerus, who acknowledges the burden proclaimed by Habakuk that
the Jewish people must bear: 'Ich trage von Ewigkeit zu Ewigkeit
diese Last . . . Aber Israel stirbt nicht'.[36] Yet the dark Angel of Death
spares none, neither Jew nor Gentile; the sculptor Kroner speaks of
the black vessel bearing the dead into a transcendent realm, and Lutz,
the dead man's son, sees that those who chanted 'Juda, verrecke!'
would likewise perish.[37] The poet von Herdberg, speaking for
Hauptmann himself, has the last word, and proclaims that suffering
is not a Jewish burden, but a universal human destiny; the apparition
of John the Baptist precludes a total identification of the play with
the Jewish holocaust. Hauptmann's grief at the fate of the Pinkus
family provided the stimulus for this meditation on the interaction of
life and death, and the omnipresence of suffering and darkness.

Die Finsternisse was a play which, obviously, could not be
performed, but Hauptmann was able to portray the horror of the new
Reich by using myth, and what could be called his greatest achievement
during those dark years was the *Atriden* cycle, an astonishing work for
a writer in his eighties and comparable only with Goethe's late
creativity. The tone of sombre violence, the themes of madness and
destructive frenzy which abound in these plays reach an almost
unbearable intensity: Julius Bab described them thus: 'Im Deutschland
von 1940 entstand dies Werk voll Blut und Grauen — schrecklicher
Triumph der Unterweltsmächte! Es ist wahrlich ein vollkommenes
Echo der Hitlerwelt. Man muß fürchten, daß diese riesige Folge von
Grauen, von Krämpfen, von Ohnmächten auf der Bühne kaum
erträglich wäre, wenn die vier Stücke je in geschlossener Folge
dargeboten werden sollten'.[38] The description of the fearful ship with

its sombre colours, full of baying hounds, and of the evil priest Kalchas
who perverts whole peoples, achieves a sinister significance; most
impressive is a speech of Kritolas in Act 2 of *Iphigenie in Aulis*, a play
which was, in fact, staged in the Burgtheater in Vienna in 1943:

> Die Erde hat gebebt. Der Menschen Städte
> erzittern, fürchten ihren Untergang.
> Was für die Ewigkeit gemauert schien,
> zerbröckelt knisternd, knirscht und wankt im Grund.
> Die Sterne werfen sich aus ihren Bahnen,
> Die Erde fiebert und der Mensch mit ihr . . .
> Vertrocknet und zersprungen glüht die Erde,
> Der Würger Hunger mordet Mensch und Tier,
> Die Pest, wie eine Wölfin, neben ihm.
> Es wird der Mensch sogar des Menschen Wolf
> Und stillt mit seinesgleichen seinen Hunger.[39]

Elektra, written in 1944, contains in the description of the place of
Agamemnon's murder that which could be used to refer to that
other place of extermination, Auschwitz, not two hundred miles east
of Agnetendorf:

> Ein übler [Ort], wie ich keinen mir ersehnt
> zeit meines Lebens. Halbverkohlte Knochen
> starren aus grauer Asche überall:
> Hier ein bezahnter Kiefer, weiter dort
> ein Schädeldach, Gebeine hier und da.
> Fluch steigt aus allem auf wie ein Gewölk:
> es ist ein mörderischer Schacht fürwahr,
> von Leben zeugend, das mir schlimmer scheint
> als hundertfacher Tod.[40]

Yet the universal horror of which this tetralogy speaks is seen as being
transient: 'Die Nacht ist dunkel, doch folgt ihr das Licht/Wie immer
in der Welt . . .';[41] this is not platitudinous optimism, but the fervent
conviction of the sage. Neither the suicide of Ida Orloff in 1945 nor
the destruction of Dresden, which he observed from afar, could crush
Hauptmann's resourceful and vital spirit. In 1933 he had announced:
'Meine Epoche beginnt 1870 und endigt mit dem Reichstagbrand',[42]
yet he survived the hectic and murderous madness of the Third Reich
and remained creative until the end, his death in 1946 coinciding with

the end of Silesia as a German country.

In a speech given in Frankfurt on 9 November 1952, Thomas Mann praised the majestic vitalism of Hauptmann, and above all his inexhaustible fecundity. The reservations concerning 'Mynheer Peeperkorn' have been forgotten, and this tribute, from one Nobel Prize Winner to another, is sincere and perceptive. Thomas Mann had not remained in Germany; throughout the Weimar period he had watched with concern the resurgence of those powers which, he felt sure, would pose a baleful threat to civilisation. He had watched the rise of Fascism in Italy with alarm, and his short story *Mario und der Zauberer* (1930) gives an excellent portrayal of the hypnotic powers used by the unscrupulous charlatan to corrupt and debase. (The 'Ästhetisierung der Politik', later discussed by Walter Benjamin in his essay 'Das Kunstwerk im Zeitalter seiner technischen Reproduzier-barkeit' and described as a necessary concomitant of Fascism, is shrewdly portrayed in this story.[43]) On 17 October 1930 Thomas Mann gave his lecture *Deutsche Ansprache. Ein Appel an die Vernunft* in the Beethoven Saal in Berlin, which was an overt criticism of Fascism and a warning against irrationalism; Arnolt Bronnen, who had thrown in his lot with the Nazis (and had forced his mother to declare him illegitimate, to avoid the taint of Jewish blood), led the demonstration against him. Thomas Mann closely observed the events leading up to the Nazi success in 1933: on 10 February of that year he gave his brilliant lecture *Leiden und Größe Richard Wagners* in the Auditorium Maximum at the University of Munich to commemorate the fiftieth anniversary of the composer's death. He discussed Wagner's 'gesunde Art, krank zu sein, seine morbide Art, heroisch zu sein' and his influence on the literature of European decadence; he saw Wagner as a European phenomenon and stressed his basic indifference to political entities. The figure of Siegfried, far from representing the Germanic ideal, was described as 'Hanswurst, Lichtgott und anarchistischer Sozialrevolutionär auf einmal',[44] and Thomas Mann deplored the reduction of Wagner to the role of chauvinistic figurehead. The outcry which greeted the address was indicative of the new mentality which prevailed in Germany (Richard Strauss and Hans Pfitzner were amongst those who signed a protest against Mann's inimitable and fascinating study), and Mann himself, who had left Germany next day to repeat the address in other European capitals, was advised not to return. Those criminal elements who saw in Wagner an apotheosis of German musical art had triumphed, and Mann saw in them the perverse conclusion of those romantic-atavistic forces which he had earlier extolled, and which his brother had always feared and attacked. The issues prevailing at the time of the *Betrachtungen eines Unpolitischen* were gone for ever, and the mouthing of worthy political precepts no longer seemed platitudinous, but a matter of desperate importance.

Thomas Mann would not return to Germany for fourteen years; he did, however, publish the first part of the Joseph tetralogy, *Die Geschichten Jaakobs*, in Germany in 1933, determined as he was to hold on to his German readership for as long as possible: the reason why he dissociated himself from his son Klaus's journal *Die Sammlung* was to keep some contact at least with his German readers, for to have incensed the Nazi authorities immediately would have meant a total ban. (The novels *Der junge Joseph* (1934) and *Joseph in Ägypten* (1936) were published in Vienna, and the fourth of the cycle, *Joseph der Ernährer* (1943) in Stockholm.) Heinrich Mann, acknowledged head of the German émigrés in Paris, published two years after *Die Geschichte Jaakobs* his vast historical novel *Die Jugend des Königs Henri Quatre* which was followed by *Die Vollendung des Königs Henri Quatre* in 1938. These novels extol in the monarch his political acumen, his sense of social justice and his abhorrence of religious fanaticism – themes, in fact, more in keeping with the preoccupations of the times than his brother's descent into myth. But to Thomas Mann the creative use of myth was an answer to the irrational distortion of myth which hysterical demagogues were perpetrating in Germany: his letter to Karl Kerényi of 18 February 1941 explained 'Längst bin ich ein leidenschaftlicher Freund dieser Combination [von Mythos und Psychologie] ; denn hauptsächlich ist Psychologie das Mittel, den Mythos den faschistischen Dunkelmännern aus den Händen zu nehmen und ihn ins Humane "umzufunktionieren" '.[45] (It was also gratifying to the Jewish people to see that here was a major writer who, in those days, treated the origins of their race with sympathy, humour and enormous erudition.) The Joseph novels certainly lacked the overtly political concerns of *Henri Quatre* and of the work of Brecht, but the exploration of eternal verities and the sympathetic view of human existence provided a sense of coherence which political savagery threatened to obliterate. (Hermann Broch defined the position of the modern mythic novelist in his essay *Die mythische Erbschaft der Dichtung*, which extolled myth for its ability to illuminate the inscrutable regions of the psyche and its power to bestow coherence at times of historical dislocation.) Thomas Mann knew well that myth must never be used in isolation from the given facts of human

existence: myth could, however, help to see things in their
immediacy and also their cosmic significance, and an order of perennial
relationships could be established beyond strife and discord. Writing
of Wagner's *Der Ring des Nibelungen* in 1937, and describing it as
being compounded in a unique and remarkable manner of the archaic
and the modern, the primitive and the subtle, Thomas Mann was
describing his own tetralogy, a tetralogy, however, more in the spirit
of late Goethe than Wagner. Ernst Bertram's book *Nietzsche. Versuch
einer Mythologie*, which Thomas Mann knew intimately, with its famous
sentence: 'Alles Geschehene will zum Bild, alles Lebendige zur Legende,
alle Wirklichkeit zum Mythos'[46] may also have acted as a catalyst.

The imaginative reconstruction of the biblical story of Joseph's exile
and his survival could not but have special significance for Thomas Mann
at this time: the 'göttlicher Schelm' or 'Hochstapler' who sees the blue
sky above even in the depths of the horrid pit, who forever lands on
his feet and, unperturbed, continues on his way, resembles Felix
Krull, and seems also a mischievous account of the author's own
passage through life, becoming the most successful of all the German
émigrés, particularly after his move to America in 1938. The old
dichotomy between the sophisticated and the conventional, the
dream-like and the real is here portrayed with playfulness and
encyclopaedic knowledge; the mediator, Joseph, moves between the
eclectic refinements of Egypt and the humble dignity of his homeland
with an almost godlike insouciance: a harmonious sympathy is
established between the ways of God and the ways of man, between
'spirit' and 'reality'. This humorous song of mankind demonstrated
the triumph of the essentially civilised Joseph, whose self-esteem
carries also with it the highest blessing. (The outcast becomes the
provider: it is even possible to see certain features of Franklin Roosevelt
in the last Joseph novel, written at the height of the war.) The image of
the rolling sphere, the alternation of God and man, the blessing of the
dying Jacob, the benediction from above and below, also the images
of fruitfulness, reflect Thomas Mann's close reading of Goethe at this
time; the novel *Lotte in Weimar* (1939) is a remarkable *tour de force*
in which, with consummate skill, Thomas Mann uses interior monologue to enter into the very mind of Goethe himself. The picture of
Weimar in 1816 was a reassuring counterbalance to the picture of
Berlin in 1939 but here, as in the Joseph novels, there is no mere
escapism, for Thomas Mann saw in Goethe a writer well aware of the
precarious balance held between order and disorder, particularly
between the blandishments of art and the claims of life. Thomas Mann

well understood Goethe's 'vampirism', the egocentricity of the greatest
artist who used other lives in his act of creation; yet art is extolled as being
the mediator between 'spirit' and 'life', and the genius of the creative
artist is praised as synthesising both into a fruitful relationship. Goethe
became more and more Thomas Mann's *alter ego*: the juxtaposition
Goethe-Wagner, proposed in a letter to Julius Bab twenty-eight years
before, and offered to the Germans as a choice, became once more
topical. 'Aber ich fürchte, sie würden "Wagner" sagen',[47] he had
predicted in 1911; the elevation of that fascinating and dangerous
artist into the Nazi Valhalla was an ominous vindication.

With the outbreak of the war no colours seemed black enough to
betray the appalling depths of barbarism into which Germany had
descended. That problematic country, whose cultural tradition
Thomas Mann unquestionably loved, seemed bent upon a path of
furious destruction and unparalleled brutality; those who, exasperating-
ly, attempted to point out a 'good Germany' failed to see, in Thomas
Mann's eyes, that the ideas of Nazism were already to be found in the
German past, particularly in German romanticism. In 1941 he explained:

> Was man Nationalsozialismus nennt, ist die virulente Entartungs-
> form von Ideen, die allerdings den Keim mörderischer Dekadenz
> immer in sich trugen, aber in the old Germany of culture and
> learning gar sehr zu Hause waren. Sie lebten dort auf vornehmem
> Fuße, sie hießen 'Romantik' und hatten viel Faszinierendes für
> die ganze gebildete Welt . . . Zusammen mit Deutschlands
> hervorragender Angepaßtheit an das technische Massen-Zeitalter
> bilden sie heute eine Sprengmischung, die buchstäblich die ganze
> Zivilisation bedroht.[48]

It was entirely appropriate that Thomas Mann's preoccupation with
the figure of Goethe should give way to an awareness of the possibilities
of using the Faust legend (he had, in fact, considered a work on
Faust as early as 1905) to describe the satanic temptation into which
Germany had fallen; the basic themes of Thomas Mann's whole *oeuvre*
— the relationship between art and disease, and the tension between
Germany and the rest of Europe — are taken in his next great novel,
Dr Faustus (1947), to literally devilish extremes. The hysteria and
demonology of the sixteenth century, when the original Faust book
was written, and the fanatical inhumanity of the twentieth are linked
in this book, and the figure of Adrian Leverkühn, so closely based upon
Nietzsche, exemplifies also the modern artist who, threatened by

sterility, turns to diabolical influences for the gift of creativity, the
Durchbruch which his country also achieved, but at the cost of her
soul.

The novel looks into Germany's past and Thomas Mann's own —
Erich Heller reviews the earlier work and declares that 'All themes
come together once more in *Dr. Faustus*, and, greatly intertwined
and infernally illuminated as they now are, make the work a *summa
demonologica* of Thomas Mann's imagination'.[49] Here the diseased
Nietzschean artist is not contrasted with a healthy society: both
artist and his fellow men, to overcome sterility in art and political
restrictions, break through to unheard-of adventures, and both reach
terrifying heights before collapsing into insanity and destruction.
The Nietzschean parallels are of paramount importance: Leverkühn's
family are described as hailing from the Naumburg area, near
Nietzsche's home; like Nietzsche, Adrian Leverkühn studied theology,
and the brothel scene is taken directly from Deussen's *Erinnerungen
an Friedrich Nietzsche*. The restlessness of Nietzsche is also shared by
Adrian Leverkühn; the disease, madness and death of both are identical,
Leverkühn dying on the same day as Nietzsche and at exactly the same
age. Nietzsche's concept of the eternal recurrence is also found in the
many repetitions and circular returns in the novel: the Kridwiss circle
seems to put forward many of the earlier views discussed by the
students at Halle, and the Bavarian farm which Adrian makes his home
greatly resembles the scene of his boyhood. But the novel also contains
elements from Thomas Mann's own life and, again, uses actual people
as models (Paul Ehrenberg — Rudi Schwerdtfeger; Ludwig Derleth —
Daniel zur Höhe; the death of Ines Rodde also contains echoes of the
suicide of Thomas Mann's own sister Carla); he is able to draw on his
Munich experiences to show once more the proximity of aestheticism
and barbarism, the sneering rejection of progress and enlightenment
from the lips of Chaim Breisacher and the prurient longing for the
beauty and blood of the Borgias by the delicate Professor
Institoris. As Thomas Mann had fastidiously sought to overcome
bohemianism in his own youthful days, so Adrian Leverkühn sought
for order and discipline in his music, a rigid dodecaphonic system in
the manner of Schönberg; as Thomas Mann went back to the
original Faustbook for his inspiration, so Adrian looks back to the
early age of music, far more complex and demanding than the
bourgeois-humane tradition in art; as Thomas Mann 'unwrites' Goethe's
Faust, so Adrian 'unwrites' Beethoven's ninth symphony. Like
Aschenbach, Leverkühn sought abandonment, a 'prangende

Unbedenklichkeit',[50] and this creative energy, traditionally held to emanate from God, now comes from Satan, from Samael, the angel of poison.

The scene with the devil (at Palestrina, a town Thomas Mann knew well from his youth), which occupies the centre of the book, is a borrowing from Dostoevski: these obvious literary borrowings do not spring from a paucity of imaginative talent, but an awareness that the late-comer on the artistic scene must needs acknowledge his indebtedness to that which has gone before. The devil ratifies and confirms the pact, the infection of Leverkühn's body by the syphilis baccili; the novel is, basically, not specifically 'Faustian' in spite of the obvious similarities (the twenty-four years of heightened genius, the scene at the end) but, rather, demonic in that the book does not concern itself specifically with the pact.[51] The Faustian parallels are obvious, but so are the political ones: German life had been infected with dangerous irrationalism long before the Nazi success in 1933. Those mentors whom Thomas Mann had never tired of heeding — Nietzsche and Wagner — had both contributed to the German catastrophe; even romanticism, with its disparagement of reason, its love of myth and worship of sub-rational urges had prepared the way. German idealist thought and German music, surely unadulterated by baseness of motive, or even 'content' itself, are equally tainted, the former by its arrogant abstraction of mind from world and subsequent solipsism, the latter by its ambiguous fusion of order and primitivity. The barbaric undercurrent, latent in German civilisation, broke through with fearful force in the twentieth century, and Adrian Leverkühn's music is a complete expression of that force.

For the modern author the problems of tradition and freedom are crucial issues: the problems are exacerbated if the German cultural tradition is dubious and suspect. But freedom is likewise suspect if it means nothing more than an arid emptiness. The bourgeois cultural tradition, with its emphasis on subjectivity and 'freedom' had, Adrian Leverkühn realised, failed to appeal to the deepest needs, indeed, had failed to take heed of the idea of a communal life, a true communion. In conversations with Serenus Zeitblom Leverkühn had rejected the highly individualistic aesthetic aspects of bourgeois culture and extolled in its place the idea of a collective cult. This position is close to that of Bertolt Brecht, who sought similarly to replace the concept of art as refined, bourgeois pleasure, and rejected the merely psychological and individualistic. (Bertolt Brecht, however, is untypical in his refusal to accept Faustian solutions, his preference for the economic rather than the metaphysical, and his cautious, wry appraisal of historical events.) But Leverkühn, like Nietzsche, in spite of his strictures concerning many aspects of German life, is 'ur-deutsch', unable to forget Kaisersaschern, his father's speculations and his indebtedness to an immense tradition of music. This music originally sprang from praise of God, but comes to contain the tone-row h-e-a-a-es, suggesting the name of a poisonous butterfly, and also the name of the Leipzig prostitute from whom he received the fatal disease. Leverkühn is essentially apolitical, seeking in music an order beyond the merely temporal; the aestheticising of politics, however, which National Socialism provided, the fusion of order and hysteria, is an appropriate parallel to his art.

Leverkühn's musical primitivism makes him very much a twentieth-century artist: aestheticism and barbarism are closely linked in their denial of bourgeois liberalism. The situation is not specifically German: Julien Sorel, Knut Hamsun, D.H. Lawrence and many others praised the primitive and the violent, but it was in Germany that irrationalism and military technology fused to such barbarous intent. For fear of concentrating too much on German 'demonism' (and, perversely, giving a back-handed compliment to those powers which he abominated) Thomas Mann puts the story of Leverkühn into the mouth of Serenus Zeitblom, whose pedantry interposes between the reader and the devilish subject matter. Serenus Zeitblom is a representative of German bourgeois culture at its finest; he upholds the highest standards of scholarship and human decency, and watches with alarm the hectic progress of his friend. But it is false to see him as a staid and rather dull foil to Leverkühn: he did not disdain to feel proud of the German victories in the First World War, and develops as the novel progresses, his very style reflecting the growing accelera-tion towards disaster. (*À propos* his style, Mann is able to parody his own prolix verbosity and mandarin dignity in Zeitblom's initial hesitations.) It is false to see in Zeitblom a 'good', and in Leverkühn a 'bad' German, for Thomas Mann, as has been shown, sees the roots of Nazism in an earlier and hitherto much valued soil. Zeitblom had likewise felt the temptations of music, and had agreed with much that Leverkühn had propounded during their long conversations; like Leverkühn he had taken little interest in politics and, as representative of a whole class of cultured *Bürger*, had unwittingly assisted in the triumph of unreason. But his humanist, 'Western' orientation must needs reject the path that Leverkühn took; having lost his serenity he has gained in knowledge and sympathy, and commands the reader's

respect, not only for his ethical standpoint, but for the fervent love
for his friend and his country:

> Deutschland, die Wangen hektisch gerötet, taumelte dazumal auf
> der Höhe wüster Triumphe, im Begriffe, die Welt zu gewinnen
> kraft des einen Vertrages, den es zu halten gesonnen war, und
> den es mit seinem Blute gezeichnet hatte. Heute stürzt es, von
> Dämonen umschlungen, über einem Auge die Hand und mit dem
> andern ins Grauen starrend, hinab von Verzeiflung zu Ver-
> zweiflung. Wann wird es des Schlundes Grund erreichen? Wann
> wird aus letzter Hoffnungslosigkeit, ein Wunder, das über den
> Glauben geht, das Licht der Hoffnung tagen? Ein einsamer Mann
> faltet seine Hände und spricht: Gott sei euerer armen Seele gnädig,
> mein Freund, mein Vaterland.[52]

When describing Adrian Leverkühn's last work, the *Doktor Fausti
Weheklag*, Zeitblom sensed, paradoxically, a transcending of despair,
a tremulous voice of hope amidst the deepest mourning:

> Nein, dies dunkle Tongedicht läßt sich bis zuletzt keine
> Vertröstung, Versöhnung, Verklärung zu. Aber wie, wenn der
> künstlerischen Paradoxie, daß aus der totalen Konstruktion sich
> der Ausdruck – der Ausdruck als Klage – gebiert, das religiöse
> Paradoxon entspräche, daß aus tiefster Heillosigkeit, wenn auch
> als leiseste Frage nur, die Hoffnung keimte? Es wäre die Hoffnung
> jenseits der Hoffnungslosigkeit, die Transzendenz der Verweif-
> lung, – nicht der Verrat an ihr, sondern das Wunder, das über
> den Glauben geht. Hört nur den Schluß, hört ihn mit mir: Eine
> Instrumentengruppe nach der anderen tritt zurück, und was übrig
> bleibt, womit das Werk verklingt, ist das hohe g eines Cello, das
> letzte Wort, der letzte verschwebende Laut, in Pianissimo-Fermate
> langsam vergehend. Dann ist nichts mehr – Schweigen und Nacht.
> Aber der nachschwingend im Schweigen hängende Ton, der nicht
> mehr ist, dem nur die Seele noch nachlauscht, und der Ausklang
> der Trauer war, ist es nicht mehr, wandelt den Sinn, steht als ein
> Licht in der Nacht.[53]

The light in the darkness, the forgiveness of the sinner – forgiveness
for Leverkühn and for Germany – these are theological concepts,
linked to the devil's belief that God bestows all things, even guilt and
sin, and that he who passes through sin may be closer to the divine

than he who abjures: Thomas Mann deliberately touches upon Luther's 'Esto peccator et pecca fortiter, sed fortius fide et gaude in Christo'. The younger writers after 1945 will increasingly reject such a theologically tinged portrayal of Nazism as untenable and even blasphemous, but to Thomas Mann at the darkest period of the war it seemed entirely appropriate. *Doktor Faustus* was Mann's crowning achievement, despite the intellectual rigours and musicological profundity abetted by Theodor Adorno; the impossibility of expressing 'as literature' what caused the German collapse into barbarism is here surmounted.

The works that followed such a daunting novel show the consummate mastery with which Thomas Mann deals with the potentially offensive: incest in *Der Erwählte* (1951), which is a reworking of Hartmann von Aue's *Gregorius*, and uterine cancer associated with the menopause in *Die Betrogene* (1953), where nature, like the later blond and blue-eyed variations on Hans Hansen, is shown as being not devoid of sinister possibilities. (The work may also be read as an allegorical and scurrilous account of the effects of Americanisation upon Europe.) It seems as though, in extreme age, Thomas Mann felt drawn to the pathological, particularly in its sexual manifestations, to demonstrate the magisterial supremacy of art: his praise of Hans Henny Jahnn vindicates the belief in the power of the writer to transfigure and redeem. Yet, playfully, the last work, written at the very end of his life, was *Felix Krull. Der Memoiren erster Teil*, begun in 1911 and taken up again in 1954, which sees in the 'Hochstapler' the perfect 'paradigm' for the artist who, able to simulate and adopt so many different roles, scarcely knows himself who he is. In the hands of a lesser writer this theme may well have been treated with unbecoming earnestness; Thomas Mann, however, parodies the *Bildungsroman* and gives a picaresque novel *à la Simplicissmus*, with a host of delicious episodes. Felix, the 'happy one', by dint of cunning, good fortune, skill, charm and irrepressible verve, moves through society with little heed for moral considerations. He is not far removed from the artist who, delighting in Imogen and Iago, basically knows that ethical values play little part in his creative work. The miraculous ease with which Felix passes through life, the Hermes motif (Hermes was the 'elegant deity' of magic, cunning and roguish metamorphosis) and the idea of infinite adaptability form a highly entertaining and stimulating novel: if art *is* simply pretence, a trick, a piece of sophisticated sleight-of-hand, then at least one should be grateful for its virtuosity and not despise its surface-sheen: the pimples on the back of Müller-Rosé should not — and do not — detract from the ease and sophistication of his performance.

The themes of survival and adaptability bring to mind that other exile from Nazi Germany who is of equal stature to Thomas Mann: Bertolt Brecht. The increasingly Marxist orientation of Brecht's work in the late 1920s and early 1930s necessarily meant that flight was inevitable after 1933: the dramatic cantata *Die Maßnahme*, performed by the Arbeiterchor Großberlin in 1930, testified to the need expressed in his work to obliterate individuality should the work of the Communist Party be jeopardised. The adaptation of Gorki's *Die Mutter*, performed early in 1932, under great difficulty, was overtly propagandist; the film *Kuhle Wampe*, also of 1932, was immediately banned by the government because of its uncompromising portrayal of the life of the unemployed. After the burning of the Reichstag Brecht fled to Vienna: he attended the meeting at Sanary-sur-mer of exiled writers (Thomas and Heinrich Mann, Arnold Zweig, Lion Feuchtwanger and Ernst Toller were also present), and thence moved to Denmark, to the province of Svendborg, where he watched events in Germany most closely. To be thus isolated, removed from the theatre and hardly likely to have a stage put at his disposal, was hardly a pleasing prospect; the senselessness of the exiled writers' situation at this time, the fear of writing into a void in spite of brave hopes, would have sapped a lesser writer of his energies and purpose. But Brecht worked relentlessly: 'das Entsetzen über die Reden des Anstreichers', described in the poem 'Schlechte Zeit für Lyrik',[54] kept him at his writing desk in an unceasing vigil. The resultant works ranged from the tedious and the arid (*Die Rundköpfe und die Spitzköpfe, Die Horatier und die Kuriatier*) through a successful portrayal of fear, menace and betrayal (the semi-documentary *Furcht und Elend des Dritten Reiches*) to the undisputed masterpieces written between 1939 and 1945 which, due to a parabolic approach achieve universality and greatness.

It is commonly believed that Brecht, deprived of a theatre, turned his attentions during his exile to formulating a Marxist aesthetic of drama, a theoretically determined system: nothing could be further from the truth. Brecht was first and foremost an artist: his plays were written to express a particular view of the world in the style which he felt to be appropriate at the time; his subsequent theorising was an attempt to explain to himself as well as to others how it happened that this or that particular work had been written and produced in a particular way. His theoretical writing reflects the way in which he reflected on his own work; there is nothing rigid or inflexibly ideological about his speculation. The tone is light, frequently wryly humorous, often curious, but always allowing for movement and renewal; a rare intelligence is at work which questions, worries, retreats, adapts and restates. Theatre, literature and politics, society and even landscape are discussed: Brecht's *alter ego* Herr Keuner, examines his basic personal attitudes, and Ziffel and Kalle, the refugees of the *Flüchtlingsgespräche*, range in their discussions from the mentality of 'Wieheißterdochgleich', the then leader of the German people, to military virtues, passports, *Ordnung* and the potential for humorous irreverence latent within Hegelian dialectics. The following rueful remark by Ziffel brilliantly sums up the situation of the man who is forced to decide whether or not to flee: 'Damit man herausbringt, ob man schon heut fliehen muß oder erst morgen fliehen darf, ist eine Intelligenz nötig, mit der man noch vor ein paar Jahrzehnten hätt ein unsterbliches Werk schaffen können'.[55] The *Messingkauf* dialogues, a four-handed conversation piece, relate more directly to theatrical problems, and see above all the need for lightness of touch, *Spiel*, and a kind of elegance in acting which contains sobriety within it; the philosopher explains:

> In dieser Leichtigkeit ist jeder Grad von Ernst erreichbar, ohne sie gar keiner. So müssen wir allen Problemen die Fassungen geben, daß sie im Spiel erörtert werden können, auf spielerische Weise. Wir hantieren hier mit einer Goldwaage, in abgemessenen Bewegungen, mit Eleganz, gleichgültig, wie sehr uns der Boden unter den Füßen brennen mag. Es mag ja auch beinahe anstößig erscheinen, daß wir hier jetzt, zwischen blutigen Kriegen, und keineswegs, um in eine andere Welt zu flüchten, solche theatralischen Dinge diskutieren, welche dem Wunsch nach Zerstreuung ihre Existenz zu verdanken scheinen. Ach, es können morgen unsere Gebeine zerstreut werden! Wir beschäftigen uns aber mit dem Theater, gerade weil wir ein Mittel bereiten wollen, unsere Angelegenheiten zu betreiben, auch damit. Aber die Dringlichkeit unserer Lage darf uns nicht das Mittel, dessen wir uns bedienen wollen, zerstören lassen. Hast hilft ja nicht, wo Eile not tut. Dem Chirurgen, dem schwere Verantwortung aufgebürdet ist, muß das kleine Messer doch leicht in der Hand liegen.[56]

The rapier thrust is preferred to the sabre blow, the elliptical precision of Chinese art to Germanic ponderousness, and the athletic form of acting to the pretentiously histrionic.

In 1940 Brecht left Europe for America; in the following year the Züriches Schauspielhaus staged his *Mutter Courage und ihre Kinder*, a 'Chronik aus dem dreißigjährigen Krieg'. This was to be the play with which the Berliner Ensemble opened in 1949: it has remained in the repertoire and has been staged by all the leading theatres of Europe and America. It provides an excellent example of 'Epic theatre', that form of theatre which eschews 'Aristotelian' forms of drama and concentrates instead upon a 'Fabel', a tale which narrates and offers a nucleus for possible discussion. In the *Kleines Organon für das Theater*, written in 1948, Brecht insisted on the importance of this 'Fabel': 'Auf die Fabel kommt alles an, sie ist das Herzstück der theatralischen Veranstaltung';[57] the various chapter headings are provided by *Spruchbänder*, stretched across the stage. The importance of alienation, stressed also in the *Kleines Organon* ('Es [das Theater] muß sein Publikum wundern machen, und dies geschieht vermittels der Verfremdung des Vertrauten'[58]) is found here in the choice of historical subject, by the encouragement of the actors to 'imitate' and 'represent' the parts, rather than identify with them, and by the use of songs to interrupt the action and drive the several points home. The stage designs likewise were chosen to create a feeling of distance between audience and stage, to emphasise the essential *artificiality* of the proceedings, in order that critical faculties should remain sharp and alert. Each scene, and there are twelve of them, is supposed to stand as a self-contained unit, indeed, they should in theory be interchangeable — but a cumulative effect is undeniable and there are moments that are conventionally dramatic, which enthral, rather than alienate, an audience. At the climax of Brecht's creativity magnificently observed characters are brought to life, such as Mother Courage herself, her two sons, the daughter Kattrin, the army chaplain, the prostitute Yvette, and the Dutch cook, who are as well drawn as the best creations of German naturalism. Yet the audience, comprised of 'Kinder des wissenschaftlichen Zeitalters',[59] must assess Mother Courage's motives and actions coolly and impartially. The reactions of the audience are complex: her resilience and courage are admirable, but her greed and stubbornness to be deplored; her love for her children contains a total indifference to others, and even this love is tempered by her mercantile shrewdness. But her love for Kattrin is beyond reproach, and the scene of her hopeless lullaby over the child's dead body is intensely moving. With Brecht, however, there is always an 'and yet . . .': she has, apparently, learned nothing and rejoins the ragged, demoralised armies, pulling her cart ever onwards beneath a wintry sky. Brecht did not approve of the reactions of the audience to the first performance: in notes to the play he added certain modifications which were intended to stress the more negative qualities of that woman who was by no means a Niobe; identification with her plight must be ruled out emphatically: 'Dem Stückschreiber obliegt es nicht, die Courage am Ende sehend zu machen . . . ihm kommt as darauf an, daß der Zuschauer sieht'.[60] Hyena of the battlefield she may be, but she does also achieve a vitality and fortitude which are life-enhancing qualities; she remains Brecht's most memorable creation and one who is immediately understood without recourse to fable, alienation, *Gestus* or any other 'non-Aristotelian' concept.

In his *Aus einem Brief an einen Schauspieler* Brecht himself admitted that several misconceptions had arisen concerning his theatrical practices. He had been forced, he claimed, to overstate the differences between conventional theatre and his own in order that certain abuses be rectified: there was nothing dogmatic or sacrosanct about his suggestions. (As early as *Aufstieg und Fall der Stadt Maha-gony* he had, in fact, stressed that an overschematic differentiation between dramatic and epic was unsubtle: it was simply a difference of emphasis. In 1937 he had written a conventional play – admittedly not one of his best – on Aristotelian lines, *Die Gewehre der Frau Carrar*, which provided opportunity for splendid acting on the part of the heroine.) Brecht turned to the critics above all and admonished them to look at his plays *as plays* without preconceived ideas and theories:

> Sähen sich die Kritiker mein Theater an, wie es die Zuschauer ja tun, ohne meinen Theorien zunächst dabei Gewicht beizulegen, so würden sie wohl einfach Theater vor sich sehen, Theater, wie ich hoffe, mit Phantasie, Humor und Sinn, und erst bei einer Analyse der Wirkung fiele ihnen einiges Neue auf – das sie dann in meinen theoretischen Ausführungen erklärt finden könnten. Ich glaube, die Kalamität begann dadurch, daß meine Stücke richtig ausgeführt werden mußten, damit sie wirkten, und so mußte ich, für eine nichtaristotelische Dramatik – o Kummer! – ein episches Theater – o Elend! – beschreiben.[61]

The year 1943 saw a performance of two plays in Zurich which demonstrated once more Brecht's skill in creating memorable

characters who have entered the standard theatrical repertoire: the
heroine of *Der gute Mensch von Sezuan* and Galileo in *Leben des
Galilei*. The former, a parable play set in modern China, deals with
the virtual impossibility of doing good in this world; the kindness
of Shen Te has to be tempered with the ruthlessness of her 'other self',
Shui Ta, to prevent the importunate demands of spongers and
parasites. Brecht utterly rejects the Christian idea of original sin: it is
the nature of man to be good ('freundlich' is an epithet used with ever
greater frequency in his later work), and it is unnatural, self-
destructive and, indeed, strenuous to do evil. The poem 'Die Maske
des Bösen' emphasises this:

> An meiner Wand hängt ein japanisches Holzwerk
> Maske eines bösen Dämons, bemalt mit Goldlack.
> Mitfühlend sehe ich
> Die geschwollenen Stirnadern, andeutend,
> Wie anstrengend es ist, böse zu sein.[62]

The outstretched hand is a more natural gesture than the clenched
fist: Brecht had long pondered the problem of doing good in this
world and had shown, in *Die Ausnahme und die Regel* of 1930, how
a natural act of kindness could be misunderstood, and hatred and
violence assert themselves as the norm. The epilogue to *Der gute Mensch
von Sezuan* exhorts the audience to think of a better solution to the
play, which terminates in Shen Te's despair at not being able to meet
the conflicting demands of charity and self-survival; a society which
has not found a solution to this problem must make way for one which
can.

    Leben des Galilei has been admired as Brecht's masterpiece: he took
endless pains over it and worked at it intermittently for over seventeen
years. His initial concern was to show Galileo as a man determined to
live, and whose cunning recantation enables the truth to be heard in
spite of the strictures of the Church; Galileo's sensualism has much of
Baal about it, his adaptability much of Herr Keuner and his ultimate
triumph akin to the triumph of water which, as the 'Legende von der
Entstehung des Buches Taoteking' depicted, 'mit der Zeit den mächtigen Stein besiegt'.[63] The ultimate triumph of reason is left in no doubt
in this first version; the new age, immeasurably encouraged by
Galileo's discoveries, would dawn and bring prosperity and intellectual
freedom to the civilised world. In America Brecht worked with the
actor Charles Laughton on an English version of the play, which

emphasised Galileo's greed for life, and his motives for recantation
were shown as springing from fear, a fear from which good eventually
came: the smuggling of the *Discorsi* out of the country. But Brecht's
faith in the ultimate triumph of reason suffered a severe setback at the
time of the discovery of the atomic bomb: his crisis has been
described as 'eine Lebenskrise, deren Rigorosität und existentielle
Bedrohlichkeit Kleists Kantkrise vergleichbar ist'.[64] In 1938 Brecht's
Galileo could believe in a time of light which would supersede the rule
of darkness; with the detonation of atomic weapons Brecht now saw
that the submission of the scientist to the state could have fearful
consequences. In a crucial declaration Galileo, in the third version of
the play, explains what submission (previously a virtue in Brecht's
eyes) could mean, and what knowledge divorced from morality could
lead to:

> Wofür arbeitet ihr? Ich halte dafür, daß das einzige Ziel der
> Wissenschaft darin besteht, die Mühseligkeit der menschlichen
> Existenz zu erleichtern. Wenn Wissenschaftler, eingeschüchtert
> durch selbstsüchtige Machthaber, sich damit begnügen, Wissen
> um des Wissens willen aufzuhäufen, kann die Wissenschaft zum
> Krüppel gemacht werden, und eure neuen Maschinen mögen nur
> neue Drangsale bedeuten. Ihr mögt mit der Zeit alles entdecken,
> was es zu entdecken gibt, und euer Fortschritt wird doch nur
> ein Fortschreiten von der Menschheit weg sein. Die Kluft zwischen
> euch und ihr kann eines Tages so groß werden, daß euer Jubelschrei
> über irgendeine neue Errungenschaft von einem universalen
> Entsetzensschrei beantwortet werden könnte . . . Hätte ich wider-
> standen, hätten die Naturwissenschaftler etwas wie den
> hippokratischen Eid der Ärzte entwickeln können, das Gelöbnis, ihr
> Wissen einzig zum Wohle der Menschheit anzuwenden! Wie es nun
> steht, ist das Höchste, was man erhoffen kann, ein Geschlecht
> erfinderischer Zwerge, die für alles gemietet werden können.[65]

The sharpest criticism that Brecht ever allowed himself to make was
made à propos Galileo who had, Brecht claimed, sold science into the
hands of the authorities and in so doing removed it from the hands
of those who could benefit most, and made it a purely specialist's
occupation, remote, abstract and amoral. Profound moral problems
are adumbrated here, and several implications are noted: some see the
play as attacking the abuse of science by the American military and
political machine, others find a veiled discussion of Brecht's submission

to the East German regime after the Second World War. The issues are
intellectual, but the play provides magnificent theatre: the portrayal
of Galileo himself, of the cardinals and the other clergy (the 'little
monk' particularly), Galileo's daughter and the Sartis belong to
Brecht's finest. Most memorable is the scene of the dressing of the
Pope, the transformation from man to institution as each layer of
clothing is added. Brecht chose to ignore the obviously dramatic
scene, that of the recantation itself (Jakob Bührer's *Galileo Galilei*,
performed in Zurich in 1933, and other plays, had used this as the
climax), but the sense of dramatic inevitability which accompanies
the action shows yet again that Brecht did not adhere to any rigid
scheme of 'epic theatre': he created living characters, in conflict at a
crucial time of man's intellectual history.

Brecht's *Arbeitsjournal* (a two-volume diary dealing with the years
1938 to 1942, and 1942 to 1945) and his return to poetry to express
a more personal reaction to the world around him reflect his mis-
givings and sense of crisis at this time: the Soviet purges and the new
aesthetics demanded by Moscow, the death of old friends (particularly Margarete Steffin) and the tentative hope that reason would
prevail in spite of all. The American situation sickened and dismayed
him: the work on the film *Hangmen also Die* with Fritz Lang made
him entirely disillusioned with the Hollywood film industry (just as
Zuckmayer, who had previously achieved success as a scriptwriter
with *Der blaue Engel*, abandoned all work in Hollywood after Warner
had asked him to write a *Don Juan* for Errol Flynn, set in Florence
and featuring the Medicis and the Borgias[66]). His own fellow exiles
disappointed him in their readiness to conform and become more
American than the Americans: Emil Ludwig and Erich Maria
Remarque are particularly censured, as well as Thomas Mann, who,
Brecht claimed, treated his brother with condescension. There is
undoubtedly a sense of isolation, but not of paralysis: Brecht reworked
the Galileo material, and took over Hašek's figure of the *Good Soldier
Schweik* to exemplify yet again the need for survival and cunning;
he turned to the American underworld to see a parallel between Hitler
and Arturo Ui, the Capone-like gangster; he had brought from Finland
Herr Puntila und sein Knecht Matti, with its rumbustious portrayal of
the drunken landowner who completely steals the play; he worked
with Feuchtwanger on *Die Gesichte der Simon Machard*. But the
most tender and perennially successful of the plays which he wrote
in the mid-forties is *Der kaukasische Kreidekreis*, based on Klabund's
adaptation of the old Chinese play. The theme of goodness occupied

him once again: 'Schrecklich ist die Verführung zur Güte!',[67] but the
basic theme concerns the rightness of giving the child, or the disputed
land, to those best able to tend or cultivate it. The problem of the
final version of *Galileo* is touched upon here: knowledge should be
given not to the ruthless politicians but to those who would treat it
with respect and humility. The play is most successful in the portrayal
of the judge Azdak, a figure compounded of the vitality and amoral
zest of Baal and Puntila, and, to a lesser extent, of Galileo himself.
There are moments of great beauty; the love between Gruscha and
Simon Chachava has a dignity and a tenderness unequalled in Brecht:

> Simon Chachava, ich werde auf dich warten.
> Geh du ruhig in die Schlacht, Soldat
> Die blutige Schlacht, die bittere Schlacht
> Aus der nicht jeder wiederkehrt:
> Wenn du wiederkehrst, bin ich da.
> Ich werde warten auf dich unter der grünen Ulme
> Ich werde warten auf dich unter der kahlen Ulme
> Ich werde warten, bis der letzte zurückgekehrt ist
> Und danach.
>
> Kommst du aus der Schlacht zurück
> Keine Stiefel stehen vor der Tür
> Ist das Kissen neben meinem leer
> Und mein Mund ist ungeküßt
> Wenn du wiederkehrst, wenn du wiederkehrst
> Wirst du sagen können: alles ist wie einst.[68]

The epic qualities of the play are also in evidence: the exotic landscape, parabolic approach, songs, stylised action and the use of masks.

Brecht returned to Europe in November 1947; Zuckmayer, his
friend from the early days of the 1920s, had returned shortly before
him with his new play *Des Teufels General*, which was staged in Zurich
in 1946. He had survived where others had not: Ernst Toller, Stefan
Zweig, Kurt Tucholsky, Walter Hasenclever, Ernst Weiss, Walter
Benjamin and Carl Einstein had committed suicide; his friend Tretiakov
had disappeared in the Soviet Union and was presumed killed, as were
Carola Neher and Herwarth Walden. The *Flüchtlingsgespräche* bear
the motto by 'Woodhouse' (P.G. Wodehouse?): 'He knew that he was
still alive/More he could not say'. The setting up of his own Theater
am Schiffbauerdamm brought little comfort: the Berliner Ensemble

was boycotted by the orthodox critics, the workers made up only a small percentage of the audience and government pressure was brought to bear at every point. *Das Verhör des Lukullus*, which Brecht had written in 1939, and which condemned war, had to be modified at the behest of the authorities, who demanded that war against aggressors be permitted, and indeed praised. It is perhaps significant that Brecht wrote nothing of original merit for the theatre after his removal to East Berlin; he adapted, produced and modified, turning his attention, amongst other things, to *Waiting for Godot*, which he annotated up to Pozzo's entrance. He withdrew again into poetry and wrote, in the *Buckower Elegien*, some of his finest. With economy, grace and sobriety he evoked a world of trees and water, silence and serenity; by the willows he is taken back to childhood on seeing a green boat and its occupants:

> Heißer Tag. Auf den Knien die Schreibmappe
> Sitze ich im Pavillon. Ein grüner Kahn
> Kommt durch die Weide in Sicht. Im Heck
> Eine dicke Nonne, dick gekleidet. Vor ihr
> Ein ältlicher Mensch im Schwimmanzug, wahrscheinlich ein Priester.
> An der Ruderbank, aus vollen Kräften rudernd
> Ein Kind. Wie in alten Zeiten! denke ich
> Wie in alten Zeiten.[69]

The unchanging quality of nature is invoked:

> In der Frühe
> Sind die Tannen kupfern.
> So sah ich sie
> Vor einem halben Jahrhundert
> Vor zwei Weltkriegen
> Mit jungen Augen.[70]

But the need for human habitation, which quietly completes the landscape, is expressed:

> Das kleine Haus unter Bäumen am See.
> Vom Dach steigt Rauch.
> Fehlte er
> Wie trostlos dann wären
> Haus, Bäume und See.[71]

The utter simplicity of these poems demonstrates Brecht's unique
ability to find beauty in the trivial. 'Rudern, Gespräche', in a few deft
touches, incomparably invokes the evening, peace and communication,
an almost classical image of friendship caught in the economy of a
haiku:

> Es ist Abend. Vorbei gleiten
> Zwei Faltboote, darinnen
> Zwei nackte junge Männer: Nebeneinander rudernd
> Sprechen sie. Sprechend
> Rudern sie nebeneinander.[72]

Before his premature death in 1956 Brecht had written:

> Ich benötige keinen Grabstein, aber
> Wenn ihr einen für mich benögtigt
> Wünschte ich, es stünde darauf:
> Er hat Vorschläge gemacht. Wir
> Haben sie angenommen.
> Durch eine solche Inschrift wären
> Wir alle geehrt.[73]

Conformity and silence, *innere Emigration* and exile – these alterna-
tives faced the German writer between 1933 and 1945. This chapter, and
this book, will finish with a final reference to Alfred Mombert, whose
radiant poetic genius transcended the horrors even of the concentration
camp. Mombert's work was discussed in chapter 4; difficult of access,
it nevertheless seemed that his poetry might reach a wider audience
at the end of the 1920s, thanks to the critical studies of Soergel and
Benz. But after 1933 his poetry was ignored or greeted with derision;
in 1936, the year of publication of part one of *Sfaira der Alte*, Hans
Carossa at least had the courage to honour his work in *Führung und
Geleit*. Ousted from the academy of writers, Mombert refused to heed
the warning voices, remaining deeply attached to the beauties of
Heidelberg and ultimately to the spirit of all that was finest and most
noble in Germany's culture. In 1940 he was seized, together with his
sister, by the Gestapo and taken to the French detention camp at
Gurs, where Carl Einstein had also been detained; in 1941, after much
tribulation, Mombert was allowed entry into Switzerland, arriving
in Winterthur a desperately sick man, who died shortly after his

seventieth birthday. In the following year there appeared for private
circulation the second part of *Sfaira der Alte* whose second section,
'In der Finsternis', is a poetic expression of the fearful winter of
1940—41, and a miraculous transfiguration of bestiality and degradation.

> Jetzt aber schau' ich mein Land —
> jetzt schau' ich meine Stätte —:
> Ich schaue die Zelte der Finsternis —:
> Ich schaue den diamantenen Glanz der Pforten der Toten-Welt —[74]

In squalor and ugliness the spirit gazes upwards towards Orion, the
Pleiades and Cassiopeia:

> In der Tiefe auferstanden
> stoß' ich mein Glanz-Schwert durchs Baracken-Dach —
> . . .
> Durch Bretter-Spalt mein Empor-Blick:
> Ihr mir Zärtlichen![75]

And yet the torturer approaches, the denigrator and destroyer, the
Demon himself:

> Ächter des Kristall-Geistes:
> Seiner Herrlichkeiten Ahnung-Loser:
> Zerstörer-Dämon der Bild-Welt —:
> auf dich blas' ich Asche der Verfluchung,
> der Verschmachtung, der Veraasung,
> in Spiegeln der Hölle leide die Verzerrung
> deiner wüsten Dämon-Flacker-Flamme . . .
>
> Chaos-Kot — dem Morast des Todes
> entkrochener eitriger Drachen —
> wälztest heran an meinen kastalischen Quell —
> vor der erglühten Götter-Burg
> jauchst du um meinen Garten der Hesperiden —
> Die Geißel dir — dir Fraß — und dann Feuer! —[76]

With imagery which anticipates that of Paul Celan the poet, Sfaira
himself, expresses the bitterness of the taste of death upon his lips;
the torturer, with the metal noose slapping against his thigh, stands

in arrogance before him:

> *Sfaira.* Nacht-Asche auf den Lippen —
> bitter-bitter —
> aber Triumph im Geiste . . .
> Als Wer möchtest du Schöner scheinen? —
> Schleuderst Flammen? — trümmerst Berge? —
> Nichts von dem.
> Doch deinen Augen, — wenn Augen benennbar sind:
> diese schaudervollen Laster-Gruben —
> entträufelt Eiter-Gift:
> wo es hinabtropft, dort krümmt sich im Ekel der Erde
> reiner Schoß; aufschrecken die Begrabenen.
> Greuel, die meine Lippe schweigt —

> *Dämon.* Ich brauche keinen Schein.
> Dir bin ich Häscher, Fänger, Würger.
> Achte nur immer, mein Freund,
> auf die geschärfte Draht-Schlinge,
> die so lustig wippt an der Stärke meiner Hüfte:
> die ist mein Wahrzeichen.[77]

In the face of insolent brutality the poet is helpless, yet the poetic *act*, the manipulation of expressive images, can transcend evil and create a luminous world of joy: *Sfaira der Alte* ends on a note of mystic rapture, a cosmic vision of light, azure and crystal. The metaphors of height and purity bring forcibly to mind Hölderlin's *Empedokles*, and *Also sprach Zarathustra*; indeed, Zoroaster is hailed as the life enhancer, the spirit of affirmation and praise. As Sfaira passes into death and final transfiguration he once more turns to the loveliness of earth, untainted by the squalor and baseness of human perversion:

> Einmal noch kehre ich ein
> bei den Liebe flötenden Nachtigallen
> an den kühlen klingenden Bächen
> — und dann niemehr! —

> Einmal noch kehre ich ein
> beim Blau-Schiller schießender Wasserjungfern
> über den mondlicht träumenden Teichen
> — und dann niemehr! —

Auf der sommerwarm duftenden Haide
bei den Bienen saugend die goldnen Blüten
— und dann niemehr! —

Einmal noch kehre ich ein
bei den Lerchen an Ufern des Rheins:
in die dunkel-treue Efeu-Wildnis,
drin zu Zeiten nistete der Orion-Sänger
— und dann niemehr! —[78]

The ultimate apotheosis, the *Geisterchor* and *Chor der Göttinen* echoes
the climax of *Faust II*; the nadir of German cultural history is also the
moment when the poet feels his affinity with the highest manifestation
of that culture. In an era of violence and hatred, both violence *and*
hatred are transmuted by love and reverence, and terror and inhumanity
are allotted only a short dominion.

Notes

1. See Wolfgang Rothe, *Schriftsteller und totalitäre Welt*, Berne, 1966.
2. Joseph Wulf, *Literatur und Dichtung im Dritten Reich. Eine Dokumentation*, Gütersloh, 1963, 113.
3. Josef Goebbels, *Michael. Ein deutsches Schicksal in Tagebuch-Blättern*, Munich, 1933, 42.
4. Ibid., 74.
5. Ibid., 51.
6. Ibid., 53.
7. Ibid., 77.
8. Gustav Sack, *Prosa. Briefe. Verse*, Munich and Vienna, 1962, 39.
9. Ibid., 106.
10. Julius Langbehn, *Rembrandt als Erzieher*, Leipzig, 1890, 39.
11. Ibid., 125.
12. *Literarische Manifeste der Jahrhundertwende*, 326.
13. See *Die deutsche Literatur VII. 20. Jahrhundert. 1880–1933*, 477.
14. Gustav Frenssen, *Der Glaube der Nordmark*, Stuttgart, 1936, 122.
15. H. Boeschenstein, *The German Novel 1939–1944*, Toronto, 1949, 3.
16. See *Die deutsche Literatur VII. 20. Jahrhundert. 1880–1933*, 1,133-1,134.
17. Hans Grimm, *Volk ohne Raum*, Munich, 1934, 1,110.
18. Ibid., 1,182.
19. Ibid., 931.
20. Oskar Loerke, *Tagebücher 1903–1939*, Heidelberg, 1956, 270 and 275-276.
21. See Wulf, *Literatur und Dichtung im Dritten Reich*, 45-46.
22. Oskar Maria Graf, *Beschreibung eines Volksschriftstellers*, Munich, 1974, 38.

23. Gottfried Benn, VII, 1,697-1,698.
24. Gottfried Benn, *Lyrik und Prosa. Briefe und Dokumente*, Wiesbaden, 1962, XII.
25. See Jahnn and Munker, *Deutsche Kulturgeschichte der letzten hundert Jahre*, Munich, 1970, 167.
26. Gottfried Benn, I, 208.
27. George, *Das neue Reich*, 134.
28. See Michael Hamburger, *From Prophecy to Exorcism*, 70.
29. Jünger, *Werke VI. Essays II*, 19-20.
30. George, *Das neue Reich*, 39.
31. See Hamburger, *From Prophecy to Exorcism*, 73.
32. Sorge, II, 23.
33. Hauptmann, VIII, 1,039.
34. See Harry Pross, 'On Thomas Mann's political career', in *Journal of Contemporary History*, Vol. 2, 1967, 75.
35. See Wulf, 133.
36. Hauptmann, VIII, 401.
37. Ibid., 415.
38. Julius Bab, *Über den Tag hinaus*, Heidelberg, 1969, 194.
39. Hauptmann, III, 890-891.
40. Ibid., 1,009.
41. Ibid., 597.
42. See Tank, *Gerhart Hauptmann in Selbstzeugnissen*, 27.
43. Walter Benjamin, *Illuminationen*, 176.
44. Thomas Mann, IX, 407.
45. Thomas Mann, *Briefe an Karl Kerényi*, Zurich, 1969, 97-98.
46. Bertram, *Nietzsche*, Berlin, 1919, 6.
47. Thomas Mann, *Briefe 1889–1936*, 91.
48. .Thomas Mann, XII, 907.
49. Erich Heller, *The Ironic German*, London, 1958, 260-261.
50. Thomas Mann, VI, 316.
51. See T.J. Reed, *Thomas Mann*, 396.
52. Thomas Mann, VI, 676.
53. Ibid., 651.
54. Brecht, *Gesammelte Werke*, 1967, IX, 744.
55. Brecht, XIV, 1,496.
56. Brecht, XVI, 643.
57. Ibid., 693.
58. Ibid., 682.
59. Ibid., 671.
60. Brecht, XVII, 1,150.
61. Brecht, XVI, 816.
62. Brecht, X, 850.
63. Brecht, IX, 661.
64. See Rémy Charbon, *Die Naturwissenschaften im modernen deutschen Drama*, Zurich, 1974, 175.
65. Brecht, III, 1,341.
66. Carl Zuckmayer, *Als wärs ein Stück von mir*, Frankfurt/Main, 1969, 414.
67. Brecht, V, 2,025.
68. Ibid., 2,018-2,019.
69. Brecht, X, 1,011.
70. Ibid., 1,012-1,013.
71. Ibid., 1,012.
72. Ibid., 1,013.

73. Ibid., 1,029.
74. Mombert, II, 555.
75. Ibid., 556.
76. Ibid., 558.
77. Ibid., 558-559.
78. Ibid., 593.

BIBLIOGRAPHY

The purpose of this bibliography is to supply hints for further study of
the period: for reasons of space it has been reduced to an absolute
minimum. Scholarly books on modern German history and literature
are legion, and each new publisher's catalogue attests to the ever-
increasing fascination exerted by both the historical vicissitudes of that
country and the influence of its major literary figures. It is Germany
above all other European countries which seems to demand
unstinting attention, particularly the period under discussion here, and
when such names as Brecht, Kafka, Thomas Mann and Rilke become
part of the framework of the modern literary consciousness, then
the compiler of bibliographies can only crave indulgence. Many of the
works listed below contain adequate lists for further reading, to which
the reader may be safely referred.

1.   General Background: Historical and Cultural
Abbé, Derek van: *Image of a People*, London, 1964
Fest, Joachim: *Hitler. Eine Biographie*, Frankfurt, Berlin, Vienna, 1973
Kohn, Hans: *The Mind of Germany*, London, 1961
Laqueur, Walter: *Weimar. A Cultural History 1918–1933*, London,
    1974
Lukács, Georg: *Die Zerstörung der Vernunft*, Neuwied, 1962
Mosse, G.L.: *The Crisis of German Ideology*, New York, 1964
Pascal, Roy: *From Naturalism to Expressionism. German Literature
    and Society 1880–1918*, London, 1973
Pross, Harry: *Literatur und Politik*, Olten, 1963
Stern, F.: *The Politics of Cultural Despair*, Berkeley, 1961
Stern, P.: *Hitler: the Führer and the People*, Glasgow and London,
    1975
Taylor, Ronald: *The Intellectual Tradition in Modern Germany*,
    2 vols., London, 1973
Toulmin, S. and Janik, A.: *Wittgenstein's Vienna*, London, 1973

2.   General Surveys of Literature
Closs, August (ed.): *Introduction to German Literature IV. Twentieth
    Century German Literature*, London, 1969
Duwe, W.: *Deutsche Literatur des 20. Jahrhunderts*, 2 vols., Zurich,

1962

Gray, Ronald: *The German Tradition in Literature 1871–1945*,
Cambridge, 1965

Hamburger, Michael: *From prophecy to exorcism: the premisses of
modern German literature*, London, 1965

Kunisch, H.: *Handbuch der deutschen Gegenwartsliteratur*, Munich,
1965

Mayer, Hans: *Zur deutschen Literatur der Zeit*, Reinbek, 1967

Mann, O. and Rothe, W.: *Deutsche Literatur im 20. Jahrhundert.
Strukturen und Gestalten* (5th ed.), Berne and Munich, 1967

Olles, Helmut: *Rowohlt Literaturlexikon 20. Jahrhundert*, Reinbek,
1971

Pasley, Malcolm (ed.): *Germany. A companion to German studies*
(chapter ten), London, 1972

Natan, A. (ed.): *German Men of Letters*, Vols. 2 and 3, London, 1963
and 1964

Raabe, Paul: *Quellenkunde zur neueren deutschen Literatur*,
Stuttgart, 1962

Wiese, Benno von (ed.): *Deutsche Dichter der Moderne* (2nd ed.), Berlin,
1969

3.   Genres and Movements

A useful series is that edited by O. Best and H.-J. Schmitt: *Die deutsche
Literatur. Ein Abriß in Text und Darstellung*, Vol. 12: *Naturalismus*;
Vol. 13: *Impressionismus, Symbolismus und Jugendstil*; Vol. 14:
Expressionismus und Dadaismus; and Vol. 15: *Neue Sachlichkeit,
Literatur im 'Dritten Reich' und im Exil*, Stuttgart, 1974. Other full
surveys in the *Paperbacks zur Literatur* series include: Manfred Durzak,
Die deutsche Exilliteratur 1933–1945, Stuttgart, 1973; Wolfgang
Rothe, *Die deutsche Literatur in der Weimarer Republik*, Stuttgart,
1974; and Horst Denkler, *Die deutsche Literatur im Dritten Reich*,
Stuttgart, 1974. The following should also be noted:

Arnold, A.: *Die Literatur des Expressionismus. Sprachliche und
thematische Quellen*, Stuttgart, 1966

Cowen, R.C.: *Der Naturalismus. Kommentar zu einer Epoche*, Munich,
1973

Hermand, J.: *Jugendstil: ein Forschungsbericht 1918–1964*,
Stuttgart, 1965

Hoefert, Sigfrid: *Das Drama des Naturalismus* (Sammlung Metzler),
Stuttgart, 1968

Huelsenbeck, R.: *Dada. Eine literarische Dokumentation*, Reinbek, 1964

Ketelsen, U.W.: *Völkisch-nationale und nationalsozialistische Literatur in Deutschland 1890–1945* (Sammlung Metzler), Stuttgart, 1976

Koreska-Hartmann, L.: *Jugendstil*, Munich, 1969

Lethen, H.: *Neue Sachlichkeit 1924–1932*, Stuttgart, 1970

Loewy, E.: *Literatur unterm Hakenkreuz*, Frankfurt/Main, 1966

Meyer, Theo: *Theorie des Naturalismus*, Stuttgart, 1973

Osborne, John: *The Naturalist Drama in Germany*, Manchester, 1971

Raabe, Paul (ed.): *Expressionismus. Aufzeichnungen und Erinnerungen der Zeitgenossen*, Olten, 1965

Rothe, W.: *Expressionismus als Literatur*, Berne and Munich, 1969

Schutte, Jürgen: *Lyrik des deutschen Naturalismus 1885–1893* (Sammlung Metzler), Stuttgart, 1976

Sokel, Walter: *The Writer in Extremis*, Stanford, 1959

Sternfeld, W. and Tiedemann, E.: *Deutsche Exilliteratur 1933–1945. Eine Bio-Bibliographie* (2nd rev. ed.), Heidelberg, 1970

Welzig, W.: *Der deutsche Roman im 20. Jahrhundert*, Stuttgart, 1967

Willett, John: *Expressionism*, London, 1970

Wulf, J.: *Literatur und Dichtung im Dritten Reich. Eine Dokumentation*, Gütersloh, 1963

4.   Specific Authors

The series *Rowohlts Monographien. Große Persönlichkeiten in Selbstzeugnissen und Bilddokumenten* (published in Reinbek/Hamburg) can be relied upon for useful bibliographies; the series serves the period 1890–1945 well, and includes such names as Gottfried Benn, Bertolt Brecht, Stefan George, Gerhart Hauptmann, Hermann Hesse, Hugo von Hofmannsthal, Ernst Jünger, Franz Kafka, Erich Kästner, Karl Kraus, Thomas Mann, Rainer Maria Rilke, Robert Musil and Georg Trakl. The 'Sammlung Metzler' (Stuttgart) series is a worthwhile one, and covers to date most of the authors listed above. Readers can also keep up to date on the most recent publications by consulting the appropriate section in the *Years Work in Modern Language Studies*. More specific details are as follows:

(i)   Gottfried Benn

Buddeberg, E.: *Probleme um Gottfried Benn. Die Benn-Forschung 1950–1960*, Stuttgart, 1962

Loose, G.: *Die Ästhetik Gottfried Benns*, Frankfurt/Main, 1961

Wellershoff, D.: *Gottfried Benn. Phänotyp dieser Stunde*, Cologne,
  1958

(ii)   Bertolt Brecht

Demetz, Peter (ed.): *Brecht. A collection of critical essays*, New Jersey,
  1966
Esslin, Martin: *Brecht. A choice of evils*, London, 1959
Fuegi, J.: *Brecht heute. Jahrbuch der internationalen Brecht-
  Gesellschaft*, Frankfurt/Main, 1971
Gray, Ronald: *Brecht the dramatist*, Cambridge, 1976
Mayer, Hans: *Bertolt Brecht und die Tradition*, Munich, 1965
Petersen, K.D.: *Bertolt Brecht Bibliographie*, Bad Homburg, 1968
Schumacher, E.: *Brecht. Theater und Gesellschaft im 20. Jahrhundert*,
  Berlin, 1973
Schuhmann, K.: *Der Lyriker Bertolt Brecht 1913–1933*, Munich,
  1971
Willett, John: *The Theatre of Bertolt Brecht*, London, 1959

(iii)   Hermann Broch

Durzak, Manfred (ed.): *Hermann Broch. Perspektiven der Forschung.*
  Munich, 1972

(iv)   Alfred Döblin

Kort, W.: *Alfred Döblin. Das Bild des Menschen in seinen Romanen*,
  Bonn, 1970
Peitz, W.: *Alfred Döblin Bibliographie 1905–1966*, Freiburg, 1968

(v)   Stefan George

Bennett, E.K.: *Stefan George*, Cambridge, 1954
Durzak, Manfred: *Der junge Stefan George*, Munich, 1968
Heftrich, Klussmann, Schrimpf (eds.): *Stefan George Colloquium*,
  Cologne, 1971
Klussmann, P.G.: *Stefan George. Mit einer Bibliographie*, Bonn, 1961

(vi)   Gerhart Hauptmann

Daiber, H.: *Gerhart Hauptmann oder der letzte Klassiker*, Vienna,
  1971
Knight, K. and Norman, F.: *Gerhart Hauptmann Centenary Lectures*,
  London, 1964
Michaelis, R.: *Der schwarze Zeus. Gerhart Hauptmanns zweiter Weg*,
  Berlin, 1962

(vii)   Hermann Hesse

Bareiss, O.: *Hermann Hesse. Eine Bibliographie* (2 vols.), Basel, 1964
Boulby, Mark: *Hermann Hesse. His mind and art*, New York, 1967
Rose, E.: *Faith from the abyss. Hermann Hesse's way from Romanticism to Modernity*, New York, 1965
Zeller, B.: *Hermann Hesse*, Hamburg, 1963
Ziolkowski, T.: *The novels of Hermann Hesse*, Princeton, 1971 (3rd ed.)

(viii)   Hugo von Hofmannsthal

Alewyn, R.: *Über Hugo von Hofmannsthal* (2nd ed.), Göttingen, 1960
Hamburger, M.: *Hofmannsthal. Three Essays*, Princeton, 1971
Hammelmann, H.: *Hugo von Hofmannsthal*, London, 1957
Weber, H.: *Hugo von Hofmannsthal Bibliographie*, Berlin, 1972
Wunberg, G.: *Hugo von Hofmannsthal im Urteil seiner Kritiker*, Frankfurt/Main, 1972

(ix)   Franz Kafka

Bezzel, C.: *Kafka Chronik. Daten zu Leben und Werk*, Munich, 1975
Binder, H.: *Kafka in neuer Sicht*, Stuttgart, 1976
Emrich, W.: *Franz Kafka*, Frankfurt/Main, 1960
Gray, Ronald: *Franz Kafka*, Cambridge, 1973
Greenberg, M.: *The terror of art: Kafka and modern literature*, London, 1971
Heller, Erich: *Kafka*, London, 1974
Järv, H.: *Die Kafka-Literatur: eine Bibliographie*, Malmö, 1961
Kuna, F.: *Kafka. Literature as Corrective Punishment*, London, 1974
Politzer, H.: *Franz Kafka. Parable and Paradox*, New York, 1962
Sokel, W.: *Franz Kafka. Tragik und Ironie*, Munich, 1964
Thorlby, A.: *A student's guide to Kafka*, London, 1972

(x)   Karl Kraus

Field, F.: *The Last Days of Mankind. Karl Kraus and his Vienna*, London, 1967
Kerry, O.: *Karl Kraus Bibliographie*, Munich, 1970

(xi)   Heinrich Mann

Matthias, K. (ed.): *Heinrich Mann 1871–1971. Bestandsaufnahme und Untersuchung*, Munich, 1973
Zenker, E.: *Heinrich Mann Bibliographie*, East Berlin, 1967

(xii) Thomas Mann

Baumgart, R.: *Das Ironische und die Ironie bei Thomas Mann*, Munich, 1966

Hatfield, H. (ed.): *Thomas Mann. A collection of critical essays*, New Jersey, 1964

Heller, E.: *The Ironic German. A study of Thomas Mann*, London, 1958

Hollingdale, R.J.: *Thomas Mann*, London, 1973

Lehnert, H.: *Thomas Mann Forschung. Ein Bericht*, Stuttgart, 1969

Pütz, Peter (ed.): *Thomas Mann und die Tradition*, Frankfurt/Main, 1971

Reed, T.J.: *Thomas Mann. The uses of tradition*, Oxford, 1974

Wysling, H.: *Thomas Mann heute. Sieben Vorträge*, Berne, 1976

  See also *Sonderheft Thomas Mann* in *Sinn und Form*, East Berlin, 1965

(xiii) Robert Musil

Baumann, G.: *Robert Musil*, Berne, 1965

Bausinger, W.: *Studien zu Robert Musil*, Reinbek, 1964

Kaiser, E. and Wilkins, E.: *Robert Musil. Eine Einführung in das Werk*, Stuttgart, 1962

Reniers-Servranckx, A.: *Robert Musil,* Bonn, 1972

Thoeming, J.: *Robert Musil Bibliographie*, Bad Homburg, 1968

(xiv) Rainer Maria Rilke

Belmore, H.: *Rilke's craftsmanship*, Oxford, 1954

Hamburger, K. (ed.): *Rilke in neuer Sicht*, Stuttgart, 1971

Holthusen, H.E.: *Rainer Maria Rilke: a study of his later poetry*, Cambridge, 1952

Jonas, K.W. and Schnack, I.: 'R.M. Rilke's manuscripts in German and Austrian collections', *Monatshefte,* LVI, 1964

Kunz, M.: *Narziß. Untersuchungen zum Werk R.M. Rilkes*, Bonn, 1970

Mason, E.C.: *Lebenshaltung und Symbolik bei R.M. Rilke*, Weimar, 1939

Obermüller, P. and Steiner, H.: *Katalog der Rilke-Sammlung Richard von Mises*, Frankfurt/Main, 1966

Ryan, Judith: *Umschlag und Verwandlung*, Munich, 1972

Stephens, A.: *R.M. Rilke's 'Gedichte an die Nacht'*, Cambridge, 1972

Stephens, A.: *R.M. Rilke's 'Malte Laurids Brigge'. Strukturanalyse des erzählerischen Bewußtseins*, Berne, 1974

(xv)   Arthur Schnitzler

Allen, R.H.: *An Annotated Arthur Schnitzler. Bibliography, editions and criticism in German, English and French*, Chapel Hill, 1966
Swales, M.: *Arthur Schnitzler. A critical study*, Oxford, 1971

(xvi)   Frank Wedekind

Best, A.: *Frank Wedekind*, London, 1975
Kutscher, A.: *Wedekind. Leben und Werk*, Munich, 1964

INDEX

Under the names of certain major authors are listed the more important works referred to in this book.